ETHICS AND THE PUBLIC SERVICE: TRUST, INTEGRITY, AND DEMOCRACY

ETHICS AND THE PUBLIC SERVICE: TRUST, INTEGRITY, AND DEMOCRACY

Susan Dimock
YORK UNIVERSITY

Mohamad Al-Hakim
YORK UNIVERSITY

Garrett MacSweeney
YORK UNIVERSITY

Alessandro Manduca-Barone
YORK UNIVERSITY

Anthony Antonacci
YORK UNIVERSITY

NELSON / EDUCATION

NELSON / EDUCATION

Ethics and the Public Service: Trust, Integrity, and Democracy

by Susan Dimock , Mohamad Al-Hakim, Garrett MacSweeney, Alessandro Manduca-Barone, and Anthony Antonacci

Vice President, Editorial Higher Education:
Anne Williams

Acquisitions Editor:
Anne-Marie Taylor

Marketing Manager:
Ann Byford

Developmental Editor:
Caroline Winter

Permissions Coordinator:
Sandra Mark

Content Production Manager:
Christine Gilbert

Production Service:
Cenveo Publisher Services

Copy Editor:
Susan James

Proofreader:
Erin Moore

Indexer:
Robert Swanson

Production Coordinator:
Ferial Suleman

Design Director:
Ken Phipps

Managing Designer:
Franca Amore

Interior Design Revisions:
Liz Harasymczuk

Cover Design:
Liz Harasymczuk

Cover Image:
KatieLittle/Dreamstime.com

Compositor:
Cenveo Publisher Services

Printer:
RR Donnelley

Library and Archives Canada Cataloguing in Publication Data

Ethics and the public service: trust, integrity, and democracy/ Susan Dimock . . . [et al.].

Includes bibliographical references and index.
ISBN 978-0-17-650442-7

1. Civil service ethics. 2. Public administration—Moral and ethical aspects. I. Dimock, Susan, 1963–

JF1525.E8E843 2012
172'.2   C2011-907929-1

ISBN-13: 978-0-17-650442-7
ISBN-10: 0-17-650442-7

We offer this book as thanks to the many hundreds of thousands of men and women who devote themselves in their professional lives to the values of good government and the common good. We offer it because we believe a professional and ethical public service is a vital part of a just and legitimate democratic government, and that it is indispensable in ensuring that government serves the public interest and that public trust in government is deserved.

We personally dedicate the book to our families, without whose love and support, we would be less than we are. Thank you to our parents and spouses, siblings, and children.

BRIEF TABLE OF CONTENTS

TABLE OF CONTENTS

ABOUT THE CONTRIBUTORS

Susan Dimock

Susan Dimock is Professor of Philosophy at York University. Dr. Dimock joined the faculty at York in 1991 after earning her Ph.D. from Dalhousie University, M.A. from York and B.A. in Philosophy and History from the University of New Brunswick. Her main areas of scholarly research are in the philosophy of law (especially criminal law theory), ethics, public policy, and political philosophy. She is the author or editor of many books, and has published articles in numerous scholarly journals.

Professor Dimock has always been keenly interested in governance issues and has been entrusted with a number of leadership roles during her 20 years at York University. She has been the President of the York University Faculty Association, Chair of her Faculty Council, Chair of the University Senate, and Director of the York Centre for Practical Ethics. Such leadership responsibilities have provided valuable opportunities for her to gain practical experience in leadership and governance in complex organizations, experience that has enriched her academic understanding of good governance. She is also an award-winning teacher, and has developed numerous pedagogical materials for university-level instruction in her fields.

Mohamad Al-Hakim

Mohamad Al-Hakim is a doctoral student in philosophy at York University. His main areas of research are ethics, public policy, multiculturalism, political theory, and legal philosophy. Mr. Al-Hakim holds an Honours B.A. and a Master's degree from McMaster University and is currently finishing his Ph.D. at York University.

Mr. Al-Hakim has published in various journals including *Criminal Law and Philosophy, New Criminal Law Review*, and *Transnational Legal Theory* and continues to work in various areas relating to ethics, multiculturalism, and law. Mr. Al-Hakim is also a co-founder and co-executive director of AB&M Advisors Inc., a boutique consulting firm concentrating on managerial ethics and training for the public and private sectors.

Garrett MacSweeney

Garrett MacSweeney holds an Honours B.A. in philosophy from Saint Mary's University, Halifax, and an M.A. in philosophy from York University, Toronto, where he is currently pursuing a Ph.D. in philosophy. Mr. MacSweeney's doctoral research is in the intersection of the philosophy of law and political philosophy, specifically looking at the political justification of *mala prohibita* offences and criminal law. Mr. MacSweeney also has as an area of specialization in business and professional ethics, having taught in the Department of Policy and Strategy for the Management Program at the Schulich School of Business, and is competent in moral and political philosophy, specifically international justice and global ethics. Mr. MacSweeney is a Fellow of McLaughlin College, York University, a graduate associate and executive board member of the York Centre for Practical Ethics, and a member of the Canadian Business Ethics Research Network. In addition to his academic work, Mr. MacSweeney is also a co-founder and co-executive director of the consulting firm AB&M Advisors Inc.

Alessandro Manduca-Barone

Alessandro Manduca-Barone is a Ph.D. candidate at York University in the process of completing his dissertation in the field of bioethics. Having degrees in both philosophy and economics, one of Mr. Manduca-Barone's interests has been the role of ethics in corporations. However, his interests vary widely, publishing and presenting articles on topics revolving around public sector ethics, international human rights, competence, and ethical standards relating to medical research. Furthermore, he is one of the co-founders and co-executive directors of AB&M Advisors Inc., a company that engages in ethical consulting for both the private and public sector.

Anthony Antonacci

Anthony Antonacci received a specialized honours Bachelor's degree in Public Policy and Administration in 2008 and a Certificate in Professional Ethics in 2009. He is currently pursuing a Master's degree at the School of Public Policy and Administration at York University. He is a freelance writer from Toronto, and is currently a Featured Columnist for Bleacher Report, the fourth largest sports media website in the United States.

Mr. Antonacci was a community blogger in his riding of Don Valley East for the *Toronto Star* during the Ontario provincial election in 2011, interviewing local candidates and writing about issues both on a local and a provincial scale. He is hopelessly optimistic that the day will come when our politicians say what they mean, and do what they say.

PREFACE

This book is offered as a primary text for the teaching of public sector ethics to students in Public Policy and Administration, Public Policy and Law, and Policy and Government programs in Canadian universities. It also includes a section specifically for managers.

The aim of this book is to provide a framework for the discussion of specific ethical challenges that members of the public service might face in the course of their work. Additionally, and perhaps more importantly, however, it seeks to explain why an ethical public service is so vital to democracy and good government. It tries to explain the value of ethics codes, the importance of independent oversight, and the contribution of ethical leadership to the achievement of public trust, political legitimacy, and the integrity of government programs. Thus it attempts not only to explain what ethical conduct consists of, but also to provide an explanation of why ethical behaviour is so valuable.

The book minimizes the use of current laws, actual ethics codes or codes of conduct, and real-world examples of ethical lapses, though some references to all three are made in the following pages. It does so in order to provide a framework for the discussion of public sector ethics that does not presuppose that any specific ethics code or legal framework is perfect (including those we have at the time of writing this book). It is anticipated that the book will be supplemented by current legislation (enacted or proposed), recent reports of Auditors General, Ombudsmen, or Integrity Commissioners, contemporary judicial decisions involving the civil service, and media reports of (alleged) wrongdoing in the public sector as supplementary educative tools. All of these materials are available free of charge and electronically, and so one advantage of proceeding as we have is that it will reduce the cost of the text. Likewise, new editions will not be required every time the law changes or the examples become outdated. Finally, such an approach allows different instructors to concentrate on different components of an ethics regime for the public service: conflict of interest, say, or procurement policies, depending upon the particular needs of their students or clients.

The book concludes with 30 sample cases for discussion. We have collected the cases at the end of the book, rather than interspersing them throughout the various chapters, because we believe that it will be worthwhile to revisit them as students' understanding of ethical principles and values expands and deepens through their studies. The use of cases is an excellent aid to comprehension, and demonstrates the complexity of the issues that public servants face in their day-to-day work. Students will no doubt wish they had additional information in some of the cases, a fact which is itself illuminating; as they analyze why they think additional facts might or might not be useful, they will be demonstrating the range of considerations that are relevant for good moral reasoning and ethical decision making.

We offer this book because we believe a professional and ethical public service is a vital part of a just and legitimate democratic government, and that it is indispensable in ensuring that government serves the public interest and that public trust in government is deserved. We offer it as thanks to the many hundreds of thousands of men and women who devote themselves in their professional lives to the values of good government and the common good.

ACKNOWLEDGMENTS

The authors would like to acknowledge the generous support they have received from York University, especially the York Centre for Practical Ethics, McLaughlin College, and the Faculty of Graduate Studies, while conducting research on this book. They would also like to thank the editorial team at Nelson Education Ltd. for their invaluable assistance, advice, professional support, and good-humoured patience. Finally, the authors thank the anonymous reviewers who read and provided comments for two previous drafts of the manuscript. While any mistakes, omissions, and oversights remain ours, the book is much better as a result of their generous and constructive advice.

List of Reviewers

O.P. Dwivedi, University of Guelph

Pierre Martel, University of Ottawa

Frank Ohemeng, University of Ottawa

Robert P. Shepherd, School of Public Policy & Administration, Carleton University

Introduction to Morality and Ethics

Public sector ethics is a particular branch of professional and applied ethics. It is related to **morality**, and draws many of its foundational terms and concepts from morality. Central among these are the concepts of values and principles, rights and duties. We offer some initial clarification of how we understand these concepts in this chapter.

You see a person or group of people acting cruelly toward another, and you judge that their behaviour is wrong. A friend lies to her parents for personal gain, and you judge that your friend's action is wrong. Another friend is considering having an extra-marital affair, and you condemn the proposal. You read in the newspaper about a terrorist attack on innocent people in some distant part of the world, and you judge that action to be immoral. You read in an historical account about the actions of armies raping the female civilians of the enemy population in order to demoralize them, and you judge such a tactic to be unjustifiable. You read that a multinational corporation has knowingly risked selling contaminated food products and you judge its conduct wrong. You read about societies that systematically exploit segments of their populations for the good of the rulers, about slave societies, or societies in which women or particular racial groups are denied basic rights, and you deem such societies unjust. You find out that your employer refuses to hire members of visible minorities and you judge such a policy to be racist. You see a person who relishes the misery of others and you judge such a person to be cruel. You see a group of young people light a cat on fire and you judge what they are doing to be bad. These are just a few examples of the moral judgments a person might make in assessing the situations he confronts in the world as we know it.

We think what makes these otherwise diverse situations or actions morally important is that they all affect significant interests of those involved in or affected by them. We suppose that burning cats, racist hiring policies, slavery, adultery, rape, cruelty, and the like are wrong and ought not to be engaged in because the interests involved are too important to be sacrificed, at least in favour of the interests that such actions serve in the cases as we have imagined them. Parents have an interest in not being lied to by their children, women have an interest in not being raped, people have an interest in being free, and so forth, and these interests are so important that we judge actions that violate them to be wrong.

Now we are supposing that everyone has a set of judgments of this kind that they have formed in reaching normal moral maturity. These judgments are pre-theoretical, and are made prior to or independently of any systematic study of moral philosophy. They are not guided by a theoretical commitment to any particular moral theory or general moral principles.

The moral judgments with which we begin our critical moral thinking are of this type. We assume that those judgments have been made under something like the conditions needed for ideal moral judging (discussed more fully in 1.5.2). To anticipate, we assume that when you make the judgments you make, you are not impaired in some way, your interests are not directly affected by actions being assessed, and more. Of course, often we do form our judgments in contexts that do directly involve our own interests. Consider the difference between the case we mentioned in which you learn that a friend has lied to her parents, and a case in which your friend has lied to you. In the latter case, you might be expected to judge your friend's actions very harshly, since it is your own interests that are in conflict with hers. Before we make a final judgment about your friend's lying, we need certain factual information, including information about why your friend lied. Did she lie to spare your feelings, to save another friend from even greater harm, or for self-serving reasons? History is a great tool of moral education, because through history we have the actions of others laid bare, and the relevant facts explained, while our own interests are not affected. Thus the judgments we make about the actions and policies of individuals and societies distant from us in history are often such that they satisfy the conditions for ideal judging. And we see, as we should expect, that there is much more agreement among individuals about the moral quality of the actions described in history than there was by the participants in those events, whose information was perhaps more limited, whose biases were directly involved, and whose competing interests were at stake.

Of the moral judgments we make, some we feel very certain about, while others we make much more tentatively. We are very sure, in other words, that some of our judgments are correct or fully justified, but others we are less sure about. Those moral judgments that we are most sure about are such that we cannot imagine changing our minds about them without radically transforming our entire moral outlook. Our conviction that slavery is wrong is one such judgment. We do not believe that any further information could be found that would make us change our minds about the injustice of slavery. And we could not revise our judgment about the immorality of slavery without changing our entire moral outlook, about the value of persons, the rights that people have, and the point of morality itself. For us, the moral status of slavery is an easy case; we have no difficulty reaching a firm conclusion about its immorality.

Consider, by way of contrast, our attitudes toward cloning or genetic engineering. Here our moral judgments concerning whether we ought to engage in these activities might be much more tentative. This will often be the case when assessing new technologies. This is in part because we recognize that we probably don't have all the relevant facts, such as the long-term health effects of these technologies on people or the environment, nor do we know the uses to which such technologies might be put in the future if they are allowed. We don't even have a clear sense of what interests are involved in using or banning such technologies, and so it is very difficult to reach a firm conclusion as to the moral status of their use. The expectation of agreement upon the morality of such issues is much less reasonable in these cases. These are moral "hard cases."[1]

It is not, of course, solely new situations that give rise to hard moral cases. The moral status of affirmative action hiring policies is often only weakly agreed upon. The same person may recognize that there are good moral reasons for hiring policies that favour members of historically disadvantaged groups (correcting past injustices, for example, and providing a more level playing field from which different people can compete for valued social positions) and also recognize that there are good moral reasons for rejecting the implementation of such policies (it will lead to hiring people for reasons other than their qualifications—the very thing that led to the need for corrective measures). If a single person is unclear regarding which course of action is correct, it is difficult to be optimistic regarding the possibility of widespread agreement.

Critical moral thinking begins with those judgments about which we have the greatest certitude, about which we feel confident that we know the relevant facts, the interests that are at stake, and the consequences of deciding between those interests one way rather than another. We begin our critical thinking with our firmest moral judgments.

The methodology of critical moral thinking then requires that we move from the level of specific moral judgments to the formulation of general moral principles. In formulating principles, what we are trying to do is find a principle or set of principles that will explain the particular moral judgments we make, explain why the easy moral cases are easy, and systematize those judgments into a coherent moral point of view. Suppose that my set of firm moral judgments includes the following.

- "Slavery is wrong."
- "The use of torture, rape, and brutality toward human beings is never permissible."
- "We ought not to lie."
- "We ought to keep our promises."
- "It is wrong to engage in terrorist attacks."
- "The intentional killing of people is wrong."

Critical morality requires that I think about *why* I think all these things are wrong. Do they have something in common that makes them all wrong, and that explains why I think they are wrong? In answering this question I am trying to formulate a general principle under which all the specific judgments will form a coherent moral point of view.

What do lying, promise breaking, killing, rape, torture, slavery, terrorism, and brutality have in common? What common interest do they offend? There are a few possibilities that come readily to mind. Perhaps these actions are wrong because they all involve inflicting pain upon the victims of the wrongful action. And so the principle I might think systematizes and explains my specific moral judgments would be "It is wrong to inflict pain upon people."

Now there are two stages to testing this proposed principle. First, does it explain all the specific judgments it is meant to explain and systematize? And, second, what implications does it have in terms of further specific judgments it supports? Consider the first test first. Does the principle "It is wrong to inflict pain upon people" explain all the moral judgments it was meant to explain? No. It does not adequately explain what is wrong with breaking our promises and lying, since both of these actions can be done without the victim knowing and so without the victim experiencing any pain as a result. This principle does not forbid some actions that are clearly wrong: promise-breaking and lying.

An alternative principle that might explain all the specific judgments that need to be explained is, "You must always respect other persons." This principle is better than the first attempt, because it covers all the cases; every wrong that I was trying to explain can be seen as covered by this principle, since cruelty, promise-breaking and the rest all fail to respect the person who is wronged.

The principle of respect for persons is not the only principle that could explain the judgments in question, however. I might instead think that the judgments are best explained by this principle: "We ought to follow moral rules that produce the most happiness for everyone whose interests are concerned." Rules that forbid torture, killing, lying, promise-breaking, and the rest are likely to produce more happiness for the people whose interests are concerned than rules that allow or require such actions, and so this principle explains the cases equally well.

When we have more than one principle that systematizes and explains the specific judgments that we make, how do we decide between them? One thing we can do is expand the range of judgments to see if both principles can accommodate the expanded set. So suppose we add the judgment that when kids light cats on fire, what they are doing is wrong. The principle "You must always respect other persons" cannot explain this judgment, since cats are not persons and so they are not covered by this principle. It cannot explain why we think burning cats is wrong. By contrast, the principle "We ought to follow moral rules that produce the most happiness for every being whose interests are concerned" can explain the judgment we make about cat burning being wrong. If cats are made very unhappy by being burned alive, and their pain outweighs the happiness that people might get from burning them, then this principle would support a rule against burning cats and, presumably, other acts of wanton cruelty toward animals just for kicks. Thus this principle explains the broader range of judgments and so would be deemed superior. The reason we use such a trivial example of an obviously wrong act as inflicting wanton cruelty on animals just for fun is because if a proposed moral principle can't explain why something so obvious as *that* is wrong, the principle is clearly inadequate.

But now we come to the second way that we test our principles. We must ask what further judgments are implied by our principles. Whereas in the first stage of critical moral thinking we moved from our firm moral judgments to the level of general principles, in this stage we move from the general principles to the specific judgments they require in further cases. Take, for example, the principle that "Killing human beings is always wrong." And suppose we stipulate that "human being" means "entity with the DNA of a *Homo sapien*." If you accept this principle, then you must accept, as an implication of this principle, that killing even in a defensive war is wrong, that killing in self-defence is wrong, that abortion is wrong, that suicide is wrong. If you are not willing to accept all of these implications, then you must refine your principle.

Critical moral thinking requires that we move back and forth between the levels of specific moral judgments and general moral principles. What we are trying to do is construct a moral point of view that is coherent, within which all of our firm moral judgments are explained by our general principles, and the implications of our principles in deciding further specific cases are acceptable. The resulting point of view should allow us to say why easy moral cases are easy, being directly explained by the basic principle or principles in the view, and why hard cases are hard. It must also provide us with guidance in deciding hard or novel cases, and its direction in such cases must be such that we can accept it as ideal moral judges.

So critical moral thinking requires that we move back and forth between the levels of moral judgments and moral principles, in order to test both. We must be willing to refine and revise our principles when we find that they are too narrow to explain all the firm moral judgments that we make, or when we find that they have implications for specific cases that would appear unreasonable to an ideal moral judge. But we must also be willing to revise our specific moral judgments when they cannot be supported by the best set of principles we have been able to formulate. Revision works in both directions. In this respect critical moral reasoning follows the path described by the American philosopher John Rawls.[2] Rawls called his method *reflective equilibrium*: we are trying to bring our moral judgments and our moral principles into equilibrium, into a coherent balance where they are mutually supportive and explanatory. Our principles are supported by their ability to explain our firmest moral judgments and our further judgments are supported by the principles from which they are derived. There is balance and mutual support between the levels, producing a moral point of view that is in equilibrium. It is reflective because it has been produced by a method that begins but does not end with a person's uncritical moral judgments. Both the principles and specific moral judgments that come to make up a coherent point of view have been scrutinized; they have been tested for fit with one another, and in terms of their implications for deciding further moral questions. When the person engaged in critical moral thinking reasons from the perspective of an ideal moral judge, the moral point of view that results from this process is reflective, and has been selected as the most coherent and rationally defensible moral position available. This is the goal of critical moral thinking. Its output is what we call *critical morality*.

What we hope to do in this book is provide the tools that public servants will need in order to engage in good moral reasoning while conducting their professional lives. The discussion thus far has been framed in terms of **moral judgments, moral principles**, and other moral terms, such as values and rights. In what follows, we will provide a general outline of what we mean by the terms morality, ethics, principles, and values.

1.1 MORALITY

What is morality and what makes an issue a moral one? Morality is a system of norms that sets standards of right and proper conduct. Those standards then play two roles within moral thinking. First, they *govern our judgments* about the rightness or wrongness of actions, the goodness or badness of certain states of affairs, the virtue or viciousness of people, and the justice or injustice of social practices and institutions. This is the evaluative aspect of morality; we use it to evaluate people, actions, states of affairs and institutional or social arrangements, as good or bad, right or wrong, just or unjust, duty fulfilling or rights violating, and as displaying virtues or vices. A people's morality includes judgments about what is right and wrong in relation to human actions, what is just and unjust in their institutional and social arrangements, which character traits are virtuous and vicious, and what is good and bad in various states of affairs. Moral judgments, then, range over a number of objects: persons and their characters, actions, events and institutions. Morality provides norms for evaluation within a group of people. It identifies (evaluates) some actions as good, right, or just, while other actions are condemned as immoral, wrong, unjust, or evil. It evaluates people according to whether their conduct and attitudes exemplify virtues (such as honesty, kindness, charity, compassion, fortitude, prudence, integrity, temperance, and courage), or demonstrate vices (such as dishonesty, cruelty, insensitivity, meanness, deceptiveness, selfishness, indulgence, laziness, and cowardice). Virtues and vices are traits of character, settled dispositions of persons over time that colour not just their conduct but their attitudes, perceptions, and personality. One is a kind or cruel person, meaning more than just that one has performed a specific kind or cruel act, but that one is inclined to notice opportunities to help or harm others, to be sensitive to the needs of others, to take enjoyment from others' well-being or misfortunes. Morality thus guides our evaluations of both actions and persons.

Morality is not just evaluative, however; it is also prescriptive or normative. It provides rules, principles, or norms that govern our behaviour, and it tells us that there are some things we must not do, and other things that we must do. It is, in other words, conduct-guiding. We use morality to determine what we should do and what we should refrain from doing. Having set the standards of right and proper conduct, morality *directs us to act* in conformity with those standards. In this way morality concerns what we ought to do. As such, it is a normative and **imperative** system: morality tells us what we must or must not do. Behaviour that conforms to the standards set by morality is prescribed as what a person ought to do, while actions that violate the standards are condemned as wrong or bad, and proscribed as what a person ought *not* to do. Thus morality governs a particular range of judgments (concerning what is right, good, virtuous, or just, and their contraries), as well as issuing prescriptions concerning what people ought to do or not do (we ought not to lie, we ought to keep promises, we ought to avoid acting cruelly, and we ought not to kill).

Now in many cases morality is silent; there are many kinds of actions or choices that morality does not regulate, that are morally indifferent, or morally permissible. There is a corresponding set of values that we recognize as being personal values, values for ourselves, but not because we think these values deserve to be held by everyone; some values are personal, unlike those other values that we think all right-thinking and right-feeling persons would also recognize as valuable. While everyone might recognize fulfilling work and loving family relations as valuable, the specific choice of a career or a spouse, for example, may be matters that morality does not regulate, at least within a set of parameters (that the career be legal and the spouse be of an age to give competent consent to marriage, for example). But on other matters, morality speaks loudly and in an imperative voice, telling us what we must or must not do. Here we might speak of duties and rights, or of right and wrong, rather than of good or bad, virtue or vice. In its action-guiding mode, morality determines what is required of us, either because we have a duty to do something or because others have rights requiring that we do that thing.

We shall be concerned in this book, not just with virtues and values, but also with the action-guiding, imperative side of morality. That is because we want to discuss what morality requires civil servants to do or not do, what duties it imposes upon them, and how they ought to conduct themselves in their capacity as members of the public service. Those standards of conduct are set by the values we expect our civil servants to adopt and pursue, the realization of which is deemed worthy of public support.

Every society is committed to a set of moral beliefs, subscribes to moral values, and enforces moral norms. Morality is learned through processes of moral education, most of which occur informally. We learn morality on our mother's knee, when we are corrected using moral terms. We learn that fairness, kindness, compassion, honesty, and trustworthiness are valued, and their contraries condemned, first through the gentle correction of caregivers, and later through such social organizations as religious centres, schools, arts and sports organizations, and through peers and friends. Morality is enforced informally: moral wrongdoing in childhood is met with censure and correction. A flourishing moral culture depends upon individuals being willing to respond to the wrongdoing of others in a way that conveys social condemnation of their actions. If a given action meets no opposition, no censure or condemnation by anyone over time, then it is fair to say that, even if that action was considered morally wrong in the past, it is no longer considered so now. Moral norms are those norms which a society informally enforces through moral education and social sanctioning and, on the positive side, reinforces through praise, encouragement, and reward. Morality becomes internalized through processes of moral education and normal socialization, the goal of which is to ensure that individuals come to genuinely identify with and support the moral norms of their community as their own.

Ethics, by contrast, is more formal than morality, and is typically both articulated and enforced through more external mechanisms and agencies. Ethics is also narrower in scope than morality. It consists of a set of values, principles, and norms that govern the conduct of particular individuals under some description that is narrower than that of "person," or "member of society," such as parent, physician, judge, elected official, engineer, or researcher. There are usually some formal mechanisms to ensure compliance with the ethical requirements that apply to persons meeting those descriptions, and wrongdoing is typically responded to more formally as well. The contrast between ethics and morality will be more fully developed shortly, but given the close relationship between morality and ethics, it may be worthwhile first to continue to explore the nature of morality and moral reasoning a little further.

1.2 RELATION OF MORALITY TO INTERESTS

Presupposed in the discussion of moral judgments at the beginning of this chapter is a view of the relationship between morality and interests that is worth making explicit. There are standards of evaluation, values, and norms governing conduct of many different kinds, drawn from many different sources. When evaluating conduct or states of affairs, for example, we might appeal to standards other than those drawn from morality, such as efficiency or prudence (self-interest). There are not only moral values, but intellectual and aesthetic values as well. And human societies have norms for guiding conduct that are drawn not only from morality, but also from religion and law. What distinguishes the evaluations, values, and norms of morality from others is, we think, best characterized by their relationship to significant interests. We believe that moral issues are those which affect the significant interests of people (and perhaps other kinds of creatures that have interests, such as animals). Morality sets the standards of proper conduct toward creatures that have significant interests. Its central content takes the form of norms governing how we ought to act toward creatures with interests, and especially toward other people. Moral values attach to those things and activities which impact significant interests; those things with positive moral value contribute to the well-being of creatures with interests, while other things have disvalue to the extent that and because they set back, impede, or retard interests. The purpose of morality, ultimately, is to assist us in interacting in ways that are mutually beneficial, to help us live more peaceful, co-operative and meaningful lives, and to enable each of us to satisfy our own interests. Morality is the set of norms that, if followed, makes us all better off as social beings living in a common world. Its most central requirements must always be universal in scope. And it receives its authority from the necessary protection of interests and the mutual benefits that it makes possible. Only those norms which in fact serve our interests, and make our interactions mutually beneficial, are truly moral norms. And given that the interests of everyone matter, only those norms which serve our interests in an impartial way will be endorsed by a rationally defensible morality.

We concentrate on interests because we think doing so provides the best explanation of why morality matters. It also explains why the moral systems endorsed and followed by different groups of people have a common, uncontroversial core. That core includes rules against imposing harm on others. Everyone has an interest in being free from physical assault causing death, pain, or disability. Thus morality condemns violence and the free use of force. Everyone also values having an extensive range of freedoms and opportunities so that they are free to live their lives and determine how they shall act, to decide for themselves what activities they shall pursue and with whom they wish to share their lives. Thus morality condemns interference with the freedom and opportunities of others. Finally, because creatures with interests value pleasure, derived from a wide variety of sources, morality condemns actions that are designed to or have the effect of depriving others of pleasure. Note that pleasure here is a very broad category, and includes not just base or physical pleasures, but the pleasures derived from friendship and loving relationships, from intellectual or artistic pursuits, from a satisfying career or the achievement of goals. Other things being equal, actions that deprive people of pleasure or impede their access to the sources of pleasure are morally wrong. Morality also contains rules requiring us to refrain from types of actions that we know tend to cause harm or misery when they are done. Morality condemns deception, breaking of promises, and cheating. This could equally be stated positively: we ought to tell the truth, keep our commitments, and play fair. Morality also requires that we take the interests of others into account in our actions, provide easy aid to others when we can do so at little cost to ourselves and significant benefit to them, and generally act in such ways that our relations with others enhance their well-being rather than making them worse off.

As described thus far, the demands of morality are quite general. And they are probably not absolute. That is, there may be situations in which it is morally permissible to violate the rules of morality. Even the rule against killing or assaulting is not considered absolute by those who allow that we may be permitted to kill or wound in self-defence, in a just war, or as retribution against those who have violated the same moral rules through state punishment. All of the rules of morality are likely subject to such exceptions or qualifications, and many of the most intractable moral disputes and agonizing moral dilemmas arise in trying to determine whether one is in an exceptional circumstance that permits violation of the normal moral rules. Such exceptions may arise because two moral rules conflict in a given situation. A trivial example might be found in the conflict between telling the truth and not causing pain that can arise when a friend asks what you think of the poem he has written; you think it not very good, but to say so would hurt your friend. Is this a case in which you may violate the duty to tell the truth or refrain from intentional deception? Such situations are commonplace, of course. And they arise when the stakes are much higher than telling "a little white lie" or hurting your friend's feelings. Thoughtful, reasonable people seem to disagree, for example, over the moral status of abortion, capital punishment, euthanasia (mercy killing), and the justice of war. Do any of these situations provide an exception to the **general rule** against killing or wounding? Reasonable people may disagree. And it is not just over issues involving death that we see moral disagreement manifest itself. Is there a duty to provide assistance to the poor? A positive answer seems to interfere with freedom, while a negative answer seems to violate the requirement that we aid others when we can. Is it wrong to use animals for food or various kinds of research? On the one hand, the animals surely have an interest in not being subjected to painful treatment, not being intentionally infected with fatal diseases, and not being caged in laboratories; all of these actions involve the intentional infliction of pain on them. On the other hand, human beings have an interest in collecting scientific data about the causes and treatment of diseases, the safety of new drug therapies and the like; actions that serve these goals are recommended by our moral principles. What these cases reveal is a conflict of interests, and indeed, we think most moral disagreement arises out of competing or conflicting interests. What people disagree about in moral disputes is which of the competing interests that are at stake should be protected or served, and which interests can be subordinated. So, for example, if we are disagreeing about whether we ought to use animals in medical experiments or not, it is helpful to think about what interests are in conflict in the case. People who disagree about the moral status of such research can usually be seen to give different weight to these competing interests. We must examine what interests are at stake, and which moral rules are implicated in the situation; how seriously will interests be furthered or set back depending on how we decide to proceed, and what moral rules will be violated, depending on how we resolve the issue?

These are difficult questions, to be sure. But there are some general things we can say about how we ought to apply reason in solving them. First, all of the interests potentially affected must be considered. This is *not* to say that some interests are not more important than others; your interest in being free from a relatively minor physical injury is less than your interest in not being killed, and so the moral rule against killing is stronger than the moral rule against the infliction of physical harm when the two compete. But it *is* to say that every interest matters, and must be weighed in the overall calculation of how various interests should be balanced when they compete.

The interest of every interest-bearer must, furthermore, be considered equally. The fact that it is the death of your enemy being considered, or the pain of animals rather than people, or the freedom of a marginalized group that might be restricted, is morally irrelevant. In morality, everyone's interests matter equally. Thus we must approach moral issues from an impartial perspective. The answer we give to a moral question, the weighting we give to competing interests in a given case, must be one that we think any person reasoning about the issue impartially could also give. This functions as a constraint on our natural partiality towards ourselves and those close to us. We tend to think that our own interests are more important than the interests of others, that the needs of our children are more important than the needs of other children, that our freedom is more valuable than the freedom of those whose lifestyles we think are unworthy. We are, in a word, partial toward ourselves and those with whom we identify. It is often perfectly acceptable, moreover, to act upon this bias in a very wide range of cases. It is morally permissible to treat your own projects as especially important in deciding how to spend your own money, for example, and it is equally acceptable to choose to spend time making your parents happy rather than spending an equal amount of time making strangers happy. But we see the danger of partiality when we think about the temptation to cheat, lie, steal, or deceive. We might want to carve out exceptions for ourselves when self-interest seems to be better served by breaking the moral rules than by conforming to them. We want to be able to cheat on a test, but we don't want others to cheat. We want to be able to lie when it will serve our interests, but we want others to tell us the truth. We want to be able to steal when we think we can get away with it, but we want others to respect our property rights and leave us in peaceful possession of whatever we rightly own.

The temptation to make exceptions just for ourselves is pervasive, and we are very clever at creating rationalizations for why *our* cheating or lying is permissible but other people's is not. This is a violation of the impartiality requirement; an impartial person would not recognize our situation as unique or as special in the way that we are inclined to view it. One way of thinking about whether one is falling into this moral error is to ask whether you would be willing to have everyone act as you want to in the same conditions. Or, to put it a slightly different way, to ask whether you would be willing to have your exception made a general and public rule. This illustrates the difference between the true qualification to the rule against killing in self-defence and the purported qualification of the rule against cheating that would permit you to cheat. We would (and in fact do) allow killing in self-defence as a public rule limiting the duty not to kill, while we would not allow as a public rule everyone to cheat when doing so would allow them to do better than they would under a fair competition. Thus morality requires us to consider the interests of everyone affected by what we propose to do if what we propose to do violates a moral rule, and it requires us to ask whether allowing the rule violation could be impartially and publicly permitted as a qualification of the rule.

So we have the view that a moral issue is one involving significant interests, moral disputes are disagreements about competing interests, and moral norms are standards governing how we ought to act toward creatures with interests. Morality requires that we conform to rules that promote or protect such vital interests as the interest in bodily integrity and freedom from pain, the interest in being able to rely on others not to deceive us, cheat us, and break their promises, and the interest in having liberty and opportunities, and to enjoy a wide variety of pleasures. Morality requires that we settle disputes when interests conflict in a way that treats the interests of all equally, that is impartial, and that can be the basis of a public rule.

1.3 CONVENTIONAL AND CRITICAL MORALITY

Morality, then, is this comprehensive set of norms, values, rights, duties, and virtues that guide us in evaluating actions, characters, situations, and institutions. They all have an important connection to the interests of those affected by the actions of others. Morality tells us that we must respect the rights of others, fulfil our duties, and abide by moral rules that enable us to live peacefully together for mutual benefit.

This use of the term "morality" is ambiguous between two meanings with important differences, however. Sometimes we talk about the morality of a particular group of people at a particular time. Thus we might contrast the morality of contemporary Canadians with that of contemporary Iranians, or the morality subscribed to by contemporary Greeks with that of ancient Greeks. In this sense we use the term "morality" in a descriptive, sociological, or anthropological sense, to refer to whatever set of moral beliefs and values a particular group of people hold or held. We can talk in this sense about morality changing over time, and differing between groups. But morality in this conventional sense may be in part a product of ignorance, prejudice, superstition, and error. It may be deeply influenced by the religious beliefs of the people, their scientific knowledge, their technological circumstances, or any number of other factors. The moral beliefs of a great many groups have included elements of racism, homophobia, and sexism; their values have been infected by such considerations, so that their valuations and prescriptions include the subjugation of some members of their own communities.

When philosophers use the term "morality" they typically do not mean the moral code of a particular society, infected as it may be by such factors as ignorance, superstition, and prejudice. They do not mean conventional morality, but rather *critical morality*. Critical morality consists of that set of values, norms, rights, duties, virtues, and rules that is most rationally defensible, an ideal moral code that, if followed, would actually make peaceful co-operation for mutual benefit possible, that would enable people to live good lives and to pursue that which is truly valuable, and that would result in a distribution of rights and duties that can be defended as serving interests in an impartial way. Hereafter, we shall speak of morality in this latter sense, meaning a moral code that is rationally defensible and that reflects our best understanding of what an impartial concern for important interests requires. It is critical morality that good moral reasoning aims at, a moral view that is coherent, comprehensive, consistent, impartial, and defensible; it is consistent with the best information we have about the world (scientific knowledge as well as social scientific and humanistic knowledge), and as free from bias and prejudice as possible.

Of course, we realize that critical morality is an ideal, an objective to be sought even if we cannot ever fully attain it. We will always be bound by our limited rationality and our incomplete knowledge of the world we live in. Mistakes, errors, and ignorance are unavoidable for imperfect creatures such as human beings. But we must work toward developing a critical morality if we are to have a tool we can use to assess and critique both the moral views and values of our own communities and those of other societies, as well as an independent normative standard against which to measure and judge other normative systems within our societies, most especially law and religion.

1.4 A BRIEF INTRODUCTION TO SOME SPECIFIC MORAL CONCEPTS

A necessary preliminary to developing a critical morality is achieving clarity with respect to the central concepts used in moral thinking. One is not likely to be able to critically evaluate a rights claim, for example, such as the claim university students are often heard to make—that they have a right to education—unless one knows what rights are or what such claims purport to be about. We therefore provide a brief examination of some of the central moral concepts used in this book before proceeding.

1.4.1 Values

Moral evaluations typically reflect the values of the people making them. Morality centrally includes a set of values held by a particular group of people that guides their evaluative judgments across a range of objects of evaluation. Values are embedded in, and partly definitive of, cultures, ways of life, and organizational ethos. Values refer to what is valued (a positive attitude or emotional response to something) on the basis that it is thought to be valuable or worthy of being valued (the evaluative component to valuing). Many things are valued by people: friendship, family, love, knowledge, beauty, loyalty, health, integrity, security, freedom, peace, leisure, and recreation, for a start. Some theorists try to find a common element that unites all valuable things and activities. Utilitarians, for example, might say that what makes those things and activities which are valued truly valuable is that they contribute to happiness. A theorist inspired by the ancient Greek philosopher Aristotle might say that what makes valued things valuable is that they contribute to human excellence. **Pluralists** about value might deny that there is any one common element to the things we find valuable, and that there are many different values which are incommensurable and distinct. Whatever one's view about the nature of value and what makes something valuable, though, it is agreed that human beings are valuing creatures, that there are things and activities that we find enjoyable, toward which we have positive feelings, that we are motivated to pursue, achieve, or attain, that we approve of and are attracted to in others. It is further agreed that we are so oriented toward those valued things and activities because we believe they are worthy of being valued and they are constitutive ingredients in a worthwhile life. Other things being equal, our lives go better when we enjoy more of what we value rather than less, and we aim in much of what we do to realize, secure, protect, and cherish those things we find most valuable. Any account of morality as a system of evaluation will give an important place to values, then, since so often our evaluations of activities, states of affairs, and social conditions will be based upon the degree to which they realize what we value and find worthy of valuing. Many public service organizations (municipalities, agencies, provincial/territorial departments, and the federal public service) have at the heart of their approach to ethics a core set of values to which they are committed and that define the ethos they aspire to realize in the organization. Values will thus be very important in what follows.

The Canadian federal public service is committed to four families of inter-related values, each of which requires decision making that realizes specific ethical principles.[3] Similar values inform public service organizations at other levels of government in Canada. We provide a few examples of ethics codes from provincial and municipal governments as appendices to this work. Our goal is to develop a framework within which to think critically about ethics in the public service, and to explain what ethical public service requires and why it is important. In what follows, we provide guidance with respect to what the various values and principles to which public service organizations are committed mean, and how they might be realized in an ethical public service organization.

1.4.2 Virtues and Vices

Virtues are traits of character extending over a period of time, traits that to a large extent determine the kind of person one is: kind or cruel, just or unjust, honest or dishonest, compassionate or insensitive, temperate or intemperate, generous or miserly, courageous or cowardly, and the like. As this suggests, we can not only talk of some positive character trait as a virtue, but contrast it with its contrary or opposite, which is a vice. In fact, Aristotle thought that each virtue was paired with *two* contrasting vices, one of excess and one of deficit, with the virtue lying somewhere in between as a mean. Consider, for example, the virtue of courage. This virtue involves a resoluteness to stand firm in the face of certain dangers. This meant especially the danger of death for Aristotle, though we can recognize courage in a wider range of cases, such as the courage required to tell one's boss that one thinks she is making a mistake. How is courage a mean between two contrasting states, of excess or deficiency? If one has an excess of courage, one is foolhardy or insensible of genuine danger. If one has a deficiency of courage, one is timid and meek, and too easily frightened to resist threats or risk perils when necessary. Courage is the mean between these two states. Aristotle thought this was a structure common to virtues. To consider another example, take **honesty**. A person is honest who tells the truth as appropriate, and this is a virtue. An excess of truthfulness, by contrast, is found in a person who tells more than necessary, who shares the secrets of others, or who tells the truth even when it will do nothing but cause pain. A deficiency of honesty is revealed by a person who withholds the truth, who lies or deceives, who tells only partial truths, or who fails to provide information, the disclosure of which is important in the circumstances. Honesty is the mean.

Those who think that the most important demand morality places upon us is to live lives of virtue and to develop good characters are known as virtue ethicists or followers of virtue ethics. Virtue ethics is not, in the first instance, an ethics of actions. It evaluates persons rather than actions. But actions are important to virtue ethics, in one of two ways, depending on the particular version of the theory in play. Actions might be important because they provide the best evidence we have of a person's character. How do we know that a person is honest, or charitable, or courageous? We look to see how she acts over time, and whether her actions display the character traits which reflect that virtue. According to this view, it is possible that a person could be courageous even if she has never in fact had an opportunity to act courageously, because she has never faced a situation of mortal danger. A different view would be that our virtues are determined by our actions, because being courageous or compassionate consists of doing courageous or compassionate things. According to this alternative, it doesn't really make sense to talk about virtues that have never been displayed in action. But regardless of this point of contention internal to virtue ethics, it is agreed that virtues cannot be fully explicated just in terms of the actions they motivate. Rather, virtues are more pervasive than that. Our virtues and vices, those lasting character traits that largely define the kind of person we are, not only incline us to act in specific ways in circumstances where the virtue or vice can manifest itself, but they also colour our perceptions and affect our sensitivities. A kind and compassionate person, for example, not only provides assistance and care to others, but he notices when others are in need of such assistance or care. He is open to the well-being of others, notices occasions when others might need help, and is attuned to the needs of others, having a range of sensitivities that allow him to see that this might be an occasion when compassion is appropriate. The callous or unkind person, by contrast, not only fails to provide care and assistance to others when he can do so and it is needed, but fails to even notice the need in the first place. This contrasts with a genuinely cruel person, who notices other people's pain or need, but revels in it, contributes to it, and makes it worse. Thus learning virtue requires developing our sensitivities, to be open to recognizing the kind of situation we are in and responding appropriately. As Aristotle said, virtue consists of doing the right thing, for the right reason, on the right occasion.[4] Consider, for example, a friend who is brutally honest in a circumstance where what his friend needs is compassion and support, or a charitable person who foists unwanted help on others who find that help degrading and shaming. It is not that being an honest friend and being charitable are not virtues, but they have been applied in the wrong circumstances or in the wrong way in these cases.

Virtues can be learned. And they are best learned by being practised. Indeed, Aristotle thought that this was the only way that virtue could be learned; we learn to become virtuous by acting virtuously, and we attain virtue once acting virtuously has become habitual. This makes having virtuous role models especially important, because we develop virtues by imitating those who are virtuous. The virtues needed in an ethical public service will also be explored in this book. Among the most important will be integrity, honesty, respect, and a sense of justice.

1.4.3 Rights and Duties

The discussion of morality has been framed in terms of values and rules, standards of evaluation, and conduct-guiding prescriptions. But morality also includes rights and duties. Both have been the subject of sustained philosophical study, and we cannot do full justice to the richness of those studies here. But a few words are in order. Let's start with rights.

Rights are entitlements. There are two kinds of rights, and three important sources of rights. One of the most common kinds of rights is called "claim rights."[5] **Claim rights** have corresponding duties. Thus we can speak of a student's right to a fair grade on her term paper, or we can speak equally well of the corresponding duty of her professor to assign her a fair grade on her term paper. Claim rights take the following form, like an equation: person P has a claim right to x against person $R = R$ has a duty to x that is owed to P. Claim rights are thus relational, governing the relation between the person with the right and the person who owes the corresponding duty. I have a duty to my government to pay my taxes = my government has a claim right against me that I pay my taxes.

What one has a right to (x in the preceding schema) is not determined by the fact that one has a right. It may be something positive or negative, and the right may be universal or particular. The right to a fair grade is positive and particular. It is positive in the sense that it requires that the right holder actually be given something, or be treated in some way, or that some state of affairs be brought about by the person with the corresponding duty; the teacher must assign a fair grade, or bring about a state of affairs in which the student receives a fair grade, or must grade the student fairly. There is some positive action required of the duty holder. And it is particular, because the right is held against a particular person, namely the teacher. Likewise with the tax example: it is owed to a particular government, namely mine, and it requires that I do something, namely pay my taxes. Claim rights can also be negative, such as in cases where the duty bearer must refrain from doing something as a result of the right. It is clear that there is a **negative right** to life, for example: I have a right to life held against you = you have a duty not to kill me. Most people think this is a universal right, because the duty it imposes applies to everyone, universally; everyone has a duty not to kill me. (Of course, if we allow that I may permissibly be killed if I unlawfully attack you and you have to kill me in self-defence, or if you may kill me if I am a combatant in an unjust war, then we may deny that the right is really universal in this sense; instead, it is a right I have only against most people. Or we might deal with this problem by retaining the belief that the right is universal, but say that in some cases we may permissibly violate a right. Different theorists prefer different ways of characterizing this phenomenon about rights.) Some rights are also universal in the sense that everyone has them. Again, the right to life (the right not to be killed) is usually considered universal in this sense too (though again the exceptions pose the same problem).

The right not to be killed is a negative right, in the sense that it imposes only **negative duties**, or duties to refrain from acting, on the person with the corresponding duty. Negative duties are easy to fulfil. I am, while writing this, fulfilling my duties not to kill you and everyone else. I can fulfil my negative duties by doing nothing at all, even while I am asleep. If my adult child has a right relative to me to choose his own mate, for example, I am duty bound not to interfere with or prevent his so choosing; I have only to do nothing to fulfil my duty.

Positive duties, on the other hand, are often very hard to fulfil, because they impose positive duties on those against whom they are held. To see the difference, consider again the right to life, but now suppose it is a **positive right** rather than a negative one. If positive, it would be the right to have whatever the right-holder needs to live. And as a universal right, it would impose on everyone else a duty to provide whatever the right-holder needs to live. This may impose significant burdens on others, and be very hard to meet, if the right-holder has particularly great needs that have to be met to live. What if, for example, what the right-holder needs to live is my kidney? Suppose I am the only suitable donor, and she will die without my organ. If she has a positive right against everyone, including me, to whatever she needs to live, then I have a duty to surrender my kidney. Whether rights are construed as positive or negative thus matters a great deal.

Many controversies have involved disputes about whether a given right is negative or positive. The United Nations Universal Declaration of Human Rights, and a number of similar international and national statements of rights, will impose very different duties upon others and upon governments depending on whether they are taken to be positive or negative. Every province and territory in Canada, as well as the federal government, has issued human rights codes which state that those governed by them have a range of **human rights**. If these rights are negative, requiring others merely to refrain from interfering with the exercise of them, then it may be easy to satisfy them; if, on the other hand, they impose positive duties, then other individuals, groups, or governments may have to do quite a bit to meet the rights articulated therein.

A second kind of right is known as a **liberty**, or a **liberty-right**. These rights do not have corresponding duties. If I have a liberty-right to pursue an education, no one need have a duty to provide me with an education. Instead, what such rights entail is that there is no corresponding duty on me not to pursue an education. Liberties entitle one to do what one has a right to, and indicate that the right-holder has no duty not to act as she has a liberty-right to act. Liberty-rights are correlated with permissions; if I have a liberty-right to do *x* then doing *x* is morally permissible for me (i.e., doing *x* would not violate any moral duty I have with respect to *x*-ing). I have a liberty-right to choose whether to marry, for example, because I have no duty to marry that is owed to anyone. Once I have promised to marry a particular person, I have given up my liberty-right and thereby assume a duty to marry. Through our own commitments we often give up liberties we have, thereby assuming duties that we did not have and would not have had but for our voluntary acceptance of them.

This brings us to the second point about rights mentioned above, namely that they may have different sources. Some rights are thought of as human rights (also called natural rights), rights we have just by virtue of being human beings. The United Nations Declaration of Human Rights articulates a comprehensive set of such rights. The grounding of such rights must be some feature of human beings that is universal and, probably, unique. Thus human rights are often said to be grounded in our common rationality, our status as rational or autonomous agents, or our status as creatures having inherent dignity or worth. Such rights are often thought to be held against other human beings, so that other people have the corresponding duties not to interfere with actions we have a right to engage in.

Other rights, by contrast, are not universal but rather are enjoyed by particular people against particular other people. Chief among such rights are civil and **legal rights**, the kinds of rights found in such things as the Canadian *Charter of Rights and Freedoms*. This document, which is part of our Constitution and so part of the highest law of our land, articulates a set of rights and freedoms enjoyed by persons in Canada or by Canadian citizens and landed immigrants whether within Canada or elsewhere in the world. The rights granted by the *Charter* are not enjoyed by all persons, just in virtue of being human beings, but rather are enjoyed by a group of people identified as being members of a given political community. They are rights enjoyed by Canadians, but not by Americans or Egyptians. And they do not hold against everyone else, even every other Canadian, but rather they are held against our governments. The duties imposed by the *Charter*, such as the duty not to discriminate against people on the basis of marital status, or the duty to treat those charged with a criminal offence as if they are innocent until proven guilty by an impartial tribunal after a fair trial, or the duty not to violate freedom of expression, are duties on our governments to act or not act as the right requires. Thus it is possible for governments to violate the civil rights of Canadians, but private individuals and institutions cannot. Membership in a particular polity is a common source of rights, and those rights extend only to members of that polity. Some members of the Canadian polity are members by birth, and so some of their rights are in some sense enjoyed independently of any choice or action of their part. Susan Dimock was born in Canada and so has the rights and freedoms of a Canadian citizen not by choice, but rather by historical accident. Of course, she could choose to emigrate, but short of renouncing her Canadian citizenship, she enjoys the rights of a Canadian through no choice of her own. Other members of the polity have chosen to come to Canada and have adopted Canadian citizenship or landed immigrant status as a matter of conscious choice. They have thus acquired their *Charter* rights and freedoms in a more voluntary manner.

Many rights and duties are similarly the product of our voluntary choices, and are specific to a role or position. Thus we might speak of the rights of members of various organizations, such as churches or universities or clubs. As a faculty member at a Canadian university, Susan Dimock has the right to participate in the collegial governance of her university, the right to academic freedom, and the right to disseminate the results of her research, for example. All of these rights are specific and are enjoyed as part of voluntary membership in a particular organization. The same is true of many duties. As a faculty member, she has a duty to conscientiously prepare material for her classes, to hold lectures as scheduled, to grade students' work fairly, and to engage in scholarly and research activities. She has these duties by virtue of her position within the university. Some of those duties she owes to her students, others to the university as her employer, and some to Canadian tax-payers generally, who support university activities through their taxes. Yet all are duties she owes in virtue of her position as a university professor. If she ceases to hold that position, many of the rights she enjoys and duties she owes would cease to apply to her. Rights and duties often arise in relation to our membership in various groups and organizations, or to roles we occupy within society. In this same vein, we might speak of the rights and duties of parents, for example. Parents have certain rights with respect to their minor children, such as the right to set a curfew or to choose where they will go to school. No one else has the right to set a curfew or choose a school for my children, and I do not have that right with respect to other people's children. I likewise have duties to my children that I do not have to anyone else, and that no one else has toward them. I have the duty to provide the "necessaries of life" to my children under Canadian criminal law, and so long as I have custody of them, no one else has this same duty; I have no such duty toward the children of other people.

So one common way of acquiring rights and duties is to assume social or political roles that are in part defined by such rights and duties, such as becoming a parent or a citizen or a police officer. Another very common way of acquiring new duties and granting new rights to others is through promising or contracting. Indeed, both promising and contracting are practices that are at least partly defined by the fact that they create rights and duties that did not exist before the promise or contract was made, and they are useful practices precisely because they allow individuals to change their moral relations with others in just this way.

Though rights and duties often hang together in the ways just described, there may be some duties that do not have corresponding rights, or that are not owed to particular other people. The nature of such duties is controversial. Perhaps we have duties to animals or the environment, which do not reduce to rights enjoyed by animals or the environment, or indirectly to other people. Perhaps we have duties toward ourselves, such as the duty to develop our natural talents; it would be odd to suggest that such duties are correlated with rights.

Duties are sometimes characterized as either perfect or imperfect. Perfect duties are duties that dictate specific actions as required in each and every case that the duty is operative. Thus the duty not to engage in an act of avoidable killing is a perfect duty, requiring that we not kill in every situation where killing is possible but avoidable. **Imperfect duties** are not imperfect in the sense of being less important, but rather in the sense that they do not dictate specific actions as necessary in every circumstance where the duty applies. So, for example, the duties to develop our natural talents and to be charitable are imperfect in the sense that they leave open a range of actions that could be taken in fulfilment of the duty, and they do not dictate specific actions in every circumstance where the duty could be fulfilled. I have considerable latitude or discretion in choosing how to fulfil these duties: I might undertake post-secondary education, or work to perfect my skill at playing the piano, as ways of developing my natural talents; I may give money to the United Way or work in a soup kitchen in fulfilling my duty of charity. It is not that I must always choose that action which would perfect my talents or express charity for others; I may choose how to fulfil these duties in any number of ways, and over time, even if that means forgoing opportunities to engage in self-improvement or charitable acts on a given occasion.

1.5 THEORETICAL AND APPLIED ETHICS

We follow the lead of many philosophers and theorists in distinguishing between morality and ethics. Often the difference is understood this way: ethics is the critical study of morality and the construction and evaluation of moral theories.

This is known as theoretical ethics. Whereas morality concerns the moral judgments, values, and norms of a given people, ethics is the study of morality itself. The aim of ethics is to develop a critical morality, a moral theory consisting of those principles, values, and norms that are rationally defensible, that if followed would make everyone living under the recommended morality better off in terms of the protection of their interests and the realization of whatever is truly worthy of being valued. Morality, we might say, is what children learn at their mothers' knee, whereas ethics is what professional philosophers and ethicists develop after critically examining a host of conventional moral systems and subjecting them to tests of good theorizing: coherence and consistency, explanatory power, predictive success, effectiveness in the impartial service of significant interests, and the ability to resolve moral controversies and uncertainties, among other criteria.

The study of critical morality is the subject matter of moral philosophy or ethics. It consists of the set of moral beliefs, norms, institutions, and practices that would be endorsed as those which are rationally most defensible. Critical morality is a corrective to **conventional morality**. Different moral theories, such as we shall examine later, attempt to identify the content of critical morality, the set of moral beliefs and practices that are most rationally defensible. They also typically provide guidance as to the right method for thinking critically about moral issues, including the issue of whether any particular conventional moral belief is defensible and so deserving of rational support.

Applied and professional ethics are sub-fields within the study of ethics. In **applied ethics**, general ethical theories—consisting of a coherent set of values, principles, rules, evaluative standards, duties, rights, and virtues—are applied to solve moral problems and answer moral questions that arise within a given field of activity, such as medical research (known as bioethics), environmental activities (known as environmental ethics), business activities (known as business ethics), or military activities (known as military ethics). **Professional ethics** is a branch of applied ethics that deals with activities that are organized around the practice of a given profession, such as medical ethics (defining the ethical values, principles, obligations, and rights of physicians), legal ethics (defining the same for lawyers), judicial ethics (for judges), engineering ethics (for engineers), accounting ethics (for chartered accountants), and public sector ethics (for public servants). These more specific areas of applied ethics locate the values, principles, virtues, rules, rights, and duties of participants against an understanding of the specific role of the relevant profession in society, the kinds of rights and responsibilities that practice of the profession requires, and the ideals and values it is trying to realize. In what follows we develop an account of ethics suitable for the public service in a liberal democracy. Public sector ethics is then an account of the moral obligations, rights, values, and principles that ought to govern the conduct of those engaged in public service organizations. In keeping with the contrast between ethics and morality drawn earlier, public service ethics are more formal, narrower, and more externally developed and enforced than morality generally.

1.5.1 Moral Judgments, Moral Principles, and Moral Reasoning

The move from conventional to critical morality, and from morality to ethics, is simultaneously the move from moral judgments to moral principles. Moral judgments are specific, and apply to **act tokens**. Act tokens are specific, concrete actions or events in a particular set of circumstances. Thus we might speak of the act token: "Jones shooting Smith." Moral judgments arise when we judge that a particular action is wrong, that a particular person displays a certain virtue, or that a particular duty has been violated. Principles, by contrast, are general and abstract. They are about *types* of actions. The shooting of Smith by Jones is an instance or example of a general action type: "killing." To illustrate the relation, imagine that you are walking down the street and see a group of young people assaulting an elderly man. You can be expected to make the immediate, pre-theoretical judgment: that what they are doing is wrong. But what we want to know when we are doing ethics is *why* the action is wrong. What is it about such an assault that makes it wrong? Once we have an answer to that question, we can begin to develop moral principles and moral theories that explain what wrong actions have in common that makes them wrong, and what types of actions are wrong and why. Then we can use our moral principles and moral theories to engage in reasoning about new situations, to resolve conflicts between our moral principles, and to critically adjust the judgments we make when they are influenced by such things as prejudice or partiality.

When thinking about critical morality, we must distinguish between moral judgments and moral principles. Moral judgments are specific judgments we make when we call some person or action or practice good or bad, right or wrong, just or unjust, virtuous or vicious. So, to return to our example, if you were to turn a street corner and see a group of young people beating an elderly person, you might be expected to make the moral judgment that what they were doing is morally wrong. Likewise, if a business acquaintance tells you that she has been interviewing candidates for a job, and that she has decided to hire a candidate from a First Nations community even though he is not strictly the best qualified for the job, you might applaud this decision as an instance of corrective justice. And if you read in the newspaper that cosmetics companies have been using animals to test their products, in ways that cause considerable pain to the animals, you might think the researchers involved to be vicious and their activities to be bad. These are examples of specific moral judgments that a person might be expected to make; other people may make different judgments, of course, and so we have moral disagreement at the level of moral judgments.

Critical moral thinking begins with the judgments that we make, but it does not stop there. We also formulate moral principles. Ethics involves the development of moral principles and the construction of theories of critical morality. Moral principles are general in a way that specific judgments are not. Principles identify *types* of actions as morally right or wrong, good or bad, and the like. These principles then form the foundations of competing ethical theories that attempt to explain what it is that makes particular actions or practices or people right or good or just or virtuous. Such principles, and the theories that are built upon them, attempt to systematize and explain the particular moral judgments that we make, to identify what properties make right actions right and wrong actions wrong, and to guide our thinking about new or difficult moral issues. Examples of moral principles are the following:

- All persons deserve equal concern and respect;
- That action is right which produces the greatest happiness for the greatest number of people affected by it;
- Every person ought to enjoy the most extensive liberty compatible with everyone else enjoying the same liberty.

These are general moral principles, which are used both to explain the specific judgments we make and to justify those judgments that conform to them.

The interplay between moral judgments and moral principles is at the heart of **reflective moral reasoning**. Critical or reflective moral reasoning must instruct individuals concerning what they ought to do. It must do so, especially, in hard cases—cases concerning which there is moral disagreement. Critical moral reasoning must help us decide between the competing claims that make up moral disputes. And it must resolve such disputes in a reasoned and principled way.

Reflective moral reasoning begins with the specific judgments we make, when we simply respond to some action or event or person as morally good, right, or just, or when we immediately respond positively or negatively to a particular action or event. The response will be moral when our reaction is centrally guided by the impact of the action on important interests, or when our evaluation of an event or situation takes into account how the event or situation affects important interests. But even though reflective moral reasoning begins with specific moral judgments, taking them as it were as data in the construction of our ethical principles and theories, not all judgments should be treated alike. Even at this beginning stage, we ought to recognize that some judgments deserve more respect than others. There are norms for good judging.

1.5.2 Reliable Moral Judgments

First, a good judge does not decide a case when she is drunk, when she is under serious emotional distress, or when she is very tired or distracted. These and other influences we commonly recognize can impair the judgment of a person and a good judge would postpone making decisions if she was influenced by such factors, or would give lesser weight to a judgment made under such influences.

Likewise, since moral judgments involve interests, a good judge never decides a case in which his own interests are personally involved. The fact that the judge's own interests would be affected by the outcome of a case disqualifies the judge. The worry, of course, is that in such cases the judge would not be impartial, and would be biased toward a solution that favoured his own interests, regardless of the relative merits of the competing positions. At the most extreme, judges must never be allowed to judge cases in which they themselves are a party to the dispute. More generally, we ought to be suspicious of any judgment we make that might be tainted by bias because our own interests, or the interests of those close to us, are implicated in what we are judging. The more impartial we can be in making a judgment the better. If we think our judgment is influenced by prejudice or partiality, to that degree we ought not to trust it.

A judge must also be sensitive in considering who has interests that are at stake in any dispute or that may be affected by any decision. Only if all the competing interests are considered will a reasoned resolution of their conflict be possible. One common reason why people find themselves in difficult conflict situations is that they fail to give due weight to the interests of those whose interests conflict with their own, dismissing the concerns of other parties as irrelevant or unimportant. A judge must never dismiss the interests of any of the disputants in this way. One of the most serious ways of being prejudiced is to have prejudged which interests are important before examining the matter.

Finally, a judge must do the best she can to ascertain any facts that are relevant in the dispute or to a decision. This is often a difficult task. But if it becomes clear that any of the conflict rests on disputes about the facts (such as whether animals really feel pain, whether imprisonment serves as a deterrent to crime, whether building a dam in a given location will undermine agriculture in the area, whether a drug is efficacious in treating a given disease, and so on), the judge must use all the methods of respectable investigation appropriate to the domain to decide which set of facts is most fully supported by the evidence. When considering how much weight to give to a particular judgment, we must consider to what degree it depends upon beliefs or assumptions about essential factual matters, and what evidence we have for the truth of those beliefs or assumptions.

These are requirements of good judging because, when they are satisfied, we can be as sure as possible that the judge has considered all the relevant moral and non-moral facts of a case, has taken full and unbiased account of all the interests that are in conflict in the situation, and has impartially weighed the competing claims of the disputants. When such a judge renders a verdict in favour of one of the disputants against the other, or settles on a compromise between their competing claims, we can be as sure as it is possible to be that that is the most reasonable judgment that could be made. We can also assume that any other similarly good judge would agree with the judgment, or at least see it as justified.

When we engage in critical moral reasoning, we must try to emulate as fully as possible the ideal of a good moral judge. We must take into account all of the competing interests, we must be impartial between the different moral positions being put forward, we must be as fully informed of any relevant facts as is possible, we must be impartial between the disputants, and we must be free of influences that distort our judgment. When we make moral judgments under such ideal conditions we can be as confident as it is possible to be that those judgments are as reasonable as could be made.

1.6 LAW AND RELIGION

Morality is only one of many normative systems typically found within human communities. Among the most important other normative systems are those of law and religion. All three are normative systems, in that they set standards of right and proper conduct, and prescribe actions that conform to those standards as what people ought to do. The relationships between morality, law, and religion in societies are enormously complex, and might be examined from any number of perspectives. We might examine, for example, the degree to which a legal system enforces the morality of the dominant social group, or the way in which religious groups reinforce the norms of morality and help their members internalize those norms.

It would be extraordinary if we did not find considerable overlap between the norms recommended by the religious, legal, and moral traditions within a given society. It would be unreasonable to think that the legal code and conventional moral code of a society could be entirely unrelated. Human beings often use law to reinforce their moral systems. Moreover, law serves many of the same purposes that morality does. It should provide rules governing human behaviour that make for peaceful and co-operative interaction in society, and mechanisms for resolving disputes when the interests of some come into conflict with the interests of others. The same may be said with respect to morality and religion. We see such overlap, for example, in the prohibition on killing: killing is condemned in most religions as a sin, in criminal law as a crime, and in morality as violation of a basic right. Thus all three normative systems include a prohibition on killing. This itself will be unsurprising if a society's conception of law and/or religion in themselves make essential reference to the important interests of those governed by the systems. If, for example, we think that law ought to, and for the most part does, aim at the well-being of individuals, at protecting them from various kinds of harm and securing various opportunities for them, then we would expect law and morality to overlap in important ways. Likewise, if we think that religion aims at the personal fulfilment and communal well-being of its adherents, then again we should expect overlap between its requirements and those of morality. Of course, whether one thinks that these are the basic purposes of law or religion, as opposed to keeping the masses under control or serving the greater glory of God, say, is an open question. But *if* one thinks that law or religion ought to and does aim to serve and protect the interests of creatures with interests, then significant overlap will be expected.

But it is important, notwithstanding such overlap, to recognize that the three are conceptually distinct normative systems. This is especially apparent when we move from conventional morality to critical morality. We begin with law. The norms of a legal system and that of critical morality may differ. We know, for example, that some legal systems have explicitly supported the institution of slavery and denied basic rights to women. Critical morality, we assume, would condemn such laws as morally unjustified, because they do not serve interests in an impartial way, nor do they provide mutual benefit; instead, they make benefits for some available only at the expense of others. We think critical morality would condemn such laws on these grounds.

One of the great benefits of attending to the separation of law and morality is that it provides us with an independent tool with which to assess the justifiability of our legal rules and practices. For, just as the conventional moral system of a society may be defective, influenced by ignorance, prejudice, and the like, so can its legal system be defective. In both cases our standard of deficiency is set by critical morality. Critical morality provides an independent standard against which we can test both the moral opinions of our fellows and the laws of our society. Ideally, both will be reformed to bring them into closer harmony with the dictates of critical morality over time. We have seen such a progression with respect to both conventional moral views and laws concerning homosexuality in recent years; we have come to see that our commitments to equality are inconsistent with moral and legal discrimination against gays and lesbians, and that our past treatment of these groups is inconsistent with the moral principles to which we subscribe.

By **law**, we are referring here to positive law, the law as posited by those with authority to make law within our legal system, which is a constitutional parliamentary democracy. "Law" includes all the various branches of law: public law, family law, criminal law, regulatory law, tort law, and more. Such laws may be wise or misguided, beneficial or harmful, just or unjust, but regardless they are the laws of the land, provided they have been enacted by the right authorities within their legislative competence and according to the procedures established for law-making. In a legal system such as ours, there is thought to be a basic division of authority between those who make laws (democratically elected legislators) and those who apply the laws that others make (appointed judges). Public servants play an interesting role within this general division of labour and authority. They are often involved in drafting laws and their attendant regulations, though they do not have ultimate legislative authority; their role is to serve democratically elected and publicly **accountable** legislators in developing legislation as determined by the legislators. Public servants also play an important role in interpreting the laws as they conduct their day-to-day affairs. While they do not have the authority to provide authoritative and final interpretations of the law (a power vested in judges, and especially in the Justices of the Supreme Court of Canada), the reality is that public servants often have to interpret the laws in order to do their jobs. There are competing theories of legal interpretation: one is to follow the plain meaning of the law; another is to follow the intent of the original creators of the law; yet another is to interpret the law so that it conforms to principles of liberal democracy. But whatever one's theory of legal interpretation, laws must be interpreted so that they comply with the *Charter of Rights and Freedoms* and other constitutional conventions, including the jurisdictional division between federal and provincial/territorial authority.

Given their role in maintaining constitutional democracy, public servants must be committed to the rule of law, as they have a very strong duty to uphold the law. If public servants act contrary to the law, they undermine the authority and accountability of elected politicians, and threaten democracy itself. Yet once we recognize that some laws may themselves be unjust or otherwise morally objectionable, this duty becomes much more complex. This will become clearer in what follows. It is noteworthy that the duty of public servants to uphold the law is consistent with attempting to have laws changed that public servants deem to be defective in one way or another.

Religion is, of course, the other important normative system within many cultures. It often influences both the legal code of a society and the moral beliefs of individuals. But it is an independent normative system. If the deity requires that we treat each other well (because he loves us, for instance), then there will be some overlap again between the dictates of religion and those of law and morality. Religious groups often play a vital role in the moral education of children, moreover, and many believers find in their religious convictions strong motivations to be moral. Being morally good is often encouraged by religion. Religion often plays a significant role in the lives of individuals, making those lives more meaningful, connecting people to a broader community, and often is a strong support to morally good action and the building of virtuous and happy characters. However, critical morality stands independent of religion; it can be studied in its own right, and appeals to religious authority alone cannot be an acceptable method of resolving moral conflicts, at least within the context of public sector ethics. Despite the fact that religion and morality are often bound up together in the moral outlook of believers, religion *per se* cannot play a role in determining the content of the moral obligations of public servants.

We must reject religion as a guide to what critical morality requires if we are trying to develop an approach to ethical decision making for members of the public service in a liberal democracy. Members of the public service must act in the interests of all Canadians, whatever their religious views, and must be able to defend their advice and decisions to the public (through their ministers, councillors, or other superiors). Such a defence cannot rest on as contested and divisive a foundation as religion. Canada is a country committed to freedom of religion and freedom of conscience, and to **multiculturalism**, religious pluralism, and toleration. There is no official religion to which we must as Canadians subscribe. To justify one's actions and decisions as members of governmental structures founded on such commitments as religious tolerance and multiculturalism, members of the public service must appeal to principles that can be endorsed from a broad range of viewpoints.[6] Members of the public service thus cannot appeal to religious authority in defence of the decisions they make; instead, they must appeal to principles that are consistent with religious freedom, religious tolerance, and multiculturalism.

QUESTIONS FOR FURTHER DISCUSSION

1. What are the four Canadian families of inter-related values? Explain each.

2. What is the relationship between morality and values? How does one relate to the other?

3. Explain the difference between evaluative and descriptive morality. Why is this distinction important for public service workers?

4. List and explain the two kinds of rights discussed. What is the main difference between them?

5. What is the difference between negative and positive duties? Give an example of each, not from the book.

6. Are all rights derived from the same source? If not, then what sources of rights might there be?

7. What are some of the ways by which we acquire rights (and their corresponding duties)?

8. What does it mean to say that morality is in everyone's interest? Is this different from saying that "what is good for me is good for you"? Explain why or why not.

9. Given that "interests" can come into conflict, what are some of the considerations that public servants should keep in mind when reasoning about competing interests?

10. Explain the difference between critical and conventional morality. In your opinion, which form of morality is most important for public service?

11. Explain, in your own words, the relationship between moral judgments and moral principles. How is one derived from the other?

12. What is reflective equilibrium and how does it work? (In your answer, be sure to consider how moral judgments, convictions, and principles interact.)

13. How might we test a proposed moral principle after it has been formulated?

NOTES

[1] By speaking of moral "easy cases" and "hard cases," we mean to draw an analogy between what makes a case a hard case in morality and what makes a case a hard case in law. In law, the notion of "hard cases" and what makes a case hard or easy is a matter of importance, and different theorists of law draw the line between easy and hard cases in different places. For examples, see H. L. A. Hart, *The Concept of Law*, 2nd ed. (Oxford: Oxford University Press, 1994) and Ronald Dworkin, *Law's Empire* (Cambridge, MA: Harvard University Press, 1986).

[2] John Rawls, *A Theory of Justice* (Cambridge, MA: Harvard University Press, 1971).

[3] See Appendix 1, "Values and Ethics Code for the Public Service," Treasury Board, 2003. http://www.tbs-sct.gc.ca/pubs_pol/hrpubs/tb_851/vec-cve1-eng.asp.

[4] Aristotle, *Nicomachean Ethics*. There are several good English translations of this text available.

[5] The contrast drawn here between claim rights and liberty-rights comes from Wesley N. Hohfeld, "Some Fundamental Legal Conceptions as Applied in Legal Reasoning," *Yale Law Journal* 23: 16 (1913).

[6] A strong version of this thesis is endorsed by John Rawls, who argues that only "public reasons," reasons derived from a commitment to a conception of persons as free and equal and sharing a sense of justice but independent of any comprehensive and contestable doctrine such as religions, are eligible for use in the political arena in a liberal democracy. We need not endorse the whole of Rawls's view on public reasons to recognize that public decisions cannot be based just on religious convictions or religious authority if they are to conform to the principles of religious freedom and multiculturalism. See John Rawls, "The Idea of Public Reason Revisited," *The University of Chicago Law Review* 64: 3 (Summer, 1997): 765–807.

Moral Principles and Moral Theories

In this chapter, we briefly describe a few of the most important moral principles that inform the thinking of most individuals in Western societies, including Canada. These principles have been so important that whole moral theories have been built around each of them. Because the reasoning supported by these moral approaches is so common, it is useful to be able to identify them so that we can evaluate their appropriateness for a given circumstance or problem, and so that we can understand their limitations as guides to moral conduct.

2.1 UTILITARIANISM, ACT AND RULE

A very common approach to moral reasoning is that found in the moral theory known as utilitarianism. Utilitarianism begins with a theory of value: what has value, ultimately, is happiness. Everything else that we value is valuable because it contributes to happiness. This point is usually established as follows. Think of all the things or activities you value: money, friends, spending time with your family, your career, your car, gardening, health, sports, enjoying the arts, or engaging in creative activities, and so on. Why do you value these things? Because they make you happy. In the case of money, its value is purely instrumental; that is, it is a means to other things that you value. Money is a means to security, health, power, comfort, leisure, and consumer goods. Why do you value money? Because you value these other things, and money is a means of getting them. Why do you value these other things (health, power, leisure, etc.)?

Ultimately the only answer you can give is that they make you happy, and their loss or absence would make you unhappy.

Some of the things you value are not merely instrumentally valuable, like money, as a means to other ends; rather they have **constitutive value** because they are partly what you think constitutes a happy life. Many of the activities we engage in are constitutively valuable; they partly constitute a happy life. Time spent with loved ones, or engaged in meaningful work, for example, is typically treated as a constitutive good. But even **constitutive goods** are valuable, ultimately, because they contribute to a good, i.e., happy, life. A theory of value tells us what is good, and utilitarians think that what is **intrinsically** good—good in and of itself and for its own sake—is happiness. Everything else is good, or has value, because it is constitutive of happiness or is a means to it. The theory takes its name from **utility**, which is just a measure of happiness.

Utilitarianism, like all moral theories, includes an egalitarian or impartiality component. For utilitarians, this means that the happiness of every person is equally valuable. It does not matter whose happiness is at stake; happiness is valuable wherever it is found. One state of affairs is better than another if it has more happiness in it than the other.

From their theory of value, utilitarians then construct their **normative principle**: we ought to always act so as to bring about the most good, i.e., happiness, that is possible. This is often characterized as the **greatest happiness principle**: always act so as to produce the greatest amount of happiness for the greatest number of people possible. Figuring out what we ought to do requires considering the implications of our various choices in terms of their outcomes for happiness. Because utilitarianism is concerned with outcomes, or consequences, and tells us to act in such a way as to bring about the consequence that the greatest amount of happiness is enjoyed, it is a **consequentialist moral theory**. We are to consider all of the people whose happiness would be affected as a consequence of our possible actions, consider for each person how much happiness each option would produce, and then add up the total amount of happiness each option would produce. We must sum up all of the positive utility associated with each of our possible choices. Then we must also consider all of the negative consequences that each option might produce, weigh up all the disvalue of each possible action for each person who might be affected by it. We then sum the negative utility of each option. Having done this, we then subtract the disutility from the utility of each possible option, and choose the action that will produce the highest level of positive utility from among our possible actions. If we are choosing between evils, we should choose the option that produces the least amount of bad or unhappiness overall.

In performing this calculus (known as the **felicific calculus** because it measures felicity or happiness), we must also consider relevant differences between kinds of or sources of happiness. For example, more intense forms of happiness are better than less intense forms, other things being equal. Likewise, happiness that is long lasting is better than happiness of shorter duration. If we are choosing between actions that might or might not produce happiness, we should choose the action that is more certain to produce happiness than an action that will less certainly produce happiness; we should likewise choose actions that will produce happiness sooner rather than later, other things being equal. And we should prefer sources of happiness that are pure and fecund (or productive), in the sense that they are more likely to be followed by future additional pleasures, rather than sources of happiness that will be followed by future unhappiness. We say that these are ways to rank sources or kinds of happiness "other things being equal," to suggest that if the only difference between two pleasures is that one is more intense than the other, longer lasting than the other, will be enjoyed sooner rather than later, is more certain, or will likely lead to even further enjoyments rather than being followed by disvalue, and that is the only difference between them, then these considerations allow us to say that one is better than the other. This kind of guidance is helpful because there are very many sources of happiness, and different experiences of happiness, that might seem virtually incomparable or incommensurate. How do we compare the happiness we derive from sex or eating a great burger, say, with that which we experience from reading a good book or skiing down a run with perfect snow, and then compare those with the enjoyment we derive from performing rewarding work or going on holiday with our family, and those again with the euphoria of using cocaine or taking a long bubble bath? Even though these various experiences of happiness may seem incommensurate, and derive from very different sources, we can use the criteria set out in the felicific calculus to aid in their overall comparison. The same considerations apply, moreover, to disvalue: other things being equal, unhappiness is worse the more intense it is, the longer lasting it is, the more certain it is, the more immediate it is, and the more likely it is to lead to even further unhappiness in the future.[1]

This is a very rough sketch of the decision procedure advocated by utilitarians. Luckily for most of us, most of the time, our actions affect the happiness or unhappiness of a very limited number of people. And we have a pretty good idea of whether what we propose to do will make ourselves and others happy or unhappy. We are quite good utilitarian calculators in our day-to-day affairs. And because the happiness of everyone matters equally, this decision procedure tempers our natural partiality and temptation to make exceptions to what morality requires for ourselves. So while I might know that I would be happier if I did not spend my weekend grading essays from the students in my Introduction to Ethics course, but instead would be much happier if I spent the weekend on a mini-vacation, when I consider the impact on the happiness of my students as well, given that there are many more of them and they would suffer even moderately by my failure to give them timely and constructive feedback in the course, I know I should do the grading.

The founders of the utilitarian school of thought—Jeremy Bentham, John Stuart Mill, and Henry Sidgwick—were not just concerned with articulating a moral principle for individuals.[2] They were also social reformers, who thought that their theory was of particular relevance to those in political power, the consequences of whose actions might affect the happiness of thousands or even millions of people. They saw utilitarianism as especially important as a political morality, as setting the standards to which public policy and laws should conform.

Utilitarianism has been a very important moral theory. Its central principle, the greatest happiness principle, has many of the features we want in a moral principle. It can explain a great many of the moral judgments we make. What is the unifying feature of lying, cheating, killing, wounding, assaulting, torturing, and exploiting that makes them all wrong? They cause unhappiness, pain, disutility. This single principle can seemingly account for a vast number of the moral judgments we make about specific acts, as well as about various political actions and policy decisions. It can also account for why such things as cruelty to animals are wrong. Because animals can be made happy or unhappy, can experience pleasure and pain, they come within the moral domain. Pain inflicted upon them without offsetting benefits to others is wrong according to the utilitarian principle. And it can explain why a number of hard cases are in fact hard cases. Hard cases arise either when we do not have sufficient information to be confident in our predictions about the consequences that will follow from our actions, or when we can only produce happiness for some by diminishing the happiness of others. The balance between such trade-offs might be very fine, especially when the kinds or sources of happiness are incommensurate.

There is a difficulty with utilitarian approaches to moral questions that will be especially vexing in the context of setting public policy, which stems from the fact that it is a maximizing view. It tells us to act so as to maximize happiness overall. But it is indifferent to the distribution of happiness itself. To see the problem this creates, consider the following choice a public official might be called upon to make: she can use a certain quantity of money either to revitalize a public park or to subsidize an opera house. If she revitalizes the park, 1,000 people will be made moderately happier than they are now. If she subsidizes the opera house, only 200 people will benefit, but they will be made significantly happier. Should she use the funds to make more people a little bit happier, or fewer people much happier? The felicific calculus does not tell us how to answer this question. And as the example also suggests, there may be other important differences between groups who might be benefitted by various options. On utilitarian grounds, it is strictly irrelevant whether the benefit goes to people who are already very well off or less well off. At least this is so up to the point of **diminishing marginal utility**.

The concept of diminishing marginal utility is important for policy purposes, and its intuitive force is easily grasped. There is a point at which, for any good, the utility of further increases in that good for a single person begin to diminish, so that the utility (happiness) derived from subsequent increases beyond that point is less than the utility derived from earlier increases in the good. A couple of examples will make this clear. Consider the utility of eating a hamburger to some individual. If he likes hamburgers and is moderately hungry, the utility derived from the first hamburger might be 5. If he is then given another hamburger, it too may produce the same amount of happiness, and so may be given the value 5. Likely, though, a third hamburger will not produce the same level of happiness as the first or second; it may only have a value of 3. And if we imagine that at the fifth hamburger the person is so full and his desire for hamburgers so satiated that he derives no value from it, then the utility has declined to 0. Many goods have declining marginal utility, including money. It has been speculated that in Canada the tipping point, the point at which the utility derived from the next dollar earned begins to decline, is about $75,000.[3] That means that any increase in a person's income above that point will produce less utility to that person than the same money would generate for a person earning less than $75,000. And this makes intuitive sense: if a person is very wealthy, it seems likely that giving her $100 will produce less happiness than that same $100 would generate if given to someone with a low income. The declining marginal utility of many goods requires that utilitarians be indirectly concerned with the distribution of happiness in society, since modest investments in low income communities or on services for relatively disadvantaged communities will likely produce a greater amount of happiness than the same investment made in communities whose members are already relatively well off.

Even though the early utilitarians were concerned to develop a moral theory that could be used both by individuals in their daily lives and by lawmakers and others holding political, economic, and social power, there have nonetheless been serious challenges to the theory. Some people object that the theory is too demanding, because it forces us to treat the happiness of everyone equally.[4] Because we do not in fact value the happiness of everyone equally, instead valuing more highly our own happiness and the happiness of those close to us or with whom we identify, we probably all violate the requirements of utilitarian morality most of the time. Consider, for example, the following. Suppose you are an average middle class Canadian, with a spouse and two children. You have a limited amount of disposable income, say $200 at some given time. You could spend that $200 taking your family to the Science Centre for the day. That would produce a certain amount of happiness for your spouse and children, as well as a moderate amount of value for others affected by your choice, such as those who work at the Science Centre. Or, you could donate the $200 to a good charity, perhaps a charity that works especially for the well-being of severely disadvantaged children. Your gift might give food to five children for one week, and provide them with vaccinations against a debilitating disease; without your gift, they would be seriously underfed during that week and it is statistically predictable that one of the five will become infected with the preventable disease and thereafter be unable to work or provide for himself. It seems obvious what you should do: you should give to the charity. But this might seem too demanding, requiring that we alienate ourselves from our own commitments and cares. It seems to require, as a moral demand, that we act contrary to our most central moral obligations, those we have to the people closest to us and to whom we have special obligations. It seems to require that we must always put the needs of others above our own, when the needs of others are weightier or shared by greater numbers of people. It seems that utilitarianism requires that we allow our own interests to be subordinated to the good of others, that we may be used for the benefit of others.

The decision procedure advocated by utilitarianism also seems to be too demanding. We must consider all of the consequences, negative and positive, of every option open to us, for every person potentially affected by what we propose to do, before we can determine which outcome would have the best consequences overall. This may require a considerable amount of information, and it may require a significant amount of speculation as well. After all, sometimes we will not be sure what the consequences of a given action might be. Then we are to aim at maximizing expected utility, which is measured in the way described above, but with probabilities also taken into account. If a good outcome from an action is not certain, but only, say, 50 percent likely, then the utility calculation must take that probability into account when determining the expected utility of the action (the value of the outcome multiplied by its probability of being realized). Given that real people have finite resources for decision making (limited time, attention, and information), the decision procedure recommended by utilitarianism demands too much of us.

Both of these objections might be overcome if we move away from the version of utilitarianism that has been implicitly assumed thus far, which is known as **act utilitarianism**. It is called that because it assesses the consequences of individual actions, and enjoins the choice of that action that will produce the best overall outcome. But we might, instead, adopt a **rule utilitarian** approach.

This version of the theory requires that we assess possible rules or principles, asking which rule or principle, if adopted as a guide to conduct, would produce the best consequences. Instead of asking every time that we might tell a lie or assault someone whether doing so would have the best consequences, we ask whether it would be better to have a general rule against lying or applying force against others without their consent. We compare the likely outcomes of adopting such a rule, to having no rule or an alternative rule, such as a rule that would permit some people to lie or commit assault, but not others. We have to make the comparison between all the possible rules we might adopt with respect to some kind of conduct, and we select the rule the following of which would have the best outcome over a range of cases. This reduces considerably the burden of decision, because once we have determined which rules will produce the best consequences, we then just have to follow the rules when they apply in a given case. We don't have to engage in the complete utilitarian calculation every time we propose to act. We just consult the rules.

Rule utilitarianism might also allow us to overcome the first objection mentioned above. If we think about how to organize our lives, and how to distribute money, it might actually produce better outcomes overall and in general if we let individuals privilege themselves and those close to them rather than having to treat everyone impartially at all times. It might produce more happiness overall if parents are allowed to devote the majority of their time and resources trying to make their own children happy, as opposed to trying to make all children happy. There are lots of reasons why special relations might give rise to special duties that a rule utilitarian would want to respect. With respect to myself and those closest to me, there is a much higher chance that my actions will directly impact my own and their happiness, and the impact is likely to be more significant. Moreover, those in close personal relationships have a much better understanding of what matters to the individuals involved, and so can make better informed predictions about what will make them happy; our knowledge of what strangers need to make them happy is less certain. For these and other reasons, there may be good reasons to allow moral rules that give those in close personal relationships special duties to each other, which are not shared by others, and to allow individuals to privilege the interests of some people over others.

Rule utilitarians think that the core of morality consists of rules that have been adopted and have stood the test of time because they are rules that, when followed, generally produce better outcomes than would result if they are violated or absent. The moral rules requiring honesty, compassion, fairness, and the like, and the rules against imposing various forms of harms, are justified because they produce the most good of any viable alternatives. Moral conduct then becomes just conduct that conforms to the rules.

On a rule utilitarian approach, the moral rules ultimately derive their authority from their service to happiness; this is what makes the view a species of utilitarianism. But the view faces challenges because no rule seems to be absolute. That is, for every rule that is justified on utilitarian grounds, it seems we can find exceptional cases in which following the rule would do more harm than good, where the best consequences would be produced by violating it rather than following it. Consider, for example, the rule against lying. Suppose you are a German citizen during the Second World War and you are hiding Jews in your attic. The authorities come to your door and ask if you have any Jews in the house. Surely, all things considered, you should lie; telling the truth would have disastrous consequences both for the Jews you are hiding and for you and your own family, whereas lying will protect all of you at just the cost of frustrating in a minor way a morally illegitimate political regime. It seems we can find such examples for virtually every proposed moral rule.

Now we might think that we can formulate the exceptions and simply produce more complex rules. But this is unlikely. The exceptions are virtually limitless, and if we tried to write them all into our rules they would lose their advantage of being able to guide conduct in a simple fashion. We would re-introduce all of the problems with the decision procedure of act utilitarianism, though now at the point of formulating our rules. So we have to live with exceptions, with the recognition that our moral rules are not absolute.

But then the rules seem to be no more than "rules of thumb," general guidelines that we may follow or not depending on the circumstances. This re-opens the possibility that we will illegitimately make exceptions to the rules for our own benefit or convenience. If, on the other hand, we say that the rules must be followed even when this would not produce the best consequences, we seem to have abandoned the consequentialist base of the theory. We will not resolve these issues here; we merely raise them to illustrate the complexity of utilitarian reasoning. Because it is the dominant form of moral reasoning in many domains, and especially in the domain of public policy, the appeal and limitations of this approach are worthy of serious consideration.

To apply utilitarian reasoning to any specific decision, the following are the kinds of questions that must be addressed:

1. What are the consequences of each option that is available in the decision context (direct and indirect, short-term and long-term)?

2. How sure are you that you have all the information needed to predict the likely outcomes of the alternatives?

3. What factual assumptions are you relying upon in assessing the outcomes of various options, and what evidence do you have for those assumptions?

4. Will your decision produce the greatest happiness for the greatest number?

5. If your decision will provide benefits for some only by imposing costs or losses on others, have you considered the pre-existing relative advantages or disadvantages of the various groups affected?

6. Have you considered all of the interests implicated in your decision in an impartial way?

Apply the utilitarian theory (either act or rule) to Cases 4, 7, 11, 18, 23, 25, and 27 at the end of the book.

2.2 DEONTOLOGY

A very different approach to moral thinking is found in deontological theories of morality. **Deontology** refers to duty-based moral theories, of which there are a considerable number of variants. Deontology is the contrary of consequentialism. Deontologists deny that what make an action right are its consequences. Rather, they think some actions are right and others wrong just by virtue of what they are; that is, actions are right or wrong depending on their intrinsic properties, rather than on any good or harm the action might do. Under extraordinary circumstances, a good action might produce very bad consequences, while a wrong action might produce significant benefits. But what matters is the motive from which the action was done, or the intrinsic properties of the act itself, not the consequences. Some actions are intrinsically right and others are intrinsically wrong, just by virtue of what they are. The contrast between deontological and utilitarian and other consequentialist approaches to ethics can be highlighted this way: consequentialism allows that good ends can justify even bad means, because the ends justify the means (e.g., deceiving research subjects to achieve a valid medical study); deontologists reject the view that the ends always justify the means, insisting that the quality of the act (means) is more important than the outcome of the act.

One of the most famous deontologists was the German philosopher Immanuel Kant. Kant rejected all hint of consequentialism, arguing instead that the only thing that is intrinsically good is a good will. Whether a good will produces good consequences is a matter of luck, and luck is not a proper basis of moral assessment. Kant offered two alternative tests for determining if an act of will is good, both as articulations of what he called the **categorical imperative**.[5] The categorical imperative is the highest moral principle within Kantian ethics.

The first formulation of the categorical imperative is the principle of universalization or universalizability. This says that a good will wills only acts the **maxim** of which can be universalized as a rule for all. The maxim of the act is, roughly, its underlying motive formulated as a principle of action. Take, for example, the act of cheating on a test. A person might be tempted to cheat on a test for any number of reasons: because she has not studied, because she fears the repercussions of failure, because success is a means to other things she cares about, and so on. The principle of universalization says that this can only be a morally right act if its maxim can be universalized as a general rule for all.

The maxim that would allow cheating for any of these reasons could not be universalized as a general rule, because it would generate a conceptual contradiction. Testing only makes sense in certain contexts, when it is important to find out if the person being tested has mastered some content. This is true whether it is a driving test or a school exam. In the case of the driving test, the context is not competitive; one person can perform perfectly without thereby creating a competitive disadvantage for others. In non-competitive test situations, everyone can perform perfectly without any loss of the value of the testing. This is the case with tests designed to ensure a threshold functioning of **professionals**, for example: every would-be physician being tested for competence in medicine could perform perfectly, and that would not undermine the point of the testing. In competitive situations (e.g., university class), by contrast, testing may not be aimed just at determining a threshold level of competence, but a comparative ranking between test subjects. Regardless of whether the situation is competitive or not, however, we could not universalize a principle that permits cheating on tests. Universalizing a rule that permits cheating would undermine the very concept of testing within which cheating is possible. Whether we are testing for a threshold of competence or testing to grade levels of performance, the very point of testing would be undermined in a context in which cheating was universally practised. This would produce a contradiction in our conception of testing itself.

Or consider the example of lying. Most people accept that lying is generally wrong, but seem quite willing to make exceptions to the rule for themselves when they find telling the truth inconvenient. The test of universalizability asks whether these people could universalize lying as a rule. And the answer is that they could not. Lying only "works" if it is believed, and that can only happen within a general practice of truth telling. If we tried to universalize a rule of deception, the concept of deception itself would become incoherent. If universalizing a given action would produce this kind of conceptual incoherence, then it cannot be morally acceptable.

Other actions we might be tempted to commit would, if generalized as a universal rule, produce a different sort of incoherence, a contradiction in will. Kant asks us to imagine a situation in which we are assessing whether to acknowledge a rule requiring us to give easy aid to others when they are in great need. We are wondering whether there is a duty of easy rescue or easy aid, or whether we are permitted to turn our backs on those in need. There is nothing conceptually incoherent in the rule "every man for himself." We could, in principle, adopt the rule that no one gives aid to anyone else. But we cannot universalize this rule in practice; we cannot support such a rule without a contradiction in will. This is so because we know that if we ourselves were in serious need of aid, and another could easily provide it, we would want him to do so. We cannot will that we ourselves not receive aid in such circumstances. Thus we cannot will a rule that permits persons to forgo giving easy aid. The deception case might also be blocked by this way of understanding the universalizability test, because presumably we want others to tell us the truth. Thus we cannot will that others comply with a rule that permits lying, because we cannot will that others lie to us, even if only in circumstances when telling the truth would be inconvenient to them. The universalizability test is a very good corrective to our natural propensity to make exceptions to the demands of morality for ourselves. Even if we occasionally want to lie, cheat, steal, assault or kill others, we would not accept the universalization of our conduct as a rule for others.

The second formulation of the categorical imperative is known as the **respect for persons principle**. Kant claims that morality requires that we treat humanity, whether in ourselves or others, always as an end in itself and never just as a means. We certainly treat others as a means to our own ends all the time. I treat the cashier at my grocery store as a means to my ends when I use her to ring up my groceries so that I may purchase them and take them home. My students use me as a means to their end of learning about ethics. The list is obviously endless. But I don't treat the cashier *merely* as a means, and my students don't treat me *merely* as a means, in our interactions. To treat someone as a mere means is to treat them as a thing, a tool to be used for the user's purposes, and in ways that ignore or deny that the other has intrinsic value as a fellow human being. The requirement that we treat others as ends in themselves acknowledges that every human being (rational creature, for Kant) has inherent dignity and worth, that every human being is an autonomous creature capable of setting ends for herself, and that a certain mode of treatment is due to them in virtue of their rationality and **autonomy**. (Autonomy just means self-rule, and refers to our capacity to set ends for ourselves.)

This idea, that every human being has inherent dignity and worth, and is entitled to respect as an autonomous rational agent, is of central importance to morality in the modern Western world. It is the foundation of theories of human rights. Because we have inherent dignity and worth, just as human beings, we enjoy certain human rights. Even though we are related by ties of family and affection only to certain others, even though only some others are useful to us, and even though different people have different entitlements based on various skills and accomplishments, all persons are entitled to a certain kind of treatment just by virtue of their shared humanity. They are entitled to be treated as ends in themselves, as valuable in themselves; they must not be used as a mere means, like things, in the service of other people's ends.

The respect for persons principle is thought to be an alternative formulation of the categorical imperative, and so it will ground exactly the same set of duties as the universalization principle will. We can see this if we think again about deception. To deceive another is wrong because it treats the person deceived as a mere means to our ends. We deceive others in order to get them to do something they would not do if they knew the truth. In this way we subordinate their ends (what they care about or are committed to) to our own. We treat them as a thing to be manipulated for our benefit, rather than as centres of rational agency in themselves. Indeed, we deprive them of the ability to act on their own ends, by manipulating their understanding of the relationship between their ends and our own. We use them in a way that degrades their true worth.

Because Kant thought human beings are ends in themselves, he thought there are a number of duties we owe to persons, others, and ourselves. It is from him that we drew, in section 1.4.3, the distinction between perfect and imperfect duties. Since we have both kinds of duties, and they are owed to humanity, whether in ourselves or others, Kant thought there were four kinds of duties. There are **perfect duties** to ourselves, duties that bind on each and every occasion and leave no room for determining how they will be fulfilled, such as the duty not to commit suicide. There are imperfect duties to ourselves, duties that do not dictate a particular action on every occasion and that leave room for determining how best to fulfil them, such as the duty to develop our natural talents. There are perfect duties to others, such as the duty not to deceive them, and there are imperfect duties to others, such as the duty to be charitable.

Kant believed that all of the duties generated by the categorical imperative were absolute, admitting of no exceptions. Lying is wrong in every circumstance. Thus even if the Nazi is asking if you are hiding Jews, you are not permitted to lie. At most, you may be silent. This is a particularly austere and demanding moral theory. It presupposes that there can be no such thing as a conflict among duties, that there are no genuine moral dilemmas in the world. Other deontologists have developed weaker versions of the theory by abandoning the view that moral duties are absolute. One such theorist was W.D. Ross, who developed a deontological theory that posited seven *prima facie* (on their face) duties. They were fidelity, reparation, gratitude, non-maleficence, justice, beneficence, and self-improvement.[6] What Ross meant by saying that these seven duties were *prima facie* was that, although they always have positive value, they may compete in a given situation, and which one is the most important in cases of conflict becomes a matter of moral judgment, taking into account the specific circumstances of the situation. In some circumstances the duty of fidelity might conflict with the duty to do no harm (non-maleficence); our Nazi case is surely such a circumstance, in which there is a conflict between these two duties and the more important one to follow in this case is non-maleficence rather than fidelity. There is no master duty, such as the categorical imperative, that we can use to rank the weight of our various duties or to decide what to do when duties conflict. Nonetheless, Ross thought that the core of our moral obligations could be captured under these seven heads of duty.

Though consequentialism (especially versions of utilitarianism) and deontology are mutually exclusive (they cannot both be true as complete theories of morality), they are by far the most common approaches to the morality of action. They are widely employed in moral reasoning and in the public justification of actions and policies. Though incompatible as complete theories, we think it likely that the enduring appeal of each can be seen in their common service to important interests. Fulfilling our duties will surely produce happy results overall, and constraining the pursuit of happiness by consistent principles will better protect vital interests than the pursuit of happiness by any means. Thus we believe the insights of both can be combined in a coherent moral theory, though we do not present that case here.

Questions that you should ask in applying deontology to a situation include the following:

1. What principles are involved in your decision?

2. Could you universalize what you propose to do as a general rule to be followed by everyone?

3. Would acting as you propose to do treat everyone involved as ends in themselves, or would it treat some as mere means to your end?

4. Would your action show respect for persons?

5. Are any duties involved in what you propose to do, and if so, will any of them be violated by your action?

6. If all of your options involve violating at least one duty, how have you weighed their relative importance in the circumstances?

7. Are you making an exception for yourself that you would not want others to follow?

8. Can you do what you propose to do openly and publicly, or is the use of deception or withholding of information vital to the success of your actions?

Apply deontological reasoning to Cases 3, 4, 12, 13, 17, 18, 22, 23, 27, and 30 at the end of the book.

2.3 VIRTUE ETHICS

Virtue ethics has a long and venerable tradition, going back to the ancient Greek philosophers, especially Aristotle. We discussed virtues above, describing them as settled dispositions or character traits. Virtues and **vices** not only incline us to act in certain ways, but colour our perceptions of our circumstances, make us notice certain morally salient characteristics of our situations, and determine to a large extent the kind of persons we are. Virtue ethics is the study of those traits of character that are virtuous and those that are vicious. It enjoins us to develop virtues and to manifest them in leading good lives. To a significant extent, moral education during childhood is aimed at producing virtuous persons; children are encouraged to be honest, thoughtful, caring, fair, compassionate, courageous, and the like. When engaged in moral education, we are ultimately aiming at producing good and virtuous people. Many social groups and organizations are likewise structured around a set of virtues, and introduction to the culture of those groups or organizations is an immersion into the virtues that structure them and give meaning to their members and participants.

There are a number of different kinds of virtues: intellectual, social, and moral, among others. **Intellectual virtues** are those needed for right thinking and serve the pursuit of truth, knowledge, and understanding. They include a commitment to evidence, impartiality in assessing evidence, attention to detail, honesty in reporting, integrity in research, perseverance, intelligence, creativity, and judgment. These are virtuous intellectual traits because those who have them are more likely to achieve truth, knowledge or understanding, and to make good judgments.

Social virtues are the kinds of traits that are especially important to living a good life in society with others. They include empathy, humour, forgiveness, respect, charitableness, wit, a sense of justice, reciprocity, and the like. Social virtues are those traits that make us easy and agreeable companions to others, that make our social interactions a source of joy, pleasure, or happiness to others, rather than the contrary.

Moral virtues are those traits of character that make us sensitive and responsive to the moral characteristics of our circumstances. The moral virtues overlap considerably with the social ones. The following were commonly considered virtues among the ancient Greeks: **prudence** (appropriate care for one's own well-being, reasonable self-interest, an ability to resist current temptations that risk serious harm to self later); **fortitude** (the strength to bear disappointments and hardship, resilience, grit, inner strength); courage (the ability to withstand or stand firm in the face of danger or intimidation); liberality (generosity, willingness to bestow benefits on others, as well as an openness to tolerate difference in judgments of others); magnanimity (a greatness or nobleness of spirit, the willingness to forgive past wrongs for which responsibility has been taken); and temperance (moderation or restraint, especially with respect to indulging passions or appetites). Other moral virtues include proper self-respect, which is contrasted with both undue pride or vanity and with servility or improper humility, and respect for others. Compassion is also a moral virtue. Justice, too, is an important moral virtue, and it is discussed below. Justice as a virtue entails a commitment to acting and judging equitably, justly, fairly, or according to law, and a commitment to make sure that people get what they deserve, are entitled to, or are due. The moral virtues consist of character traits that enable those possessing them to be sensitive to their own and other people's interests, to defend those interests when they are under threat, and to have due regard for how their actions will affect the well-being of others.

Aristotle understood the virtues as consisting of a **golden mean** between two extremes, of a deficit (too little) on the one hand, and an excess (too much) on the other, of the character trait in question (as mentioned in Chapter 1). Thus liberality is contrasted both with excessive generosity, as exemplified by a person who gives away money he will need to support his own children, say, as well as with miserliness, exemplified by a person who refrains from giving even when giving would be a significant benefit to another without appreciable loss to the miser. An excess of generosity might likewise be displayed by a person who gives to those who are unworthy of such generosity, or who do not really need it. It is an excess of generosity, too, rather than the real virtue of generosity, to give for the wrong reasons, such as when a person makes a large gift to a charity in order to receive public praise, or to create feelings of indebtedness in the recipient. The virtuous person adopts the mean between these extremes, being generous to the right degree, in the right way, for the right reasons, at the right time. Aristotle thought all the virtues were to be found in the mean between such extremes of deficiency and excess.

To provide a different example, drawn from the intellectual virtues rather than the moral virtues this time, we might consider the virtue of perseverance in research. The virtuous person will persevere in her research to the degree needed to achieve her goals of truth, knowledge, or understanding. She will display a deficiency of that virtue should she conduct sloppy research, cutting corners, taking matters on faith that should be investigated, giving up the search for relevant information before she knows all she needs to know in the context and given the questions being addressed, and so on. The vice of deficiency will be a kind of laziness with respect to the activity, and a willingness to consider inadequate evidence enough so as to avoid doing the tough work that is necessary to get to the bottom of the topic being researched. On the other side, a person might fail to exemplify the virtue of perseverance in research through an excess of attention and care. She might refuse to accept evidence even on very good authority, continue to make inquiries after all reasonable people would have been satisfied that they have reached the truth, refuse to consider matters as reasonably settled that should be so taken, and fail to complete the project because she simply refuses to or cannot see that she has attained sufficient knowledge to stop. Some perfectionists are like this; they fail to rest content with what others would consider a complete and fully adequate job, and as a result they are often paralyzed, unable to complete tasks because they are forever unsatisfied that they have done enough or that their work is good enough. The true virtue lies as the mean between these extremes, and at the edges we cease to talk of virtues but actually speak of vices. To be such a perfectionist that one cannot complete tasks or take pleasure in one's accomplishments is a vice, as is being miserly, or cowardly (to refer again to an example spelled out in the first chapter). Likewise, being foolishly liberal with money or other goods, or being sloppy in one's intellectual pursuits and trusting before trust is warranted, or being rash or reckless in the face of danger are all vices.

Aristotle believed that we acquire the virtues by habit: it is by doing virtuous things that we come to be virtuous people. Only after doing the right thing, for the right reason, on the right occasion, to the right degree becomes habitual can we be said to fully have the virtue in question. Once acting virtuously has become habitual, it has become part of our character, partly defining the kind of person we are. Then it is appropriate to speak of a person as kind, or honest, or compassionate, or just, or courageous, or as having integrity or being trustworthy. For a virtue theorist, what is ethical is just what a virtuous person would do; to know what we ought to do to act ethically we have to ask what a virtuous person would do in our circumstances and act as he would. We learn to be virtuous by emulating the conduct of those who are virtuous, and being virtuous just is what it means to be ethical.

Because we learn virtues by example, and become virtuous by acting as a virtuous person would, it is crucially important that we have positive, virtuous role models to emulate. This is true with respect to children, for whom moral education often depends upon having good role models to emulate and mimic, role models who can be held up as exemplars of the virtues. Role models may come not just from immediate family, friends, and social acquaintances, from religious institutions and schools, from sports and arts organizations and the like, but also from literature, history, and popular culture. Children who lack virtuous role models are at a serious disadvantage in terms of their moral development.

Given that virtues are learned through example, it is also important that we attend to the moral culture or ethos of organizations. Only if ethical behaviour is modelled throughout the organization will acting virtuously within it be easy. If those in leadership positions, or members of the organization generally, act viciously (display vices in what they do), this will have a corrosive effect on everyone in the organization, tending to degrade the ethical character of everyone involved. Vices, as well as virtues, are acquired when acting viciously becomes habitual and the vices become ingrained features of a person's character. Thus it is crucially important that virtues be modelled within organizations, including public service organizations, as part of the ethos or culture, if persons are to behave ethically within those organizations. As we will see, among the most important virtues for public servants are respect for the rule of law, integrity, honesty, respect for others, empathy and compassion, and justice, as well as the intellectual virtues. The list of virtues mentioned above, and here, is not complete, and will be fleshed out in greater detail as needed in what follows.

Among the questions you should ask in applying virtue ethics to a situation are the following:

1. What character traits will my decision or action exemplify?

2. What effect will my action have on my character, in the short term and long term?

3. What effect will my action have on the character of others, in the short term and long term?

4. Would what I propose to do show me to be an admirable and trustworthy person, or the contrary?

5. If others displayed the same traits I would express in my action, would that make my organization better or worse?

Apply virtue ethics to the situations described in Cases 1, 3, 5, 8, 9, 12, 14, 15, 17, 19, 22, 23, 24, and 29 at the end of the book.

2.4 ETHICS OF CARE

Another approach to ethics is found in **care ethics** (also sometimes called **relational ethics**). This approach to ethics arose out of empirical research conducted into differences between how men and women think about ethical problems, especially as found in the work of the moral psychologist Carol Gilligan.[7] She observed that while men often rely upon abstract principles (especially principles of rights and justice) in deciding how to resolve moral dilemmas, women by contrast typically approached moral issues in a more concrete way, attending to the specific context, the relationships between the parties to the dispute, and the needs of the individuals involved. Women employing a care approach tended to try to find ways of resolving moral conflicts that would enable relationships to be maintained and strengthened. This approach focused on promoting the well-being of those involved in a decision, and attempted to find solutions to moral problems that would promote continuing relationships among those involved.

We can see the contrast between the *justice approach* and the *care approach* in the following recent case. A community group has for some years held an African-centred festival every summer in Toronto in a particular public park. The festival got so large that there was a risk of damage to the public park, and as a result, city officials considered denying the organizers the licences they would need to hold the festival there again. One could approach this issue from the perspective of justice or rights. One could, likewise, approach the matter from a utilitarian perspective. In either case, however, the result would tend to be an either–or decision: either the cultural group has a right to hold the festival or it doesn't, either overall utility would be served by holding the festival or it would not. But those who use the care perspective think of the matter differently. They would try to figure out how the competing interests and needs of the various stakeholders could best be served together, so as to maintain good relations between the organizers, the African-Canadian community, and the city. They would look at the specifics of the case, in its particular context, including the need to improve race relations in the city, and the need to ensure that marginalized groups feel included and valued within the broader society. They would look at the specific impediments to the festival going ahead as planned, in light of potential damage to the park. When they looked at the specifics, it became apparent that a major issue was the damage done by vendors' carts in the park during the festival. A compromise was proposed: move the vendors to the streets surrounding the park, rather than having them in the park itself. This would largely eliminate the damage caused to the park, and would allow the space to accommodate the expected number of participants. The festival could go ahead, with modifications, thus meeting the needs of all the players. Relations were maintained, needs met, and individuals took responsibility for ensuring that the concerns of the others would be attended to. This was an example of municipal workers trying to find a compromise position that met the needs of everyone, as the care perspective recommends.[8]

Questions relevant from a care perspective include:

1. In what ways might a decision damage relations between the parties?

2. Is there a compromise that can meet the needs of the parties and allow them all to move forward in a constructive way?

Apply the care perspective to Cases 3, 4, 7, 9, 12, 13, 19, 22, 24, and 29 at the end of the book.

2.5 CONTRACTARIANISM

Another major moral theory was developed by a number of historical thinkers, including Thomas Hobbes, John Locke, and Jean-Jacques Rousseau.[9] It is known as **contractarianism**, or the social contract tradition. Its most important contemporary proponent is David Gauthier.[10] Contractarians invite us to think about society as "a cooperative venture for mutual advantage."[11] They think of morality as a system of norms that, if followed, will make everyone living under them better off. The idea of mutual constraints (on our narrowly self-serving actions) for the sake of mutual benefit is at the heart of contractarian reasoning. Morality is that set of mutual constraints, norms that limit how we go about achieving what we want, that forbid the pursuit of our own advantage at the expense of others; contractarian morality is a set of norms that limit the achievement of one's own good in ways that make others worse off.

Contractarianism is a theory whose proponents believe that what justifies any normative system is that its norms would be agreed to by those who are governed by it. Contractarians believe that all norms need justification, because they limit the freedom of individuals, and the only acceptable justification is that the norms in question would be agreed to by those whose behaviour they regulate. This basic reference to norms makes clear the scope of contractarian justification: it can be applied to any norm-governed activity. Not all human activity is norm-governed, of course. Norms are used for a particular purpose in particular sets of circumstances. The purpose they serve is to co-ordinate the behaviour of individuals in circumstances of social interaction, when such co-ordination is necessary for each of the parties to the interaction to benefit fairly by it. Not all conventional norms are justified, because not all ensure that the benefits of co-ordination are fairly shared. Only those that would be agreed to by the people interacting are justified, and this notion of hypothetical agreement is grounded in a theory of practical rationality.

The theory is often called *social contract theory* because its early proponents asked us to imagine what norms people would agree to be governed by, as though they were forming a social contract to live by. Only norms that individuals could rationally consent to be governed by are legitimate. In order to conduct this thought experiment, the early contractarians asked us to imagine choosing a set of moral norms and political institutions from a pre-moral (Hobbes, Rousseau) or pre-political (Locke) **state of nature**.

Beginning with the assumption that all human beings are utility-maximizers, who when acting rationally act in ways they expect will maximize the satisfaction or fulfilment of their preferences (for utility is just a measure of preference for contractarians, as it was a measure of happiness for utilitarians), contractarians suppose that only those norms that maximize utility would be agreed to. Thus contractarianism is the view that norms are justified just because they co-ordinate behaviour in utility-maximizing ways. Moral norms are distinguished from political ones only in terms of their enforcement mechanisms: moral norms are enforced informally and non-coercively, and internalized as virtues, while political norms are enforced formally and coercively, through such external mechanisms as the judicial system. We concentrate on moral norms here.

The circumstances in which moral norms play their basic role can be understood most easily by considering circumstances in which they are not needed or possible. First, situations in which an individual's choice is the sole determinant of the eventual outcome do not require moral norms. In such cases, provided the individual understands her options, she has merely to decide which of the available options she most prefers and choose accordingly. Such situations are known as "parametric choice situations," meaning just that the choices of a single actor determine which state of affairs results. In parametric choice situations there is no need for co-ordination and so no need for norms.

Suppose, for example, that you are choosing between going to see a movie and staying home to read a book. So long as you understand your options, and can determine which of the two you most prefer, you simply have to choose the option you most prefer in order to act rationality; the outcome that results will be determined by your choice alone, so you don't need to consider anything other than what you most want to do. An implication of this view is that Robinson Crusoe, when stranded alone on his desert island, had no need of morality.[12] He no doubt benefited from having a number of personal and intellectual virtues (courage, perseverance, intelligence, and the like), but he had no need of the moral or social virtues. Contractarians believe that morality is needed only in situations of interaction.

Most of what human beings do involves situations of interaction, in which the eventual outcome that results does not depend on the choice of just one party to the interaction, but the combined choices of them all. These are situations of "strategic interaction" or "strategic choice," because the outcome that results will depend not just on your own choice but on the choices of others as well. Suppose you are trying to rent an apartment. Whether you succeed in doing so will depend not just on your choices, but on the combined choices of you and the potential landlord, as well perhaps as others, such as your references and your bank. The would-be landlord might act as you expect, and after many interactions you might obtain the apartment. Provided she is letting it freely and you are renting it freely, we can assume that this was a mutually beneficial transaction: you both are better off, by your own lights, after you have concluded your transaction. But of course, things might not go as you expect: she might lead you to believe that she will rent it to you and then renege on the agreement; she might have deceived you about the cost or the condition of the apartment; she might take your deposit and run. In all of these ways, and countless others, she could disappoint your expectations, violate your agreement, or treat you in ways that make you worse off for the encounter. She has made her position better by worsening yours, so that your interaction is not one of mutual benefit. Contractarian morality forbids such terms of interaction, because the person who loses from them would not rationally have consented to norms permitting him to be so treated. And this is the core of contractarian thinking: it insists that morality, to be rational and so generate genuine obligations to obey it, must provide mutual benefits. A justified moral code does not require some to sacrifice for the good of others, with no corresponding benefits. Morality does not make some the slaves of, subservient to, or the doormat for, others. This highlights one of the important differences between utilitarianism and contractarianism: because utilitarianism is concerned with overall happiness, but not its distribution, it allows that we might sacrifice the good of some for the greater good of others; contractarians wonder why the losers would possibly agree to such an arrangement.

Contractarians also differ from utilitarians in terms of their theory of value. Whereas utilitarians have an objective and agent neutral theory of value—happiness is valuable, for everyone—contractarians do not specify what is valuable *per se*. Rather, they say what is valuable is whatever a person prefers; what is valuable is whatever a particular person values. Thus value is relative and subjective; my values are mine, and yours are yours (relative), and what is valuable for me is so just because I value it (subjective). This does not mean that persons' values are selfish or egoistic; if I care about the well-being of another, or about a cause, then those things are good for me. But whatever it is that we prefer, we rationally must want to maximize the satisfaction of our preferences. We are self-interested in this sense: we want to achieve, fulfil, or satisfy our preferences as fully as possible. We are rational utility-maximizers.

Contractarians typically adopt further assumptions about persons and their environment.[13] Persons are assumed to have limited benevolence. We care deeply about the well-being of ourselves and only a small group of others, those with whom we are in close personal and social relationships, or with whom we identify. We don't have strong ties of benevolence to others generally. And, on the flip side, we don't have strong negative feeling for most others either; we don't typically desire the misery or failure of others. They make this assumption because if we were led by fellow feelings so deep that we desired the well-being of others as much as our own, we would not need the full range of moral norms; we would not need to constrain our maximizing behaviour if what we most wanted was the good of others impartially. (We would still need rules to solve co-ordination problems, but we would not need the rules against exploitation, coercion, oppression, and violence that we have, because perfectly benevolent people would not be tempted to harm others in these ways.)

Our environment is characterized by limited scarcity and competition. There are not enough of the things people want for everyone to fully satisfy their desires; there is limited scarcity in the world. Again, this is assumed because if there was either perfect abundance or complete scarcity and want, there would be no need or no use for morality. If there was perfect abundance, so that everyone could fully satisfy their wants without limiting the ability of others to do so as well, then we would not need the rules settling exclusive property, for example. If there was complete scarcity, so that nothing we could do would make it possible for everyone to satisfy even their most basic needs (as we see in cases of severe natural disasters, for instance), then the rules of morality would be in vain; we would not restrain our own pursuit of survival in a situation of pure scarcity. This insight is reflected in the common adage that "necessity knows no law"; it licenses farmers to break into grain stores in cases of extreme famine, for example, or survivors of a boating disaster to take whatever they can find that might contribute to their self-preservation. The normal circumstance of human beings lies between these two extremes. It is characterized by limited scarcity. As a result, it is also characterized by competition. We compete for the scarce goods that are necessary to the satisfaction of our preferences. Thus we need moral norms to govern the terms of competition. We must make room for the kind of competition that free competitive markets make possible (for reasons we will explain shortly), but we must limit actions that make competition unfair. Most especially, we must adopt rules that limit force and fraud, violence and deception, as competitive means.

One might find the description of the human condition given thus far—limited benevolence, limited scarcity, and competition—rather bleak. But contractarians also recognize that human beings can improve their natural condition through co-operation. Through co-operation, individuals can expand the set of goods available for the satisfaction of their preferences, and make sources of value available that would otherwise be lacking. And the idea of society as a co-operative venture for mutual advantage is at the heart of contractarian reasoning.

Co-operation has two principal benefits. First, it allows us to overcome certain kinds of interactive situations that make the parties to them both worse off. These kinds of situations are modelled by the **prisoners' dilemma**.[14] Here is an example. Suppose that Farzad and Fred are neighbouring farmers. They have no strong fellow feelings for each other, either positive or negative. They are strictly self-interested utility-maximizers. Farzad has a field of corn, and Fred has a field of tomatoes. Farzad's corn will be ready to harvest two weeks before Fred's tomatoes. Neither can harvest his whole crop alone; if each has to harvest his crop alone, each will have crops die in the field, which will be a straight loss to them. But together they could harvest all of Farzad's corn, and then all of Fred's tomatoes. Ideally, then, they should co-operate and assist each other in bringing in their crops. But here is the problem. Fred reasons as follows. If I help Farzad harvest his corn in mid-July, Farzad will then have no reason to help me at the end of the month when it is time to harvest my corn. After all, he will have already reaped the benefit of our agreement to offer mutual help; when it comes time for him to return the favour, doing so will be straight loss for him. It would be irrational for Farzad to help Fred once his corn has already been harvested. Being equally rational, Fred and Farzad can both anticipate that it will be irrational for Farzad to do his part after Fred has already done his. They both anticipate that Farzad will renege on any agreement they might have made to render mutual assistance. Thus they will not make the agreement, and thus they will both be worse off than if they had been able to co-operate and provide mutual aid.

The problem has the following structure: each most prefers that the other help him without him having to provide aid to the other (on the assumption that they lack fellow feelings and are interested only in maximizing their harvest at as little cost or effort to themselves as possible). The outcome that is worst for each is that in which one helps the other, but the other does not help him. Then the one who has helped the other has expended time and energy for no benefit to himself. For each, the second-best outcome is the one in which they help each other. Then they get their full harvest, though at the cost of helping the other, which is what makes it second best. Finally, each ranks as third the option in which neither helps the other. Then they will both do less well than they might have, with some of their crop rotting in the fields, but at least they have not been exploited by the other by helping and then not being helped in turn.

First choice for each: receive help but give no help.

Second choice: each helps and receives help.

Third choice: neither gives nor receives help.

Fourth choice: give help but receive no help.

This kind of situation is remarkably common. (Arms races can be nicely characterized as prisoners' dilemmas, for example.) Because the outcome that results is the product of both of their choices together, this is a case of strategic choice. If each individual reasons from a straightforward maximizing point of view, each will wind up with the outcome represented as his third best option. Yet if they could co-operate, make an agreement, and stick to it, they would each do better, achieving their second ranked option rather than their third. Contractarian morality thus encourages the keeping of mutually beneficial agreements. It would tell Farzad and Fred to keep their agreement to render mutual aid in the harvesting of their crops. If Farzad then takes Fred's help, but does not reciprocate when it is his turn to help, he acts immorally, achieving a benefit at the expense of his partner. Contractarian morality condemns such exploitation.

Solving prisoners' dilemmas requires that individuals forgo their most preferred option (getting what they want but only by making their interactive partners worse off) in favour of pursuing the mutually beneficial second-best option. This requires co-operation and a commitment to keep mutually beneficial agreements. Doing so is rational because it makes it possible for people to achieve their second-best outcome, rather than their third-best, which is what will result if each tries to pursue his own advantage at the expense of his partners. Thus it is rational to be moral in strategic choice situations like prisoners' dilemmas. The disposition to pursue the co-operative outcome, to accept mutual benefits rather than pursuing maximum personal benefit when that can only be attained at the expense of others, is at the heart of the contractarians' theory of virtue. It is the basic moral disposition. All the classic virtues, and familiar moral rules and principles, are then justified if and because they help us to attain mutually beneficial co-operation.

Co-operation has another benefit, besides solving prisoners' dilemmas. It makes possible co-operative surpluses that would not be otherwise available. Co-operation, in other words, helps us overcome natural scarcity. This is evident from the example of the farmers above: if they co-operate, they will harvest their complete crops, and more food will be available than if they don't co-operate. And this is true generally: people can produce more of whatever is valued through co-operation than they can by their own efforts alone. The very division of labour upon which modern societies depend is itself dependent on co-operation.

Co-operation makes possible co-operative surpluses, sources of utility that are not otherwise available to people. Contractarians insist that co-operation is rational whenever such surpluses can be achieved, provided that the parties to the co-operative activity share the proceeds of their co-operation according to a rationally acceptable principle of distribution. In any co-operative activity generating a surplus, individuals will rationally insist on two basic conditions of distribution. First, they share only the surplus; whatever anyone brings to the co-operative venture remains exclusively hers. Second, the distribution must make rewards proportionate to contributions. In a two-party case, where both are necessary to achieve the co-operative dividend, they share the proceeds equally. In cases involving more than two persons, they share the surplus in a way that accords with relative contribution. In order to ensure that resulting distributions are fair, what one brings to co-operative activities must be restricted to those things one has acquired without violating the rights of others to their bodies and capacities, and what they properly acquire through their use.

This description of the need for and benefits from morality, i.e., co-operation, also explains why contractarians give special place to free competitive markets. Market transactions involve social interaction, yet the market is a **morally free zone** in contractarian thinking.[15] This is because we don't need to constrain our individual utility-maximizing behaviour to reap mutual benefits from the free competitive market. Within a genuinely free and competitive market, each individual acting just so as to maximize his expected utility will bring about results that are also optimal (such that no one could do better without someone else doing worse). If I have a book that is worth only $5 to me (I would be willing to sell it for any price above $5), and you have $8 that you are willing to pay for it, then our exchange will leave us both better off. I will exchange something worth only $5 to me for $8, resulting in a net benefit to me of $3. If you are rational, then obviously the book is worth more to you than the $8 you are willing to pay for it, so the transaction benefits you as well. We are both better off. This is the idea behind Adam Smith's famous claim that the market achieves mutual benefit as though through "an invisible hand": each individual pursuing his or her own good achieves a result that is good for everyone overall.[16] In such circumstances, people need only make decisions parametrically in order to bring about the best results for all. One important *caveat* here, of course, is that the optimal results achieved through free market behaviour are also fair only if "the initial factor endowments" of the participants (what they can bring to the market) are themselves fairly determined.[17] If I robbed Suharshi of her book, and then sold it, the resulting distribution of goods would not be fair; thus I cannot bring a stolen good to the market as part of my factor endowments. Nor can I hold a gun to my prospective buyer's head and say "$8 for the book or your life." Thus, while the free market itself does not require moral norms to govern its operations, the conditions that make free market activity possible (a prohibition on force and fraud), and a commitment to fair terms for determining what people can bring to market interactions, are required as preconditions of market activity. Very briefly, what is required is that a right to our own bodies and capacities be recognized, along with the right to whatever material goods we can acquire through their use, provided that we do not use our bodies and capacities in such a way that we benefit ourselves at the expense of others. Slightly more carefully, we must not better our situation in a way that worsens the situation of others, and then use the resulting competitive advantage in free market transactions or co-operative relations between us in the future. But so long as the preconditions of fair market activities are met, market mechanisms are to be supported, because they necessarily result in mutual benefits. Thus we must think carefully about whether a given good should be supplied by the market or by non-market mechanisms such as government programs.

Questions to be asked in applying contractarianism include the following:

1. What are the preferences (desires, wants, needs, goals, objectives) of the parties to this interaction?

2. Whose choices will combine to determine the eventual outcome of your decision?

3. What would count as a mutually beneficial outcome in this case; conversely, what would count as one or more parties benefitting at the expense of others?

4. Is the norm you propose to employ in resolving an issue one that everyone involved could consent to?

5. Can your conduct be characterized as co-operative?

6. Does what you propose to do show you to be a trustworthy co-operative partner?

Apply contractarian reasoning to Cases 1, 3, 5, 6, 15, 18, 24, 25, and 29.

2.6 INTUITIONISM AND PERSONAL CONSCIENCE

Moral intuitionism is a theory of moral knowledge (moral epistemology). It has two branches: one rationalist and the other empiricist. All moral intuitionists are moral realists: they believe that moral qualities or moral properties (such as the property of being morally good) exist in the world independently of our knowledge of them or our use of them. Their intuitionism is a theory about how we know such properties, how we come to have moral knowledge, for example, that killing other people is morally wrong. Both groups of intuitionists think that we come to know moral truths directly and non-inferentially. That is, we do not reason to moral truths from other kinds of knowledge, such as knowledge of what makes people happy, or what they prefer; we do not infer that killing people is wrong from further facts, either about people (such as, they don't want to be killed) or about killing. Here the difference between the two types comes into play.

Rationalist intuitionists think that we acquire moral knowledge through an exercise of reason, and that moral knowledge is *a priori*. *A priori* just means prior to experience. Many people think that our knowledge of mathematics is *a priori*. We know that two plus two equals four, not from any experience with things in the world, but rather directly from our understanding of the concepts. If you understand the concepts of two, four, equals and plus, you just know that two plus two equals four. We don't infer the truth of this claim from our knowledge of other things. Our moral knowledge is likewise *a priori* and non-inferential, claim rational intuitionists.[18]

An earlier branch of ethical intuitionism existed among the **moral sense** and **moral sentiments** philosophers, such as Francis Hutcheson, David Hume, Adam Smith, and Thomas Reid.[19] They were empiricists, who believed that we acquire knowledge through experience of the world. Knowledge, for empiricists, is *a posteriori*, or after experience. Though there were important differences between these theorists, their general orientation was towards thinking that we either have a moral sense, analogous to our sense of hearing and sight, by which we come to know moral properties, just as we come to know physical properties of objects in the world, or that we have natural moral sentiments through which we come to know moral facts. We feel that certain actions are right or wrong by the sentiments they produce in us: we feel outrage, or indignation, or revulsion, or shame, and this is just to feel that the actions giving rise to such sentiments are morally wrong. Our moral knowledge is acquired by exercising a kind of perceptual ability, just as we acquire knowledge of physical objects through direct perception. We might draw an analogy between moral sentiments/sense and aesthetic perception. We perceive certain objects or forms or sounds as beautiful and others as ugly. To explain our aesthetic knowledge we might posit an aesthetic sense or sensibility, which responds directly to the aesthetic qualities of objects; likewise, actions and events seem to us to be morally good or bad, right or wrong, and we might posit a moral sense or sensibility which responds directly to such moral properties.

As a theory of moral epistemology, intuitionism has fallen out of favour. That is in part because moral realism has fallen out of favour. The idea that morality is a human construct, something we have created because it serves important purposes for us, seems to fit many of the facts about morality better than moral realism, including the fact that there is considerable variation in the moral systems of different societies. Moral differences, and moral disagreement, are difficult to explain on an intuitionist theory. Why don't we have the same level of agreement about morality that we do about, say, mathematics, if they are both subjects we have direct *a priori* knowledge of? Even in the case of the empiricist version, it is difficult to explain the pervasiveness of moral disagreement. Why don't we have the same degree of agreement about moral judgments as we do about judgments of colour, if they both are judgments we draw from experience of their objects? If two people have differing intuitions about a given case, there are no further facts that can be appealed to in order to settle the dispute, and so there is no mechanism available for resolving moral disagreements.

But intuitionism is colloquially associated with another claim that does stand on firmer ground and is worth mentioning. That is that we all seem to have a moral conscience, which is informed by our emotional responses, that is worth listening to. Acting ethically requires judgment. But it is not a wholly intellectual exercise. All morally mature and morally healthy adults have a more or less well-developed personal conscience as well, that is a matter as much of feeling as of thought. Our emotional reactions, and especially our moral emotions, can be useful aids to good moral judging. Sometimes we just feel uncomfortable with what someone asks us to do. Sometimes we feel shame or guilt at the prospect of acting in certain ways or having acted in a particular way. At other times we experience reactive attitudes, such as resentment and indignation, when others have treated us in ways we think are contrary to our true worth or inherent dignity. While we might feel angry or frustrated by some natural calamity befalling us (such as a storm knocking down our shed), we do not resent the storm or feel indignation toward it. These attitudes are suitable only as reactions to the actions of other persons, and only when the actions of those others treat us in ways that we do not deserve to be treated. Likewise, we can regret many decisions and actions we take, say because they have tragic but unforeseen consequences, but we only feel shame and guilt if we think we have done something morally contemptible or morally wrong. The moral emotions, and the feelings of conscience, should also be relied upon in making complex ethical decisions.

Many emotions are **amoral, immoral**, or even pathological. Sometimes we can be swept away by emotions, unhinged by them. But the emotions we are recommending here are not of those types. They are appropriate in the circumstances, and in some cases it would be monstrous not to feel them; a person who has committed a heinous crime, without excuse, yet who feels no shame, guilt, or remorse, for example, is worse than someone who has done the same wrong and then experienced the normal moral emotions of guilt and remorse. Anger, hostility, aggression, cruelty, sadism, envy, jealousy, self-loathing, and vindictiveness are generally unhealthy and immoral emotions. They differ in important ways from the moral emotions of due pride and resentment of demeaning treatment, resentment of wrongs done either to yourself or others, guilt if you have done wrong sufficient to warrant feeling guilty and judging that you deserve to be punished, shame if you have acted in shameful ways unworthy of a person with due regard for herself, and so on. The use of moral emotions in the moral education of young persons ("you should be ashamed of yourself," "how would you feel if I did that to you?", "how do you think I should feel?") is an extremely powerful tool, and once the moral emotions have developed into a mature moral conscience, it can be a reliable guide to moral insight.

Among the ways to use our personal conscience in reaching ethical decisions are the following:

1. How will acting in a given way make me feel?

2. Will I be able to look myself in the mirror, look my loved ones in the face, live with myself, or sleep soundly, if I do what I am thinking about doing?

3. Will I feel guilt, shame, embarrassment, humiliation, or remorse?

4. If someone else did to me what I propose to do to another, would I feel resentment or indignation?

5. How would I feel if a complete and accurate account of my decision and action was plastered on the front page of every newspaper and social media site in the country?

6. Is my action compatible with proper self-respect?

Apply the test of moral emotions to Cases 3, 5, 8, 14, 15, 16, 17, 22, 23, and 29.

2.7 JUSTICE

Justice is commonly found both on lists of duties and lists of virtues. Justice is typically rendered as the disposition to give persons their due or what they are owed. Thus to know what justice requires we must know what people are due or owed, what they are entitled to, and by whom. Justice is complex, in part because there are at least four different kinds of justice: *retributive, compensatory, distributive,* and *procedural.*

Retributive justice requires that we give people what they deserve, where what they deserve is based on whether they have purposely benefitted at the expense of or wrongfully harmed others. At its most general, retributive justice requires that we return good for good and evil for evil. The requirement that we return good for good grounds our duties of gratitude and reciprocity. Those who have done something good for us deserve that we not act in ways that make them regret their kindness or favour, at a minimum, and that we reciprocate with kindness toward them in turn. We ought to display gratitude toward our benefactors. Likewise, the requirement that we return evil for evil is at the heart of our retributive criminal justice system, in which persons are punished for wrongfully harming others, because that is what they deserve. Punishment, or discipline, is given as matter of justice when it is given because it is deserved for a wrongful act.

Compensatory justice concerns what persons who have suffered harm deserve or are owed. The harm may be wrongfully imposed, as is generally the case in tort law, through which individuals seek compensation for harms they suffer as a result of others' negligence (failure to take reasonable care), or as in the case of compensation paid to victims of historical wrongs, such as that paid to survivors of the residential school system.[20] It may also be a harm that persons suffer through no fault of anyone, a harm that is not also a wrong, as in cases involving compensating people for damages caused by a natural disaster such as a fire or a flood.

People suffer harms or losses all the time. The issue of compensatory justice is to determine when the costs of those harms should fall where they lay (just bad luck that your house got swept away by the hurricane, but you bear the cost), when they should be compensated either by the person who caused the damage (you drove through my shed in the snow storm, and even though it was an accident for which you were not at fault, it is right that you pay to repair my shed), by the people in general through their government (bad luck that your house got flooded and we will share that cost collectively by providing public compensation rather than leaving the burden of the loss on you alone), or be shared between those who might cause and those who might suffer such harms through some kind of insurance scheme, which might be mandatory or optional (motor vehicle insurance, crop insurance, home insurance, disability insurance, or workers' compensation insurance, all of which provide mechanisms for sharing the costs of compensating those who might suffer harms).

Distributive justice concerns the distribution of goods and service, burdens and benefits, in society. There are many potential principles of distributive justice, based upon assessments of what people are owed or entitled to. Among these principles are individual merit, need, contribution, ability, and equality. There are some goods that we think should be distributed equally to all, regardless of differences between them, and unequal provision of such goods will be deemed unjust regardless of why it is imposed. Elementary school education, police protection, and basic health care are among such goods that Canadians have decided should be made available equally to all. If educational opportunities, police services, and critical health care are denied to any members of our society, this will constitute an injustice. Under this approach, the lack of clean drinking water on hundreds of Aboriginal Reserves throughout Canada, for example, is unjust.

Other goods and opportunities we think should be distributed according to merit, such as employment opportunities and innumerable awards and distinctions (literary awards, public service awards, grants, competitive prizes, and so on). It is usually recognized that merit-based systems of distribution will only be just against a background of equal opportunities; if some people have been deprived of equal opportunities by being previously deprived of something that ought to be distributed equally, such as education, then merit-based systems of distribution may simply perpetuate that past injustice rather than serving justice. This is the insight that motivates **affirmative action** and other programs aimed at ameliorating the effects of past injustice: some people may not be able to compete on an equal footing now under a merit-based system because they continue to suffer the effects of past injustice, and so relying on a pure merit-based system of determining entitlements may perpetuate injustice into the future.

Yet other goods ought to be distributed according to need. This is the thought that motivates much of our public **welfare systems** and our social safety net. Some people have basic needs that they cannot meet, through no fault of their own (through natural misfortune, accident, illness, and so forth), and so we make provision to meet those needs through public systems of wealth redistribution, operationalized as systems of social security, welfare, and disability schemes. Such benefits are available only on the basis of need, rather than merit or contribution.

Some other kinds of goods we think should be distributed on the basis of contribution. This is the foundation of free competitive markets. People should be able to bring their talents and contributions to the market, and if they thereby offer goods or services that others find valuable and are willing to pay for, those who contribute them are entitled to the profits they reap from their own efforts. Deciding what goods and services ought to be left to markets to distribute, according to principles of competition and supply and demand, is a fundamental question of justice. Our decision that basic education and critical health care should not be left to the market, and made available only to those who can pay for them, reflects our judgment that the distribution of these goods should be based on a principle of equality rather than contribution.

Governments are not productive entities; they do not generate wealth, as do participants in the market. Rather, they redistribute wealth. They take money from some, through taxation, and give it to others (directly as income supplements or indirectly in the provision of goods and services such as health care, education, police services, and roads). It is a question of distributive justice how our taxation system should be structured, and what goods and services should be provided by redistributing wealth in society. As we have seen, some of these decisions are based on a conception of basic human needs. We have determined that persons are entitled to have their basic human needs met, even if they cannot meet those needs themselves. Operationalizing this decision requires that we have some way of distinguishing basic needs from mere wants or desires. I may want to live in a penthouse apartment and to drink fine single malt scotch; if I am not able to satisfy these desires without public assistance, alas, I must do without them. But if I want food sufficient to meet my caloric needs for minimum health and basic shelter, I may receive assistance should I not be able to secure these goods for myself. We need a theory of basic needs to draw these distinctions. We also need to determine what goods should be left to markets to provide, and what goods should be regulated or removed altogether from market mechanisms.

Why do we think governments should provide roads and military protection from foreign enemies, but not cars and refrigerators? Part of the answer lies in the distinction between public and private goods (and bads). Most of the goods we use and enjoy in our daily lives are **private goods**. They are private in the sense that they are exclusive and rivalrous. If a good is exclusive, then the person who owns it can exclude others from its use; its being available to one person does not entail that it must be available to others. If a good is rivalrous, then its use by one person is incompatible with its use by others, or its use by one person diminishes the amount of it available for use by others. Most consumer goods are private in both senses. When I buy a particular car, I can effectively exclude others from using it, and it is now not available for the use of others.

The contrast is with what economists call **public goods**, which are non-excludable and non-rivalrous. Consider a lighthouse. Suppose I build a lighthouse to aid my safe passage though a rocky strait of water. Once it is built, I cannot effectively exclude others from using it; they derive benefit from it, even though they did not contribute to its construction. And their use does not rival or compete with mine. The benefit others derive from it in no way diminishes its usefulness to me or its availability to me. Air is a pure public good in this sense; no one can exclude others from using air, and the use by others does not diminish my access to the good or the benefit I can derive from it.[21]

There are few public goods in this technical sense. Some people think national defence is an example of a public good, because if a country provides national defence no one in the country can be excluded from the benefit, and its enjoyment by some does not diminish its availability for others. A more obvious example might be television signals. Once a television signal is broadcast, it is available to everyone with the equipment to receive it and some receiving it does nothing to diminish access to it for others. Digital music and books have the same features. In order to render such goods excludable, artificial barriers must be put in place (proprietary software, copyrights, or patents, for example), to exclude some from accessing them.

More common are goods that have one but not both features of public goods: they are either non-excludable or non-rivalrous, but not both. Music, art work, literature, and public parks (up to a point) are typically non-rivalrous;

their use or enjoyment by some does not diminish their availability for use or enjoyment by others. But they are excludable, because access to them can be restricted. Some natural resources, such as fish stocks, are non-excludable, but they are rivalrous in the sense that their use by some leaves others with diminished access to or use of them. Health care in a system such as ours is non-excludable, because it is available to all, but it too is rivalrous, in the sense that its use by some may leave less for others or access to it more restricted for others.

A discussion of public goods is relevant here because many people think that it is a matter of justice that certain public goods be provided by the state equally to all, paid for through taxation. In everyday parlance, such things as education, clean air and water, public parks, police services, emergency services, national defence, and the arts are called public goods. Most of these goods are not, technically, public goods, because their use by some leaves less for others, or their provision for more users increases their costs. But they are public goods in another sense: they provide benefits to more than their immediate consumers or those who access them. They provide indirect benefits to society in general. It is appropriate that governments provide public goods, because their provision tends to be undersupplied by the free market, given that some can enjoy them without paying the costs of their production or delivery. In other cases, regulations such as copyright provide incentives to produce such goods by creating artificial barriers to their free distribution.

Few people believe that justice requires equality of outcomes, wherein everyone enjoys the same level of goods and services in society. We recognize that extraordinary talent and contribution can give rise to inequality of income and other desired goods. Those who work harder, are more talented, take greater risks, are more creative, and maybe even those who are just luckier, deserve to reap the rewards from their extra efforts or contributions to society. But this depends upon a just distribution of opportunities as a backdrop to distributive schemes based on competition, merit, or contribution. And provision of the goods and services necessary to ensure fair terms of competition and equality of opportunity depends upon distributive justice.

Finally, some matters of justice fall under the heading of **procedural justice**. Justice requires that the terms of competition be fair, if competition is to lead to just outcomes. The administration of law must also meet the requirements of procedural justice, which requires among other things that judges who decide disputes do so impartially, that everyone has an opportunity to present his or her case, that like cases be treated alike, and more.

Theorists have tried to identify what all these aspects of justice have in common, what makes them all matters of justice. In liberal democracies, it is generally assumed that justice requires that governments treat all their members with equal concern and respect. Equal concern is shown through the provision of social welfare programs designed to ensure that every person has their basic needs met. Provisions against discrimination that make equality of opportunity possible are necessary to ensure equal respect.

One of the most significant forms of injustice comes in the form of discrimination, and it is not surprising that we have laws prohibiting discrimination on the basis of morally irrelevant factors, such as race, ethnicity, gender, sexuality, religion, marital status, and the like. We have a guarantee of equality in the *Charter of Rights and Freedoms*, which guarantees that governments will not discriminate against members of society on prohibited grounds. It reads:

> 15. (1) Every individual is equal before and under the law and has the right to the equal protection and equal benefit of the law without discrimination and, in particular, without discrimination based on race, national or ethnic origin, colour, religion, sex, age or mental or physical disability.
>
> (2) Subsection (1) does not preclude any law, program or activity that has as its object the amelioration of conditions of disadvantaged individuals or groups including those that are disadvantaged because of race, national or ethnic origin, colour, religion, sex, age or mental or physical disability.*

We also have rights to be free from discrimination on prohibited grounds set out in provincial, territorial, and federal human rights codes, which protect us from discrimination at the hands of others besides government. Equality guarantees are necessary to ensure that all enjoy equal opportunities and access to the benefits our society makes possible. They provide, in other words, one of the essential conditions under which other principles of justice can operate, such as merit-based and market-based competition. They ensure that all are treated with equal respect.

Finally, we must acknowledge that what someone is due is often times determined by their prior undertakings, such as their prior agreements or contracts. Often justice will involve ensuring that persons keep their agreements, and receive benefits for which they have contracted, independently of whether the agreement or contract was fair from some ideal standpoint. So long as the agreement or contract was freely entered into (itself a question of considerable complexity, especially if the parties have unequal bargaining power) by competent

Canadian Charter of Rights and Freedoms

people, and its terms are not grossly unfair ("unconscionable" in law), justice requires that the parties get what they bargained for.

Questions raised by justice are too numerous to list exhaustively, but include the following:

1. Is the provision of some good or service to be conducted under a principle of equality, merit, competition, or market forces?

2. Is this particular good related to basic needs?

3. Will a particular program help to ensure equality of opportunity?

4. Is the operation of some program fair?

5. What do the individuals involved in a particular situation deserve?

6. Are the goods that are the concern of your organization public goods or private goods?

7. Are the participants in your program treated according to principles of procedural justice; that is, are like cases treated alike?

8. Are there assumptions built in to your program that discriminate against some members of society?

9. Are the effects of a program discriminatory?

Consider Cases 1, 2, 3, 4, 7, 12, 13, 23, 24, 25 , 27, and 29 with an eye to determining what the parties are owed as a matter of justice, and whether an injustice has occurred.

2.8 FEMINISM, CRITICAL RACE THEORIES, DISABILITY STUDIES, AND INDIGENEITY

A number of fields of study have arisen in the modern era that address particular forms of injustice in society: most especially sexism, ableism,[22] racism, and discrimination against Aboriginal and indigenous peoples. Feminism in its most basic form is comprised of two claims, one factual and one evaluative. The first is that human societies, including our own, have been and continue to be sexist, to systematically and systemically subordinate women. The second is that the oppression of women is morally wrong and unjust. Taken this way, virtually everyone is a feminist. But of course feminism is not universally subscribed to. That is because the ways in which women have been subordinated by men is so thorough and systemic that women's subordination has been thought natural and rendered invisible. Feminism challenges the naturalism of women's subordination, pointing out that it is a product of social arrangements rather than biology.

Critical race theory, disability studies, and theories of indigeneity similarly explore the ways in which social structures discriminate against persons of colour, persons with disabilities, and Aboriginal persons. They have in common a commitment to demonstrating that the disadvantages experienced by marginalized groups are not natural or unavoidable, but are instead a product of the intersection of unjust laws, economic arrangements, access to education, health care, and meaningful work, and other social forces that are not immutable or unchangeable. It is necessary, if we are to genuinely express equal concern and respect for persons, that we be attentive to the ways in which our practices and social arrangements work to exclude or marginalize some, even if that is not their intended effect.

One feature that all these perspectives have in common is an attention to inequalities of power in society, and a commitment to challenging those power imbalances. When power imbalances are used to deny equal concern and respect for some on the basis of morally irrelevant characteristics (such as race or physical ability), or to restrict the access of some to equal opportunities, critical social theories demand that we recognize such imbalances as producing injustice.

Among the questions asked by those influenced by critical social thought are these:

1. Are there power imbalances between the various parties to some dispute or who will be affected by some decision?

2. Does my decision affect the well-being or opportunities of historically disadvantaged groups?

3. Am I relying on assumptions about the natural abilities or disabilities of individuals in my thinking?

4. Will my action(s) promote opportunities for participation among those who have historically been excluded from or marginalized in decision making?

Consider the situations described in Cases 1, 4, 6, 7, 9, 14, 28, and 30 as opportunities to apply the insights of critical social theories.

QUESTIONS FOR FURTHER DISCUSSION

1. What is the normative principle of utilitarianism?
2. What does it mean to say that utilitarianism is a consequentialist moral theory?
3. How might a public servant rank sources or kinds of happiness?
4. In what ways might utilitarianism be useful for ethical thinking?

5. Explain what *diminishing marginal utility* means. Why might this idea be important for drafting social policy?

6. List and explain three difficulties with utilitarianism as it relates to ethical practices.

7. Explain the difference between *act utilitarianism* and *rule utilitarianism*.

8. In what ways might *rule utilitarianism* avoid the objections raised against *act utilitarianism*?

9. According to *deontological theories of morality*, what makes an action right or wrong?

10. What is the central difference between consequentialist (e.g., utilitarianism) and deontological theories of morality?

11. Explain, in your own words, Kant's categorical imperative.

12. How does Kant's *respect for persons* relate to the categorical imperative? How can respect for persons be universalized?

13. List and explain Kant's four kinds of duties.

14. What are some of the virtues thought to be important for being a good public servant?

15. What is the difference between intellectual, social, and moral virtues? Give examples of each that is *not* from the text.

16. How does *care ethics* differ from utilitarianism and virtue ethics?

17. What are the four kinds of "justice" discussed? Explain each.

18. What features help differentiate between a private and public good. Explain the difference.

19. How can we determine what rational individuals would agree to? Why is rational endorsement relevant to moral acceptability?

NOTES

[1] Jeremy Bentham, *An Introduction to the Principles of Morals and Legislation* (1780, 1823 revised). There are many fine editions of this text available.

[2] John Stuart Mill, *Utilitarianism* (1861); Henry Sidgwick, *Methods of Ethics* (1874).

[3] See Daniel Kahneman and Angus Deaton, "High income improves evaluation of life but not emotional well-being," *Proceedings of the National Academy of Science* (Sept. 7, 2010).

[4] See Peter Railton, "Alienation, Consequentialism, and the Demands of Morality," *Philosophy and Public Affairs* 13:134 (1984).

[5] Kant actually offers four formulations of the categorical imperative, but we will focus just on the two that have been widely adopted and that guide much moral thinking today. Immanuel Kant, *Groundwork for the Metaphysics of Morals* (1785). There are many acceptable translations and editions of this work widely available.

[6] W. D. Ross, *The Good and the Right* (Oxford: Oxford University Press, 1930).

[7] Carol Gilligan, *In a Different Voice* (Cambridge, MA: Harvard University Press, 1982).

[8] Although Gilligan finds the justice perspective and care perspective to be correlated with the different genders, the correlation is a loose one. Men and women can and do use both perspectives, even if one tends to dominate more in their ethical approaches. And it is not surprising that women have developed a care-based approach to ethics, given that they have been the primary caregivers in society, are more often charged with meeting the needs of particular persons in the family, and often play the role of mediator in family disputes, where finding a compromise that can allow maintenance of the relationships involved is of paramount concern.

[9] Thomas Hobbes, *Leviathan* (1651); John Locke, *Second Treatise on Government* (1689); Jean-Jacques Rousseau, *Du Contrat Social, Principes du droit politique* (*Of the Social Contract, Principles of Political Right*) (1762). There are excellent editions of all these texts available in English. German philosopher Immanuel Kant is often included in the family of social contract theorists, but since his views have been used to illustrate deontology, and we can describe the social contract tradition without reference to Kant, we ignore his version of the theory in what follows.

[10] David Gauthier, *Morals by Agreement* (Oxford: Oxford University Press, 1986) and *Moral Dealing: Contract, Ethics, and Reason* (Ithaca: Cornell University Press, 1990).

[11] This phrase actually comes from John Rawls in *A Theory of Justice* (1971), though he subsequently moved away from his early contractarian leanings in his later work.

[12] Daniel Defoe, *Robinson Crusoe* (1719).

[13] This description draws heavily from another Enlightenment philosopher: David Hume. Though Hume rejected an actual social contract, through which morality or political systems were justified by consent, his theory has many affinities with hypothetical contractarianism. Here we draw on what has become known as Hume's description of the "circumstances of justice," the circumstances in which morality is both necessary and possible, in describing the human condition. See *A Treatise of Human Nature* (1739–40) and *An Enquiry Concerning the Principles of Morals* (1751). There are many good editions of each widely available.

[14] The original description of the dilemma involved prisoners. Suppose two people, A and B, have committed a serious crime together. They have been detained by police, and all each wants is to minimize his own jail time. The prosecutor offers each of them the following deal: if you confess and your partner doesn't, I will pin most of the blame on him; you will get 1 year, while he will get 10 years. Of course, if he confesses and you don't, the opposite will occur. The prosecutor does not have enough evidence to convict you of the serious offence you have committed, but she is quite confident she can get you on a

lesser charge if you both keep quiet: 3 years each. But if you both confess, then she will have you on the serious charge and you will each get 7 years in jail. You reason as follows: if my partner confesses, then I should confess (7 years rather than 10); if my partner doesn't confess, then I should confess (1 year rather than 3). Whatever I think my partner is going to do, I should confess. Both reason the same way, both confess, and both wind up being sentenced to 7 years. But they could have gotten off with just 3 years each if they had just kept their mouths shut and not confessed. Not confessing is the **co-operative strategy** in this game. It requires that each forgo their highest ranked outcome (getting only 1 year by letting their partner take most of the blame), and pursue the mutually beneficial second-ranked choice instead. See Gauthier's *Morals by Agreement* for an excellent description of the dilemma and its history.

[15] See Gauthier 1986 for the argument.

[16] See Adam Smith, *An Inquiry into the Nature and Causes of the Wealth of Nations* (1776).

[17] See Gauthier 1986 for discussion.

[18] Rational intuitionism was popular in the early 20th century, especially among English analytic philosophers. See, for example, G.E. Moore, *Principia Ethica* (Cambridge: Cambridge University Press, 1903); H.A. Prichard, "Does Moral Philosophy Rest on a Mistake?" *Mind* 21 (1912); Michael Huemer, *Ethical Intuitionism* (NY: Palgrave Macmillan, 2005).

[19] Francis Hutcheson, *Inquiry concerning Moral Good and Evil* (1725) and *Illustrations upon the Moral Sense* (1728); David Hume, *A Treatise of Human Nature* (1739-40); Adam Smith, *A Theory of the Moral Sentiments* (1751); and Thomas Reid, *Essays on the Active Powers of the Human Mind* (1788).

[20] The residential school system was a policy adopted by the government of Canada in the 20th century under which Aboriginal children were removed from their communities and sent to residential schools, where they were forbidden to use their native languages and were subjected to a school experience designed to assimilate them into the mainstream, non-Native, culture of Canada. It had devastating consequences for its victims, who were forcibly removed from their communities and deprived of access to their languages, heritage, cultural traditions, and families. Some were further victimized by sexual, physical, or psychological abuse. But the greatest harm done by the residential school system was to Aboriginal communities as such. For multiple generations they were derived of the ability to parent their children, thereby losing the capacity to parent effectively. Consider how one learns to be a good parent. One looks to one's own family, and those of friends, for successful role models. One thinks about those parents who seemed to have struck the right balance between freedom and control, an effective mix of discipline to discourage bad behaviour and incentives for good behaviour, successful approaches to resolving family disputes, and so on. In removing generations of children from their families and their communities, the residential school system deprived Aboriginal communities of the capacity for effective parenting and healthy family relations. As a result,

incidence of family violence, family break-up, and substance abuse are higher in many Aboriginal communities than in their non-Aboriginal counterparts.

[21] See Paul Samuelson, "The Pure Theory of Public Expenditure," *Review of Economics and Statistics* 36:4 (1954): 387–389.

[22] "Ableism" refers to the way in which social arrangements favour those who are physically and mentally able (functioning within some normal range of abilities), and discriminate against or disadvantage those who are disabled (functioning below the normal range).

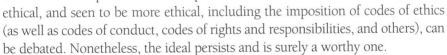

CHAPTER 3

The Value of Ethics Codes and of Ethics in the Public Service

It might seem as though talk of "public service values," "ethics in the public service," and "ethics codes" should be as old as the public service itself. It's not so. Our current approach to ethics in the civil service has its beginnings in the 1960s, and the widespread use of ethics codes is an even more recent development. The efficacy of various attempts to make the public service more ethical, and seen to be more ethical, including the imposition of codes of ethics (as well as codes of conduct, codes of rights and responsibilities, and others), can be debated. Nonetheless, the ideal persists and is surely a worthy one.

Although in what follows we stress the potential benefits to be hoped for from the articulation of organizational values and the adoption of an ethics code, we are not unmindful of their limitations and dangers. A great deal depends upon the *processes* by which a set of organizational values come to be assembled and articulated. It is crucial to the future effectiveness of the statement of values as inspirational and unity-building that all interested parties be given a voice in their selection and expression. The values articulated must actually express the aspirations of the people in the organization, be aligned with its core activities, and be realizable in the context of those activities. And reference to context reminds us of a further limitation: it is extremely unlikely that there can be a one-size-fits-all approach to constructing ethics codes for organizations in the public service. Codes must be appropriate for the purposes of the organization, which vary widely across the various levels of the public service. The kinds of values emphasized by such codes must, likewise, be sensitive to the kind of clients the organization serves, and the degree to which its activities are politicized. The values appropriate for a procurement department, for example, may differ considerably from those of a department whose purpose is to aid victims of crime, which will differ again from those needed in a department tasked with forestry management. With this in mind, we make some general remarks about ethics codes and their value in what follows.

Ethical conduct cannot be assured simply by the adoption of an **ethics code** (or code of conduct, or statement of values and principles). But ethical conduct *can* be learned, promoted, encouraged, and valued. While some may be under the impression that Canada's public service is largely ethical and corruption-free, especially when compared to certain other countries, in actuality:

> There are few areas of unethical conduct for which we cannot find a Canadian illustration. In any event, comparison of the level of ethical conduct in various countries is an exceedingly difficult and a largely fruitless endeavour. Since many instances of misconduct are never discovered, it is difficult to measure even the number, much less the type and gravity, of offences committed. Moreover, the excesses of officials in other countries do not justify excesses of our own.[1]

Ethics codes are vital, for they have an important role to play in developing an ethical culture, or promoting an **ethics regime**, within complex organizations like the civil service.

A major source of resistance to ethics codes is founded in the idea that everyone (or, almost everyone) is ethical, knows the difference between right and wrong, and will do what is right. Thus ethics codes are thought to be superfluous at best (articulating what everyone already knows and does), or they are insulting at worst (assuming that people cannot determine what is right or that they will not voluntarily do the right thing).[2] But this underestimates the value of ethics codes and the role they can play in complex institutions.

3.1 GUIDANCE AND CLARITY OF EXPECTATIONS

The first benefit of an ethics code is that it provides clear guidance for members of an organization. It establishes a set of common expectations that are easy to read and understand. Thus an ethics code can establish a baseline of expectations about conduct that makes reliance on others and trust in them more reasonable. We do not have to figure out whether each individual within an agency is personally of high moral character in order to predict what he or she might do in a given situation. Rather, we can assume that all agency staff will act in conformity to the code.

Expectations are extremely important in social life, including in the workplace. For example, consider a friend who voluntarily creates expectations in others: that he will be somewhere at a particular time, that he will keep a secret shared in confidence, that he will repay a loan on a given date, that he will do his share of a joint assignment, that he will take care of some task, and so on. If your friend fails to meet the commitments he has undertaken, without a good excuse or justification, he has, among other things, disappointed the expectations of others. Others have determined their own course of conduct in light of those expectations. Serious harm may be done by the commitments not being fulfilled. But separate from any harm or damage that might result from your friend not fulfilling his commitments—you miss an important appointment or are left stranded, someone's reputation is seriously compromised, the person to whom the money was owed cannot pay her own rent because the loan was not repaid on time, the assignment is not completed and all the members of the group receive a failing grade, or the task is not finished, with whatever negative consequences that might cause—his failure to fulfil the expectations that he has himself created is a moral wrong and a harm to your relationship. Some of the most common forms of immorality—promise breaking, lying, cheating, and infidelity in personal relationships—have in common the disappointment of legitimate expectations. When a person knowingly creates expectations, and then fails to meet them, it is impossible for others to reasonably trust him in the future. His word is no good. He cannot be relied upon. He cannot, in short, be trusted. And without trust, healthy social relations are impossible.

Ethics codes and similar devices are valuable because they create a common set of expectations, and are "recognized as providing an essential foundation and framework for guiding individual and organizational behaviour."[3]* They are often fairly minimal expectations, such as a criminal code, setting a minimum standard of conduct that is expected rather than expressing a high ideal to be aimed for. Nevertheless, they have value insofar as they make known a set of shared expectations. Misunderstanding and harm often result when expectations are unclear, when one person has expectations that the other does not. "I thought you were going to do it," followed by "I didn't think it was my responsibility to do it," expresses a common exchange based on different expectations. Ethics codes can help people avoid such misunderstandings and so better determine how to act, given their understanding of how others are going to act.

*Kenneth Kernaghan, "The emerging public service culture: values, ethics, and reforms," *Canadian Public Administration* 37: 4 (1994), p. 616.

3.2 EMBODY PRINCIPLES AND VALUES OF THE ORGANIZATION

Every organization embodies a set of values and has ideals it is trying to live up to as well as goals it is trying to accomplish. Ethics codes can be valuable because they often articulate those values, ideals, and goals. Successful businesses rarely have "Make as much money as possible!" as their corporate motto. Instead, they have values: Providing quality service at a fair price, Helping seniors live better, and so on. A statement of values provides a common understanding of the organization, and can unite workers in a common cause. They make the work more meaningful, and are important in inspiring loyalty. Among the values important to the public service are the traditional values of "integrity, accountability, efficiency, effectiveness, responsiveness, representativeness, neutrality, fairness and equity,"[4]* as well as **democracy**, the common good, and **justice**. The values of an organization are those ends that are thought worthy of pursuit or support, that provide its *raison d'être*, and that give meaning to its activities.

The principles of an organization are the central practical commitments that help realize its values. So, for example, an organization committed to the value of equity or equality would hold inclusivity as an important action-guiding principle. An organization that values democracy would be committed to principles encouraging participation and access to information to promote informed decision making. This organization would recognize the principle that the public has the right to know the people's business.

Ethics codes provide a venue through which organizations can express what their values are, and should embody a set of principles that will aid participants in the organization to realize those values. The principles might be quite abstract, such as to treat people fairly or to act with professionalism, or they might be quite specific, such as not to disclose confidential information. But a good ethics regime is one that articulates a set of values that are worthy of pursuit, around which the organization's activities are co-ordinated, and a set of practical principles, the following of which will help its members achieve those objectives. This applies to ethics codes in the public service, for "the real challenge is to give not only guidance as to what will not be tolerated but also inspiration as to the values that should inform public service,"[5] such as "honest dialogue, speaking truth to power, acknowledging conflict, aiming for balance, equity and synthesis."[6]† In this sense an ethics code is often aspirational, setting out ideals to strive for, as well as more concrete minimum standards of conduct.

---

*Kenneth Kernaghan, "The emerging public service culture: values, ethics, and reforms," *Canadian Public Administration* 37:4 (1994), p. 615.

†John Tait, "A Strong Foundation: Report of the Task Force on Public Service Values and Ethics,"*Canadian Public Administration* 40:1 (1996), p. 1.

The minimum standards of conduct will often include rules of both prohibition and prescription, rules that dictate what members must refrain from doing as well as what they must do. So, for example, public servants must avoid conflicts of interest, and they must provide honest advice to their Ministers, agency heads, or Council members. The first is a prohibition, while the second is a prescription. Ethical conduct will require refraining from prohibited conduct and performing that which is prescribed, but it will also require at least a good faith attempt to meet the more lofty aspirations and ideals of the organization, and a commitment to acting in ways that express and help realize its values. Ethics codes, insofar as they articulate the value set of an organization, further "provide an analytical tool, or framework, for explaining past, current, and emerging developments in public administration, and serve increasingly as a management tool, especially in the areas of strategic planning and organizational change."[7]*

This emphasis on values, and principles to realize them, is a relatively recent development in Canadian public service organizations, and it has been embraced most enthusiastically at the federal level. The values approach is often contrasted with a "rules approach," which focuses much more heavily on rules and regulations, proscribing particular kinds of activities on the part of public servants, often with a fair amount of specificity. Rules prohibiting conflict of interest, or moonlighting, or post-employment lobbying activities, are ready examples of the rules approach. Advocates of the values approach often justify their advocacy in terms similar to those used just above, and the values approach has been thought attractive if one wants to empower individuals within public service organizations and make them more democratic. Yet the values approach does have significant limitations, a few of which are worth mentioning.

The values approach faces several serious challenges. First, actual codes that are expressed in terms of values and the principles to realize them (such as that of the Federal Public Service, see Appendix 1) often contain a *very long list of values*. This is problematic for a number of reasons. To begin with, values statements can deliver the benefits mentioned above only if they refer to a set of "core" values. But there has been a significant proliferation of values expressed in such codes, which tends to water down their effectiveness as aspirational and inspirational statements.

More seriously, the values expressed are often quite *abstract or general* (e.g., professionalism, integrity, accountability), and to this extent they may fail to provide practical guidance to those who are expected to act in accordance with them. Moreover, if a multitude of values are expressed, situations will surely arise in which they conflict with each other. The mere articulation of a set of values does nothing to help individuals decide how to resolve such conflicts of values when they arise.

*Kenneth Kernaghan, "Codes of Ethics and Administrative Responsibility,"*Canadian Public Administration* 17:4 (2008), p. 530. Copyright © 2008 John Wiley & Sons. Reproduced with permission of Blackwell Publishing Ltd.

And perhaps more seriously still, there is often a *gap* between the values expressed and the principles to be adopted to realize them. What principles must be adopted if one is to act loyally, respectfully, equitably, or with integrity? Unless there are managers within the organization who have expertise in applying the values and adopting principles appropriate to realizing them, the action-guiding usefulness of values will be negligible.

Related to the previous points, it is not clear how appeal to values can help public servants resolve moral dilemmas or *decide what to do* in hard moral cases. Especially if there is a large set of "core" values in the organization, the public servant will almost certainly decide what she thinks she should do (often based on consequentialist reasoning, considering the impact of the options on those affected), and then simply find a value that supports that decision. In such cases, the values are not doing any of the moral work.

Finally, many codes that are written in the language of values and principles contain not just a large number of values, with no way to weigh their relative importance in cases of conflict, but the values are of significantly *different types*. This is explicitly so in the federal case, which is organized around four "families of values": people, professional, ethical, and democratic. When a code includes values drawn from very different domains (such as ethics and management theory), it may lack internal coherence. Even if we would expect values drawn from a single domain to be reconcilable or scalable in terms of their relative importance, the chances that values drawn from very different domains will be likewise capable of giving coherent advice to their addressees is slim at best.[8]

Yet this critique of the values approach to ethics in the public service is itself not without difficulties. First, the contrast between rules and values is itself problematic. It is extremely unlikely that rules alone could inspire ethical conduct in the public service. But more than that, rules could not even be understood unless those to whom they apply have some sense of the values they are designed to realize or protect. The rules derive their moral authority, moreover, from those very values they help realize; without this, they would be nothing but imposed constraints, to be complied with for pragmatic reasons, perhaps, but empty of genuine normative force. The critique also ignores the effect a statement of enduring values can have in creating an institutional culture, rather than merely being a guide to individual decision making. Ralph Heintzman, an able apologist for the emphasis on values in public service organizations, stresses both of these points.

Codes play more than one role for the professions, like the public service, they define and inspire. A code for a public service does not serve only to "maintain and enhance public confidence in [its] integrity," important as that may be. It also serves to "strengthen respect for, and appreciation of, the role played by the Public Service within Canadian democracy." And the second is the precondition for the first. In this mode, by establishing the standards and first principles of the profession, a code also instills the pride and motivation without which the rules would remain a dead letter, perhaps observed only in the breach, as in so many countries. A values and ethics code should set out not just the rules but, more important, the vision of the good— the public-service good—that inspires public servants to do what they do, every day. Not a new vision, but the one that is already implicit in the idea of public service itself."[9]*

We agree with Heintzman that statements of values can be valuable to public service organizations, and an aid to ethical decision making within them.

3.3 RIGHTS, OBLIGATIONS, DUTIES, AND RESPONSIBILITIES

Ethics codes are also useful insofar as they articulate or provide the basis for clear rights, duties, and obligations of public servants within the hierarchy of a department or agency. Such codes make clear the obligations of public servants in the performance of their duties, as well as with respect to outside activities (part-time employment, participation in political activities, and so forth) and with respect to post-employment interactions with government (restricting lobbying of departments with which the public servant had significant involvement in the previous 12 months, not using information obtained as a public servant upon leaving the public service, and so on). Again, the specification of duties can be helpful in clarifying expectations, and as an educative tool.

Codes of conduct or ethics codes also explain the obligations of civil servants, some of which are general, such as the obligation to obey the criminal law, and others more specific, such as avoiding anything that will bring the Crown into disrepute or the duty to report serious wrongdoing.

Yet ethics codes also define a set of rights enjoyed by civil servants, such as the right to a workplace free of **harassment** and **discrimination**, to be evaluated on the basis of merit[10]† and to be free from reprisal if one makes a good faith report of wrongdoing. These rights are complementary to any rights a civil servant might enjoy under a collective agreement or other terms of employment.

*Ralph Heintzman, "Public-service Values and Ethics: Dead end or strong foundation?" *Canadian Public Administration* 50:4 (2007), p. 573–602.

†Kenneth Kernaghan, "Codes of Ethics and Administrative Responsibility," *Public Administration* 58:2 (1980), p. 215.

Finally, codes of ethics can be valuable because they articulate a clear line of responsibility for various activities within a department or agency. More specifically, they lay out who has the responsibility for ensuring compliance with the ethical requirements of public servants. They vest responsibility for establishing an ethics regime with a designated senior public servant, such as a deputy Minister, an ethics officer, or an integrity commissioner. By identifying personnel who have direct responsibility for ethics in an organization, codes clarify from whom advice should be sought if an ethical question arises, to whom suspected wrongdoing should be reported, and express a general commitment to ethical conduct.

But codes cannot do it all. Codes are only one element in building an ethical public service. And ethics officers do not have sole responsibility for achieving that outcome. What matters is not what an organization says, but what its people do. Since an "organization's performance should reflect its espoused values, it is essential to assess the extent of the organization's commitment to these values."[11]* There is a well-documented tendency within organizations that have serious ethical lapses for everyone to point to someone higher up in the hierarchy as being the source of ethical failure. But that can't be right. The ethics of an organization is a function of its everyday practices, and is determined by the conduct of everyone in it. It is true that one of the best ways of developing an ethical organization is for senior managers to "**walk the talk**," to exemplify ethical conduct in their day-to-day activities. "It is especially important that the leaders of the organization 'live' its espoused values; otherwise, the commitment of employees to these values will fall—and their cynicism will rise."[12]† Ethics must be modelled, not just mandated. As Canada's former **Auditor General** so succinctly put it, "Value statements can be a strong positive tool, but management must be consistent and act accordingly. Announcing them and then not living by them is deadly."[13]

The ethical character of an organization is determined by "how things are done around here" rather than how they are described. But ethics codes can contribute to ethical conduct in their educative capacity and by making clear what exactly the "talk" is that we hope is walked. An organization whose managers (not just senior managers but middle managers too) explicitly use the language of ethical principles and values and incorporate rights and duties into discussions and decision making is more likely to embody and exemplify public service values than one that does not. While there is a great deal of discussion about how to "walk the talk," it is important to note that members of an organization must first "talk the talk." Ethics codes can make that vocabulary more accessible and easily shared.

*Kenneth Kernaghan, "Codes of Ethics and Administrative Responsibility," *Canadian Public Administration* 17:4 (2008), p. 619. Copyright © 2008 John Wiley & Sons. Reproduced with permission of Blackwell Publishing Ltd.

†Kenneth Kernaghan, "Codes of Ethics and Administrative Responsibility," *Canadian Public Administration* 17:4 (2008), p. 619. Copyright © 2008 John Wiley & Sons. Reproduced with permission of Blackwell Publishing Ltd.

By establishing mechanisms under which civil servants can get advice about ethically problematic situations, ethics codes assist civil servants in navigating a range of complex and potentially controversial matters. They encourage a direct engagement with the ethical implications of various decisions or judgments the public servant might be called upon to make. Codes provide support for good decision making, where it is understood that the common objective is to find the ethically best solution to a complex problem rather than to ignore the problem or wish it away. This engages ethics and values in a lived way, taking them from the code but then applying them, using them, exemplifying them, and modelling them. When that happens an organization is positioned to make good decisions. Even if the outcome remains controversial, decisions made after full consideration of the ethical implications of the factors involved are much more easily defensible, both within the organization and to the public.

3.4 CONSISTENCY AND FAIRNESS, DUE PROCESS, AND ADMINISTRATIVE JUSTICE

Ethics codes also contribute to good government because they provide a set of standards against which the evaluation of employee conduct can be fairly judged. It is generally unfair to hold people accountable for breaches of rules they were not informed about, of course. Thus by providing clarity about expectations and announcing the standards of conduct to which public servants are to conform, ethics codes help an organization avoid a very basic kind of **injustice**. They provide advance notice to public servants about the rules that apply to them, and if a breach of the rule occurs, then a civil servant can be properly held accountable for that breach. Ethical requirements for public servants are here treated analogously with legal requirements for citizens generally: ignorance of the law is no excuse, and persons are expected to make themselves familiar with the rules governing their conduct.

But ethics codes are not valuable because they enable punishment of wrongdoing *per se*. Rather, they are valuable because they encourage right-doing and provide a framework under which wrongdoing can be identified and dealt with fairly.

By establishing a common set of expectations, ethics codes make possible the consistent and fair treatment of public servants as employees. Whether wrongdoing has occurred can be determined against a public and common set of expectations, rather than being decided on an *ad hoc*, arbitrary, and potentially inconsistent basis. Codes reduce the possibility that one manager might find a certain conduct acceptable while another would not, creating confusion for employees and the appearance of arbitrariness among managers. With a Code, civil servants will be less likely to have to guess at what their managers might consider to be unethical conduct. This makes it possible to have consistency in the application of the rules, which is essential for a department or agency to function well. Having a Code also leads to fair judgments, both because a common set of rules is being applied and because it provides a framework for comparable outcomes.

Due process and **administrative justice** are absolutely central values to the rule of law and ethical organizations. Administrative justice requires that the conduct of people be evaluated according to rules or standards with the following characteristics: the rules are made known in advance; the rules are applied prospectively; the rules are clear and consistent with one another; and persons are judged according to the rules, in ways that are fair and satisfy the principle that "like cases should be treated alike." Codes contribute to these values, and the justice and fairness they realize, by making the rules clear.

Once an organization has clear rules and common expectations, it becomes easier to develop effective dispute resolution mechanisms, as well as procedures for identifying and rectifying wrongdoing. First, the rules put in place clear lines of responsibility for ethical leadership within the organization. In addition, they identify certain officers as having responsibility for providing ethical advice and resolving questions of ethics. This is a very important role in an ethics regime. Making space for individuals to safely raise ethical questions can go a long way toward promoting good conduct.

But even in the best organizations, it is to be expected that some individuals will breach the expectations of the organization and act in unethical ways. Thus it is absolutely vital that public service organizations have in place good monitoring systems for the early detection of wrongdoing. Effective oversight is not incompatible with trust and a presumption of ethical behaviour within an organization, and is essential if the public service is to act in the **public interest**. Whether the issue is ensuring that the government is getting value for its money when it contracts for goods or services from private entities, the efficacy of inspection regimes, or the accounting practices of ministries, everyone in an organization must respond appropriately to "red flags" or warning signs that something is amiss. There must be clear lines of responsibility and reporting, but there must also be a common understanding that the organization intends to act ethically accompanied by a shared presumption that management wants to know about ethical breaches so as to correct them. When unethical conduct happens, it is vital that mechanisms be in place to report wrongdoing in ways that provide fairness and administrative justice to the accused and protect the person reporting the wrongdoing from reprisal. We further discuss the disclosure of wrongdoing below, but here we note that codes again play a valuable role in this area. They do so by making it known what the standards of conduct are, so that breaches can be more readily identified, reported, and corrected.

3.5 RIGHT-DOING, PUBLIC TRUST, AND DEMOCRACY

By setting expectations for the conduct of the civil service, ethics codes contribute to right-doing. Through their educative role, their facilitation of consideration of ethical implications in decision making, their encouragement of seeking ethical advice, and their enabling of the fair investigations of potential wrongdoing, ethics codes contribute to building ethical practices. They not only set minimum standards of conduct, but also articulate the ideals and values of the organization. This contributes to a sense of common purpose among members of the organization, and promotes loyalty and collegiality within it.

Ethics codes also contribute to public trust in the civil service since "in the grey area between behaviour that is clearly forbidden and behaviour that is clearly honest and ethical, codes of conduct and ethical rules are particularly useful, to reassure the public and to protect public office holders themselves."[14*] The public more easily accepts the power of government when that power can be shown to be directed at ethically proper ends. But from the public's point of view, of course, what the civil service *does* is much more important than what it *says*. Codes of conduct and ethics codes are merely the beginning to building trust, not the end. Insofar as they actually encourage right-doing, and assist public servants in avoiding unethical behaviour, codes contribute to making the public service worthy of the public's trust. This, in turn, contributes to good government and political legitimacy, as well as public engagement with and support of the activities of the public service. This enhances democracy.

Ethics codes can achieve these many important objectives only if they find the right balance between **generality** and specificity, between the expression of lofty aspirations and statements of abstract moral principles, on the one hand, and very specific and detailed prescriptions, on the other. A code that simply articulates a few values to be aimed for provides too little practical guidance to be of use for real people deciding real moral problems or dilemmas. But a code that tries to formulate a rule prohibiting every kind of wrongful conduct imaginable, that contains pages of legalistic rules saying what public servants must not do in all possible detail, is too dense, too unreadable, and too unmanageable to be useful as well.[15†] Thus a good ethics code must strike a balance between these two extremes. It must be detailed enough to provide practical advice for resolving ethical problems, without trying to resolve those problems in advance and for all possible contingencies. A good ethics

*John Tait, "A Strong Foundation: Report of the Task Force on Public Service Values and Ethics,"*Canadian Public Administration* 40:1 (1996), p. 13.

†Kenneth Kernaghan, "Codes of Ethics and Administrative Responsibility," *Canadian Public Administration* 17:4 (2008), p. 538. Copyright © 2008 John Wiley & Sons. Reproduced with permission of Blackwell Publishing Ltd.

code must be detailed enough to be enforceable, without so constraining public servants that there is no room left for creative problem solving and flexibility in the delivery of services. Ideally, an ethics code should articulate the values of the organization and provide general guidance as to acceptable and unacceptable conduct, which can then be applied by specially trained ethics officers in providing advice to civil servants when a difficult case arises.

Ethics codes must not be used to undermine individual responsibility, creativity, and sensitivity, however. Even if an organization has a very good ethics code, its members must still exercise individual judgment in the performance of their work, and they will still have to exercise discretion in carrying out their responsibilities. They will still face competing claims and conflicting interests. They will still face ethical dilemmas, either because different principles are in conflict in a given case, or because different ethical approaches point toward different decisions. Ethics codes can never eliminate the need for moral deliberation and ethical decision making. As experts in Public Administration J. Bowman and R. Williams put it, ethics codes are useful to the extent that they promote a philosophy of excellence and a sense of personal responsibility. "[C]odes of ethics demand more than simple compliance; they mandate the exercise of judgment and acceptance of responsibility for decisions rendered—the real work of ethics."[16] Ethics, in this view, does not mask or shun the ambiguities and complexities of work in the contemporary public service, or shy away from the multiple values implicit in public service, but instead offers an interpretative framework within which ethical dilemmas can be analyzed and resolved.

We provide four examples of ethics codes as appendices to this book. Look at each and ask the following questions:

1. What values does it articulate?

2. What principles would be necessary to translate the values into action? Are those principles spelled out in the Code or left to be worked out by practitioners in the area?

3. What moral approach (utilitarian, deontological, virtue ethics, contractarian, justice-based, or critical) is implicit in the various provisions of the Code?

4. Does it strike the right balance between generality and specificity, between inspiration and practical guidance? Why or why not?

5. Is it well suited to achieve the kinds of benefits we have described above? Why or why not?

6. To what extent does the Code reflect a rule-based approach or a values-approach?

3.6 WHY ETHICS IS IMPORTANT TO THE PUBLIC SERVICE

Ethical behaviour contributes to a vibrant and respected public service in a large number of inter-related ways. Unethical conduct by public servants undermines essential democratic values, is contrary to the public good, erodes trust in public institutions, and makes service in public institutions less fulfilling for individual public servants. Both the public and its servants benefit from the development of high ethical standards and from mechanisms that enable and reward ethical conduct.

Perhaps the most visible benefit of ethical conduct among public servants, conduct that not only complies with but exemplifies ethical behaviour in an integral way throughout their professional activities, is that ethical conduct promotes and enhances public trust and confidence in the public service. The public service is a vital part of our national, provincial, territorial, and municipal governments, and its proper functioning is essential to the achievement of good government and the legitimacy and efficacy of our democratic institutions. A public service that operates in accordance with ethical principles and democratic values is one that deserves the public trust because it serves the public good.

3.6.1 Public Values

Governments are in the business of providing public goods and services (both in the technical and informal senses of public goods), and serving the common good or collective interests of citizens. As philosophers and political scientists Dean Geuras and Charles Garofalo put it, "The public agency is created to serve values that the public considers worthy. In funding groups such as those that oversee the environment, assist the impoverished, or provide care for the aged, the public is asserting a moral value in saying that these social benefits are worth the sacrifice of public funds. . . . [M]ost people support the activities of government to help the society as a whole rather than just themselves. A society must be moved by values above mere profit to charge a public agency with tasks and provide funds for those tasks."[17]* This simple point is profoundly important.

Governments, through the activities of public servants and the departments, agencies, and other public organizations in which they work, have as their fundamental responsibility designing and delivering programs and services that society collectively considers worthy of public support. The agencies a society creates, and the programs and services it provides and funds through its system of public administration, express that society's values and commitments. The work of the public service, then, is inescapably value-laden and morally important.

*Dean Geuras and Charles Garofalo, *Practical Ethics in Public Administration*, p. 17. Copyright © 2002 Management Concepts Press.

Public servants are public stewards. In addition to being fiscally responsible, they must act in ways they judge will advance society's values.

> The public administrator is also often forced into an ethical
> decision when the public interest conflicts with that of his
> agency. It may be in competition with other agencies for
> public funding. As committed as the administrator may be
> to the goals of his or her own division, the first consider-
> ation of the public steward is attainment of society's values.
> The ideal public administrator would sacrifice his or her
> own interests for those of the public. While the ideal public
> administrator, like the ideal human being, may not exist,
> the acknowledgement of ideals has a magnetic appeal.[18]*

The functions of government are generally those that have widespread public
support, such as national defence, emergency services, education, programs for the
disadvantaged, basic health care, support for the arts, environmental protection, and
health and safety regulations. Only if the goods and services the government provides are seen as serving the public interest and as especially important or valuable
will there be the social support needed to sustain them. There must also be a reasoned decision supporting the decision to provide a given service or good through
government mechanism rather than the free market. Given the general benefits of
free market activities, there must be a compelling rationale for providing a given service through non-market mechanisms such as governments typically employ.

Many contemporary disputes resolve around this very issue: when should a
service be delivered by government rather than the market? One general way of
marking the divide between conservative and liberal political orientations is along
this line, with conservatives generally favouring market mechanisms and liberals
generally favouring public systems (though, of course, this is terribly rough and
ready as a distinction). Often this division manifests itself over decisions of whether
to privatize services that had previously been delivered by government, such as
public housing, day care, or garbage collection. This example highlights the real tension that can develop between public service organizations and their political bosses,
because it is generally good for public service organizations themselves to retain
control over services, while politicians may think privatization is better for fiscal or
ideological reasons. Both should decide the matter by appealing to what is actually
in the public interest, though even that, as we shall see, is a contested concept.

What is important here, however, is that their service to the public interest
and the special importance of what they do imposes moral obligations on those

*Dean Geuras and Charles Garofalo, *Practical Ethics in Public Administration*, p. 19. Copyright © 2002
 Management Concepts Press.

tasked with delivering public services. To quote Geuras and Garofalo once more, "If government does something, it must be important. That importance imposes a special ethical demand upon public organizations and their employees. Moreover, that importance may be a major factor in attracting people with a strong social commitment to public service."[19]*

3.6.2 Efficient and Effective Design and Delivery of Public Services

An ethical public service assists the duly elected government in establishing policies, laws, and programs that serve the public good. The setting of political objectives and policy goals does not rest in the first instance with the public service, but rather with elected officials who are given a mandate to govern by the people and are accountable to them in regular general elections. Yet the public service is vital to good government, at both the front and back ends, as it were.

First, elected governments depend crucially on information given to them by, and expertise acquired by, the permanent public service. Elected governments come and go, but the public service remains and continues when governments are not sitting and when the writ has been dropped and an election is underway. In order for governments to develop effective programs and good policies, they rely upon the public service to provide background information and legal advice. Unless public servants provide timely, accurate, and complete information to their political bosses, elected politicians will not be able to develop policies that are based upon the best evidence available. And unless there is good communication across government departments and ministries, there will be no way of limiting duplication of efforts and expenditures, or even worse, inconsistent requirements and rules.

As the repositories of vital information, public service organizations have tremendous power; in this case, the old adage that "knowledge is power" is certainly true, and information is the beginning of knowledge. A recurring challenge for public sector organizations is to find ways to support effective information sharing, within organizations, between government units, and with elected politicians and political staffers, boards of directors of public agencies, and others who need access to the information to effectively perform their roles within complex modern governments. In reality, information is often held in silos, and treated as a proprietary good of a particular department. There is an obvious reason for this: having information is good for whoever has it, and often the benefit of having information is relative: it is most valuable to have information that others don't have but want or need. Information hoarding can equally well occur within departments, with individuals holding it as a personal good rather than a

---

*Dean Geuras and Charles Garofalo, *Practical Ethics in Public Administration*, p. 21. Copyright © 2002 Management Concepts Press.

communal asset. To see the damage this kind of attitude can cause, consider the following real life example. An organization has a labour-management committee that is empowered to resolve disputes between the parties between rounds of collective bargaining. Through its work, interpretations of the collective agreement are reached, specific disputes are resolved, and agreements are made. The staff person to this committee on the labour side, however, refused to share the results of the committee's work with other staff members in the office, and even with officers of the union. As a result, the union leadership often found itself violating the agreements made at the committee level, continuing to employ officially rejected interpretations of the collective agreement, and failing to follow up on the agreements made to resolve specific disputes and unable to apply them to new cases. This is hardly a recipe for effective or efficient activity. Yet it is surprisingly common. To overcome it, public servants must be encouraged to see information as a collective and communal asset rather than a personal or departmental advantage. They must also put in place effective systems for sharing information across agencies and departments, and even across levels of government.

Elected officials also rely upon public servants in the design of programs to deliver public services. Public servants have extensive experience in the design and delivery of public services. They know from experience what works and what doesn't. They have the information necessary to determine how much institutional support a program will require (personnel, IT, physical, etc.), and how much it will cost to develop and run. Without this kind of information, elected officials cannot design effective services efficiently. New programs can face serious delays or gross cost overruns. When this happens, the confidence of the public is shaken, and the wisdom of even good policies can be called into question.

Public servants are also vital to the delivery of services. Often public servants are directly involved in the delivery of public services (we say more about the ethical requirements for good delivery of services to the public below). And they must report on the delivery of those services to the elected government. Without careful and ethical delivery of public services, and accurate and full reporting of the effectiveness and costs of those services to government, neither politicians nor the average citizen can evaluate the value of the services. The annual or semi-annual reports of the Auditor General and provincial **Ombudsmen** are rife with poorly delivered and poorly monitored government services, and in virtually every case one can identify ethical failures in the delivery of those services. The federal sponsorship program, tainted blood scandal, and gun registry come readily to mind, as do spending scandals in municipal and provincial governments, such as in eHealth Ontario in 2008.

In order for public servants to provide to government the information needed for the effective and efficient design and delivery of public services, they must be committed to providing timely, complete, and accurate information to their political bosses. This includes information about risks, factors about which there is uncertainty, and considerations that speak against a particular proposal. It is important that public servants be able to tell their ministers when they think a proposed policy or program cannot be delivered well, when there is evidence that it is not in the public interest, if there are better ways of achieving the desired result, if the costs are prohibitive, and so on. This is often described as the need for public servants to "speak truth to power." Public servants must communicate all relevant information, even if it is not what their political bosses might want to hear.

The duty to provide timely, complete, and accurate information to superiors within the public service is a difficult duty to fulfil. Not only must individual civil servants avoid such personal vices as hubris or undue pride, suggesting that they can accomplish things they cannot, or that they know things about which there is actually considerable uncertainty, but public servants must also avoid filtering information through political or ideological biases, their own or those of the governing party. This is a challenge even for persons with the best of intentions. Knowledge does not come to us in pure form, and how we receive, interpret, and understand information is influenced by our prior commitments, assumptions, biases, prejudices, passions, and a fair bit of wishful thinking. Civil servants have additional challenges: as persons with considerable experience in government, who have chosen careers of public service, it is only reasonable to think that they also have fairly firm political and ideological commitments, and views about what makes good public policy and what is in the public interest. While the duty to provide information to their political bosses does not require that they set such commitments aside—something that is probably impossible to do—they must be aware of their commitments and attentive to how those commitments may influence their interpretation of information and evaluation of evidence.

Civil servants, as participants in government, have a responsibility to provide advice that is based upon the best available evidence, and is grounded in considerations that are proper in the public realm of a free and democratic society of equals. In our private lives we may make decisions based upon any number of commitments and doctrines: political, religious, aesthetic, and philosophical, as well as on the basis of what will advance our personal interests. But those who make decisions on behalf of the public, including public servants, must make decisions based on **public reasons**, reasons that can gain acceptance by all members of the polity, regardless of personal differences in interests, affections, religion, or philosophy. They bear what political philosopher John Rawls called the "burdens of judgment." Reasonable people bear the following burdens of judgment, burdens that make agreement difficult to reach, even among reasonable and rational persons. We have to recognize that evidence, empirical and scientific, is often conflicting, complex, and thus difficult to assess and evaluate, as is its relevance. Even when we agree on the evidence and its relevance, we may assign different weight to different kinds of evidence. Moreover, the various concepts that we use are to varying degrees vague, or indeterminate, requiring interpretation. Consider, for example, the concepts of harm, growth, inflation, environmental degradation, or security. It is widely recognized that moral, political, and other normative concepts (such as goodness, justice, fairness, and right and wrong) are subject to reasonable disagreements as to precise meaning, scope, measure, and interpretation, but so are non-normative concepts. Different kinds of considerations, normative and non-normative, may also compete with respect to a given judgment, as when security must be balanced against freedom, or environmental protection against growth. Finally, there are a limited number of values that can be pursued or realized by any government at one time, and so priorities must be set and limitations placed upon the pursuit of various goals, and reasonable people may disagree about such matters.[20] All of this is important because it calls upon us to recognize that there is reasonable disagreement about the various matters about which political decisions must be made (in addition to unreasonable disagreement). This recognition should constrain our dismissal of those who disagree with us as obviously unreasonable **dogmatists**, ignorant, self-serving, or prejudiced. But it also illustrates the need, in fulfilling their duty to provide good advice to their political masters, for public servants to be guided by the best evidence there is, to make explicit the way that evidence has been weighted and its relevance judged, and to make explicit the degree to which certain value assumptions are embedded or reflected in the advice they are giving.

The reference to evidence in the above description of the duties of public servants allows us to introduce an important recent development in public service organizations, namely, the increasing emphasis on and demand for "evidence-based" policy making. The idea of evidence-based decision making arose first in health care settings.

Applied generally to the arena of public policy, its proponents hold out great hope for evidence-based policy initiatives. Consider the following, from Policy Horizons Canada:

> Evidence-based, evidence-informed or knowledge-based policy development refers to an approach that levers the best available objective evidence from research to identify and understand issues so that policies can be crafted by decision makers that will deliver desired outcomes effectively, with a minimal margin of error and reduced risk of unintended consequences.

Compared to subjective values, the factual interpretations of special interests and advocacy groups, and selective or ideologically driven viewpoints informing the policy development process, an evidence-based approach has as its great advantage neutrality and authoritativeness. This stems from sound, rigorous, comprehensive and unbiased policy research, which improves policy development in many ways, including by:

• Reducing uncertainty,

• Increasing logical clarity and consistency,

• Providing new perspectives and understandings of policy issues,

• Providing increased accountability to the public,

• Providing reliable facts and knowledge, and

• Improving the quality, inclusiveness and constructiveness of public policy debate.

The major goal of evidence-based policy development is to ensure that the experience, expertise and judgment of decision-makers is supported and resourced with the best available objective evidence and systematic research. Policy research is not expected to produce the solutions or decisions. It is meant to provide accurate, reliable and credible information, knowledge and analysis to inform public policy. The knowledge base it produces provides an important ingredient for the policy development process to reduce risk and improve outcomes, but it is not a substitute for the process.[21]*

Evidence-based management has been embraced more or less wholeheartedly and more or less widely in most public service organizations, not just in Canada but throughout the Commonwealth. Its introduction into the contemporary policy process is widely credited to the New Labour government in Britain in 1997, with their call to make sure that government does "what works best."[22] The idea of evidence-based decision making began, however, in the rather different context of health care delivery and clinical practice. "The rise of evidence-based clinical practice was prompted in part by the existence of unexplained wide

*Policy Horizons Canada, 2009. *"Capacity, Collaboration and Culture: The Future of the Policy Research Function in the Government of Canada,"* Ottawa: Policy Horizons Canada.

variations in clinical practice patterns, by the poor uptake of therapies of known effectiveness, and by the persistent use of technologies that were known to be ineffective."[23] Evidence-based health practice, at its simplest, is a commitment to make health care decisions and base clinical health practices as far as possible on evidence gathered from well-conducted research into the effectiveness of available health care interventions. It is a commitment to use the best information available from medical research (double blind randomized controlled trials and peer reviewed clinical results) and statistical meta-analyses (research that synthesizes results from a wide range of clinical studies, epidemiological studies, and the like) in making treatment decisions. As part of the attempt to introduce evidence-based decision making into clinical health care settings, governments have partnered with universities and other health agencies, networks, and research centres to develop sites through which the latest evidence on the effectiveness (or not) of various medical procedures is made available in usable form to medical practitioners. From its origins in health care, evidence-based approaches have been embraced in other areas of important policy, such as education, early childhood development, criminal justice and policing, and more. The view among governments increasingly is that policy should be informed by the best available scientific and social scientific evidence about "what works."[24] As planning and policy expert Heather Campbell pithily remarks, "There was a time when 'evidence' was what detectives looked for in making up their minds. As Sherlock Holmes said, 'It is a capital mistake to theorize before you have all the evidence. It biases the judgement.' But nowadays, seemingly, 'evidence' is as necessary to political conviction as it is to criminal conviction."[25]

And who could be against evidence-based policy? It is difficult to imagine anyone arguing that policy should be based in anything but the best available evidence. The concept of evidence-based policy has an intuitive, common sense logic, which partly explains how it has become naturalized in a diverse range of policy settings. As Tilley and Laycock argue, "rooting policy in evidence has all the appeal of motherhood and apple pie. The rhetoric is cheap and easy" (2000, p. 13). "The term acts as a catch phrase for 'scientific,' 'scholarly,' and 'rationality,' which taken together can be understood as an attempt to modernise policy-making and professionalise human service practice."[26] Does anyone want to be "unscientific," "unscholarly," "irrational," or unprofessional? Yet under the crust of this apple pie lies a quagmire.

Proponents of evidence-based policy setting often describe it as promising a way to make decisions that are depoliticized or non-ideological. It is thus seen as an important companion to the professionalized civil service. This view is taken by those who think of science and empirical research as tools for the collection of ideologically neutral information or evidence.

The image of empirical research, scientific or social scientific, as delivering objective truths and being ideologically neutral is, of course, a fiction. From the very framing of research questions (e.g., what are the most effective strategies for dealing with the problem of youth crime, can governments or the private sector best provide long-term care facilities for elderly citizens, what level of mercury in fish is safe for human consumption) to what counts as reliable or credible evidence, who is recognized as an expert in the field, and how research results are interpreted and translated into plans of actions, human judgments are required, and those judgments include ideological and other biases and unexamined assumptions.

The problem runs even deeper than this in the case of research in the humanities and social sciences. Though the emphasis is on "good empirical research," there is often no empirical reference for the research categories employed in the fields most relevant to public policy settings. Consider "unemployment," "poverty among seniors," "crime rates," "childhood obesity," "health," "endangered species," and infinitely more: there is no obvious empirical referent for any of these research categories. All depend on assumptions and stipulations. Consider unemployment. What counts as being unemployed? Does one have to be available and willing to work but not working to be unemployed? Why do we consider those who cease looking for work after a certain time as no longer unemployed for statistical purposes? How few hours of paid employment must a person who wants full-time work do before she is considered unemployed, rather than underemployed? Why does only paid work count? How is self-employment factored into the count? Why are students in post-secondary educational institutions not counted in unemployment statistics? And so on. And this is just to set the referent of study. Additional normative or evaluative assumptions are made when we frame a research subject as a "problem," like the problem of youth crime or the problem of poverty among seniors. Policy researchers Greg Marston and Rob Watts provide an excellent discussion of the breadth and depth of these problems, and provide a case study using "juvenile crime" to illuminate the choices that inform empirical research into matters of public policy.

These observations challenge claims that empirical evidence is objective and non-political. But they should not be taken too far. There are some matters that seem more amenable to empirical evidence than others. Consider the following examples given by experts in policy and management Huw Davies, Sandra Nutley, and Peter Smith: "On the face of it, there are numerous issues in, say, education, which could be resolved by such methods—for example, identifying the most effective approach to teaching reading; or assessing the impact of calculators on the child's mathematical development; or evaluating the introduction of a new homework policy."[27] Other matters are much less amenable to the kind of randomized controlled trial that is the gold standard of the evidence-based approach. To use another example from Davies et al., what result legalizing soft drugs would have on subsequent use of hard drugs cannot be studied directly through a randomized trial, and so the evidence we do have about this issue (for example from looking at jurisdictions that have removed criminal restrictions on the use of soft drugs) is contestable, because we cannot be sure that we have isolated the variable we are interested in. Suppose we know, to make this just a bit clearer, that in jurisdiction X the rate of hard drug use declined over the first five years that the use and sale of soft drugs was decriminalized there. Can we be sure this effect is caused by the change in criminal law, rather than the fact that those five years happened to be a time of greater economic prosperity, that over those five years the average age of the population of X increased, that as a result of the decriminalization of soft drugs, police and prosecutors were able to devote increased resources to the detection and prosecution of traffickers of hard drugs, thereby reducing their availability over that time period, and so on? In the context of health care, the objectives to be achieved and a conception of what counts as "working" are relatively uncontested: we want to lengthen life span and reduce morbidity, at least. But in other areas, the very objectives of our interventions are contested (are we trying to ensure a fit retributive punishment for young offenders, or are we trying to design our interventions to reduce the rate of future offending); in establishing public housing goals, are we trying to reduce the incidence of homelessness, trying to provide stable housing to support interventions for persons suffering from mental health challenges, or trying to provide mechanism through which new immigrants can be quickly assimilated into the labour market? When the objectives are unclear, multiple, or conflicting, determining what works will be correspondingly more difficult. The one conclusion we can draw for sure is that measures of what works will be always in part political questions and their answers will be context specific; there is no measure of success that applies to all public service organizations, and no single methodology for employing evidence in the policy process that will make sense across the board.

Rachel Laforest and Michael Orsini have traced a more insidious consequence of the move to evidence-based policy setting. They have studied the effect the insistence that policy initiatives be based on a systematic appraisal and review of empirical research findings has had on the relationship between the voluntary sector/civil society organizations and governments. They conclude that, "While voluntary organizations are increasingly being consulted and engaged in policy-making, the basis of these interventions too often lies in their capacity to generate empirical evidence and data, not in their ability to articulate the interests of their constituents."[28] This is having a profound effect on the way civil society organizations now interact with governments in attempting to set public policy objectives and in the design of public service delivery.

Governments are increasingly involving third parties (universities, think tanks, citizens' groups, civil society organizations, research communities, stakeholders, and others) in policy making, that is, in developing, designing, and implementing public policy. Such moves are vital for democratic legitimacy and citizen engagement. But the nature of such partnerships is being radically transformed, and in some ways narrowed, by the requirements of evidence-based policy making. This is because who counts as an expert, and the ways that external groups can intervene in setting public policy, are now set by and must conform to the norms of "good empirical evidence." It is important to stress here that certain forms of evidence occupy a privileged position in the "hierarchy of evidence," with statistical research and economic modelling near the top of the hierarchy and "lay forms of evidence" such as public consultations or focus groups at the bottom. Not surprisingly, old-fashioned advocacy occupies a marginal place in the new lexicon.[29]

That some forms and sources of knowledge will be privileged over others within evidence-based policy processes is widely acknowledged. Scientific research, statistics, policy evaluation, economic modelling, and expert knowledge are given more weight than other forms of evidence. "This comment on the preferred forms of evidence uncovers the potential problems of adopting a narrow view of what counts as valid knowledge. Lay forms of evidence, such as social service user input and public consultations, are placed further down the hierarchy of evidence. If knowledge operates hierarchically, we begin to see that far from being a neutral concept, evidence-based policy is a powerful metaphor in shaping what forms of knowledge are considered closest to the 'truth' in decision making processes and policy argument."[30] As feminism and other critical social theories have taught us, we must beware of the introduction of new forms of social hierarchy that serve to exclude and marginalize some; in the case of hierarchies of knowledge, with their attendant impacts on access to and influence within policy settings, this new hierarchy may be particularly insidious, especially since it comes cloaked in the motherhood ideas of science and rationality, objectivity and impartiality.

Civil society organizations are increasingly having to engage in empirical research, or frame their interventions in the language of empirical sciences, if they are to be welcomed as participants in the creation of public policy. The imperatives implicit in the move toward evidence-based policy can be seen, for example, in the Accord and Codes developed by the Voluntary Sector Initiative, a program of the federal government designed not only to increase the role of the voluntary sector in developing policy, but to set the terms of that interaction as well.[31] Such initiatives do not just privilege some kinds of evidence over others; they also privilege those organizations that have the capacity and willingness to engage in or utilize empirical research over those who prefer to use other methods and forms of engagement.

More than a decade ago, Graham Leicester identified seven "enemies" of evidence-based policy, which still persist today to a greater or lesser extent.[32] The first is bureaucratic logic, the logic that supports the status quo in any complex organization as "the ways things are done around here," and that "reinforces traditional interpretations of policy problems by only noticing evidence that fits the existing analysis."[33] The second is focus on the bottom line, or a reliance on quantitative measures of policy effectiveness, at the expense of consideration of quality (e.g., wait times in health care rather than impact on patient health). The third is consensus, which is encouraged as the goal and measure of effectiveness by the demands of consultation and stakeholder participation; fourth is politics, which provides input into the policy process that may be at odds with and trump evidence (likely the explanation for the persistence of what are surely failed policies in crime control and the war on drugs). Fifth is civil service culture, in which external expertise and knowledge are viewed with suspicion if not hostility; sixth is the related cynicism that civil servants are forced to adopt if they recognize that policies are not actually based on evidence but on political and other considerations; and finally, the lack of time that characterizes the work of modern public servants, in which there is scarcely time to think, let alone gather and critically assess all the information relevant to a policy problem. Together these forces work against the adoption of evidence-based policy processes, and result in the perpetuation of policies civil servants know to be ineffective, thereby undermining individual responsibility and system responsiveness. The result is a system that requires cynicism for survival: "This is the culture that allows us to go along with the 'company view' or the 'conventional wisdom,' even when we know it to be false, since our professional lives and career advancement depend on maintaining the lie. We show that we are aware of the deception and therefore not tainted by it by sounding off about how ridiculous this way of operating is in the pub with colleagues after work, complaining about how senior management must be crazy if they think they are fooling anyone. But we do nothing to change it, or to challenge formally the 'company truth'."[34]

There is a tension between evidence-based policy and the politics of policy that is important to note, because it has important implications for democratic engagement and the role of civil society. "There is a risk that 'evidence-based policy' will become a means for policy elites [to] increase their strategic control over what constitutes knowledge about social problems in a way that devalues tacit forms of knowledge, practice based wisdom, professional judgment, and the voices of ordinary citizens."[35]

Angela Packwood prefers to talk about "evidence-*informed*" approaches to public policy, because this makes room for the reality that policy is influenced by considerably more than just "evidence" understood as research results. Such factors include "financial, economic and strategic factors, and practitioner knowledge."[36] We must also acknowledge that there are considerable selection biases operating in the policy context (as is probably true elsewhere too), which limits the kinds of evidence sought, sources consulted, and relative weight given to evidence when it supports different conclusions. At the very worst, we must recognize that "research evidence may be dismissed as irrelevant if it does not match the preferred outcome."[37] Of course, when this happens, we have abandoned any pretence of being informed by evidence, as evidence is understood in the sciences and scientific method. Yet we must admit that in many cases a conclusion has been reached and those in the policy process then simply search out evidence supporting that conclusion, while dismissing any that opposes it. Strategic objectives may trump evidence about what is effective in any given policy setting. Furthermore, "there may be a lack of consensus about the nature of the evidence provided by the research because of the complexity of the issue being researched, or because there is controversy over the methods used to gather the evidence or because the evidence is open to different interpretations."[38] The importance of this final point cannot be overestimated: evidence generated by research can be interpreted in different ways and put to different uses, and so even good evidence may not produce a consensus about what should be done on the basis of it.

Evidence-based policy is changing the nature of relationships between governments and universities in ways that may profoundly affect the nature and role of universities in free and democratic societies, including Canada. It has the power to direct (or at least directly influence) what gets researched by Canadian university academics, in part through research funding practices and priorities, as well as to fundamentally undermine the academic freedom of those university researchers who partner with governments in the production of the evidence needed in the policy process.[39]

Ken Young and his colleagues have traced developments in the evidence-based policy project that apply as well to Canada as they do to Britain (which was their focus). They note that contemporary society is characterized by its utilitarian approach to research; the instrumentalization of knowledge and research is a companion of the evidence-based policy movement. Many in society, including governments, now insist that science, including social science, 'should be useful.' Government departments have in many cases become the dominant funders of social science research, and in those cases the research agenda is dictated by the perceived needs of the department. Charities have likewise begun to place increasing emphasis on research that is instrumentally valuable to the realization of their social priorities. And governments are more and more funding academic research through programs specifying strategic priorities, set by governments themselves. Within this framework, academic research is seen as a means to economic and social development rather than a public good or cultural resource, valuable in itself.[40]* This trend toward the instrumentalization of research is evident in Canada, and can be readily seen in the recent revisions to the architecture of the Social Sciences and Humanities Research Council of Canada and current funding priorities within the Canadian Institutes for Health Research.

Young and his colleagues have usefully identified five possible models for thinking about the way research knowledge and the policy process might interact or intersect. These models differ in how they characterize the relationship between policy and evidence, or how "the policy process handles the input of knowledge. [They] term these the knowledge-driven model, the problem-solving model, the interactive model, the political/tactical model, and the enlightenment model."[41]† There is something to be said for each, though, like Young and his colleagues, we prefer the enlightenment model for both descriptive and normative reasons, as we will explain below.

We need provide only brief descriptions of the five models—describing the way knowledge might be treated as an input to the policy process—here, because what is most important is to note that there is a choice to be made about this. And that choice influences our subsequent view of how public servants serve democracy.

In the *research-driven model* of policy, research (or experts) leads policy. In this model, science and technology direct policy, thereby replacing political processes with technocratic ones. This model is descriptively inadequate, given the wide range of cases in which policy decisions fly in the face of the best evidence we have (in education, criminal justice, poverty reduction, environmental protection, and many more); it ignores the fact that a great deal of social research exists that could inform policy decisions, a great deal of research is done by external parties and sent to governments, and yet decisions rarely reflect that research. It also ignores the fact that research results might be equivocal or conflicting, or subject to multiple interpretations, and that there remains a gap between research results and practical decisions that must be filled by something other than more evidence.

By contrast, in the *problem-solving model*, policy shapes and directs research. Research is employed to solve problems identified by policy makers. Neither of these

*Ken Young, Deborah Ashby, Annette Boaz and Lesley Grayson, "Social Science and the Evidence-based Policy Movement," *Social Policy and Society* 1:3 (2002), p. 215–224.

†Ken Young, Deborah Ashby, Annette Boaz and Lesley Grayson, "Social Science and the Evidence-based Policy Movement," *Social Policy and Society* 1:3 (2002), p. 215–224.

models is fully adequate, because they present the relationship between researchers and policy makers as linear and top down (either the researchers set the agenda or policy makers do, and the other is but a servant of the primary driver). These models overlook the degree to which the implications of scientific research might be unclear or contested, as well as the potential lack of correspondence between expert knowledge and lay understandings; consider matters as diverse as crime control and the genetic modification of crops and the limitations of these models become clear.

The *interactive model* seeks to accommodate these facts, and posits "a much more subtle and complex series of relationships between decision makers and researchers. It portrays research and policy as mutually influential, with the agenda for both research and policy decision shaped within 'policy communities' which contain a range of actors located across the whole spectrum from central policy making to the laboratory and research team."[42] Think tanks and other research organizations that routinely advise governments on matters of mutual interest perhaps best fit this model. It may, however, also be the model that most directly gives rise to the kinds of concerns raised by Laforest and Orsini, namely that third-party organizations will be utilized in policy making on the basis of their ability to generate empirical evidence and not on their ability to advance the interests of those concerned.

The model most closely related to a *realpolitik* vision of the policy process is the *political/tactical model*. In the political model, policy is seen as the outcome of political processes. Research agendas are politically driven to serve an independently specified goal. Research is "commissioned and/or used to support the position adopted by the government of the day, the relevant minister, or perhaps the civil servants most closely concerned."[43]* Such a view surely accurately characterizes much of the government funded research currently being done under innovation partnerships and through targeted research opportunities through which governments and researchers partner on projects, the terms of which are set by governments. This model most clearly carries the danger that social science research will become politicized, a result that benefits no one in the long run (researchers, governments, or the public), yet it is a danger inherent in the current instrumentalization of research.

Finally, there is what Young and his colleagues call the *enlightenment model*. Whereas in the political model, research is tailored toward explicit political goals, in the enlightenment model, research is carried out in the spirit of disinterested enquiry, and knowledge and understanding are valued for their own sake. In this model, researchers are at a distance from policy decisions, and the relationship between research and politics is indirect. Research is driven by the interests of the researchers, and typically is not addressed to specific policy questions asked by political actors. Instead, such research can inform such questions by

*Ken Young, Deborah Ashby, Annette Boaz and Lesley Grayson, "Social Science and the Evidence-based Policy Movement," *Social Policy and Society* 1:3 (2002), p. 215–224.

providing valuable background information, by providing a framework within which political decisions can be made. "Research conducted within this model seeks to illuminate the landscape for decision makers."[44] Researchers provide valuable information on a whole host of issues relevant to policy makers, and to the extent that that information is used by such decision makers, we can speak of policy that is "evidence-informed" even if not "evidence-based."

Young and his colleagues prefer the enlightenment model for two reasons.

> First, much of the best social research is inspired by an urge to understand, illuminate and explain, rather than by a compulsion to provide policy solutions. Secondly, the idea that research can be problem solving is based on a misconception of the nature of the political process, which is rarely characterised by rational decisions made on the basis of the best information. Indeed, information may be complicating and inconvenient, obscuring the clarity of choices most easily made under conditions of relative ignorance. As Keynes reportedly said, 'there is nothing a government hates more than to be well informed; for it makes the process of arriving at decisions much more complicated and difficult'. The core beliefs of policy makers are unaffected by information, as policy change is driven by external factors, not by ideas and analysis.[45]*

If one thinks about such issues as responses to crime, for example, one can easily see their point. Virtually all the evidence points to the fact that long periods of incarceration do not deter crime nearly so effectively as early interventions into at-risk communities and families, and yet 'get tough on crime' agendas are popular across the political spectrum, with no party willing to be portrayed as 'soft on crime.' And this all within a context in which rates of violent crime have been steadily declining for 30 years. In the face of such facts, we must accept that crime policy is being driven by something other than evidence drawn from social science research.

We would add to the reasons of Young et al. in advocating for the enlightenment model two other considerations, one drawn from the role of universities in a free society and one drawn from democracy. Universities occupy a unique position in a free and democratic society that it is important to protect. While many individuals and organizations, industries and think tanks, including governments themselves, conduct research, it is only at universities

---

*Ken Young, Deborah Ashby, Annette Boaz and Lesley Grayson, "Social Science and the Evidence-based Policy Movement," *Social Policy and Society* 1:3 (2002), p. 215–224.

that research can be driven by the disinterested desire to know, understand, and explain. All other research is conducted within a context that sets ends (or goals) for the research itself. Only university researchers are free to pursue research wherever it takes them. And only university researchers are free to disseminate the results of their research as they see fit. These roles are protected by academic freedom. To see the value of this freedom, and the activities it makes possible, one only has to look to societies where researchers do not enjoy academic freedom, either the freedom to decide what to research or the freedom to disseminate their research, including in the classroom. These are not free societies. And in our own society, just consider for a moment the extent to which university researchers are called upon by the media (especially, perhaps, our national broadcaster, the Canadian Broadcast Corporation (CBC)) to provide critical commentary on current events, claims by governments and industry, and scientific developments. University researchers are called upon to critically assess the claims of other actors in society because only they can do so from a disinterested perspective. This vital role must be protected, and it is threatened by the problem-solving model, the interactive model, and the political/strategic model. It is not threatened by the research-driven model of policy, but that is the most unrealistic of them all. And even if the research-driven model was not a poor descriptive model, because it ignores the extent to which policy decisions are made for strategic and political reasons, it would give undue weight to experts in setting policy, a situation that would be at odds with our commitment to democratic values. Thus only the enlightenment model is compatible with the robust protection of universities as sites of disinterested research and the academic freedom that makes it possible.

The enlightenment model is also the only one compatible with vibrant democratic processes. It values the knowledge and understanding created by social science research, but sees it as but one among many inputs into the policy process. Policy should be informed by evidence, but it should not be solely dictated by experts. To allow the experts to run the show is to abdicate political responsibility. Instead, research results and the understanding generated by social research should inform public discourse on policy issues. Research is often more valuable as an input to the democratic process than to the decision making process. Such a conclusion seems to be supported by the realities of the policy process itself. Young et al. contrast the perception of policy making presupposed by the advocates of evidence-based policy with a more realistic picture, which is worth quoting in full. Remarking upon the "paradox" that policy seems to be so little influenced in fact by good evidence, even within governments that are supposedly committed to the evidence-based approach, they say:

> The roots of this paradox are to be found in misconceptions about how the policy process typically works. In the traditional or ideal type of policy process, policy research is used as an instrument of the problem-solving process, to aid the making of choices. Decision makers set goals and engage in systematic thinking and research to identify the best means of achieving them. Information is supplied which is objective, and possibly conclusive, reducing uncertainties about the relationship between policies and outcomes. Public opinions and preferences are neither focused nor articulated, with the interests of a passive public communicated by professionals. The policy process itself is linear, stable, and incremental, reflecting the capture of the process by established political, bureaucratic, and professional interests.
>
> The realities are very different, and may be characterised in the following way. Goals are ambiguous, and the means of achieving them uncertain. Decisions are less about projected consequences and more about process and legitimation. Politics is about shaping interpretations and expressing preferences. Information is never conclusive but reflects the indeterminacy of cause and effect relationships; it is infused with values. Public opinion can be highly attentive and mobilised by activists who seek to frame issues. The policy process is characterised by competition over agenda setting, over jurisdictions, and over interpretations. The positions that contesting parties adopt rest on underlying, and generally tacit, structures of appreciation and belief, giving rise to . . . "frame conflicts".[46]*

If this is the messy reality of public policy setting, evidence-informed processes are probably the best we can hope for. And such an approach opens up a space wherein evidence can inform not only policy makers, but other participants in the policy process, such as the public and activists. If our goal is to make information available to all the parties to the policy process, then having mechanisms for the widest dissemination of results possible, ideally free of charge, should be

*Ken Young, Deborah Ashby, Annette Boaz and Lesley Grayson, "Social Science and the Evidence-based Policy Movement," *Social Policy and Society* 1:3 (2002), p. 215–224.

supported. This requires, among other things, that we see universities as cultural assets, institutions that provide a fundamental public good.

Vibrant democracies require more than just regular elections. They require an engaged civil society. In civil society organizations, big and small, citizens come together to articulate goals, through dialogue and deliberation. Those organizations then play a role both in building community and in engaging community in the political process. Well designed policy processes can themselves play an important part in facilitating and supporting the work of civil society in building connections between citizens and their governments.

Given that policy is often set through complex processes involving multiple players, public service organizations in the contemporary setting cannot be seen as mere service providers or problem solvers. Rather, they must act to help citizens articulate and achieve their shared interests, through processes of negotiation and collaboration during which problems can be defined and solutions sought. They must bring together multiple groups with multiple and partly competing interests and agendas, in an effort to create coalitions and broker solutions to complex social problems.

The goal of having open and accessible policy processes is not a simple one of finding a compromise position that everyone can live with, however. That is perhaps the least lofty goal public service organizations can have. Instead, the goal should be to bring people together so as to allow them to develop a shared vision of the public interest or public good. Politicians, public administrators, and citizens must be engaged in processes of dialogue and deliberation that permit the emergence of a shared vision with respect to the future direction of the municipality, province, country, or specific governmental agency or department, depending on the context. Thus the search must be for more than solutions to immediate problems, but rather should aim at a collective sense of the goals to be sought and the values to be realized through public action. Good policy processes will begin with the specific interests brought to the table by the various individuals and groups affected by a given issue, but it will not stop there. Instead, it will invite the participants to take a larger and longer term view of what is in the public interest, and support the participants in articulating such a conception of the public good; it will encourage mutual understanding of the competing interests and perspectives of the various parties, and mutual respect for reasonable differences.

If civil service organizations move beyond an understanding of themselves as service providers, and instead embrace a self-image that places them within a nexus of activities designed to enhance community activity and democratic engagement, they will embrace a model of government that is open, accessible, responsive, and inclusive. They will have as their primary goals serving citizens and creating opportunities for citizen engagement in community and governmental processes. They will see themselves as important facilitators of democratic activity. This requires a policy process that goes beyond involvement of citizens and civil society organizations in identifying solutions to social problems; it requires that citizens and civil society continue to be engaged in the implementation of those solutions, too, and that they share responsibility for taking the actions necessary to achieve the shared goals that have been articulated through dialogue and deliberation. Thus the public must be involved in the practical, strategic steps taken to achieve the public interest. This will allow patterns of mutual responsibility to develop, wherein public servants are responsible and responsive to the concerns of the public, and the public is likewise responsible and responsive to the concerns of the public service, in the implementation of shared policy goals. Governments will seem more effective in such a model, because they will be more effective, and citizens will experience a heightened sense of responsibility for and empowerment in the achievement of public objectives.

Public service differs in important ways from private sector, for-profit service. Governments do not serve citizens in the same way that business serves clients or customers. Urgings for governments to operate more like business must be rejected. The main flaw in analogies between the public service and business lies in the fact that governments serve citizens, *qua* members of the political community, rather than customers, *qua* narrowly self-interested consumers. The interests are different in very important ways. In business, the customer might always be right, but that is not so in public service. Public servants, in both the design and delivery of public services, must take the public interest, and not just the immediate interests of the individual, into account. Closing a school, granting a mining contract, reclaiming sewage water, the level of funding for public housing or child care, the investment in new physicians, whether to support a particular cultural festival, and so many more, may all be decisions about which individuals have strong views. If the public service is to serve democratic values in a meaningful way, however, it is not enough to take those views at face value, informed as they may be just by narrow self-interest. Instead, public servants must play an educative role: they must make sure that all interested parties have access to all the information being relied upon by policy makers, as well as an opportunity for those on conflicting sides of the issue to engage one another, to share their concerns and aspirations in constructive dialogue, and establish collaborative processes for moving forward toward a decision. They must also create the conditions in which members of the public can consider the public interest, and not just their narrow self-interest, in assessing the various options. This is very important. Participants in the policy process must be encouraged to move beyond positions defined by narrow self-interest and to adopt instead the perspective of the common good, to consider what is good for their community overall and in the long run, and to engage with the public values that are truly at issue in the decision. This will require that public servants have appropriate training in negotiation, mediation, and even arbitration, for all these skills will be necessary to build collaboration between different stakeholders. This is a model, however, that ultimately empowers the participants, and encourages them to develop a sense of responsibility for communal decisions, rather than being a top-down process in which citizen interests are interpreted and weighed along with other relevant considerations by the person making the decision. It is also different than a model which sees public servants as the passive servants of the public, even when the public is ill-informed or making demands that are contrary to the public interest.

Public servants are stewards of public resources, and are to make decisions through processes that respect democratic values and the right of citizens to participate in policy making. They are not entrepreneurs, and maximizing efficiency should not be their goal. Instead, serving the public interest, identified through processes that are collaborative and value driven, should be the goal of the public service. They must be prepared to work in collaboration with other government departments and agencies as necessary to achieve goals and in the delivery of government services. It is imperative that every individual in the public service be charged with the responsibility, and given the authority, to aid members of the public. This will often require accessing assistance from others outside of one's own department. Thus the public service as a whole must move beyond limited views of jurisdiction and responsibility, the limited views that result in silos rather than collaborative processes, in which public resources (including information) are treated as the property of individual public servants or specific agencies rather than public resources to be utilized for the public good. This will mark a profound shift in thinking, but is necessary if public servants are to operate in an environment that recognizes that government is owned by the people, and has as its overarching imperative service to the people.

3.6.3 Serving the Public Interest

Ethical conduct in the public service requires that decisions be made in the public interest. Though the concept of acting in the public interest may seem imprecise, at the very least the "concept enshrines two assumptions which, arguably, are essential to the public good: first considerations of a wider, public interest in the public sphere, take precedence over private, personal or sectional interests, that is, conflicts of interest are to be resolved in favour of the public interest; and secondly, public practices and policies should be subject to a process of open and public justification."[47]

This "public interest" requirement on the public service stems from the fact that "unelected public officials are entrusted with public money. Corresponding with that trust is power over people's lives [and thus] they assume responsibility in a significant way, for protecting the rights and interests of the public."[48] Yet civil servants are in a unique position with respect to their service to the common good. Their role in serving the public interest is mediated by their position as public servants. Rather than directly determining what they think is in the public interest and acting accordingly, their service to the public interest is indirect, consisting of serving those who have been elected to directly determine what is best. Thus the first duty of public servants is to support the decisions of the duly elected government in carrying out its lawful objectives.

This structural fact should not blind us, however, to the central role of public servants in determining what is in the public interest. As mentioned just above, public servants have a duty to tell elected officials when they think a given policy or law is contrary to the public interest. They also have enormous influence, given their expertise, as repositories of information, and in their capacity as advisors to government. Insofar as a public servant has an opportunity to influence government policy or government operations, he must exercise that influence only in ways that he believes are in the public interest. His own good, the good of others with whom he has close personal relations, the good of his department or colleagues, or even the good of the current government itself, are not what he ought to aim at. If the good of the public stands in any way in conflict with the good of any of these others, he must choose in such a way as to serve the public interest. We discuss conflicts of interests below.

As we argued above (3.6.2), the public service plays a vital role in helping citizens to develop a shared sense of the public good. Many of the most intractable social problems, and many of the issues that generate the most response from activists and civil society organizations, involve competing and contested visions of the public good. Civil servants cannot establish a conception of the public interest, but they can and should play a role in facilitating the development of such a vision by bringing together the various stakeholders and interested parties, by making relevant information available to them so as to encourage informed dialogue, and by establishing policy processes that are inclusive and promote mutual understanding among the participants. Such processes will invite participation from citizens *qua* citizens; it will challenge them to find shared values and a conception of the public interest that is informed by, though it need not satisfy, all of the competing interests of the parties involved. Through education, facilitation, negotiation, and collaboration, public servants should help those who have input into the policy process to think in terms of the public good, recognizing its contested and fluid understanding.

3.6.4 Democracy and Loyalty to Government

The civil service persists through changes in elected governments in democratic political systems. Public servants continue to deliver government services and implement its laws and policies. In order to contribute to good order in this way, it is important that public servants maintain a position of **political neutrality**. This important principle, and what political neutrality requires of public servants, is discussed below. But the role of the civil service in upholding democracy deserves special mention in the general description of the benefits of a civil service that conforms to relevant ethical principles.

Many of the ethical duties that apply to civil servants do so because of their role in maintaining democratic institutions. The first responsibility of public servants is to the Crown, to the government of Canada as an institution, or to the provincial, territorial, or municipal government, as the case may be. They owe duties of loyalty and **fidelity** to the Crown or government, and must not act in ways that would bring shame upon it or undermine its legitimacy.

Though loyalty is ultimately owed to the Crown or government as an institution, public servants typically discharge that duty by performing faithful service for the actual specific government of the day. Thus they have, generally, a duty to support their elected minister or councillor in carrying out his or her lawful objectives. Civil servants must both participate in shaping good policies, by providing information and advice to their minister or councillor, and must act to implement decisions taken by the duly authorized government. They must execute the objectives of their political bosses responsibly, professionally, and in good faith. They must demonstrate loyalty to the democratically chosen government, using their influence to assist it in realizing the mandate to govern it has been given. By assisting duly elected governments, civil servants directly contribute to the maintenance of democratic institutions. By acting ethically, they contribute to the legitimacy of government, and promote public confidence in and participation in public life.

But there are also substantive values involved in the commitment to democracy, many of which we mentioned earlier in this chapter: inclusiveness, participation, collaboration, dialogue, and the like. The values inherent in liberal democracy also include equal concern and respect for all members of the polity, inherent human dignity, order and security, **political legitimacy**, full participation of all members of society, the most extensive liberty compatible with equal liberties for all, the conditions of a decent human life regardless of morally arbitrary factors, the rule of law, the supremacy of democratic legislative processes, the accountability of elected politicians to the people, and commitment to the public good.

Though the claim that public servants must display loyalty to the Crown in all they do has the status of yet another "motherhood and apple pie" proposition, it is in fact more complex than what has been said so far might suggest. Typically, this requires loyalty to the duly elected government and its ministers. But the duty of loyalty is said to be to the Crown rather than any particular government or any particular person, which is shown not only by the fact that the duty of loyalty continues when no government is sitting, but more importantly when a public servant makes a good-faith judgment that an elected member of the government is engaged in such serious wrongdoing that it must be reported. Disclosure of wrongdoing by government officials may cause serious damage to the government, and may even lead to its collapse in some instances. It may, nonetheless, be a duty of a public servant to report such wrongdoing, as a matter of fulfilling her duty of loyalty to the Crown. That duty includes the requirement that public servants not participate in wrongdoing so serious as to bring the Crown into disrepute, or that would cause imminent danger to the life or health of members of the public or the physical environment. We discuss disclosure of wrongdoing below.

Leaving aside the (we hope) extraordinary cases in which government officials are engaged in serious wrongdoing, public servants normally discharge their duty of loyalty to the Crown by acting loyally to the elected government. They do so by providing good faith advice to the government in the formulation of policies, facilitating the development of policies through legitimate democratic processes, and then professionally executing the policies adopted.

That the duty of loyalty owed by public servants is to the government of Canada as an institution, rather than to any particular government or minister, is very important. Public servants are accountable to specific ministers, but their loyalty is owed to the position rather than the person. This is obvious if you think about the impact of routine cabinet shuffles. Ministers are moved from one portfolio to another; perhaps new members of the legislature are brought into cabinet and given ministerial responsibilities; others may be removed from their positions as ministers. In such shuffles, public servants continue to owe a duty of loyalty to the ministry to which they are accountable, rather than to any particular individual (the former minister or the new minister).

The duty of loyalty includes not only providing accurate and relevant information to the minister with respect to policy options being considered, but also politically sensitive advice. It is proper for public servants to provide ministers with advice as to the likely political reaction to various policy options, and political sensitivity is an important asset in high ranking civil servants. Thus if a public servant is aware of public polling results, say, that indicate that a particular policy would be extremely popular or unpopular with a given segment of the population, his duty of loyalty requires that he appropriately advise his minister of that fact. But political sensitivity is not political support. It is not the job of public servants to keep the current government in office, or to ensure its popularity with the public. This is essential for understanding one of the most important duties of public servants, which is to maintain political neutrality. We discuss this very important duty below.

The complexity arises when governments pursue policies that seem contrary to democratic values themselves, when they act in ways that are believed by public servants to be not just contrary to but harmful to the public interest, or when the bureaucracy differs in fundamental ways in its conception of the public good from the view held by the government. In these cases, public servants face a conflict of obligations. The standing possibility of such a conflict was made dramatically apparent in the minority government of Stephen Harper's Conservatives in March of 2011, when it was found in contempt of Parliament. Since respect for Parliament is necessary for democracy, this situation created a direct conflict of duties for the federal public service: if they fulfilled their duty of loyalty to the government of the day, they would be violating their duty to support democracy. It also appeared that there was a fundamental conflict between the government's understanding of what the public good consists of and the conception guiding the bureaucrats. Normally we might think such a conflict has to be resolved by acting loyally to the government, because it has been authorized precisely to make such determinations on behalf of the people, and so loyalty to the government is required by the commitment to democracy; however, part of what was at stake here was competing visions of who government serves. The government position seemed to be that it should serve the interests of just some members of Canada, while the public service was guided in its conception by the substantive values of democracy and the view that government has to serve the interests of all citizens as a matter of justice. These were deep divisions and rested on competing visions of the central values being discussed in this book: competing visions of democracy and the public good. Situations in which public servants find themselves in this kind of deep value conflict with the government of the day pose among the most complex challenges for public servants. Perhaps hearkening back to the point that loyalty is owed to the institution of government, rather than any particular government, can help resolve them, though we doubt even this basic principle can resolve all the tensions created. If public servants resolve the tension in favour of their preferred conception of the public good, it is vital that that conception itself has been arrived at through legitimate democratic processes of the kind described above. If they are guided by a conception of the public interest that is informed by good evidence, and arrived at by participatory and inclusive processes, and shared by the parties with whom they deal, the worry that they are acting undemocratically by privileging their conception of the public interest over that of duly elected political leaders may be blunted, if not wholly overcome. Public servants must be able to live with their decisions, and it may be that some public service cultures become so degraded in terms of the relationship between the elected members of government (and their political staffers) and the public service that resignation is the only available option. In such a case, going public with one's concerns may be the only way of maintaining one's personal integrity and commitment to democratic values. Allowing situations to deteriorate to such a point is a major political failing of a government, and it erodes the capacity of governmental institutions to make good decisions.

3.6.5 Promote the Value of Careers in the Public Service

Ethical conduct for civil servants requires not just faithful service to the democratically elected government, but also behaviour that exemplifies the value of public service as a career. Public servants must maintain a high level of professionalism in their work, collegiality in their processes, and respectful service to the public. Public service workplaces must be free of discrimination and harassment. Employment in the public service, as well as promotion within it, must be based on merit, rather than nepotism, **political patronage**, or other forms of favouritism.

> Public organizations must maintain a careful balance: they should protect merit, equity and neutrality, even as they pursue efficiency, responsiveness and organizational performance. A public organization does not and cannot enjoy the "flexibilities" of private sector organizations. It will always have to meet higher standards of transparency and due process in order to allay any fears of favouritism, whether internal or external.[49]*

Careers in the public service must be, and be perceived to be, accessible to all on the basis of clearly defined and justified qualifications. An accessible public service distributes participation in government and government decision making in ways that provide equality of opportunity for all citizens. It ensures that the public service is representative of the diverse and multicultural heritage of Canadians. This is one reason why affirmative action programs are so important to the public service: they help to ensure that although an applicant must reach a defined level of ability, certain other factors, such as race, ethnicity, and gender, also play a

---

*John Tait, "A Strong Foundation: Report of the Task Force on Public Service Values and Ethics," *Canadian Public Administration* 40:1 (1996), p. 9.

role in the hiring process, so as to help mirror the face of the public service with the face of the population. This, again, contributes to political legitimacy, and to the perception of legitimacy. Government is seen to be by the people and for the people when government programs are designed and delivered for the public good by a broadly representative and merit-based civil service.

An ethical public service, then, is one that contributes directly to democratic values and the common good. Service in the public service is valued, because it is seen as meaningful professional work. Appointment to and promotion within the public service is recognized as a mark of contribution to good order and public service. An ethical public service avoids corruption, being guided in its actions and its advice by considerations of the public good rather than personal advantage. It thus avoids participating in activities that result, when made known to the public, in the kinds of scandals that bring government into disrepute. By acting ethically, the public service contributes to public confidence in the government, and the perception of its legitimacy.

In constructing ethics codes for the public service, we should be guided by the specific values that ought to guide public servants in their work, the principles of conduct they must follow to achieve those values, and the personal virtues that ought to be cultivated in public servants to facilitate right action. We should be guided by considerations concerning what duties must be imposed upon them, and what rights they must have, in order to fulfil their role in realizing the values of liberal democracy. Given our approach to these subjects, we think it is preferable to develop statements of rights and responsibilities rather than ethics codes or codes of conduct. Statements of rights and responsibilities highlight that public servants must be empowered to perform their functions in the service of good governance, as well as to articulate their responsibilities across the range of activities in which they engage. But whatever we call them, the move to articulate public sector values and the principles required to achieve them has been an overall welcome development in public sector management.

QUESTIONS FOR FURTHER DISCUSSION

1. What are some of the benefits to having an ethics code? Why might we need such codes?

2. How do ethics codes relate to values?

3. Do ethics codes only establish negative rights (and duties), or can they also create positive duties? Explain your answer, using examples.

4. Should ethics codes aim to embody all the ethics of an organization or company? What other elements might be necessary for ethical conduct?

5. How can ethics codes lead to consistent and fair treatment of public servants?

6. What is the relationship between ethics codes and administrative justice?

7. Now that we have seen some of the values that ethics codes embody (and promote), can you think of how the moral theories (e.g., utilitarianism, virtue ethics, deontology) relate to the ethical promoting of values?

8. Elected officials are said to rely on public servants in important ways. What are some of those ways?

9. List and describe any two responsibilities of public servants. Be sure to explain the importance of each responsibility in as much detail as possible and to provide examples.

10. What does it mean to say that public servants serve the "public interest"? What constitutes "public interest"?

11. In what ways do public servants contribute to democracy and legitimacy?

12. To whom do public servants owe their first and foremost loyalty?

Consider Cases 1, 4, 5, 6, 7, 9, 10, 11, 14, 15, 20, 21, 27, and 29 in light of the material in this chapter.

NOTES

[1] Kenneth Kernaghan, "The emerging public service culture: values, ethics, and reforms," *Canadian Public Administration* 37: 4 (1994): 614, p. 616.

[2] Kenneth Kernaghan, "Codes of Ethics and Administrative Responsibility," *Canadian Public Administration* 17:4 (1974) 529, p. 530.

[3] For more on the idea of unwritten ethics codes and the disadvantages of them, consult Kernaghan 1974, *op. cit.*, p. 532.

[4] *Ibid.* 615. Kernaghan (1994) treats effectiveness, representativeness, fairness, and equity as traditional values because they have been at the core of the public service since the early 1960s.

[5] Stephen Potts, "Ethics in Public Service: An Idea Whose Time has Come," in *Public Sector Ethics: Finding and implementing values*, ed. Charles Sampford and Noel Preston, with C.-A. Bois. (NY: Routledge, 1998): 85, p. 89.

[6] John Tait, "A Strong Foundation: Report of the Task Force on Public Service Values and Ethics," *Canadian Public Administration* 40:1 (1997), p. 1. See also the work of Aaron Wildavsky, American political scientist and a founder of the contemporary discipline of public policy from the 1960s: *Speaking Truth to Power: The Art and Craft of Policy Analysis* (NY: Little, Brown, 1979).

[7] Kernaghan 1994, p. 615.

[8] For a good discussion of the history of the move toward values in Canadian public service organizations and their limitations, see John Langford, "Acting on Values: An ethical dead end for public servants," *Canadian Public Administration* 47:4 (2004): 429–450.

[9] Ralph Heintzman, "Public-service Values and Ethics: Dead end or strong foundation?" *Canadian Public Administration* 50:4 (2007): 573–602, p. 596, internal references omitted.

[10] While an ethics code for public officials may outline certain "constraints on political activity [which] are justified primarily by the desire that public employees both serve and appear to serve the public and their political superiors in an objective, non-partisan manner…[it is also] argued that under such circumstances, public servants are much more likely to be appointed and promoted on the basis of merit rather then party affiliation." (Kenneth Kernaghan, "Codes of Ethics and Public Administration: Progress, Problems and Prospects," *Public Administration* 58 (1980): 207, p. 215.

[11] Kernaghan 1994, p. 619.

[12] Kernaghan 1994, p. 619.

[13] Office of the Auditor General, Report of the Auditor General (Ottawa: Supply and Services, 1990) p. 193.

[14] Tait, p. 13.

[15] These "two extreme alternatives may be described as the 'Ten Commandments' approach and the 'Justinian Code' approach. At one extreme, a code may be phrased in such vague and nebulous language that it amounts to little more than a declaration of pious hopes. At the other extreme, a code may be so specific and detailed that it amounts to a lengthy and elaborate document in which an attempt is made to incorporate all existing statutes, regulations, and guidelines relating to ethical conduct and to cover every possible contingency. Neither approach seems to offer a workable solution," Kernaghan 2008, p. 538.

[16] J.S. Bowman and R. Williams, "Ethics in Government: from a winter of despair to a spring of hope," *Public Administration Review* 57 (1997): 517–526, p. 522.

[17] Dean Geuras and Charles Garofalo, *Practical Ethics in Public Administration* (Vienna, Virginia: Management Concepts, 2002), p. 17.

[18] Geuras and Garofalo 2002, p. 19.

[19] Geuras and Garofalo 2002, p. 21.

[20] John Rawls, *Political Liberalism* (NY: Cambridge University Press, 1993/1996), esp. pp. 54–58.

[21] Policy Horizons Canada: http://www.horizons.gc.ca/page.asp?pagenm=2009-0010_02. Accessed July 14, 2011.

[22] See references to follow in this section.

[23] Kieran Walshe and Thomas G. Rundall, "Evidence-based Management: From Theory to Practice in Health Care," *The Milbank Quarterly* 79:3 (2001): 429–457, p. 430.

[24] See Rachel Laforest and Michael Orsini, "Evidence-based Engagement in the Voluntary Sector: Lessons from Canada," *Social Policy and Administration* 39:5 (2005): 481–497.

[25] Heather Campbell, "'Evidence-based Policy': The Continuing Search for Effective Policy Processes," *Planning Theory and Practice* 3:1 (2002): 89–90. Internal references omitted.

[26] Greg Marston and Rob Watts, "Tampering With the Evidence: A Critical Appraisal of Evidence-Based Policy Making," *The Drawing Board: An Australian Review of Public Affairs* 3:3 (2003): 143-163, pp. 144-145.

[27] Huw T.O. Davies, Sandra M. Nutley, and Peter C. Smith, "Viewpoint: Editorial: What Works? The Role of Evidence In Public Sector Policy and Practice," *Public Money and Management* 19:1 (1999): 3-5, p. 3.

[28] Laforest and Orsini 2005, p. 482.

[29] Laforest and Orsini 2005, p. 484.

[30] Marston and Watts 2003, p. 145.

[31] See http://www.vsi-isbc.org/eng/index.cfm. Accessed July 15, 2011.

[32] Graham Leicester, "Viewpoint: The Seven Enemies of Evidence-Based Policy," *Public Money and Management* 19:1 (1999): 5–7.

[33] Leicester 1999, p. 5.

[34] Leicester 1999, p. 6.

[35] Marston and Watts 2003, p. 158.

[36] Angela Packwood, "Review Article: Evidence-based Policy: Rhetoric and Reality," *Social Policy and Society* 1: 3 (2002): 267–272, p. 270.

[37] Packwood 2002, p. 270.

[38] Packwood 2002, p. 271.

[39] See Marston and Watts 2003.

[40] Ken Yong, Deborah Ashby, Annette Boaz, and Lesley Grayson, "Social Science and the Evidence-based Policy Movement," *Social Policy and Society* 1:3 (2002): 215-224; in part quoting W. Solesbury, "Evidence-based policy: whence it came and where it's going," ESRC, Centre for Evidence-based Policy and Practice (Working Paper 1). Available at http://www.evidencenetwork.org.uk. It should be noted that the authors were, at the time of writing this paper, affiliated with the ESRC UK Centre for Evidence-based Policy and Practice.

[41] Young et al. 2002, p. 216.

[42] Young et al. 2002, pp. 216–217.

[43] Young et al. 2002, p. 217.

[44] Young et al. 2002, p. 217.

[45] Young et al. 2002, pp. 217–218 (internal references omitted).

[46] Young et al. 2002, p. 218 (internal references omitted).

[47] Noel Preston. *Understanding Ethics* (Sydney: The Federation Press, 2007), p. 151.

[48] Preston 2007, p. 153.

[49] Tait, p. 9.

CHAPTER 4

Corruption, Conflicts of Interest, and Other Unethical Conduct

In this chapter we examine a number of the most egregious forms of unethical conduct in government, ranging from outright corruption to conflicts of interest and the improper use of government resources. We then present some further cases for reflection, where the line between ethical and unethical conduct may be less clear than in the case of receiving or soliciting bribes, or hiring one's own family members.

4.1 CORRUPTION

Ethical conduct among public servants is necessary to good government. At the most basic level, ethical behaviour prevents government corruption. **Corruption** is quite possibly the largest barrier to good government and the public good in the world today. It is now generally acknowledged that "corruption can be a source of political instability."[1] Corruption is problematic for fairly obvious reasons. Given that democratic governments depend upon the consent and support of their citizens, the rise of corruption in democratic states undermines the political legitimacy of the state's institutions. The fight against government corruption is becoming a high priority for both government and non-governmental organizations. Corruption can primarily be addressed by either government prosecution or prevention. "In practice, both prevention and prosecution are necessary in order to keep the threat of corruption in check . . . [However] enforcement systems may be overwhelmed if there are no effective preventive measures in place to reduce the burden on investigators and prosecutors . . . [Apart from the benefits already discussed, ethics codes function as a preventative measure and] reduce the need to invoke the more drastic measures of prosecution, administrative discipline and punishment."[2]

Transparency International (TI), a well-respected international non-governmental organization (NGO) that studies and fights corruption throughout the world, defines corruption as follows:

> Corruption is operationally defined as the misuse of entrusted power for private gain. TI further differentiates between "**according to rule**" **corruption** and "**against the rule**" **corruption**. Facilitation payments, where a bribe is paid to receive preferential treatment for something that the bribe receiver is required to do by law, constitute the former. The latter, on the other hand, is a bribe paid to obtain services the bribe receiver is prohibited from providing.[3*]

When considered in the context of public service organizations, corruption involves using the power one has as a government agent for personal gain, or for the benefit of family, friends, or specific others, rather than for the public good. This could take any number of forms: safety inspectors taking bribes from businesses seeking government approval of their operations; public servants receiving gifts of travel or entertainment in exchange for a favourable review of the giver's tender for government work; civil servants requiring a bribe or personal benefit in exchange for issuing permits, licences, or other government permissions to conduct business or engage in a desired activity; public servants such as police officers extorting money in exchange for police services, as a means of avoiding arrest, or as protection from police harassment; or the establishment by civil servants of fraudulent service contracts with private agencies, who instead of providing the service or product for which the government is paying, kick back some of their revenue from the government contract to the civil servants who approved or oversaw the contract. The examples can be multiplied almost indefinitely, and the history of every country (including stable western democratic ones) includes a number of high-profile corruption scandals. There are doubtless many more instances of corruption that have gone undetected or unreported to the public.

*Reprinted from *Frequently Asked Questions About Corruption* <www.transparency.org/news_room/faq/corruption_faq>. Copyright © 2011 Transparency International: The global coalition against corruption. Used with permission. For more information, visit http://www.transparency.org.

While bribery is often associated with developing countries rather than stable democracies like Canada, and is generally more of a problem in emerging democracies than in developed ones, corruption exists everywhere and is a constant threat against which governments must pro-actively protect themselves. Bribe-taking and bribe-demanding are particularly acute forms of corruption, but they are not the only forms that unethical conduct can take, as we shall see in further sections of this book. But even if such explicitly corrupt practices as taking bribes are relatively rare among civil servants in Canada, it is still important to understand why corruption is such a serious problem and ethical breach. The negative effects of corruption highlight some of the ways in which the unethical conduct of civil servants can seriously hinder good government, and the real harms such unethical behaviour can cause.

It is important to note that some positions may be more susceptible to corruption than others. Psychologist Gary B. Brumback calls these "**seductive positions**"; their holders have extraordinary access to power, discretion, and money. Such positions test the moral character of those holding them.[4] It is no coincidence that corruption is often found in police departments, among those charged with awarding government contracts and overseeing government procurements, and among those engaged in licensing and inspections, since these positions all provide ample opportunity for inside dealing, kickbacks, and bribes.

Though we cannot provide an exhaustive discussion of the causes of corruption, or the conditions most likely to give rise to it, a few general remarks are in order. First, corruption corrupts. Corruption can only flourish in an environment where individuals are corruptible or have been corrupted. Corruption, in other words, always involves a degradation of the virtues and conscience of the persons involved. Thus corruption most easily gets established when individuals feel alienated from the organization, when they do not identify with its values, when they feel insecure or devalued within the organization, or when they have acquired their position through corrupt processes. If access to positions or promotion is governed by corrupt practices, individuals are much more likely to take a wholly instrumental view of their position; if it costs them to get the job, they will expect the job to pay off. If they feel insecure or devalued within the organization, they are also more likely to think in terms of what they can get from the job in the short run, rather than what they can contribute to it over the longer term. It is important for these reasons that access to the public service be based on merit through genuinely competitive processes, and that public servants be paid a living wage. In many parts of the world, public servants are paid so inadequately that they must resort to corrupt practices, like bribe demanding, in order to make a living. More generally, if corruption is to be avoided, it is important that individuals see themselves as valued members of a team working toward valuable ends; if individuals think of their position from a purely instrumental viewpoint, by contrast, they are much more likely to consider actions acceptable that benefit themselves at the expense of the organization or those it is supposed to serve.

If roles and responsibilities are ill-defined or conflicting, this too can have a corrupting effect. It is impossible in such an environment for public servants even with the best of intentions to perform their jobs well or to avoid failure. If they are given too much personal discretion in determining what they should be doing, this may erode an organization's capacity to achieve its goals. If goals are poorly defined or conflicting, then those who would benefit from moving in one direction rather than another may be able to use that excess flexibility to induce public servants to exercise their discretion in ways they prefer; this kind of influence is often acquired through corrupt practices.

Corruption is also enabled by weak transparency measures. Evil flourishes in dark corners; it is much more difficult to engage in corruption if the actions of government are transparent—to the public, to those within government structures who have audit and oversight functions (legislative committees, ombudsmen, integrity commissioners, ethics officers), and to the media. Lack of government transparency, and constraints on freedom of information—including freedom of the press and a responsive access to information regime—make it possible for corruption to develop and become ingrained in organizational cultures. One of the most powerful tools against corruption may turn out to be the Internet. Government agencies now provide a great deal of information about their operations and activities, as well as personnel, on Web sites that are freely available. Through government Web sites, individuals and civil society organizations can obtain a vast amount of information about what government does, and how it does it.

Weak financial or accounting practices can also enable corruption to flourish. If individuals handle cash in an environment of few controls and little oversight, the motivation to abuse such positions might be overwhelming. This is not the most common kind of case, however. Instead, weak accounting practices, procurement policies, contracting policies, and the like make possible widespread corruption, from kickbacks to bribes. We discuss some of these below.

There are many ways for government structures themselves to become dysfunctional. If the government of the day demonstrates contempt for democratic values and the interests of the people, or indifference to considerations of the public good, this will have a corrosive effect within public institutions, including the public service. If government is not explicitly directed toward the common good, it is natural for those operating within it to adopt a more selfish and instrumental view of their work; if they are not working for the people, they must be working for the good of themselves and those with whom they identify. If there is considerable tension between the government of the day and the public service in terms of their understanding of the common good and the values that animate their work, this may be another kind of dysfunction that can be corrupting. Once public servants feel entitled to substitute their own judgment about what to do for that of the duly elected representatives of the people, a significant bar to corruption is gone.

Social conditions can also affect the amount of corruption within public institutions. Poverty and economic hard times are broadly correlated with increased government corruption. So too is lack of literacy and general education among the public, since an uneducated population will be less likely to critically monitor government actions, to recognize wrongdoing when it is happening, and to call them to account for corrupt activities. Citizen apathy is similarly enabling of corruption, for largely the same reasons. Government actors do not have to avoid corruption if nobody cares what they do, or if citizens are unwilling to call them to account. Relatedly, and for reasons touched on in Chapter 8, lack of strong civil society organizations can make corruption easier. This is so for a number of reasons. First, without a strong civil society, citizens are less able to effectively interact with governments and participate in the policy process. They are also less likely to be able to act collectively and to articulate shared public values. Finally, without a robust civil society, individuals may not be able to obtain the information needed to formulate policy alternatives and critically review the actions of government.

We know, too, that corruption is most likely to occur in local governments. This is so for a number of reasons, most especially the extensive ties that exist between those in government organizations and the community. It is more likely that civil servants will have close personal and other ties to members of the community they serve in local governments. If those communities themselves are organized along clan or clique lines (religious, familial, ethnic, linguistic, etc.), in which nepotism and favouritism are accepted and expected, it may be exceedingly difficult for members of the public service to rebuff requests for special treatment from their own groups. Loyalty to their family or group may conflict with their professional responsibilities, and this may create considerable inducement to corruption.

As we know from the experience of failed states and dictatorships, one of the greatest protections from corruption comes from the rule of law and an independent judiciary. Thus these must be protected and valued if corruption is to be avoided, and if serious wrongdoers are to be punished.

Finally, the size of public service organizations can make a difference to the amount of corruption they can sustain. If public service organizations become too large, they may lose the capacity to respond effectively to concerns or complaints, either from within or without. Individuals must believe that potential remedies are available if they are to take the time and trouble to ask questions or raise concerns. Ombudsmen and similar positions can help here, but more important is creating an environment in which every member of the organization is responsible for and enabled to respond effectively to such criticisms and concerns.

The effects of corruption are corrosive in any organization (business, government, non-governmental organizations, etc.). Transparency International highlights four kinds of harm caused by corruption: political, economic, social, and environmental.

4.1.1 Political Costs of Corruption

Transparency International describes corruption as "a major obstacle to democracy and the rule of law. In a democratic system, offices and institutions lose their legitimacy when they are misused for private advantage."[5*] This is an important claim, raising complex issues of political morality, about the legitimacy of political offices and institutions and about democracy. Legitimate political power is exercised "for the people"; political power is legitimate only when it is used for the good of the governed, the common or public good, rather than the private gain of those who govern. In democratic societies, we have decided that the best method of ensuring that political power is exercised for the good of the people is to vest that power in the people, to have rule "by the people." Thus we have democratically elected governments that must propose policies which will elicit the approval of a majority of voters in popular elections, and that can be removed by the people in subsequent elections should they lose that approval. The ethical requirements that must be met by elected officials is not our subject in this book, though refraining from corruption is obviously vital in our public officials if we are to have good government and decision making in the public interest.

Our concern here is with the civil service that supports the activities of our elected political officials. When civil servants act in corrupt ways that are contrary to the decisions of elected officials, the negative impact on democracy is plain to see. If the elected government adopts criminal laws, or health and safety regulations and inspections, or licensing requirements, or restrictions on the use or extraction of natural resources, for example, and civil servants help individuals, organizations, businesses, corporations, and others to "get around" these laws and regulations for private gain, the civil servants are obviously acting in ways that impede the elected government from carrying out the mandate given to it by the people. Inhibiting the ability of a duly elected government from executing its lawful political agenda is in direct conflict with the values of democracy. It substitutes the judgment of the corrupt civil servant for the elected officials authorized to make decisions for the people. These are cases of "against the rule" corruption as distinguished by TI.

*Reprinted from *Frequently Asked Questions About Corruption* <www.transparency.org/news_room/faq/corruption_faq>. Copyright © 2011 Transparency International: The global coalition against corruption. Used with permission. For more information, visit http://www.transparency.org.

This might suggest that "against the rule" corruption only occurs when public servants circumvent or violate the orders of their political superiors, but this kind of corruption need not take this form. Sometimes public servants engage in against the rule corruption at the behest of, or under orders from, their political bosses. In such cases, elected officials direct public servants to violate the rules or regulations set by the government, either for the personal benefit of the elected official or the benefit of his or her political party. In such cases, politicians attempt to shield themselves or distance themselves from the wrongdoing by ordering others to do it. This is every bit as much an affront to good government and democracy as corruption undertaken by civil servants on their own initiative, though placing public servants in an even more difficult situation. Civil servants may feel vulnerable and unable to resist such orders because of their relative powerlessness, because they fear reprisal from their boss, say, or think that they must comply in order to secure a good performance review or promotion. They may also feel the tug of loyalty to their boss, which may incline them to comply with unethical and even illegal orders. This is a case in which wrongdoing may need to be disclosed; that is, the public servant may have to blow the whistle on his or her boss. We discuss the disclosure of wrongdoing below. Without minimizing the difficulty of the position that public servants face in such circumstances, it is important to remember that "I was just following orders" is never a good excuse for bad behaviour. And civil servants owe their primary duty to the Crown or government institution, rather than any particular elected official or government. Again, we say more about this in what follows.

When civil servants act contrary to the rules established by government, they undermine the **rule of law**. The "rule of law" is contrasted with the "rule of men." In order to have the rule of law, rather than arbitrary exercises of power, it is essential that those exercising power do so in accordance with established rules. The rule of law can only be enjoyed when people are governed by general rules, made known to them in advance, and applied fairly and consistently by those who are authorized to do so. These basic principles of administrative justice are vital to good order; without them, individuals dealing with government cannot plan and guide their behaviour according to the rules. They cannot be sure that their individual cases will be dealt with fairly and impartially, rather than arbitrarily and in ways that they cannot predict. Interaction with government becomes something to fear; citizens lose confidence that their good faith efforts to comply with the law will protect them against government action. The effects are a loss of confidence in the rule of law, loss of trust in government officials, and loss of trust in the administration of government services. All of this has, of course, a corrosive effect on civil society and government/citizen interaction, as well as public support for and confidence in their political institutions.

Corruption in a civil service can also impede good government when it is "according to rule" corruption. When a civil servant demands payment or other personal gain to perform his or her public service job—to issue licences, to perform a fair inspection, to make recommendations about government contracts, to hire other civil servants, to do, generally, the job he or she is employed by government to do—the efficiency of government is directly undermined. Decisions are no longer being made on the basis of a good faith assessment of what is in the public interest, or what would best implement the government's objectives, but rather by what will benefit the individual public servant. The delivery of public programs will become less efficient and effective, and individuals dealing with government will lose faith that the government is operating for the public good, impartially and fairly. This erosion of public trust in the operations of the government is a direct threat to the perceived legitimacy of government.

4.1.2 Economic Costs of Corruption

Transparency International describes the economic costs of corruption in the following terms:

> Economically, corruption leads to the depletion of national wealth. It is often responsible for the funnelling of scarce public resources to uneconomic high-profile projects, such as dams, power plants, pipelines and refineries, at the expense of less spectacular but more necessary infrastructure projects such as schools, hospitals and roads, or the supply of power and water to rural areas. Furthermore, it hinders the development of fair market structures and distorts competition, thereby deterring investment.[6]*

It may not be obvious why corruption in the public service imposes these economic costs upon society. But it may have such effects if public servants recommend expenditure on projects from which they stand to benefit. If a public servant receives a kickback from a developer, industry, or organization wanting to do work for government, it automatically raises suspicions as to whether the public servant is recommending the project or the particular provider for personal reasons rather than because evidence suggests that this is the best use of public funds or the best supplier of public services. If public servants receive funds from private lobby groups, the same suspicions arise. "In economic terms, corruption misdirects resources and discourages investment by the private sector. A study by the International Monetary Fund concluded that high rates of investment by the private sector are linked to low levels of corruption (Mauro 1996)"[7]

Perhaps more insidious is the fact that corruption makes every corrupt transaction more expensive. As ethicist Stephen Potts points out, "in an increasingly competitive global economy, countries can no longer afford the cost of corruption. It simply makes them non-competitive in world markets."[8] In short, corruption must be controlled if developed or developing countries are to have a chance at promoting their economic systems. Civil servants have an obligation to keep corruption out of the public service, as this would have devastating effects on the state's economy. If, for example, a civil servant demands a bribe for doing his job, the delivery of government services becomes more expensive. If a civil servant recommends a provider for a government service or product that would not be selected through a fair procurement procedure, government will spend more for the product or service, or receive less for its money. Genuine competition will be undermined: "who a private agency knows" in the civil service will become more important than the quality of their service or the competitiveness of their bid. This is why corruption undermines market structures and fair competition. Government services will be delivered less effectively, and/or cost more than they would without the corruption.

4.1.3 Social Costs of Corruption

Transparency International also identifies social costs of corruption:

> The effect of corruption on the social fabric of society is the most damaging of all. It undermines people's trust in the political system, in its institutions and its leadership. Frustration and general apathy among a disillusioned public result in a weak civil society. That in turn clears the way for despots as well as democratically elected yet unscrupulous leaders to turn national assets into personal wealth. Demanding and paying bribes become the norm. Those unwilling to comply often emigrate, leaving the country drained of its most able and most honest citizens.[9]*

Obviously every country has a strong interest in protecting the reputation and integrity of its political institutions from this kind of damage. Honest business people will not bring their services and goods to government if they don't think there will be a genuinely open and competitive bidding process for government work. Average citizens will become cynical about government claims to act in the public interest if they know or suspect that decisions are being made for the private gain of government actors. And the incentive to participate in democratic institutions will be undermined if there is a perceived disconnect between the values and rules publicly proclaimed and the actual operation of the government and public institutions.

In addition to the damaging effects corruption has on society as a whole, it often adversely affects a particular group within society the most. For the "truth is that the poor suffer the most when government is corrupt. Goods intended for them are siphoned off for illicit purposes. Funds needed for programs to provide transportation, schools and medical care are misdirected to less socially beneficial ends. Corruption makes it virtually impossible for the poor to lift themselves out of poverty."[10]

4.1.4 Environmental, Health, and Safety Costs of Corruption

Finally, Transparency International identifies damage to the environment as a cost related to corruption:

> Environmental degradation is yet another consequence of corrupt systems. The lack of, or non-enforcement of, environmental regulations and legislation has historically allowed the North to export its polluting industry to the South. At the same time, careless exploitation of natural resources, from timber and minerals to elephants, by both domestic and international agents has led to ravaged natural environments. Environmentally devastating projects are given preference in funding, because they are easy targets for siphoning off public money into private pockets.[11]*

Environmental regulations, like those governing health and safety, food quality, and more, are only as effective as their enforcement. The public service is charged with overseeing inspections and other monitoring activities and licensing programs that operationalize environmental protection and safety laws. Only if inspectors carry out their activities impartially and in accordance with the rules can the public be sure that the food they eat, the pharmaceuticals they consume, the water they drink or swim in, the buildings they occupy, and the roads and

*Reprinted from *Frequently Asked Questions About Corruption* <www.transparency.org/news_room/faq/corruption_faq>. Copyright © 2011 Transparency International: The global coalition against corruption. Used with permission. For more information, visit http://www.transparency.org.

bridges upon which they travel are safe. Governments enact significant public welfare and regulatory law to protect the public from undue risk of harm, to ensure the safety of workers and consumers, and to protect the natural environment. Unless those regulations are applied fairly, and for the common good, they cannot provide the security that is their aim. Public servants have an indispensable role to play in enforcing those legislative and regulatory schemes. Thus offering and receiving bribes are egregious violations of a public servant's duty and are both considered criminal offences under the *Criminal Code of Canada*.[12]

4.2 CONFLICTS OF INTEREST AND CONFLICTS OF COMMITMENT

Public servants have a duty to avoid all forms of **conflict of interests**. "We may distinguish between an ***apparent* conflict of interest** (when it appears that an official's private interests may have the potential to interfere with the proper performance of that official's duties) and an *actual* conflict of interest (when a reasonable person, in possession of the relevant facts, would conclude that the official's private interests are likely to interfere with the proper performance of that official's duties)."[13]* Though it may seem clear that a public servant ought to avoid actual conflicts of interest, for the last few decades society has begun to recognize the severity of even apparent or potential conflicts of interest. For the seriousness of even just an apparent/potential conflict of interest was recognized in a decision made under the federal *Public Service Staff Relations Act*.[14]

> The adjudicator upheld the suspension of a federal employee who established a company offering services that could lead to a conflict of interest with his official duties. The Board found that the appearance of conflict was enough to establish a conflict of interest. According to the adjudicator, "it is not sufficient for the public servant or his associates to be convinced of their own innocence and integrity. Nor is it necessary to prove that they have been disloyal to the employer. Even in the absence of evidence of wilful wrongdoing, a conflict of interest or the appearance thereof can be easily recognized by an intelligent citizen as contrary to public policy."[15]†

*Noel Preston. *Understanding Ethics* 2/e. pg. 156–157. Leichhardt, N.S.W.: Federation Press, 2001.

†Kenneth Kernaghan, "Codes of Ethics and Administrative Responsibility," *Canadian Public Administration* 17:4 (2008), p. 529. Copyright © 2008 John Wiley & Sons. Reproduced with permission of Blackwell Publishing Ltd.

This reasoning not only demonstrates that potential conflicts of interest ought to be avoided, but also suggests a third type of conflict of interest, specifically, a perceived conflict of interest. Apart from actual and potential conflicts of interest, it is crucial that situations that may be perceived as conflicts of interest are avoided, especially if public trust and confidence in the public service is to be upheld. Thus public servants must avoid perceived, actual, and potential conflicts of interest. If a conflict of interest does arise, they have a further duty to resolve it in favour of the public interest.

Conflicts of interest arise whenever a public servant stands to personally gain from a particular government decision that the public servant can influence, even indirectly. To avoid such conflicts, civil servants must have no private interests that would be affected by the government actions or decisions they participate in. Though every jurisdiction has conflict of interest guidelines for public servants, there is no canonical definition of what a conflict of interest is. But conflicts of interest can be generally described in the following terms:

> A conflict of interest is any situation in which a public employee, either for himself or herself, or for some other person(s), attempts to promote a private or personal interest that results in or appears to result in either of the following:
>
> (a) an interference with or impediment to the objective, neutral, and impartial exercise of his or her duties in the public service, or
>
> (b) a gain or advantage by virtue of his or her position in the public service.

Conflicts of interest arise when the private interest of a public servant can be advanced by his or her employment in the public service or when the pursuit of a private interest might lead the public servant to act in any way that is contrary to the proper performance of his or her public sector duties.

Public servants are permitted to participate in their communities in numerous ways. They may serve on the board of a charity, or hold a position on a parent-teacher association or the board of their condominium, for example. Such activities do not pose a conflict of interest as long as the following conditions are met. First, the organization with which the public servant is involved must not engage in business with her ministry, department, or agency, or any ministry, department, or agency that she may be directly dealing with in her capacity as a public servant. Second, the public servant must not disclose any information obtained in the performance of her duties as a public servant to the outside organization that is not readily available to the public. Third, she cannot use her position in the civil service to provide an unfair advantage or preferential treatment to those with whom she has personal relationships or private dealings. She likewise cannot help private persons or entities in dealing with government where this might be perceived as providing preferential treatment. Fourth, she cannot use government resources or property to further the ends of private associations or for personal gain.

Public servants must not only avoid disclosing confidential information to private persons or entities, but they must avoid using information obtained in the performance of their duties for their personal good or the good of close family and friends. If information is not readily available to the public, it is possible that it can provide an unfair advantage or opportunity for those who have it. So, for example, a public servant might come to know about plans for development of land, or government investment in a particular industrial sector. Based on that information, the public servant can predict that the value of property in the area or the value of shares in a range of companies is likely to increase when the information becomes public or the government policy is executed. This creates the possibility of using that information for personal gain. This may be one of the most problematic conflicts to detect, because the public servant need not use her position to influence government policy that creates the opportunity for private benefit. Thus it might seem that no harm to the public good can come from her profiting from her inside knowledge after the decision has been made. Nonetheless, using confidential information in this way is prohibited. To use information in this way is a conflict of interest and, if discovered, would discredit the objectivity and impartiality of the public service.

Clearer cases involve the opportunity to influence government decision making in ways that will personally benefit the public servant. If a public servant has assets of any kind, the value of which can be influenced by government decisions in which she plays a part, there is a potential conflict of interest.

Cases of what is known as "self-dealing" provide clear examples of conflicts of interest. If a public servant owns a private business, or is a partner or significant shareholder in a private company, there is a potential conflict of interest should that company seek to do business with the government, especially the department for which the civil servant works. If the civil servant awards a contract to the private company which he also owns or in whose profits he shares, he is in an actual conflict of interest. The same can be said of firms owned or operated by his family or friends. He has provided a benefit to himself, his family, or friends in his private capacity through his public function. This will be true even if he does not directly make the decision about whether to award the contract to his company, if he influences or even attempts to influence that decision in his favour. Such influence may extend even beyond his own department, if he uses contacts in another department to secure a government contract from which he stands to benefit personally.

The public servant might be tempted to influence the decision in such a way as to increase the value of her asset, even if that is not the best decision from the point of view of the public good. Assets that might pose a conflict of interest must be reported confidentially to an official designated within the public service organization for this purpose. Among the assets in this category are any publicly traded securities of corporations and foreign governments; self-administered RRSPs and RESPs that are composed of these securities (if the security is held directly, not in mutual funds or similar instruments); interests in partnerships, proprietorships, family businesses (especially those that control shares in public companies or do business with government); commercially operated farm businesses; real property that is not for the private use of the public servant or her family members; commodities, futures, foreign currencies held for speculative purposes; assets placed in trust or from an estate, from which the public servant is a beneficiary; secured or unsecured loans granted to non-family members; any asset or liability that can give rise to real or apparent conflict given the nature of the duties of the public servant; any direct or contingent liability in respect of the assets already discussed. This list is not exhaustive. Public servants have a duty to disclose all such assets, and must keep their disclosure up to date. They cannot avoid this duty by transferring assets to immediate family members, as this too would constitute a perceived, if not an actual, conflict of interest.

If a potential, actual, or perceived conflict does arise because a public servant has private interests in any of these types of assets, it must be reported to the public servant's deputy head (or other official designated for this purpose). The deputy head will determine what course of action is most appropriate to limit the conflict. The deputy head must consider what the public servant's specific duties are; the value and types of assets and type of interest involved; the actual costs incurred by divesting the assets or interests compared with the potential that the asset or interest represents as a conflict of interest. By considering these various factors, the deputy head engages in a balancing test, weighing on the one hand the value of the asset to the public servant and the costs of divesting it, and on the other, the degree to which holding the asset creates a conflict of interest, given the public servant's responsibilities and relationship to the asset. If a conflict does exist because of a public servant's holding of an asset or participation in a private entity that does business with government, various remedies to end the conflict may be proposed. The public servant may have to withdraw from the private entity, or the asset may have to be sold or put into a blind trust over which the public servant exercises no direct control.

Though public servants allow this limited intrusion into their private affairs in an effort to detect potential conflicts of interest before they arise, and to resolve them if they do arise, they retain the right to hold a range of assets and enter into a range of relationships. They need not report any residences, recreation properties, or farms used privately by themselves and their family; household goods and personal effects; art, collectibles, or automobiles; cash and deposits; Canada saving bonds, fixed investments issued by any government or government agency; RRSPs and RESPs that are not self-administered; any investment in an open-ended mutual fund; guaranteed investment certificates and similar instruments; annuities; life insurance policies; pension rights; money owed by a previous employer, partnership, or client; or personal loans receivable from immediate family or small loans receivable from others.

Another form of conflict of interest is known as **influence peddling** and is against the law. It is closely aligned with soliciting or receiving bribes, which is also against the law. In both cases, the civil servant solicits or accepts some kind of benefit in exchange for exercising her authority or influence within government for the benefit of the person or organization providing the benefit. At its most extreme, this form of criminal activity is the epitome of corruption, which was discussed above. The benefit that is solicited need not be financial. An immigration officer who offers to use his influence in reviewing refugee claims for the benefit of a refugee claimant in exchange for sex is engaged in influence peddling. So is a public servant who offers to fast-track a developer's application for building permits in exchange for free work on his home or cottage. Likewise, when a public servant offers to use her authority to assist a friend or family member who is seeking some benefit, aid, or contract from the government, she is engaged in influence peddling. She is attempting to use her position in government for the private benefit of herself or those with whom she has a personal relationship, and to do so requires that she be committed to influencing the outcome of government decision making so as to secure that private benefit, even if doing so would not otherwise be in the public interest, or be the result obtained through the objective and impartial performance of her public sector duties.

Another area of potential conflict of interest arises when a public servant takes outside employment. A civil servant may wish to take additional employment outside the public service. He may, for example, wish to write a newspaper column for pay, or teach a course in a post-secondary institution. If the public servant is employed by the civil service full-time and not on leave of absence, then such outside employment must be only part-time. And a number of general conditions apply to ensure that the potential conflict of interest does not become an actual or perceived conflict: the organization he proposes to work for cannot be in direct competition with his government employer; the organization he proposes to work for cannot do business with his ministry or department; he cannot disclose confidential information to the private sector employer; he cannot use government property or resources in performing his outside activities; he must perform his outside activities on his own time; and his employment generally must not interfere with the performance of his duties as a public servant. Public servants must receive approval from their minister or equivalent before taking outside employment.

Likewise, a civil servant may wish to engage in a business enterprise, and may do so provided her private interests in the undertaking do not conflict with her responsibilities as a public servant or interfere with or detrimentally affect her ability to perform her duties to the Crown. In engaging in such outside activities, the civil servant must ensure that no person derives an advantage from the fact that she is also a public servant.

Public servants have a duty to exercise their influence on government decision making only for the public good. When they have a private interest that could be served by a government decision, they are in a conflict of interest. They must not participate in decision making by the Crown if they can influence the decision in the course of their duties in such a way that they (or their family or close friends) can benefit from the decision. Likewise, if they belong to an outside organization or group, they should not engage in decision making within that organization or group if there is a conflict between the interests of that group and the interests of the Crown, or if they can influence the organization or body because of their position as a public servant. When conflicts of this type arise, public servants have a duty to disclose the conflict to their deputy head or ethics officer, and to the private organization or group as well.

Similarly, public servants must not participate in decision making when they have a conflict of commitments. The clearest case of such a conflict arises with respect to hiring, promoting, or contracting with a person with whom the public servant has a close personal relationship. This is a special type of conflict of interest, which we call a *conflict of commitments*. Even though the public servant may not stand to gain in any material sense from the employment, advancement, or contract with another with whom he has a close personal relationship, he may have commitments to that person that create a potential, actual, or perceived conflict. We said above that employment and advancement in the civil service must be based on merit rather than **nepotism**, favouritism, or political cronyism. This principle is compromised when civil servants participate in decision making situations involving those to whom they have commitments that could result in bias, favouritism, or unfair advantage. This type of conflict has led to various scandals, including the recent eHealth Ontario scandal, in which it was revealed that "a consultant was paid $30,000 for 78 hours work, and the son of board chairman Alan Hudson worked for a firm closely connected to the agency."[16] A public servant should declare such conflicts, and the personal relationships that give rise to them, to their deputy head or ethics officer, and may then be required to withdraw from the decision making situation.

Though conflicts of interest may be the most common form of corruption in government, and may be the kind of wrongdoing that the public most readily identifies as wrongdoing, it is important to recognize that it is only one of many forms that corruption can take. **Integrity Commissioners** at the federal, provincial, and municipal levels, the Ethics Officers of the House of Commons and the Senate, Auditors General, and various ombudsmen have sometimes been (rightly) criticized for taking an unduly narrow view of ethics so that in practice it precludes only conflicts of interest. This is an unacceptably narrow conception of corruption, and must be avoided.

A different kind of conflict of commitments situation involves the receipt or acceptance of gifts, and is dealt with in its own right immediately below.

4.3 GIFTS

The line between gifts and bribes is, at best, a blurry one. Thus some of what was said under the heading of corruption applies to the topic of gifts. But even when a gift is offered without any explicit commitment on the behalf of the civil servant receiving the gift, receiving gifts can compromise the impartiality and integrity of the civil service. Thus the general rule is that civil servants shall not accept or solicit any gifts that could compromise their impartiality or create obligations to the giver.

The receipt of gifts has created a number of scandals at almost every level of the public service. To receive gifts from organizations or individuals who contract with the government or who otherwise stand to benefit from government decisions, or who are under the regulatory or licensing control of government, creates a perception of undue influence or bias. The public rightly thinks that private individuals or agencies who wine and dine civil servants, or who provide them with gifts of sports and entertainment, and the like, expect something in return. The givers must expect to receive some advantage from their generosity, and this compromises the integrity of the civil servants receiving the gifts. Thus public servants are barred from receiving gifts of any significant value from any private entity that does business with their ministry or department. This includes not only gifts of cash, but gift cards, complementary membership in clubs, tickets to sports and entertainment events, travel, and services.

Public servants may think that they can receive gifts without their objectivity or impartiality being compromised, but there is reason to doubt this. Receipt of gifts creates a conflict of commitments, because receiving a gift generates felt duties of reciprocity in those who receive them. It is a very basic feature of social life that we are positively inclined toward those who give us gifts, and there is an expectation of reciprocity toward those who do so. The virtue of gratitude exemplifies this expectation: we ought to return kindnesses with kindnesses. Thus there is a psychological pressure, however subtle, that is exerted when one enters into a relationship of gift giving and gift receiving that can compromise objectivity and fairness.

There are additional social and cultural factors that must be taken into account in understanding the rules around the receipt of gifts, however. Some gifts are offered as part of the normal standards of hospitality, courtesy, or protocol. To refuse such gifts may be considered rude or culturally insensitive. In other cases, the gift may arise out of official activities or events in which the public servant is expected to participate, in the course of performing her official duties. In such cases, the receipt of such gifts may be acceptable, provided they are of minimal or symbolic value. Timing may be relevant, that is, *when* the gift is offered or given; a gift given at the end of an interaction, as a token of appreciation, may be less worrisome, in terms of influence on the recipient, than a gift offered or given prior to or at the beginning of an interaction. The general test, again, is whether the receipt of the gift would compromise or appear to compromise the **integrity** of the public servant or her organization, or place the public servant under an undue influence of the giver, or create a perception of reciprocal duties to the giver that could compromise the integrity of the civil servant. Public servants are advised to seek advice from their deputy head before accepting gifts. And they must notify their ethics executive or deputy head when they have received gifts in the normal course of fulfilling their official duties.

Public servants have a duty to avoid conflicts of interest and conflicts of commitments. When such conflicts arise, they must resolve them in favour of the public interest. They must act in ways that maintain the integrity of their organization, and act in good faith. Thus they must avoid situations that create the potential for bias, favouritism, partiality, or conflicting loyalties. When such biases exist, they must abstain from decision making on matters involving those toward whom they have commitments that could conflict with their duties to the Crown.

4.4 USE OF GOVERNMENT RESOURCES

Public servants may have access to various government resources, and they have a duty to protect such resources and not use them in improper ways. A variety of duties fall under this heading. Public servants must use their time at work on government business, for example. It is improper for public servants (like all employees) to spend any of the time for which they are being paid by their employer to do work for themselves or another, whether that other work is remunerated or not. Similarly, employees are supposed to spend working hours working, rather than idling away the hours surfing the Internet, playing computer games, or engaging in personal correspondence. Likewise, public servants must use government resources, such as computers and vehicles, only for the performance of their official responsibilities.

Public servants must also ensure that they make only ethical use of expense accounts. It is acceptable for government employees to be reimbursed for reasonable expenses incurred in the course of performing their official duties: travel, meals, hospitality, and accommodation expenses are allowable expenses, subject to reasonable limits. Reasonable limits may be specified by particular rules, or left to the discretion of individual agencies. But common sense is a good guide. What constitutes a reasonable limit will depend upon one's position within the organizational hierarchy, since where one might be expected to eat, for example, will depend upon where one is travelling and with whom one is dining. If it is expected that a civil servant will dine with high ranking foreign officials and dignitaries, for example, it can be expected that dinners will be in more expensive restaurants than he or she might frequent during private travel with family. Some expenses are always suspect, including alcohol. While a modest consumption of alcohol may be permitted, costs for alcohol should be kept to a minimum or should be paid for by the public servant personally. Many government officials, elected and non-elected, have been found putting on their professional expense accounts what are clearly personal expenses unrelated to their positions and providing no benefit to their employer or the public, and the public expresses in no uncertain terms its condemnation of such practices. Installing a swimming pool or building a deck on one's private residence is not an acceptable use of public funds, and neither is using government vehicles for private purposes.

4.5 ETHICAL PROCUREMENT, CONTRACTING, AND CONSULTANTS

Governments contract for many goods and services from "suppliers": private entities, businesses, consultants, and so forth. Such contracts have given rise to some of the most serious breaches of ethics, and public scandals, seen in recent years. Consider, for example, the sponsorship scandal that plagued the federal government between the late 1990s and 2005, and which is widely credited with a dramatic drop in popular support for the federal Liberal governments of

Prime Ministers Jean Chrétien and Paul Martin. Investigations into the sponsorship scandal indicated that an amount as high as $100 million was misspent by Public Works on contracts to promote Canada in Quebec after the narrow defeat of a separatist referendum in 1995. These contracts produced little value for the Canadian public, and were awarded to various private entities (especially advertising companies) that had close ties to the Liberal Party of Canada and to various ministers within the Liberal government. Consider, with respect to this scandal, the point made earlier about the importance of clarity of objectives. What did the objective "promoting the federal government in Quebec" mean, and how could this be done without promoting the interests of the ruling federal party?

More recently, the provincial government in Ontario has come under fire because of allegations that the provincial agency eHealth spent millions of dollars on consultants who had ties to the agency's CEO or board chair, through a process of untendered contracts. Here the problem did not seem to be lack of clarity in the objective to be sought by the agency; the creation of a system of electronic medical records seems clear enough. But there was a lack of financial controls and oversight, accompanied by poor procurement practices. The examples could, unfortunately, be multiplied.

Such scandals reveal a number of important considerations for building an ethical public service. First, it is absolutely vital that government contracts for goods or services, including consulting services, be awarded through a competitive and transparent tendering process. While it is reasonable to expect that public servants, elected officials, or board members of a government agency may have prior professional or personal relations with those who bid for government contracts, it is important that any prior relationships be declared. In this way, potential conflicts of interest can be disclosed and the parties affected can be removed from decision making involving those with whom they have such relationships. When it is revealed, usually by the media, that a significant government contract has been awarded to a company headed by the child or spouse of a government official, to a company that has contributed large amounts of money to the ruling political party, or to a company that has close personal or professional relationships with senior civil servants, the public is rightly suspicious that the reasons for choosing that company were personal rather than based on an assessment of its competitive advantages. These concerns can only be allayed by proof that the contract was awarded through an open and competitive bidding process, and that the nature of the relationships had been disclosed during that process.

Having open competitive bidding processes for government contracts is also important for ensuring that there is good value for tax-payers' money.

Governments, at least in Canada, do not own productive resources (for the most part) and so we must remember that the money governments spend is actually tax-payers' money. The public has a right to expect that its money will be spent effectively, in the provision of goods and services that have real value. While disclosure that a company doing business with government has prior ties to that government raises concern, full-blown scandals that bring government and the civil service into disrepute always include allegations that the government did not receive appropriate value for its expenditures. This was the case in both the sponsorship and eHealth scandals. When millions of tax-payers' dollars are spent on services that are of little or no value, the public is rightly outraged. Politicians and civil servants have a duty to ensure that public money is spent wisely and to diligently monitor the value of their expenditures. The best way to ensure that public money is well spent is to put in place procurement policies that are open and competitive.

There are some limitations to this general position. While open competitive bidding processes for government contracts are the ideal, governments also have to consider the cost of such processes. They delay the provision of services, and increase the direct costs. Thus it may sometimes be appropriate for governments to put in place preferred service providers for the delivery of ongoing goods and services, for example, rather than putting every contract out for competitive tender. But the process by which a private entity becomes a preferred service provider must itself be competitive and include provisions for the ongoing disclosure of any potential, perceived, or actual conflicts of interest. It might also be the case that governments adopt policies that allow for the awarding of untendered contracts below some threshold of value. Small contracts for the one-time provision of a good or service, including consulting services, might be awarded non-competitively. But if they are, the amount of such contracts must be fairly minimal. Suppose, for example, that a government decided that contracts for consulting services under $10,000 need not be put out for competitive tender. If so, protections need to be put in place to ensure that such a system cannot be used to by-pass the normal competitive process. It must be impossible for a private entity to receive multiple contracts of this type in any one year, for example. Without such protections, such a scheme would be open to serious abuse.

Government procurement policies must also include mechanisms for the ongoing monitoring of value-for-money. Many instances of the misspending of public money are revealed by the media or in the reports of the Auditor General or his provincial or municipal counterparts (e.g., provincial ombudsmen). We say more about such independent auditors below. But here it should be emphasized that public trust is much better served by governments adopting internal and ongoing value-for-money assessment mechanisms than by waiting for such reports to identify problems. Assessment mechanisms can reveal problems as they arise, and before they reach such significant amounts that the public trust is shaken by their revelation. The public service plays a vital role in ensuring that government money is not misspent.

Many spending scandals involve the employment of private sector consultants. Consultants often have expertise that is very valuable to governments in developing policies or implementing programs. It may sometimes be the case that governments can operate most efficiently by hiring such consultants for specific tasks, rather than trying to ensure that all forms of expertise are reflected in public service employees. Thus the use of private consultants may be perfectly legitimate. But governments are well-advised to be sure that they have clear policies with respect to the use of such consultants, including making sure that the nature of the work to be performed is clearly specified, with time lines for deliverables, and a framework for the amount such consultants can charge for various activities and costs. There must be a reasonable upper cap to the fees that consultants can charge governments for their services, and that cap must be made public and justified. Similarly, there ought to be clear limits on amendments to existing agreements, and a procedure by which amendments are approved and monitored. The same ought to be true especially with respect to cost overruns, a perennial problem with government contracts, which often throws even worthy projects into disrepute with the public.

Value-for-money narrowly construed is not the only value that governments ought to pursue through their procurement policies. It may also be appropriate for governments to use their procurement policies to support local industries and service-providers. It may likewise be proper for governments to use their procurement policies to build capacity in semi-private sectors such as universities. Public-private partnerships (or PPPs) might be an effective way to bring government resources together with private sector expertise and labour to provide public goods. Supporting local industries and building capacity in the private and semi-private sector are worthy goals that should also influence government purchasing and contracting decisions.

Whether the purchase of a particular good or service is of benefit to the local economy is determined by a complex set of factors. The good or service purchased has to deliver appropriate value to the public for the cost. But this cost-benefit analysis must itself be determined by a life-cycle formula which takes into account such factors as durability, energy use, transportation, long-run costs, maintenance, and spin-off jobs. These are all considerations that ought to go into the genuine costing of goods and services, and ought to be included in the assessment of value-for-money and local benefits of government purchasing policies.

Governments should also make purchasing decisions in a way that reflects a number of other values. Most especially, government purchasing policies should reflect the values of sustainability and environmental protection, as well as social responsibility and human rights. Consideration of the environmental impacts of purchasing decisions is imperative, and might include at least the following kinds of factors. Purchasing policies should be good for the natural and physical environment, or at least minimally damaging if there is no environmentally neutral or beneficial alternative available for an essential good or service. Environmental effects must be conceived across a broad spectrum: production, delivery, and disposal. Use of fossil fuels should be kept to a minimum; procurement policies must aim to reduce the use of hazardous material; government purchasing must prevent unnecessary waste; it must protect biodiversity, clean air, clean water, species' habitats, and natural capital. When unregulated, governments should use the safest course of action; governments should use only products the production, use, and disposal of which are environmentally safe as determined by appropriate regulatory standards, though it should treat such regulations as establishing minimal requirements, and be open to the possibility that genuine environmental protection may require more than compliance with such minimal standards.[17] When the cost of goods and services includes an analysis based on environmental and health impacts, the marginal costs of those goods and services typically increases. But such genuine costs must be considered and calculated. Only in this way can externalities created by the production, distribution, and use of those products be internalized, and the true costs of goods and services be determined.

Likewise, the impact of procurement policies and decisions on human populations must also be considered. Government purchasing policies should be good for the social well-being of the people associated with the production, delivery, and disposal of the goods it purchases. Social responsibility is a responsibility shared by governments. All government purchasing decisions should respect the United Nations Declaration of Human Rights and the United Nations International Labour Conventions. No government ought to purchase products the production or delivery of which has involved the use of child or forced labour (known as "no sweat" policies). Governments ought not to do business with any private sector organization that harms the health of any worker, that denies decent wages and appropriate benefits to its workers, or that engages in discrimination that is contrary to human rights. Governments must also ensure that the disposal of products purchased by them is undertaken in ways that protect vulnerable peoples; governments in Canada have an obligation to ensure that their hazardous wastes and toxic materials are not "dumped" in the Third World or in vulnerable communities within Canada, for example, where this endangers the life, health, or social well-being of persons in those locations.

Providers of goods or services who do not protect these values, and whose production processes degrade the physical environment, are unsustainable, or involve the exploitation of vulnerable populations or the violation of human rights, whether in its own jurisdictions or elsewhere, ought to be avoided, even if they could provide the good or service at the lowest cost. Thus procurement policies ought to be, in part, tailored to promote and reward corporate social and environmental responsibility. Likewise, in Canada, procurement policies ought to be responsive to the goals of employment equity, multiculturalism, and Aboriginal development.

In the interests of transparency and accountability,[18] all government contracts ought to be published, and such reporting should include the nature of the project, the contractor and any subcontractors employed, the dollar amount of the contract, and the final price for the work. The value of transparency is central to ensuring that these values are being met and public sector principles are being complied with. As it is the responsibility of public servants, especially senior public servants, to recommend, research, organize, and facilitate government procurement policies and procedures, there ought to be ongoing education and training for public servants involved in government procurement with respect to the values and principles that are necessary for sustainable and ethically responsible procurement policies and decisions.

4.6 POST-EMPLOYMENT

Conflict of interest rules continue to bind public servants even after they have permanently left their public service position.[19] Post-employment conflict of interest rules are designed to ensure that former public servants and public office holders not use contacts and relationships made within government, or knowledge acquired as public servants, for their own personal gain or for the benefit of private sector organizations.

> The public's confidence in the integrity and impartiality of the public service may be diminished if an official accepts employment from a firm with which he conducted official business before his resignation or retirement from government service. There would be grounds for suspicion that the official might have conferred benefits on the firm in the hope of future employment or that the firm might gain a competitive advantage by hiring an official who has had access to confidential information, including trade secrets.[20]*

*Kenneth Kernaghan, "Codes of Ethics and Public Administration: Progress, Problems and Prospects," *Public Administration* 58:2 (1980), p. 207–223. Copyright © 2008 John Wiley & Sons. Reproduced with permission of Blackwell Publishing Ltd.

Thus, when former public servants exploit their connections or information in proscribed ways, public trust and confidence in the fairness and impartiality of the public service is compromised. Managing such conflicts is part of every ethical government's attempt to introduce greater accountability and transparency into government workings, in order to build public trust.

The conflict of interest rules for public servants and former public servants in the *Public Service of Ontario Act*, for example, have five central provisions.

1) Prohibition on seeking preferential treatment.

Former public servants or public office holders have a professional and ethical duty not to use their former positions to seek preferential treatment from their former colleagues in the public service. Once a public servant has left the public service and is acting on behalf of a private sector entity or agency, he must not try to exploit his relationships with public servants to influence decision making in favour of the private sector entity or organization. To do so would compromise the integrity and impartiality of the public service, and could result in decisions that are not in the public interest but in the interest of the former public servant and those with whom the former public servant is now involved or on whose behalf he is now working.

2) Disclosure and misuse of confidential information.

Former public servants may have confidential information that they obtained in the course of performing their public sector duties. They have a duty not to disclose such information to any private party or entity once they leave the public service. This is, in part, related to the previous prohibition on seeking preferential treatment, because a former public servant might be able to use confidential information to obtain an unfair advantage in subsequent dealings with government. Using confidential information to obtain preferential treatment, or to obtain an unfair advantage in competition with other private sector organizations or entities, is a misuse of confidential information.

Information is generally considered confidential if it is not readily, easily, and widely available to members of the public. This could be information about government plans and priorities, government operations, and the like. But it might also be information about specific individuals or private sector organizations that has been obtained in the course of performing one's civil service duties (e.g., financial information about a person or organization obtained through work in a relevant government ministry such as Revenue Canada, medical information obtained through work in a health ministry, or information about private sector or university-based research obtained through an industry or education department). Having such information might provide a clear advantage to former public servants when they leave the public service and engage in private sector activities. Such information cannot be used for unfair advantage, whether the advantage would flow to the civil servant individually or to an organization or entity with which the civil servant becomes involved, whether as an employee, a consultant, or a partner. Likewise, former civil servants must not use personal information obtained about the status or activities of another person or entity for personal profit or competitive advantage.

3) Restrictions on lobbying.

Post-employment measures for public servants include restrictions on lobbying government. Every person or entity who lobbies the federal government is now bound by the *Lobbying Act*, which requires that all lobbying activities be registered. This provides an ongoing record of who is lobbying which government officials, in which government departments or agencies, and for what purpose. This promotes the value of transparency and is an important step in establishing public trust in government decision making.

But many public servants who have left the public service have themselves become lobbyists to government on behalf of private persons (perhaps even themselves) or organizations. Indeed, it would be naïve to deny that at least some of the value a former public servant brings to a private organization is his or her contacts in government, personal relationships with civil servants, and knowledge of government operations. But allowing these very relationships and insider knowledge to influence government decision making compromises the impartiality and fairness that we demand of government. Thus there are restrictions on post-employment lobbying activities by former public servants. The exact nature of the restriction may depend, in part, on the seniority or level of responsibility of the public service position in which the former civil servant was employed. Greater levels of responsibility within the public service typically are correlated with more extensive contacts and greater access to confidential information, and so are relevant to the post-employment duties that an individual is bound by.

But it must also be recognized that once a person leaves the civil service, he or she must enjoy the general rights and privileges of any member of society. While we impose significant restrictions on public servants while they are in the public service—restrictions on their freedom of expression insofar as they are not permitted to comment publicly on government policies or to criticize the decisions of their minister, for example, and restrictions on their rights to participate in democratic politics by the requirement of political neutrality—such restrictions surely cannot bind former public servants indefinitely once they leave the public service. Many public servants go on to stand for election, establish businesses in which the expertise they gained through their work for government is utilized, take up teaching positions in post-secondary institutions where they rely upon the knowledge they gained as public servants to inform their teaching and research, and so on. We must balance the rights of individual public servants against the interest we all share in having a neutral and fair public service. The balance has been struck by imposing time-limited restrictions on post-retirement lobbying, often for one year.

Public servants are generally restricted from lobbying another public servant who worked in a ministry or public body where the former public servant was also employed, for one year. Former public servants cannot lobby a ministry or minister where the public servant worked in the previous year. They generally ought not to lobby anyone who worked in a ministry where they also worked, again for one year.

4) Restrictions on employment.

Some former civil servants, by virtue of their senior position within the public service, may face further restrictions on their post-employment activities, in particular, restrictions on the kinds of positions they may take after leaving the civil service. Those who have served in designated senior positions in the public service may be restricted from certain kinds of employment once they leave the civil service, again for a period of one year. This restriction will be imposed on persons who have had substantial involvement with a public body, person, or entity while performing as a civil servant, and where that involvement gave the former civil servant access to confidential information that, if disclosed about the public body, person, or entity, could result in harm to the Crown. If, in discharging their responsibilities to a new employer or entity, former public servants would have to use information gained through their work as public servants—information that could give an unfair advantage to one or more persons—they again may be barred from taking up that employment for a period of one year. The same applies with respect to other post-employment activities, such as serving on a board of directors.

5) Restriction concerning certain transactions.

Anyone who advised the Crown regarding a particular matter as a public servant shall not advise or assist any private sector body, person, or entity with respect to the same matter. However, a former civil servant may continue to assist or advise the Crown on the same matter after leaving the public service.

The details of the specific rules governing post-employment activities of former civil servants are governed by relevant legislation, and differ across jurisdictions. Public servants must make a point of being aware of their duties in this respect. But though the rules vary in their details, the values underlying these post-employment restrictions are values we have seen before: democratic values, loyalty to the Crown, avoidance of conflict of interest, and fairness and impartiality.

The Treasury Board takes a pro-active approach to avoiding post-employment conflicts of interest, by requiring that government ministries and agencies put in place appropriate disclosure mechanisms. Under these mechanisms, public servants are to disclose their intentions with respect to future employment in a confidential report, and to discuss potential conflicts with their deputy head. This is designed to avoid perceived conflicts of interest before they occur. The deputy head will consider various factors in determining whether other activities need to be restricted besides those discussed above. Among the factors the deputy head should consider are the circumstances under which the termination occurred; general employment prospects of the former public servant; the significance to government of any information now possessed by the former public servant by virtue of his or her civil service position; the desirability of rapid transfer of skills from government to private sector or non-governmental organizations; the degree to which an employer might gain unfair advantage from the former civil servant's involvement in the organization; the ability of a prospective employer to gain an unfair bargaining advantage from the former civil servant's activities; and the degree or level of authority and influence that was possessed by the former civil servant while in public service.

Generally there is a limitation period of 12 months in which the post-employment activities of former civil servants are restricted. During this time they cannot be appointed to a board of directors or accept employment with entities with which they personally or through subordinates had significant official dealings during the last 12 months of employment in the civil service. During the period of restriction, they may not make representations for or on behalf of persons or organizations to any organization or department with which they personally or through subordinates had significant official dealings during their last year in the public service. And they may not give advice to clients using information that was acquired through their employment in government that is not generally available to the public. These restrictions are required to limit influence peddling, conflicts of interest and conflicts of commitment, and unethical lobbying activities. More positively, they help to ensure the impartiality, fairness, and confidentiality of the public service. They promote public confidence in the civil service and the perception that decisions made by public servants are in the public interest.[21]

QUESTIONS FOR FURTHER DISCUSSION

1. What does corruption entail in the context of public service organizations?

2. What are some of the more serious consequences of corruption for the public service?

3. How can corruption undermine the legitimacy of a government?

4. Does loyalty require that public servants fulfil all of their political bosses' requests or instructions? Why or why not?

5. What are the four kinds of costs associated with corruption? In your view, which one is the most serious, and why?

6. Explain the difference between apparent and actual conflict of interest.

7. In what circumstances do conflicts of interest commonly arise?

8. What are some of the ways public servants can avoid risk of conflict of interest?

9. Can conflicts of interest exist outside the public service workplace? If so, then how?

10. Under what (limited) conditions might public servants accept gifts?

11. How would you, the public servant, differentiate between a bribe and a gift? What might qualify something as a bribe (or gift)?

12. In what ways might public servants misuse government resources?

13. How can procurement policies contribute to ethical conduct?

14. What are some of the limitations to having open and competitive procurement policies?

15. What kinds of considerations should public servants consider when drafting procurement policies?

16. List and explain all five ways that conflicts of interest can occur even after employment in the public service has ended.

17. Have you experienced corruption in other employment situations you have been involved in? If so, what form did it take and what do you think were the principal causes of it?

In applying the information provided in this chapter, consider Cases 2, 3, 5, 6, 7, 8, 10, 15, 16, 18, 22, 23, 25, 26, and 29.

NOTES

[1] Stephen Potts, "Ethics in Public Service: An Idea Whose Time has Come," in Charles Sampford and Noel Preston, eds., with C.-A. Bois, *Public Sector Ethics: Finding and Implementing Values* (NY: Routledge, 1998): 85, p. 86. See also George T. Abed and Sanjeev Gupta, eds., *Governance, Corruption, and Economic Performance* (Washington DC: International Monetary Fund, 2003); Frank Anechiarico and James B. Jacobs, *The Pursuit of Absolute Integrity:*

How Corruption Control Makes Government Ineffective (Chicago: University of Chicago Press, 1998); Arnold J. Heidenheimer and Michael Johnston, eds., *Political Corruption: Concepts and Contexts*, 3rd ed. (London: Transaction Publishers, 2002); Robert Klitgaard, *Controlling Corruption* (Berkeley: University of California Press, 1991); Robert Klitgaard, Ronald Maclean-Abaroa, and H. Lindsey Parris, *Corrupt Cities: A Practical Guide to Cure and Prevention* (Oakland, CA: ICS Press, 2000); John Langford and Allan Tupper, eds., *Corruption, Character and Conduct* (Toronto: Oxford University Press, 1994); Peter Larmour and Nick Wolanin, eds., *Corruption and Anti-Corruption* (Canberra: Asia Pacific Press, 2001); Seumas Miller, Peter Roberts, and Edward Spence, *Corruption and Anti-Corruption: An Applied Philosophical Approach* (New Jersey: Prentice Hall, 2002); Noel Preston and Charles Sampford, eds., *Encouraging Ethics and Challenging Corruption* (Sydney: Federation Press, 2002); Susan Rose-Ackerman, *Corruption and Government: Causes, Consequences and Reform* (Cambridge: Cambridge University Press, 1999).

[2] Potts 1998, p. 86.

[3] Transparency International http://www.transparency.org.news-room/faq/corruption-faq[4].

[4] G. Brumback, "Institutionalizing Ethics in Government," *Public Personnel Management* 20 (1991): 353.

[5] Transparency International http://www.transparency.org/news_room/faq/corruption_faq [4].

[6] Transparency International http://www.transparency.org/news_room/faq/corruption_faq [4].

[7] Potts 1998, p. 85.

[8] Potts 1998, p. 85.

[9] Transparency International http://www.transparency.org/news_room/faq/corruption_faq [4].

[10] Potts 1998, p. 86.

[11] Transparency International http://www.transparency.org.news-room/faq/corruption-faq[4].

[12] See Part IV of the *Criminal Code*: Offences Against the Administration of Law and Justice.

[13] Preston 2007, pp. 156–157.

[14] Public Service Staff Relations Act Decision, Between Maurice Dudley Atkins, Grievor, and Treasury Board (Ministry of Transport), Employer, March 21 1974, File 166-2-889 (internal references omitted).

[15] Kernaghan 1974, p. 531.

[16] Karen Howlett. "$30,000 for 78 hours: Scandal grows at eHealth Ontario." *The Globe and Mail*. Aug. 13, 2009. This example will be revisited again below.

[17] See, for example, http://www.sdinfo.gc.ca/ and http://www.tpsgc-pwgsc.gc.ca/services/ntrprss-bsnsss-eng.html for relevant federal policies and procedures.

[18] See Mel Dubnick, "Clarifying Accountability: An Ethical Theory Framework" in Charles Sampford and Noel Preston, eds., with C.-A. Bois, *Public Sector Ethics: Finding and Implementing Values* (NY: Routledge, 1998): 68; and John Tait, "A Strong Foundation: Report of the Task Force on Public Service Values and Ethics," *Canadian Public Administration* 40:1 (1996), p. 1

[19] See Preamble to *2006 Conflict of Interest and Post-Employment Code for Public Office Holders* (federal), which consolidates rules from the Treasury Board and the *Public Service Ontario Act.*

[20] Kernaghan 1980, pp. 213–214.

[21] See Treasury Board Web site for a brief history of efforts from 1978 onwards to limit the influence of former public servants once they have left government (e.g., the Grandy/Reisman affair).

CHAPTER 5

Professional Values

We treat public service as a profession in itself. Those engaged in government work may also be members of further professions, such as research scientists, physicians, engineers, accountants, and lawyers. Professionals, such as physicians, lawyers, accountants and engineers, share certain characteristics that distinguish them as professionals and their work as a profession. First, professionals have mastery of a specialized, esoteric field of knowledge. Second, they wield a considerable amount of authority. Their judgments must typically be accepted at least in part as a matter of trust. This second characteristic is tied to the first. It is because they have specialized knowledge that they have authority. It is typically not possible for an average member of the public, or their clients, to fully evaluate the advice they receive from professionals, because the knowledge the professional has is not readily attainable without considerable study or research. Third, professionals have considerable autonomy in the exercise of their professional responsibilities. They are largely self-directed in the practice of their professions. They are, furthermore, self-regulating. They determine within their professional bodies the standards of competent practice for their members, and determine and apply their own codes of conduct. Because of the considerable authority professionals enjoy, and their self-regulation, professionals stand in the relationship of fiduciaries with respect to their clients. That is, professionals are duty bound to use their knowledge to make decisions that are in the interests of their clients, rather than in their own personal interest. They must exercise their authority for the good of their clients rather than for personal gain. Thus **fiduciary** relationships involve an important element of trust. In exchange for accepting the authority of professionals, their clients expect them to exercise their authority for the latter's benefit, and the regulations that professionals impose upon themselves are designed to maintain the trustworthiness of the professionals in their practice.

It is a matter of some controversy whether civil servants as a group are professionals or not. Given that professionals are characterized by multiple interrelated criteria, and so some groups might meet some but not all of the conditions, the designation of various groups as professional or not is not always easy to make. But the civil service shares many characteristics of professions. And to the extent that they are a professional group, public servants have the fiduciary duties that come with that status.

In order to know what the fiduciary duties applying to civil servants are, however, we need to be clearer about who is the client of this profession. And again the mediated relationship between the public service and the Crown/government and the public is evident in our answer. It is for the good of the Crown/government and the public that civil servants ought to apply their knowledge and exercise their authority, yet typically this requires in practice that they act in the best interests of their minister or equivalent government official. They act in the interests of the elected government by performing their duties honestly, conscientiously, and, well, professionally. They must use the specialized knowledge they have to provide the best advice they can with respect to policy options. They must make recommendations based on an honest and good faith assessment of the relative merits of those options. They must exercise their authority in the service of the interests of the government and the interests of citizens, rather than their own interests. As we saw in Chapter 3, public servants may find themselves in a very difficult situation when their assessment of what is good for the government differs significantly from what they think will be good for citizens or the common good. Despite the vast differences in the kinds of work performed by public servants, there are some common requirements of professional responsibility that apply to public servants generally.

5.1 KNOWLEDGE AND EXPERTISE

Professionalism requires adherence to six basic principles:

- objectivity,
- professional competence,
- due care,
- integrity,
- confidentiality, and
- trustworthiness.

Public servants must be *objective* in how they employ their expertise. They must adopt practices that are relevant, reliable, comparable, or replicable, as the case may be. They must utilize quality evidence in the development of their recommendations and advice. They must also avoid conflicts of interest, bias, and undue influence from others in fulfilling their duty of objectivity. If their advice is tainted by personal interest, by considerations extraneous to the matter in question, or by personal biases, then the objectivity of their advice is compromised.

Professionals have specialized knowledge, and they have a duty to maintain their knowledge at a very high level, to be aware of developments in their areas of expertise, to keep abreast of new developments within their area of knowledge, and to be aware of best practices in their areas of responsibility. Insofar as their work involves the employment of technical expertise, they must develop and maintain their technical skills. This class of duties might be called duties of *competence*. Public servants are required to maintain their professional knowledge and skills at a level that enables them to competently perform their employment responsibilities. They must also exercise *due care* in the performance of their duties. They must employ their skills carefully, on the assigned task or mandate, in a timely manner. They must make known to their superiors any limitations that might compromise their ability to competently execute their responsibilities.

Integrity refers to a set of inter-related practical virtues. To act with integrity requires that a person act honestly. Honesty, in turns, requires more than just refraining from saying things that one knows to be false. One can mislead by withholding relevant information, and giving partial truths. Integrity requires that one not deceive by any means. It also requires that one not make reckless statements, or draw conclusions based on inadequate evidence, or over-state the evidence for one's opinions. It requires full disclosure, not only of relevant information, but an honest reporting of the strength of one's evidence for any advice, along with a frank admission when one's knowledge is incomplete, and of any weaknesses in the evidence supporting a particular recommendation, and the degree to which there is reasonable disagreement with respect to some matter. Integrity requires recognition of one's own fallibility, and honest reporting of the relative strength of competing positions with respect to the matter at hand.

Public servants often receive or have access to confidential information in the course of performing their duties. They accordingly have two duties to maintain *confidentiality*. First, they must protect against the wrongful disclosure of such information. And, second, they must not use confidential information for personal gain or benefit, or for other wrongful purposes.

Finally, public servants must act in ways that do not bring disrepute to their profession. They must not promise things they cannot deliver, exaggerate their level of competence or ability, or engage in actions that compromise the *trustworthiness* of the civil service. These characteristics of professionalism are also important in enhancing the public perception of the stability, coherence, and legitimacy of the institutional structure of government. Like the perception of conflict of interest, the perception of unprofessionalism of the civil service, whether it is a perceived or actual lack of objectivity, competence, integrity, confidentiality, or trustworthiness, adds to a general breakdown of public confidence in the institutional structure of government as a whole, or the specific ministry being represented. Either way, unprofessionalism leads to a lack of confidence in government.

5.2 POLITICAL NEUTRALITY

Political neutrality is considered one of the most important requirements for good public service, but it is also one of the most difficult ideas to implement in society. This is so primarily because of the balancing act that must go into trying to respect the political rights of public servants as citizens, on the one hand, and the need for public servants to remain politically neutral as public servants, on the other. That is to say, there is "an enduring tension between political rights and political neutrality for public servants."[1]* Kenneth Kernaghan has written widely on the delicate balance between political rights and neutrality. While we do not engage this particular debate in this book, it is important to point out that there are several arguments for both sides of the debate. The issue is not to pick a side of the debate, but to try to find ways of securing the citizenship rights of public servants while simultaneously ensuring that their public service remains neutral with respect to public policy, acts, and so on. In what follows, we flesh out what the idea of political neutrality means for the public sector.

Political neutrality is essential for building and maintaining trust between politicians and public servants. Its advice cannot be partisan; its delivery of government services cannot be contingent on public servants sharing the political values, ideological or philosophical perspective, or party affiliation of the government enacting the policy. The public service is charged with the execution of political decisions made by those entrusted by the public to make such decisions on their behalf. The continuity of the public service depends upon its ability to serve the government of the day, irrespective of political affiliation. Thus public servants are required to refrain from any activity that would impair their political neutrality or the neutrality of the public service, and to avoid the appearance of political partiality. Political neutrality supports the impartial administration of the administration of law, as well as impartiality in the implementation of public

*Kenneth Kernaghan, "Political Rights and Political Neutrality: Finding the Balance Point" *Canadian Public Administration* 29:4 (1986), p. 639–652.

policy, and in the delivery of public services, all of which constitute the core activities of public servants. One way of ensuring such impartiality is to insist that individuals be appointed to the public service on the basis of merit rather than on the basis of political affiliation, but it may also require further ongoing restrictions on partisan political activities by civil servants once they have joined the public service in order to ensure that they perform their central functions impartially and are perceived to be impartial by members of the public.

Kernaghan has provided the standard framework for thinking about the requirement of political neutrality, distilled into six principles. Those principles are

1. that there should be a clear division of labour between politicians and public servants,

2. that appointments to the civil service ought to be based on merit,

3. that public servants should not engage in partisan activities,

4. that public servants should not publicly comment on political decisions,

5. that public servants should provide full and frank advice to the politicians they advise, and

6. that public servants must faithfully implement the decisions taken by their political bosses.

First, there is a basic *division of labour* between public servants and their political bosses. Politicians make policy decisions, and may properly be influenced by overtly political considerations in doing so. Public servants, by contrast, are charged with the administration of such policies. Public servants execute the decisions made by others. Of course, this is something of a fiction, and it is in part because civil servants, especially those relatively highly placed in the organizational hierarchy, exercise considerable influence on the development of policy that we must be concerned to develop an ethics regime in the public service.

Second, public servants must be appointed and promoted to positions based on *merit*, rather than political party affiliation or support for a particular political party or candidate. Having a merit-based civil service is important for ensuring the highest quality public programs, and political neutrality helps to ensure that civil service positions are based on merit rather than political affiliation. It is also important for ensuring that the civil service is broadly representative of the members of Canadian society and that opportunities within it are genuinely open to all. The contrast to a merit-based public service is all-too-familiar: appointments are based not on professional qualifications or experience but on who you know. The public service becomes a site of cronyism, favouritism, and political patronage. Those who contribute to the success of a particular politician, or who donate large sums of money to a political party, are rewarded with plum patronage appointments in the civil service. The requirement of political neutrality operates as a check to such abuse.

Third, to realize the perception of political neutrality, public servants may be barred from participating in *partisan political activities*, or their right to participate in such activities may be limited without being banned outright. Prohibited activities may include holding office in a political party, campaigning for a candidate in an election, fund-raising for a particular party or candidate, or donating to a political party. They may also include seeking nomination as or running as a candidate in an election. More generally, carrying on any activity in support of or within or in opposition to a political party, or carrying on any activity in support of or in opposition to any political candidate before or during an election, may be activities deemed inconsistent with the requirement of political neutrality.

Although described by Kenneth Kernaghan and John Langford as a "constitutional convention," there is actually considerable variation across federal and provincial/territorial jurisdictions in Canada with respect to prohibitions on participation in partisan political activities.[2] Some provinces, such as British Columbia, allow considerably more political activity among civil servants than others do. Other provinces allow such activities, but require that public servants receive prior permission from their deputy minister or other designated official in advance, or that they take a leave of absence from their position in the public service while engaged in the activities. But even when political activities are allowed, the civil servant must ensure that her activities do not compromise her ability to perform her duties impartially, and do not create a perception of partiality that could bring the civil service into disrepute.

Civil servants may thus be asked to accept, as a condition of employment, restrictions on a range of political activities that are otherwise lawful and ethical in a free and democratic society. Their rights as members of Canadian society to engage in political activities must be balanced with need for political neutrality and impartiality in the public service. Governments try to strike the right balance between the rights of political engagement and participation, on the one hand, and the restrictions on political activities necessary for a well-functioning civil service, on the other. The most permissive jurisdictions allow engagement in any political activity so long as it does not interfere with, or is not reasonably perceived to interfere with, the ability of the public servant to perform her duties in a politically impartial manner.

The restrictions on public servants that prevent perceptions of partisan bias and protect political neutrality vary from one jurisdiction to another, and change over time. But all public servants will face some restrictions, whether on explicit political activity such as running for election, or on post-employment activities when they leave the civil service. While some specific restrictions have been held by courts to be excessive, the general right to restrict partisan activities by public servants has been upheld as a permissible infringement of their rights. As the Federal Court of Canada (Trial Division) explained, "[A] public servant entering the public service must or should realize that the political neutrality required will necessarily result in some curtailment of his or her partisan political activity even if this involves some restriction on freedom of speech or freedom of association. These restrictions should be as few as possible and no more than are necessary to attain the objective of political neutrality."[3]

Fourth, public servants must *refrain from publicly commenting* on the policies adopted by government. Public servants are expected to neither criticize nor defend the policy decisions of elected officials. Public servants do not comment on or debate the wisdom of policy decisions. This requirement poses a serious restriction on the freedom of expression enjoyed by public servants, and the precise contours of the restriction are unclear. First, a distinction is drawn between public *comment* and public *criticism*. This is necessary because civil servants are often called upon to explain policies and to account for the administration of policies, to the media, parliamentarians or councillors, and the public. To fulfil this function, they must be able to comment on and provide relevant factual background information with respect to the policies they administer. But they must not offer evaluations of those policies, either positive or negative. It is not the role of public servants to defend policy decisions or to criticize them. Second, it is important that public servants do not disclose advice or recommendations given to ministers. Nor should they speculate publicly about future policy options or directions. Finally, public servants must refrain from using their position in the civil service to give additional weight to their purely personal opinions about political issues.

While this description seems sufficiently concrete to provide practical guidance to civil servants, many issues with respect to the restriction on public criticism of government policies remain obscure. Should these restrictions be limited to commenting on policies that are directly related to the public servant's duties or department? Should they be allowed to criticize another department or government? Should an engineer working for one department be allowed to criticize proposed changes to an income supplement policy, for example, or should civil servants in a provincial or municipal government be allowed to criticize policy emanating from the federal government? Different jurisdictions respond to such issues differently, and the prudent public servant will seek advice from his or her administrative superior or deputy minister for clarification before engaging in public evaluation of government actions.

As we shall see below, when we discuss whistle-blowing, or disclosure of wrongdoing, the restriction on public criticism is further limited to lawful actions. The duty to refrain from public comment on political policies extends only to policies that are lawful and ethical. If a public servant is aware of government activities that are illegal, or that pose a serious risk of harm to the life, health, or safety of persons or the environment, he might have a permission, or even a duty, to publicly expose the wrongdoing or risk.

Fifth, public servants must fully and frankly *express their opinions* about the wisdom of various policy options in private to the government officials they advise. In exchange, politicians do not disclose those opinions or the advice they receive from individual civil servants, and take public responsibility for the decisions taken by their department or agency. Politicians, not public servants, defend the decisions of government in public.

While we might have brought up the following point anywhere in this discussion, we note here that the political neutrality demanded of public servants is one side of a coin, the other side of which is ministerial responsibility. While ministers (cabinet or its municipal counterparts) are collectively responsible for the decisions made by government, individual ministers are personally responsible for both the adoption and administration of policies within their own departments and related agencies. Ministers answer to the legislature or council for everything that happens in their departments; they must explain and defend all actions and decisions taken within their departments. If serious error, mismanagement, incompetence, breach of law, or serious breach of ethics occurs, the minister should take responsibility for the failing and resign. Public servants are protected from having to answer to the legislature in either of these ways by their political neutrality; they answer instead to their minister.

Sixth, and finally, public servants *execute the decisions* taken by their political bosses loyally and in good faith, regardless of their personal opinions about those decisions. In return, civil servants enjoy job security through regime changes and security of tenure, and can be dismissed only for cause.[4] Thus, while even civil servants might be laid off if the government decides it must reduce the size of government in times of financial constraint or if government operations are reorganized in such a way that some staff members are no longer needed, they cannot be fired just because the government of the day was defeated in a political election and a different political party has been elected. To say that they can be fired 'only for cause' is similarly to say that they cannot be dismissed because their own political affiliations differ from those of the new government, but instead requires a failure to satisfactorily perform their professional responsibilities.

This model of the politically neutral and ideologically impartial civil service is, of course, something of an ideal, not fully realized or even realizable in the world as it is. Civil servants are people, after all, and they have political persuasions and loyalties that this picture masks. Nevertheless, the ideal is a worthy one, describing a separation of responsibilities that enables a professional, merit-based, continuous public service to persist through changes of government, and that contributes to good government by providing honest and objective advice to politicians in their development of policy. No doubt some civil servants have considerable influence in the development of government policies, and perhaps rightly so, given their expertise, experience, and access to information. But if governments are to trust the advice they receive, and believe that their decisions will be effectively implemented and their programs properly administered, the requirement of political neutrality in the public service is of central importance. If appointments to the civil service were to be based on political patronage, or the performance of the public service in executing government decisions and delivering government services were to be contingent on civil servants sharing the political convictions or affiliation of the politicians adopting such policies, or if civil servants were to work to actively undermine the credibility of government decisions because of political rivalry, or if a sizable portion of the public service were to be replaced every time a new political party or council was elected, good government would be impossible. The public good could not possibly be served under an overtly partisan public service.

To weaken in any significant way the requirements of political neutrality in the public service would have serious repercussions on the relationship between public servants and their ministers, and between public servants and the people. If public servants had to answer to the legislature or council not just for their performance of designated or delegated administrative matters, but for their contributions to policy development or adoption, this would necessarily politicize the public service. It would undermine individual ministerial responsibility, involve public servants in political controversies, link specific policies to individual public servants, and undermine the system of public service tenure.

The requirements of political neutrality have become even more complex in the age of the Internet, and especially with the widespread use of popular social networking sites such as Facebook, Twitter, LinkedIn, and MySpace. Public servants who maintain personal social networking sites or pages may well be tempted to include information about their work, or to make personal comments about government activities (including but not limited to those with which they are directly involved) on their personal pages. Such a practice is fraught with danger, however. Posting to social networking sites should be treated as public comment; it should be treated as equivalent to making comments to the media or in public forums. Thus the duties to protect government information and to refrain from public criticism of government policies or practices extend to public expression on the Internet.

Through a series of initiatives begun in 1918, successive governments in Canada have worked to stem the degree to which appointment to the civil service in based on patronage and political loyalties.[5] As a result, patronage is much less rampant in our civil service now than it used to be. Patronage still exists, of course, especially in appointments to the boards and senior management of Crown agencies and commissions, and through the employment of individuals outside the permanent public service through contracts and consulting arrangements. No doubt these areas of government will come under increasing scrutiny in the coming years.

Yet this model of political neutrality and ministerial responsibility seems to have come under threat in recent years. Despite its fundamental importance to maintaining an independent and professional public service owing loyalty to the Crown, a number of very high profile public servants have recently felt the need to publicly expose what they considered to be serious wrongdoing or mismanagement in government. Linda Keen, former President of the Canadian Nuclear Safety Commission, was fired and publicly denounced by the federal government after making allegations of safety violations in the operation of a Canadian nuclear power plant; Richard Colvin's testimony at the House of Commons special committee on the Canadian mission in Afghanistan, in which he alleged that the Minister of Defence knew Afghan detainees were being abused by Afghan security forces once they were handed over by the Canadian military, has led to repeated allegations against him by federal government spokespersons.[6] These and similar cases challenge the model described above. In these cases, public servants raised their concerns with their political bosses and were ignored or ordered to keep quiet. When they felt compelled to bring their allegations to the public, they were denounced, ridiculed, and subjected to relentless negative propaganda by the government. Both their motives and their competence were questioned. Their treatment, and the treatment of other public servants who have felt compelled to bring concerns about government actions to the public, threatens the relationship between public servants and elected officials. It offends the principle of ministerial responsibility and the political neutrality of the civil service, at least in the mind of the public, when they are told that the allegations are politically motivated. Such cases should be kept in mind when reading the section on whistle-blowing below.

5.3 RESPONSIBILITY

Political neutrality should not be confused with ethical neutrality or used as a shield for unethical conduct. Individual public servants must take responsibility for their decisions and their actions in the workplace. The challenge has been characterized well by Geuras and Garofalo:

> It is often difficult to identify the responsible party in large organizations. Individuals can easily hide behind what Dennis Thompson (1985) calls the "ethic of neutrality" and the "ethic of structure." With the ethic of neutrality,

> the public administrator is expected to be compliant, even
> blindly obedient, to the dictates of elected officials and orga-
> nizational superiors, while the ethic of structure mandates
> that no single individual may be held responsible for deci-
> sions and actions, since it is the organization itself that is
> responsible. To the extent that the ethic of neutrality and the
> ethic of structure are operational in public agencies, there is
> a corresponding absence of individual responsibility.[7]*

Public servants have a duty to move beyond these incentives to avoid responsibility. They cannot rely on the "many-hands" problem to escape responsibility for their own judgments and decisions. And when armed with good tools for moral reasoning, they will not need to.

Drawing on the work of Geuras and Garofalo, as well as that of Carol Lewis, we can identify six principles relevant to the issue of personal responsibility. One cannot evade personal responsibility by

1. hiding behind superiors ("I was just following orders"),
2. hiding behind subordinates ("I told Bob to do it"),
3. claiming ignorance ("I didn't know it was being done"),
4. failing to exercise whatever discretion one has ("My responsibility was just . . . "),
5. justifying wrongdoing in the name of good objectives ("Good ends don't justify bad means"), and
6. accepting incompetence ("I did the best I could").

First, it is never an adequate justification for wrongdoing to say that one was "*just following orders*." "[O]ne principle relating to personal responsibility is that we cannot hide behind our boss or our desk to escape it."[8]† Even if you just "go along to get along," that is a choice for which you must bear responsibility.

Likewise, we cannot *hide behind our subordinates*, blaming our failures on those below us in the organizational hierarchy. Managers are responsible for the decisions and conduct of subordinates, whether they were personally aware of such decisions or conduct or not. With increased authority in the organizational structure comes increased responsibility, and managers have a duty to provide effective oversight of subordinates; failure in this obligation does not excuse.

---

*Dean Geuras and Charles Garofalo, *Practical Ethics in Public Administration*, p. 111. Copyright © 2002 Management Concepts Press.

†Dean Geuras and Charles Garofalo, *Practical Ethics in Public Administration*, p. 112. Copyright © 2002 Management Concepts Press.

Third, *ignorance is no excuse*, and you cannot use ignorance to escape responsibility. "The third principle of individual responsibility is that we cannot hide behind our own ignorance. As Lewis contends, '[A] profession is defined largely by its specialized knowledge, on which its privileges rest. Ignorance here undercuts all members' (68). Furthermore, 'specialized knowledge is a source of considerable power in today's information society . . .' (69). Therefore, as a manager, you must decide and act, in the public interest, on the basis of the most accurate, complete, and up-to-date information available."[9]* We agree, but think this is true of all public servants, not just managers.

Fourth, as individuals we are responsible both for what we do and how we do it if we have any *discretion* at all. "Our discretion and expertise are critical elements in meeting our responsibilities, whether we are at the top, in the middle, or at the bottom of the organization, whether we are policy analysts, human resources specialists, or so-called street-level bureaucrats such as police officers, teachers, or life guards. Our choices count and affect citizens in many different ways. So the responsible use of our discretion and expertise matter."[10]†

A fifth principle is that *both means and ends matter*. Using immoral means even to achieve good ends, and using moral means to protect, preserve, or accomplish immoral ends, are both unethical. (To this extent, we are not pure act utilitarians.) An ethical public servant evaluates both means and ends, and takes responsibility for judgments concerning both.

Finally, individual responsibility extends to basic *competence* on the job. It is unethical for public servants to perform incompetently, and unethical for incompetence to be tolerated. "Public agencies . . . must move to a culture of performance and a commitment to competence as an ethical standard—if the idea of advancing the public good carries any weight among serious public administrators."[11]‡ We will return at the end of this chapter, after discussing the other central elements required for professional public service, to the notion of competence as an ethical requirement, and summarize the capacities that make up professional competence in the public service.

The emphasis here on individual or personal responsibility is not meant to deny that organizational culture and institutional ethos are also important in achieving an ethical public service, nor to deny that good people often engage in wrongdoing because of poor organizational structures and institutional cultures. But it is to insist that even the best institutional culture can achieve ethical conduct

*Dean Geuras and Charles Garofalo, *Practical Ethics in Public Administration*, p. 112. Copyright © 2002 Management Concepts Press.

†Dean Geuras and Charles Garofalo, *Practical Ethics in Public Administration*, p. 113. Copyright © 2002 Management Concepts Press.

‡Dean Geuras and Charles Garofalo, *Practical Ethics in Public Administration*, p. 114. Copyright © 2002 Management Concepts Press.

only if its members take personal responsibility for making ethically sound judgments and decisions. Rationalizations of unethical conduct ("everyone does it," "it's not my responsibility," "if I don't do it someone else will") cannot be tolerated from any member, regardless of their place in the organizational hierarchy.

5.4 CONFIDENTIALITY AND USE OF INFORMATION

Public servants at all levels are governed by a range of confidentiality requirements. Such federal legislation as the *Privacy Act* (1985), the *Security of Information Act* (1985), and the *Personal Information Protection and Electronic Documents Act* (updated 2006) govern the conduct of federal civil servants. Parallel legislation exists with respect to provincial, territorial, and municipal employees. Additional legislation or regulations exist for employees who work with sensitive information, such as health records, taxation, immigration, statistics, corrections, law enforcement, and national defence, or are involved in labour negotiations or litigation. The requirement that government employees maintain the confidentiality of any information available as a result of their duties has been a feature of public service since 1867, and the common law origins of this duty extend considerably farther back in British legal history. In addition to the clarification of the duty of confidentiality to be discerned from the common law and the various governing statutory and regulatory legal schemes, public service employees are typically required to take an oath of office or oath of secrecy as a condition of their employment in government. Such oaths, along with other confidentiality provisions in codes of conduct or ethics codes, are designed to ensure that all public employees are aware of the confidentiality requirements that apply to them. Given the multiple layers of legislation, however, and the rapidity of change in this area as governments scramble to keep up with evolving information technologies, government departments are well advised to provide regular training with respect to the confidentiality requirements that apply to any particular group of workers. Prospective public servants may find the services of the federal **Privacy Commissioner**, or provincial Information and Privacy Commissioners, helpful.[12]

There are actually two different duties with respect to information and confidentiality. The first is that public servants must safeguard any personal information collected by their agency or ministry. The second, as we have already mentioned, is the duty not to misuse confidential information for private gain. Public servants must not knowingly take advantage of, or benefit from, information obtained in performance of their duties, where that information is not readily available to the public. We have discussed this duty earlier, under the Conflicts of Interest heading (4.2). The duty not to misuse information acquired in the course of performing one's official duties or by virtue of one's position in the civil service also includes a requirement that such information not be used for illegal purposes, such as aiding a terrorist organization, a criminal organization, or a foreign enemy.

5.5 SAFEGUARDING CONFIDENTIAL INFORMATION

Public servants have a duty to safeguard public assets, including information. What information a public servant should legitimately access will depend upon the mandate of his or her organization, of course, and public servants ought not to access information that is not needed to fulfil their responsibilities. A public servant working in national defence should not use her contacts in government to gain access to the financial information of a person she is dating, for example. Every government department or agency should have operating procedures and a policy framework to protect the private information of citizens, and public servants ought to respect the jurisdictional boundaries safeguarding confidential information about citizens and residents. Moreover, any confidential information that public servants legitimately obtain with respect to the personal information of citizens must be shared only with those within their organizations who have a legitimate need to know it. Any and all information retained about particular individuals by either government departments or agencies must be kept as safe as possible. What exactly this latter duty requires will vary with innovations in technology and evolving protocols for information safety.

The duty to safeguard information, however, includes more than just information about private persons and non-governmental or private entities such as corporations, charities, and businesses. It also includes a duty to safeguard government information. It is a, perhaps regrettable, fact that effective government often depends upon secrecy and the safeguarding of government information. New policies often cannot be announced until they are ready to be implemented. Consider, for example, changes to the tax system, gun control, interest rates, military procurements, or land development. It is easy to imagine (or recall) the difficulty that can be occasioned if news of changes to these and innumerable other government policies is leaked in advance of their official announcement and implementation. If a public servant violates confidentiality and tells private persons about such changes, there is a possibility of insider trading occurring or other actions being taken that provide unfair benefits to those individuals who can take advantage of the information for private gain. In other cases, advance information may make it possible for some people to circumvent the intention of the changes, for example, by purchasing weapons that are about to be made illegal before the change is announced, or by converting investments from one form to another prior to such changes being prohibited. In the case of high-ranking public servants, the effect of leaking or selectively disclosing confidential information can be extremely damaging to government, as when a public servant discloses information about the government's strategy in labour negotiations, or litigation strategy before an international trade tribunal, or with respect to domestic law enforcement or external military operations. Obviously disclosure of such information is inconsistent with the duty of loyalty to the Crown.

Yet good government depends upon the open flow of information between ministries and other government agencies, as well as between civil servants. It is an oft-heard complaint by the public in dealing with government that "the left hand doesn't know what the right hand is doing." When there is inadequate information sharing between various government departments, inefficiencies arise. These take many forms; duplication of work is one of the most common, with different agencies researching the same issue or developing policies to address the same problems. But even more seriously from a public service point of view, without adequate information sharing between government departments, genuinely inconsistent policies can arise, which often work to the detriment of citizens. Citizens facing genuinely inconsistent requirements, directions, regulations, and policies cannot effectively order their own affairs to comply with such directions or regulations, or effectively access services. Citizens find themselves being shuffled from one government department to another, often while each department passes the buck with respect to which department is responsible for ultimately dealing with the issue. Examples of this kind of inefficiency are numerous, and they leave citizens feeling confused at best, completely frustrated at worst. To avoid these inefficiencies, it is essential that information sharing at a high level of institutional position take place.

We have also noted that one of the most important duties of public servants is to provide full and accurate information to ministers. This may require sharing information obtained from other departments, and specific operational policies must be in place that indicate clearly who is authorized to obtain information from other government departments or agencies, for which purposes, and to whom such information may be disclosed. But the bottom line is that ministers or other elected officials are entitled to any information that civil servants have obtained in the course of fulfilling their responsibilities.

Many public servants are professionals and members of professional associations, such as lawyers, accountants, physicians, and engineers. As such, they are also governed by specific professional codes that may contain provisions respecting the use of confidential information. Information sharing for such individuals must comply not only with their duty to the Crown, but their professional obligations under such codes.

Although public servants are responsible, in the first instance, to their ministers, they are often called to account to parliamentarians in parliamentary committees or to advise such committees. This again requires the sharing of confidential information. Parliamentarians must be able to monitor the implementation and administration of government programs, and their ability to do so often depends upon information from public servants. If public servants are permitted to keep secret relevant information from elected officials, then abuses of administrative authority, corruption, and mismanagement may be hidden.

Without full information, including relevant background information and information about the way decisions have been made, parliamentarians would be unable to perform their oversight function. Such a situation would also vest extraordinary power in public servants. Information often is, indeed, power, and if it is held by only a few very high-ranking public servants, those people would have undue power within government. Decisions cannot be fully evaluated without relevant background information, including information about which options were considered, why those that were rejected were rejected, and why those chosen were chosen. Without such information, it would be impossible to determine if decisions were being made that reflect ignorance or inadequate research, failure to consider viable options, personal bias or interest, wilful blindness or other improper considerations. Thus while public servants must not disclose the bases of policy decisions, and the advice given to ministers, to the public directly, they must make such information available to parliamentarians, councillors, or board chairs.

5.6 THE PUBLIC'S RIGHT TO KNOW THE PUBLIC'S BUSINESS

While it seems obvious that public servants must safeguard and not misuse information obtained in the course of their employment for personal gain, or in ways that provide unfair advantage to others, or in ways that would undermine the effectiveness of government policies, secrecy in government is increasingly challenged. It stands in opposition to other important values, most notably transparency and accountability. This set of interests is also reflected in legislation, such as the *Access to Information Act* (1985), and similar legislation at the provincial and municipal levels. It is reflected in such policies as those requiring that city council meetings be open to the public, and in the creation of positions of auditors-general and ombudsmen, who oversee the activities of government and report to legislatures and the public. And it is reflected in the absolutely vital protection we afford to freedom of the press.

The tension between the need to safeguard confidential government information, on the one hand, and the values of open and accountable government, on the other, creates some of the most difficult ethical problems facing public servants. To navigate these potentially treacherous waters, we have distinguished between sharing of information within government, between public servants and their ministers, between public servants and parliamentarians (usually at the committee level), and between public servants themselves, on the one hand, and the sharing of information between public servants and the public at large, including through the media, on the other. We now address the latter.

Although the buzz words "open and transparent government" are commonplace, they are, as we have argued above, ultimately unrealistic. In many instances governments must keep secrets, in either the short term or the long term, including secrets from their own populations. Yet such secrecy obtains, excluding national defence and crime control perhaps, only with respect to *prospective* government policies. It does not apply to government decisions once they have been taken, or to the implementation and administration of government policies. The public does have a right to know about government operations, the actual costs and benefits of various government policies, and the administration of government programs.

Much of the information that the public has about government operations comes from the reports of auditors-general, ombudsmen, integrity commissioners, privacy commissioners, and the like. These are officers of government who report to the legislature and the public. We also receive information through the media, and various public interest groups, who obtain information about government operations and policies, often through Access to Information or Freedom of Information requests. And, finally, the public is informed about government actions through communications from ministers, councillors and board chairs, and government agencies and departments, themselves. Indeed, it is probably safe to say that the public has never enjoyed the level of access to information about government that it enjoys today. Government Web sites contain a wealth of information about government activities, which is supplemented with departmental reports of a wide variety, performance reports, internal audits, and evaluation reports, proactive disclosure of such items as expenses and contracts awarded, and much more.

Public servants have a duty to support such legitimate information sharing with the public. They have a duty to co-operate fully with the officers who are charged with overseeing government operations such as the Auditor General, to comply with Access to Information requests, and to answer media inquiries, subject to the constraints of political neutrality and the division of responsibilities between public servants and elected officials.

A number of high profile violations of this duty to let the people know the people's business have occurred over the years. The most recent at the time of writing this book followed a familiar pattern: biologist Kristi Miller, with the Department of Fisheries and Oceans, had conducted research into declining numbers of salmon in the Fraser River. She was forbidden to discuss her findings publicly, however, by "top bureaucrats in the Privy Council."[13] The pattern involves those who conduct research within government structures, government scientists most often, who are then forbidden to disclose the results of their work. This treats information gathered by government officials, through research financed by tax-payers, as the exclusive property of the government department or agency under whose auspices the research was conducted. This is a direct violation of the right of the public to know, and cannot be tolerated. The findings of any research conducted by public servants must be made known to the public, unless disclosure of it would violate the law or put the country at significant credible risk of an identifiable and serious harm.

Public servants who deal directly with the public in the provision of services have additional duties, namely, to be proactive in informing their clients of government services that pertain or may pertain to them. And public servants who are aware of serious wrongdoing in government also have duties, discussed in more detail in Chapter 9, to disclose such wrongdoing, either to their institutional superiors, to an Integrity Commissioner or equivalent, or even to the public directly if they in good faith believe that there is a serious and imminent risk of danger to the life, health, or safety of persons or the natural environment. This duty obtains even if fulfilling it requires the disclosure of confidential government information. Of course such a course of action must only be taken when there is a genuine risk that has been identified by someone with the proper skill set, who has assertively attempted to convey such information and risk through the proper channels with no success. That is, due diligence and due process must be followed before such a drastic action is to be undertaken.

Finally, as we discussed in Chapter 3, modern policy setting processes require the sharing of information ("evidence") between multiple parties to the policy process. We there urged a democratization of public policy, which would require systems for effective sharing of information among the parties to the policy process. This is essential if citizens and civil society organizations are to be able to understand the competing interests and values a policy might affect; it is essential for meaningful dialogue, and for effectively building a shared conception of the public interest. Only if all relevant information is available to all interested parties can we avoid the kind of "rule by experts" that would subvert meaningful community engagement and democratic legitimacy. Thus we should think of the public's right to know as, indeed, a right, one that imposes corresponding duties upon public servants to make available the information necessary for robustly democratic policy processes.

5.7 ACCOUNTABILITY

We often hear demands for accountability, and public organizations typically include accountability as one of their values or principles. Accountability has a close relationship to responsibility, but we treat it as a topic in its own right here.

To be accountable is, literally, to stand in a position to give an account of oneself, of one's decisions and actions. Accountability is a relational concept. One person is accountable to some other person or group. Elected politicians are accountable, ultimately, to the public; it is to the public that they must account for their decisions and actions. But to whom are public servants accountable?

The simple model of public servants treats them as just that—servants—of political masters, which might suggest that they are accountable to their political bosses. That is partly, but only partly, true. The fact is that public servants work in complex organizations, in which there are multiple hierarchies of authority, responsibility, and accountabilities. Thus most public servants (all but those functioning at the highest level) are accountable to public administration managers within their organizations. They are also directly accountable to the public, in two ways. First, those who deal directly with the public are accountable for their competence in delivering public services. We speak about public service delivery below. Secondly, they are also accountable to the public through participation in the oversight function of the Auditor General, Ombudsmen, regulatory watchdogs, and so on. We speak more about this hereafter too. And, as we have discussed at length above, public servants' accountability to the public is often executed through public service policy processes. The public service must be inclusive, participatory, and democratic in its policy setting processes, and it is accountable to the public for the performance of its responsibilities in this regard.

Accountability is owed by those on whom authority has been conferred or delegated and to whom responsibilities have been assigned to explain as well as justify or defend their actions (or the actions of their subordinates) to a superior from whom the authority and responsibilities have been granted. The superior has an obligation to hold those to whom authority has been given and responsibilities have been assigned to account for the use of that authority and the fulfilment of those responsibilities. Thus delegated authority creates reciprocal duties: on the part of superiors, to call those to whom authority has been delegated to account for what they have done with that authority, and on the part of those to whom responsibilities have been delegated, to account for the actions taken in fulfilment of those responsibilities. In the context of democratic governance and public service administration, such calls to account and the rendering of accounts should both subject to public scrutiny and oversight. And if it is determined that delegated authority has been misused, or delegated responsibilities have been unmet, the superior has an obligation to take appropriate remedial steps and to make those public as well.

One approach to achieving accountability in the public sector is to implement accountability frameworks. Public agencies are expected to develop strategic plans, identify outcomes, and assign responsibility for achieving those outcomes, and to measure the achievement of outcomes through performance reviews. "Planning, benchmarking, and evaluation are among the essential tools of public managers in this national [USA] emphasis on increasing government productivity, performance, and accountability."[14]*

This approach reflects what is commonly called the "compliance model" of public administration. Drawing on the work of Carol Lewis and John Rohr, Geuras and Garofalo describe the compliance model's approach to accountability this way:

> Public administration tilts toward the legalistic, or compliance, mode. John Rohr (1989) calls it the "low road" or "adherence to formal rules" (60). "Ethical behaviour is reduced to staying out of trouble," which results in "meticulous attention to trivial questions" (63). In Lewis' words, the compliance mode is "largely proscriptive, coercive, punitive, and even threatening . . . designed to spur adherence to *minimum* standards and legal prohibitions" (9). What this means for public [service] managers, not surprisingly, is oversight, controls, and sanctions. For, after all, this is familiar terrain. Compliance is embedded in government operations; it is fundamental to how public agencies function; and public [service] managers are expected to be accountable.
>
> . . .
>
> In considering the compliance mode in public sector ethics, we must first acknowledge its value. Again, to cite Lewis, "compliance is fundamental to the way the public business is conducted. As guardians of political relationships and political goals, *controls are accountability implemented*." (10) Such controls, for example, can be found in the traditional managerial functions of budgeting and personnel . . . .
>
> The essential issue, however, concerns the nature and scope of accountability, whether it translates into simple compliance or obedience to statutes or regulations, as though they are clear in and of themselves, or whether public administrators should be expected to demonstrate

*Dean Geuras and Charles Garofalo, *Practical Ethics in Public Administration*, p. 2. Copyright © 2002 Management Concepts Press.

> independence of mind by exercising judgment and dis-
> cretion in meeting their obligations as public servants.[15]*
> ....

Geuras and Garofalo rightly go on to reject this stark either–or dichotomy. Accountability requires both compliance and independent judgment, of course.

Canada has been less dominated by the compliance model than our sister institutions in the United States. We use, for example, ethics officers extensively in the public service as a proactive means of facilitating proper conduct through advice rather than reacting punitively to wrongdoing once it has occurred. Yet we seem to be moving closer to the compliance model since the adoption of the federal *Accountability Act*.

There is no denying, furthermore, that accountability is linked to performance measures. Results-based performance measures are used to improve reporting by departments and agencies as a means to increase accountability to ministers and councillors, to Parliament and Council, and ultimately to the public. Performance reviews have become a large part of efforts to improve accountability by measuring results. Results-based or performance-based reporting in the service of increased accountability has become commonplace across Western democracies, as well as within many private sector organizations. Such monitoring measures both outputs (the goods and services provided in the pursuit of government objectives) and outcomes (the actual effects, positive and negative, of the achievement of the outputs). Public servants are responsible for developing and administering government programs that provide desired outcomes efficiently and effectively. While politicians accountable directly to the public must decide what public goods and services they want as outputs, at what specific level of quantity and quality, and what budgetary resources will be committed to each output, public servants are accountable for the administrative implementation of the resulting programs.

Those who have full accountability to Parliament or its equivalent (ministers, commissioners, and chairs of boards of directors of arm's length agencies) must provide both descriptive or factual explanations for actions taken within their ministries and justifications or defences of their actions and decisions. They are accountable in this robust sense because they have authority to act and are responsible for fulfilling specified statutory obligations; they are accountable for exercises of their authority and for the fulfilment of their responsibilities.

Public servants, by contrast, may be called to give an account of actions and decisions taken within their area, but they are not accountable to Parliament and Council; they are merely answerable. Thus there is a difference between full

*Dean Geuras and Charles Garofalo, *Practical Ethics in Public Administration*, p. 7–8. Copyright © 2002 Management Concepts Press.

accountability and mere answerability. Public servants are not fully accountable in the sense of providing a justification or defence of the policies, programs, or actions of their departments (except for deputy ministers, who occupy a unique role in government). They may, however, properly be called to provide factual information to Parliament or Council with respect to activities undertaken within their department or with respect to the administration of programs and delivery of services for which they have delegated responsibility. In other words, ministers may delegate authority and responsibility, but not accountability. Though this applies to the federal government, the point is generalizable and reflects a basic division of responsibilities and accountabilities between elected politicians and professional civil servants.

In order for accountability to be an effective part of good public governance and good public management, a number of conditions and instruments of accountability must be in place. Some of those conditions are political and so are outside of the realm of the public service, such as: robust democratic processes in which citizens are engaged and through which competing conceptions of the public good can be contested; opposition groups within government that are willing and able to hold those governing to account for how they exercise power; and a strong commitment to ministerial responsibility. Others directly concern how those with political authority provide effective oversight of public administration, policy implementation and service delivery, such as: external audits, whether in the form of value-for-money audits or reviews of how public services are administered; independent evaluations of policies, programs, and services, which again might be designed to evaluate the targeted policy or service against any number of desiderata (efficiency, public satisfaction, fulfilment of a specified objective such as reduced class sizes in elementary schools or reduced wait times in hospital emergency rooms; internal monitoring processes designed to ensure that applicable rules, regulations, and procedures are being followed, such as policies concerning procurement; and performance reporting to relevant parliamentary or council committees). These latter are primarily concerned with how those with primary responsibility effectively oversee those to whom responsibilities have been delegated are fulfilling those responsibilities, and how those who are fully accountable to Parliament or Council meet their duties to provide such accounts. Still other mechanisms that enhance accountability concern relations between the public at large and the public service, such as: mechanisms through which members of the public can participate in the development of public policy and the design of public programs and services, and provide input with respect to their satisfaction with existing services; effective processes ensuring public access to government information; and a free media. Finally, accountability is enhanced by processes through which members of the public or members of the public service can report suspected cases of serious wrongdoing within government and be protected from reprisal for doing so. As this list suggests, accountability is multifaceted and complex, and therefore it requires a number of instruments and processes to achieve. It is most fully realized when all branches of government put in place the mechanisms that are needed to ensure that all those with authority or responsibility provide appropriate accounts to those with whom they are in accountability relationships. And it requires a commitment to meeting responsibilities and accounting for exercises of authority throughout public organizations at all levels.

Thus some elements of the compliance framework are needed to ensure proper monitoring of performance. It is further necessary that the information made available through these various accountability instruments should be acted upon appropriately: that good service be rewarded, inadequate service be corrected, and if necessary, penalized, and problems identified be corrected.

When we take this approach to accountability, the specification of results and who has responsibilities for achieving them become extremely important. Such a focus is evident, for example, in the *TBS Management Accountability Framework*, which requires that "Accountabilities for results are clearly assigned and consistent with resources, and delegations are appropriate to capabilities." It further specifies the following accountability commitments: "Clarity of accountabilities; Delegations regularly reviewed; Executive committee oversight of performance management and regular review of performance; Alignment of individual with corporate commitments."[16]*

The relationship between control, performance, and accountability has been widely examined. In 1997, then Auditor General Denis Desautels remarked, in comments to the Association of Professional Executives of the Public Service of Canada, that if public servants wanted fewer controls and central regulations (something the Auditor General favoured), then they needed to put in place two things: values and performance measures aimed at increasing accountability. His remarks are worth quoting at some length.

> Stripping away detailed rules and controls can be a recipe for a highly effective organization. It can unlock the creativity and inherent desire to do a good job that is in all of us. But it can also be a recipe for disaster. You can end up with a Microsoft, or a Corel . . . but you might end up with a Barings Bank, or even a Bre-X. Stripping away detailed controls can lead to loss of control unless two things are put in place.

TBS Management Accountability Framework, http://www.collectionscanada.gc.ca/webarchives/ 20071116052225/http://www.tbs-sct.gc.ca/maf-crg/documents/booklet-livret/booklet-livret_e.asp, Treasury Board of Canada Secretariat, 2011. Reproduced with the permission of the Minister of Public Works and Government Services Canada, 2011.

The first is strong values. Effective control can come as much from values, ethics, trust and a shared sense of purpose as from rules and regulations. These are what we accountants refer to as informal controls, and we see these as just as important as formal controls. So here is yet another reason to push ahead on the values and ethics file—with shared values, the need for detailed rules diminishes.

The basic idea is to give people some broad parameters within which to work—tell them a few fundamental rules and make sure they understand the objectives, and then give them room to use their judgment.

But strong values are not enough without the second element. Streamlining rules and shared values takes you only so far. The second element is accountability or performance management. Values and accountability— they fit and work together.

In a way, accountability or performance management is the catch that comes with more freedom from central dictates. The catch is that if managers want greater discretion they must demonstrate that they have used it wisely, and have used it to achieve results.

. . .

I am convinced that the key to better accountability is to pay more attention to informing others about results. Forgive me for borrowing an overused line, but what Canadians and parliamentarians are really saying to government is "show me the results." . . .

Results in the public sector means more than "ends," it also covers "means." Managers must demonstrate that they have adhered to due process, fair treatment and the like. More transparency in the day-to-day activities of government would help.[17]*

*Opening remarks by Denis Desautels, Auditor General of Canada to the Association of Professional Executives of the Public Service of Canada Symposium (Ottawa: 28 May 1997). Reproduced with the permission of the Minister of Public Works and Government Services, 2011.

Governments at all levels continue to try to find the right balance between control and compliance, on the one hand, and personal responsibility and empowerment, on the other. As the Auditor General points out, values, ethics, and accountability for performance and results are essential if we are to escape a compliance approach that stifles creativity and enable members of the public sector to do good work. Among the benefits of increased accountability are 1) constraint of controls so that they do not hinder effectiveness and creativity, 2) assurance to government and the public that public authority and resources are being used well, and 3) promotion of a commitment to continuing improvements in public administration, and the design and delivery of public programs.

One element of ensuring accountability in the Canadian administrative culture is the role of independent oversight bodies, such as those of the Auditor General, ombudsmen, regulators, ethics officers, budget officers, and the like. We turn to their role in ensuring accountability for results next.

5.8 INDEPENDENT OVERSIGHT: OMBUDSMEN, AUDITORS GENERAL, AND OTHERS

While the goal of public sector ethics is to ensure that government programs are well designed, efficiently and effectively managed, and fairly and ethically provided, accountability for achieving these ends cannot depend just upon self-reporting from public agencies. Genuine performance evaluations, and assessments of value-for-money, depend as well on effective independent oversight. And across the levels of public administration in Canada there are a number of persons charged with providing such oversight. These include a number of arm's length regulatory officers, such as the Canadian Nuclear Safety Commissioner, as well as Ombudsmen of various kinds (for everything from veteran's affairs to prisons to child welfare), city and provincial Ombudsmen, the Auditor General of Canada, federal, provincial and municipal Integrity Commissioners, Ethics Officers of the House of Commons and the Senate, as well as their provincial and municipal counterparts, and many more. Independent oversight ensures that procurement policies are ethically sound, serve the political objectives of the elected government, avoid conflicts of interest, and provide value for money; it is important for accountability that there be opportunities for regular independent monitoring of government spending. Thus it is vital that there exist in each jurisdiction an independent auditor or ombudsman who is authorized to conduct value-for-money audits and review government spending. The persons authorized to perform such audits must be free from political influence, independent from government, and have access to all relevant government documents and materials in order to conduct thorough investigations. There must be similar independent oversight of performance reviews for all government programs and services.

It is frequently through reports of such independent overseers that mismanagement of public spending, and serious conflicts of interest in procurements and contracting, are brought to light, as well as mismanagement and other kinds of failure to produce the outcomes desired from public programs. While in the short run such disclosures of mismanagement and unethical contracting practices shake the confidence of the public in government and the public service, there are long-term benefits from such oversight systems. By bringing to light serious wrongdoing in government agencies and departments, governments are forced to put into place better procurement and contracting policies. Those who have knowingly engaged in serious wrongdoing, especially for personal or political advantage, need to be identified and removed from office. Potential risks may be identified before they produce real harm, especially when the mismanagement occurs in a regulatory context. Such oversight enables those to whom accountability for performance is owed to monitor the effectiveness of government programs and services, so that deficiencies can be identified and service enhancements made when needed. And, finally, such independent oversight may reduce the costs of litigation borne by governments.

QUESTIONS FOR FURTHER DISCUSSION

1. What are some of the characteristics of professionals?

2. Explain, in your own words, fiduciary duties.

3. List and explain the five basic principles of professionalism.

4. What two restrictions, or duties, do public servants have in respect to maintaining confidentiality?

5. What dilemma does political neutrality create for public servants?

6. What are the six principles of political neutrality, as identified by Kernaghan?

7. If public servants do seek to engage in personal political activities, what are some of the restrictions they must observe in order not to violate political neutrality?

8. Explain the difference between public comment and public criticism. Why is this distinction important?

9. Even though political neutrality might be impossible to achieve in practice, what are some of the reasons for wanting to pursue this idea nonetheless?

10. Since public servants cannot fully defer responsibility to their superiors and thus will need to take personal responsibility for some actions, what are the six principles of personal responsibility?

11. What are some of the ways that public servants can safeguard public assets and information?

12. One ethical dilemma faced by nearly all public servants concerns the need to balance confidentiality and transparency. How might a public servant approach this issue? Are there different ways to share information?

13. Is there a difference between responsibility and accountability? If so, how might you explain the difference?

14. Is there a difference between accountability and answerability?

15. To whom are public servants accountable?

16. What is the "compliance model"?

17. What are some of the benefits of increased accountability?

18. What role do Ombudsmen and Auditor Generals typically play?

19. For whom do Ombudsmen (and other similar individuals) work?

Consider Cases 1, 3, 6, 7, 15, 20, 21, 22, 23, and 27 in thinking about the issues raised in this chapter.

NOTES

[1] Kenneth Kernaghan, "Political Rights and Political Neutrality: Finding the Balance Point," *Canadian Public Administration* 29:4 (1986): 639–652.

[2] Kenneth Kernaghan and John Langford, *The Responsible Public Servant* (Halifax, NS: IRPR and IPAC, 1990), p. 56.

[3] *Randy Barnhart, Linda Camponi, Michael Cassidy, Ken Clavette and Heather Stevens v. The Queen, Court File No. T-163-84 Aug. 22, 1986*, pp. 33–34; quoted in Kernaghan and Langford 1990, p. 62.

[4] Ibid. See also Bill C25 *Public Service Modernization Act*, which amended the *Public Service Employment Act*, Dec. 31, 2005.

[5] For a very good survey of the evolution of this concept see Kenneth Kernaghan, *A Special Calling: Values, Ethics and Professional Public Service* (Ottawa: Canada Public Service Agency, Treasury Board of Canada Secretariat, 2007).

[6] We recognize that these are not ideal examples, because they involve Officers of Parliament, who are appointed by an order of council and are accountable directly to Parliament or the Senate (or both), and so not members of the merit-based public service *per se*. But they serve to illustrate the kind of tension we wish to comment on.

[7] Dean Geuras and Charles Garofalo, *Practical Ethics in Public Administration* (Vienna, Virginia: Management Concepts, 2002), p. 111; quoting Dennis Thompson, "The Possibility of Administrative Ethics," *Public Administration Review* 45 (1985): 555.

[8] Geuras and Garofalo 2002, p. 112; Carol Lewis, *The Ethics Challenge in Public Service* (San Francisco: Jossey-Bass, 1991).

⁹ Geuras and Garofalo 2002, pp. 112–113.

¹⁰ Geuras and Garofalo 2002, p. 113.

¹¹ Geuras and Garofalo 2002, p. 114.

¹² Office of the Privacy Commissioner of Canada at www.priv.gc.ca.

¹³ See http://www.canada.com/technology/Feds+silence+Nanaimo+scientist+over +salmon+study/5163289/story.html and http://www.cbc.ca/news/technology/ story/2011/04/26/science-federal-cswa-letter.html?sms_ss=twitter&at_ xt=4db7386d8f4fa222,0. Accessed July 29, 2011.

¹⁴ Geuras and Garofalo 2002, p. 4.

¹⁵ Geuras and Garofalo 2002, pp. 7–8, drawing on Carol Lewis, *The Ethics Challenge in Public Service* (San Francisco: Jossey-Bass, 1991) and John Rohr, *Ethics for Bureaucrats* 2nd ed. (NY: Marcel Dekker, 1989).

¹⁶ Treasury Board of Canada Secretariat, *TBS Management Accountability Framework* at www.tbs-sct.gc.ca/maf-crg, downloaded April 2011.

¹⁷ Opening remarks of Denis Desautel, Auditor General of Canada, to a Panel Discussion of the Association of Professional Executives of the Public Service of Canada Symposium (Ottawa: 28 May 1997) available at www.oag-bvg.gc.ca/ internet/English/meth_gde_e_26997.html. Accessed April 2011.

CHAPTER 6

Public Service Values

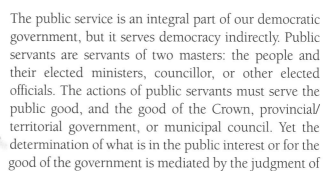

The public service is an integral part of our democratic government, but it serves democracy indirectly. Public servants are servants of two masters: the people and their elected ministers, councillor, or other elected officials. The actions of public servants must serve the public good, and the good of the Crown, provincial/ territorial government, or municipal council. Yet the determination of what is in the public interest or for the good of the government is mediated by the judgment of our democratically elected and publicly accountable political representatives, their political bosses. Thus public servants serve the public interest indirectly in most cases. They do so by providing professional, honest, impartial, and frank advice to ministers, and by loyally executing the decisions of our democratically elected leaders.

This traditional view masks, however, the extent to which public servants are involved in the articulation of the objectives of their organizations and the understanding of its value to the public, their role in engaging the public in developing policies that have democratic legitimacy, and their capacity to influence the values of the public and elected politicians. In what follows, we shall have to move beyond the classic understanding of the role of public servants in creating public values. Public servants also serve the public interest by refraining from using their positions within government for their private interest rather than the public good. We have already addressed the importance of public servants advising their political masters impartially and in ways that reflect the best evidence available to them, as well as the requirement that they avoid conflicts of interest and abstain from using their position in the public service for personal gain. Here we concentrate on the relationship between public servants and the value of democracy.

6.1 CANADIAN ADMINISTRATIVE CULTURE

In order to fully appreciate the role of the public service in Canadian democracy, we must make brief reference to the Canadian administrative culture. Like all "cultures," administrative culture is complex and multifaceted. Our culture provides our framework for understanding the world, and provides the central symbols through which we interpret the world and find meaning it in. Our culture refers to the values and patterns that constitute our way of seeing, judging, interpreting, and understanding the world around us. It is influenced by a myriad of factors: technology, economy, demography, geography, religion, language, history, and political, legal, and social structures. Administrative culture is part of the broader political culture of Canada. It refers to the cognitions, perceptions, and values of those involved in public administration, and the perceptions and understandings of public administration held by members of the public at large.[1]

Canadian administrative culture is determined by the values, norms, standards, and activities of hundreds of organizations, departments, agencies, and occupational groups. It is also influenced by non-governmental organizations, civil society groups, and citizens, and their interactions with government agents. Together, these components create a partly shared and partly contested and continuously negotiated set of collective values. Those values identify the characteristics and qualities most valued in public servants, as well as norms for evaluating public policy. Among the qualities valued in public servants are discipline, stewardship, fairness, and the cardinal virtues of prudence, temperance, justice, and courage or fortitude. Among the standards for evaluating public policy are **instrumental values**, such as efficiency, effectiveness, and legitimacy, and substantive values, such as acceptability, equality, authenticity, and justice. These are the collective values of our administrative culture.

Our administrative culture is influenced by a number of factors: our physical environment, including the regional nature of Canada; our social values, which include elements drawn from our Judeo-Christian heritage, such as community, authority, and tradition, and other more modern values based on individualism, competition, and personal achievement and responsibility; our economic situation, including our heavy dependence on natural resources and foreign trade; and our political culture, including our understanding of the *British North America Act*, our bilingual heritage, our constitutional values, such as the division of power between federal and provincial/territorial jurisdiction, more recently the *Canadian Charter of Rights and Freedoms*, and our commitment to multiculturalism. While many of our values are shaped by our proximity to and close relations with the United States, our own administrative identity is in part determined by how we understand the differences between American values and our own. More recently, our administrative culture has been influenced by trends in internationalization and globalization, and the increasingly diverse nature of the Canadian population, as we welcome more immigrants from countries that do not share our history within the British Commonwealth or the Judeo-Christian heritage that characterized earlier generations of immigrants. Our history has included a strong commitment to the values of a peaceable kingdom: peace, order, and good government, fairness and equity, community and mutual aid, and civility and gentleness.

At the foundation of our administrative culture, given its relationship to government, not surprisingly, is a set of political and legal commitments: to the Westminster Parliamentary system based on liberal-democratic ideals and representation; the federal system of governance; the *Charter of Rights and Freedoms*; and the rule of law.[2]

The more specific elements of Canadian administrative culture (many of which we have already touched upon) flow from these various collective values. Given our commitment to democratic participation, liberalism, constitutionalism, and the rule of law, we insist that members of our public service comport themselves in specific ways. We thus insist on a merit-based system of admission to the public service, rather than allowing the public service to be staffed through political cronyism and nepotism. We insist that the public service be politically neutral to the extent necessary for it to be able to serve the government of the day loyally and to retain legitimacy through changes of government. The demand for political neutrality was once much stricter than it is today. It used to be, as well, that members of the civil service were granted anonymity and secrecy. This was thought necessary, given our commitment to ministerial responsibility as a cornerstone of the parliamentary system. To ensure ministerial responsibility, we demanded political neutrality and anonymity from public servants. Civil servants were to be protected from public scrutiny for their actions. This was thought to support their freedom to provide advice to the ministers regardless of party. Ministers could (and still can) accept or reject the advice of their public servants, and bear the responsibility to defend their choices to the public. It was within these constraints that public service accountability was to be understood.

This traditional way of thinking about the relationship between public servants and elected officials, and between public servants and members of the public, no longer accurately describes the reality of a complex modern public service in a country such as Canada. Public servants are now highly scrutinized (no longer serving with anonymity or secrecy); their role involves considerably more than merely executing the will of others; and their accountability relations are much more complex than just extending to political bosses. Given their role in articulating public values and the objectives of public service organizations, their role in setting public policies, their role in engaging with external communities (industry partners, commissioners, and others contracted to deliver public services, the media, the judiciary, civil society organizations, researchers, citizens, and service users) in the design and delivery of public services, and their role in securing democratic legitimacy through interactions with the public, the simple model must be replaced with one that more accurately reflects the multifaceted nature of contemporary public service. And those new realities must be accommodated in our understanding of the contribution of the public service to democratic values within our Westminster parliamentary system of government.

6.2 MULTICULTURALISM AND THE *CHARTER OF RIGHTS AND FREEDOMS*

Canada is a multicultural society both in fact and in values. Factually, Canada is a country built upon immigration, populated by peoples from virtually every country, ethnicity, race, and religious, linguistic, and cultural group. Thus Canada is a multi-racial, multi-ethnic, multi-linguistic country. We are a country that is pluralistic along virtually every conceivable line. This gives us great strengths and opportunities, and vibrancy in our ever-changing population. But it also creates challenges that a more monistic society does not have.

First, our commitment to immigration creates challenges for those who must directly deliver immigration services. Government employees working for Citizenship and Immigration Canada must ensure that all applicants for immigration to Canada are treated with fairness, dignity, and respect. They must work to overcome the barriers potential immigrants face in light of such diverse challenges as language barriers, cultural and religious impediments to accessing immigration services, corruption and bureaucratic inefficiencies in their home countries, as well as racism and other prejudices within Canadian society. They must also decide difficult questions with respect to refugee claimants and others seeking entry to Canada on humanitarian or compassionate grounds. They must balance the individual needs of potential immigrants against the projected need for immigrants with various labour skills and considerations of regional balance within Canada. And all of this must be done within a context of global terrorism, international smuggling of drugs, arms, and people, and other security concerns. The task is daunting, and the work of those delivering immigration services is often hampered by inadequate resources and the resulting backlog of applications.

The multicultural nature of the Canadian population creates challenges with respect to the delivery of services for new immigrants as well. Most new immigrants settle, at least at first, in the major metropolitan centres of Canada, creating serious resource challenges for our large cities. From employment and housing assistance to education for those with English or French as a second language, cities are responsible for providing a host of services to new immigrants to help them transition successfully to life in their new country. Making sure that new immigrants can access health care (a challenge when language or religious barriers impede the delivery of care), have their foreign credentials recognized, gain Canadian experience in the labour market, and more, are essential if Canada is to benefit fully from its recent immigrants, and if recent immigrants are to have a real chance to contribute to their new country and fully participate in all aspects of life here.

But multiculturalism is more than a social fact about Canada; it is also one of our fundamental values, one important enough to be enshrined in the *Canadian Charter of Rights and Freedoms*. We are committed to being an inclusive society, in which all of our diverse populations have a fair opportunity to participate and succeed. Our cultural differences are to be treated as a source of strength rather than just as impediments to be overcome. Our goal as a multicultural society is not to assimilate newcomers as quickly as possible, throwing them in a melting pot to erase their differences. Rather, we recognize that cultural identities are fundamentally important to individuals' feelings of selfhood and that group membership is important to peoples' sense of well-being, meaning, and self-respect.[3] Thus individuals may identify with the groups they see themselves as belonging to, and retain the markers of their unique identities (religious beliefs and practices, language, rituals, food, clothing, marriage and family practices, and more), while being full members in good standing within Canadian society.

Being a genuinely inclusive society requires that members of minority groups within Canada have an opportunity to participate fully in the social, cultural, political, professional, and economic life of society. To do all this requires an absence of discrimination against individuals based on their group membership, as well as public accommodation of different practices and beliefs, based on an understanding and recognition of cultural differences as being equally entitled to respect.

Multiculturalism places a range of burdens on governments at all levels, and on those who design and deliver government programs. Some of these burdens, those deemed most essential to ensuring the equal right of participation and making sure that all members of our society are treated with equal concern and respect by governments, are enshrined in the *Charter of Rights and Freedoms*. Among these are the right to freedom of expression, freedom of religion and conscience, freedom of movement, freedom of association, and guarantees of equality.

The *Canadian Charter of Rights and Freedoms* applies to all government actions, and protects a range of fundamental rights and freedoms against unreasonable infringement by government. It is the highest law of the land, being part of our Constitution. It articulates a set of rights and freedoms that individuals hold against their government. It thereby places duties upon governments that correspond to the rights of individuals, and thus the courts are empowered under the *Charter* to strike down legislation that unreasonably restricts a *Charter* right or freedom.

Many of the rights and freedoms protected by the *Charter* are essential to a free and democratic society. Freedom of association, religion and conscience, expression, and movement are vital to a free society. If government could impose restrictions upon its citizens with respect to how or what they worship, with whom they may associate, where they may live, work, or travel, or what sentiments or opinions they may say or write or otherwise express in public, then our most fundamental freedoms would be threatened. It is not just that having the freedom to say what we think, to choose our friends and companions, and to act as dictated by our faith or conscience is important to each of us as individuals, though it no doubt is. But the value of these rights runs deeper than this, to the very heart of a free and democratic society. They also deeply implicate the value of multiculturalism.

The threat to freedom and democracy that attacks on freedom of expression (including freedom of the press) involve are widely known from unhappy real-world examples; we don't need to resort to imaginary cases to appreciate the danger that restrictions on freedom of speech and freedom of the press create. Dictatorships and one-party states require substantial restrictions on the free exchange of opinions and information in order to sustain themselves. Conversely, thriving democracies depend upon the widest range of expressions being heard, on the free exchange of information, and on dissenting opinions being voiced. As the English philosopher John Stuart Mill reminded us many years ago, society benefits from having virtually unlimited freedom of expression, in matters of science, politics, morality, religion, economics, and in social matters.[4] All that is necessary to see the truth of this is recognition that we are fallible; we are capable of being wrong, even about those matters with respect to which we are most certain. The history of human progress is a history of those mistakes, and their correction. If we are fallible, then for all we know the person voicing an opinion we think utterly false or abominable may, we must acknowledge, be right. Even if he is not wholly right, his opinion may contain a part of the truth. In either case, such truths will be suppressed if we allow only those who agree with us to be heard. But, and here is the real genius of Mill, even if what another says is utterly false and without any merit, society still benefits from letting him speak and subjecting his ideas to rigorous debate and scrutiny. After all, he might be persuaded of the error of his opinions. But even if not, we all benefit from the exercise of refuting him and defending what we believe to be the better view. We all benefit from having our most cherished convictions and most settled opinions challenged, and from defending them.

Consider, for example, the views you are most confident about: in matters of science, politics, morality, economics, or any other area. What could you say to someone who simply disagreed with you, and asked your reasons why you believe what you do? Why do you believe that global warming is occurring and that human activity is at least partially responsible for it? Why do you believe that the financial system needs to be regulated by government? Why do you believe that putting kidnappers in prison is the right response? Why do you believe that racism is morally wrong? Insert your own examples and Mill's point remains: whatever you most firmly believe, you benefit from having to answer challenges that make you articulate why you believe as you do. If you don't have to answer such challenges, and recall the reasons why you believe what you do, then you will hold even the truths you know as dead dogmas rather than as living truths. You will be like a child or parrot who can say the right thing, but who has no idea *why* it is the right thing. Our truths are alive, and held for good reasons, only when we remember why we think they are true. So we benefit from allowing those who would challenge even our most settled convictions to speak their minds, issue their challenges, and voice what seem to us to be utterly wrongheaded opinions. In a free society, there is little to fear from freedom of expression, and much to be gained.

In a flourishing democracy, freedom of expression has additional benefits, of course. If we are to have a genuine political contest between competing visions of our society, with different economic, international, educational, and social policies, for example, then the contestants must be free to articulate their vision for consideration. And we the people must be able to subject their visions, and the facts on which they rely, to scrutiny and debate.

Freedom of expression is not an easy right to respect, however. It has value only when there are others who disagree with us, especially about those things we hold most dear or with respect to which we feel the most confidence. We would hardly need to protect freedom of expression if we all agreed with one another, would we? Freedom of expression recognizes the right of others to say things that we might not only disagree with, but which we might find offensive, sacrilegious, immoral, or irresponsible. The right protects the freedom of others to do all of these things and more. It is, thus, a difficult right.

The right to free expression, like all *Charter* protections, is not unlimited. We can place reasonable restrictions on *Charter* rights, restrictions that can be demonstrably justified in a free and democratic society as reasonable limits to the rights. Thus we can restrict the expression of hate propaganda, false advertising, advertising aimed at children, and statements that are defamatory (as slander or libel). These have been deemed reasonable limits on the right to freedom of expression because they serve a pressing and substantial objective or strike a reasonable balance between the competing interests of different individuals or groups in society, and are not forms of expression at the heart of a free and democratic society.

Similar claims can be made about the other fundamental freedoms protected in the *Charter*. While not unlimited, they protect vital interests of persons and are necessary for a free and democratic society, and they must be respected by governments. Many of them not only protect our shared interest in having a free and democratic society, but they also protect the interests of vulnerable minorities within society and so contribute to realizing the value of multiculturalism. Freedom of expression allows individuals to publish newspapers, newsletters, and blogs in languages other than English or French, for example, which may be very important within recent immigrant communities. It allows members of the gay/lesbian/bisexual/transsexual communities to advocate for an end to discriminatory practices under which they have suffered. It allows members of ethnic communities to stage peaceful protests to encourage the Canadian government to take action against injustices in foreign countries. In these and countless other ways, the right to free expression contributes to the right of minority groups to participate in Canadian society while retaining their identification with their minority culture or group. Freedom of association plays a similar role.

Perhaps the most important *Charter* right for minority groups within Canada, as minority groups, is section 15, the equality guarantee. Section 15 really guarantees four equality rights:

- the right to equality before the law,
- the right to equality under the law,
- the right to enjoy equal protection of the law, and
- the right to equal benefit from the law.

Although the equality guarantees protect all individuals from discriminatory treatment by government, they are most important for protecting vulnerable minorities, who have suffered from systemic and widespread social discrimination. Ending such discrimination, at least as it is perpetrated by governments through their laws and policies, is the object of section 15.

A number of minority groups have benefited directly from the equality guarantees since section 15 came into effect in 1985 (three years after the rest of the *Charter,* so as to allow governments time to review their laws and identify and eliminate discrimination within them). The rights of individuals in same-sex relationships, for example, have been dramatically advanced: the right to receive spousal benefits and pensions, the right to adopt children, and finally the right to marry. Likewise, the position of persons with disabilities and that of religious minorities have also been improved under the *Charter*.

Many of the advances have come as a result of recognizing that law and regulations that seem facially neutral (that seem, on their face, to treat everyone equally) have differential impacts on differently situated groups. A government policy that says sign language interpreters are not provided by the state for those seeking medical services or participating in legal proceedings, for example, treats everyone alike: it denies to everyone the benefit of state-funded sign language interpreters. But such regulations have very different impacts on hearing persons and deaf persons. They do not provide *equal benefit of the law*. Likewise, simple government regulations like those requiring the use of a helmet while riding on a motorcycle, or a uniform cap for transit workers or RCMP officers, treats everyone equally. But they differentially impact those whose religion requires them to wear a different head covering, which cannot itself be covered with anything else. They are barred by such regulations from participating in the activities in question. Now you might say that they have a choice: if they want to ride a motorcycle or take an occupation that requires wearing certain head gear, they will have to give up their religious practice. If they choose not to, that is their choice. No one needs to ride a motorcycle or work for a particular organization, after all. But consider this: for members of the population who are not members of a religious group with this restriction on their conduct, they can have both; they can ride a motorcycle or work for an organization that requires wearing a cap and maintain their religious traditions. They don't have to make a choice. So our commitment to multiculturalism and religious pluralism requires that we consider whether the regulations can be modified for members of this group, so that they may participate fully in society (in all the ways others can) without having to give up something as vital as their religious practices. If such exceptions can be made without risking pressing and substantial public interests, our commitment to equality requires that they be made. In this way we have adopted, not **formal equality** (treating all cases alike, regardless of relevant differences), but **substantive equality** (treating persons with equal concern and respect, in ways that accommodate their differences when necessary to allow them to be full participants in all of the goods Canadian society makes possible) as our goal.

Our commitments to substantive equality and to multiculturalism require that those who design and implement government programs consider not just how those programs will impact the statistically average Canadian (whatever and whoever that might be), but also how they will affect those who are differentially situated: whether because they belong to groups that have suffered serious systemic discrimination in the past, or because they have needs not shared by the majority of the population. The ultimate test of whether a government policy or program is discriminatory makes essential reference to the dignity of the person, and whether that is compromised or threatened by the policy or program. Unless public servants design and deliver government programs in such a way as to respect the inherent dignity and equality of all persons in our society, they will run afoul of *Charter* values.

All public servants are bound in their work by the *Charter*, and have a duty to be conversant with its provisions. Which *Charter* rights will be most important to a given civil servant will depend upon his or her areas of responsibility. Those working within ministries of justice, for example, will need to know that the *Charter* protects individuals from being subject to criminal punishments that do not comport with principles of fundamental justice, that individuals have a right to be presumed innocent, tried in a timely way, and more. Understanding how the various *Charter* rights have been interpreted by the courts is also essential to faithful public service, and public service organizations are encouraged to provide regular training for their members on developments in *Charter* interpretation as they pertain to their operations.

6.3 PUBLIC VALUE

We would like to end this chapter with a discussion of a relatively recent development in the study of public management that we think holds significant promise and involves an orientation that is properly focused on the unique function of public service: the view known as "public value."[5] Although adopting the public value approach requires modifying our traditional understanding of the role of public servants and their relationship both with the public and elected officials (especially under the Westminster parliamentary system), it seems to be a model ideally suited to sustaining a desirable focus on values and to supporting a greater role for public participation within government operations, policy setting and service design, delivery and evaluation.

Public value management begins with the recognition that public services are different than others. The most important difference is that "public services are characterised by claims of *rights* by *citizens* to services that have been authorized and funded through some *democratic* process."[6] Thus public services differ from private services delivered through markets in at least the following ways: they are services people have (or at least claim) a right to, and not just a desire for; they are provided to persons *qua* citizens, rather than *qua* consumers; and their provision is authorized by democratic political processes, rather than the laws of supply and demand. These constitute quite radical differences, and suggest that attempts to mirror government activities on those of the market are missing the point of public services.

The fundamental activity public value enjoins is an articulation of the goals or purposes of every public sector organization. Every public sector agency is charged with articulating what their service is for, what value(s) it aims to realize, what objectives it serves to meet. We said before that the move to introduce public service values into the public service was an important innovation, and through the lens of public value we can see why. This first question focuses attention on what the public finds valuable in the services provided by government.

It is no easy question to determine which values or objectives are those of any given organization. Consider, for example, the provision of park and recreation services. Why do we provide such services? Among the possible objectives such a service might aim at are at least the following: to distribute good quality jobs throughout the jurisdiction; to provide summer employment opportunities to high school and post-secondary students; to preserve species, ecosystems, or habitat; to provide public spaces for individuals and families, regardless of their ability to pay; to provide green spaces within the jurisdiction for air and water quality purposes; to limit land development; to protect public resources for future generations, and so on. Depending on which of these you think is the primary purpose of park services, you might decide a number of issues differently: whether fishing or hunting should be permitted on park lands; whether some commercial or residential development should be permitted; whether a user fee should be charged; the degree to which park lands should be cultivated or left in a wilder state; whether park personnel should be reduced in times of financial constraints. This demonstrates the importance of articulating clearly what value is being realized by the service, and what its central objectives are, for they will (more or less) determine how to answer a number of possible questions about how the service is designed and delivered.

Public value insists that the objective of public service organizations has to be worked out through processes that engage the public and service users. It cannot be set either by elected officials or public managers (alone or working together); instead, there must be processes for meaningful engagement with and involvement of the public in establishing public service objectives. Public value is articulated through processes of deliberative governance or deliberative democracy. Public input is needed, on this view, for both legitimacy and effectiveness of public services.

A great deal of work has been done by organizations like The Work Foundation studying various mechanisms for engaging the public in identifying the value of public services, and then in the design, delivery, and evaluation of those services, against that shared understanding of their purpose.[7] We recommend this work to interested readers, though our focus will be less on how to implement public values than on its ethical appeal. How the public is engaged, and which mechanisms are most appropriate, will vary depending upon the kind of service being provided: regulators of telecommunications, for example, might engage the public quite differently than school boards or local hospitals or police services. Such differences must be attended to in the design of approaches to community engagement. Yet a few generalities seem to hold across contexts.

First, it is imperative that the public agency understand clearly what they seek to get out of public consultation and engagement, the extent to which the public will impact decision making, and that they have communicated their expectations about these matters clearly to the public.

Second, public consultation must be as broad-based and inclusive as possible, protecting the process against capture by well-organized interest groups or domination by the most vocal minority.

Third, public engagement must include a more-or-less substantial commitment to education on behalf of the civil servants involved. Relevant information must be shared, assumptions must be communicated, constraints (fiscal or other) must be explained, strategic priorities justified, and so on.

Fourth, the public must be engaged with as citizens, rather than as consumers or voters or political donors or taxpayers. Finally, the engagement with the public must be ongoing and iterative; the model advocated is one of continuous dialogue, rather than a one-off survey or public opinion poll. The point is to establish processes through which informed dialogue can occur. As David Coats and Eleanor Passmore put it, "public value is grounded in the idea that service effectiveness is best defined by *responsiveness to refined public preferences*."[8]

The idea of "refined public preferences" is extremely important. Public value does not involve catering to ill-informed public demands, ruling by opinion poll, or giving people everything they want. The point is not to make government more popular, but to make it more responsive to the actual needs of citizens. Citizens must have an opportunity to convey their needs to those charged with meeting them, of course, but they must also have an opportunity to think about issues from the point of view of public value and the common good, rather than from just their own narrow perspective. It is *informed* public preferences to which services should be responsive, and the degree to which services meet those preferences must constitute a considerable measure of their success or failure. It is in order to ensure that public preferences are informed that processes must be ongoing and iterative, and must include significant sharing of information from public servants to the community groups and individuals so engaged. It is expected that public opinion will both inform and be informed by good processes for engagement in public services.

One way of thinking about the public value approach is to contrast two possible views one might take toward public services: the inside-out and the outside-in views, we might call them. The inside-out approach views public service decisions as the purview of public managers and elected officials, perhaps aided by experts, who determine what services will be provided and how. It then measures the effectiveness of services against a set of benchmarks (targets or outputs, such as wait times in health care, class sizes in elementary schools) that have been established within the organization itself. By contrast, adopting an outside-in perspective asks public servants to examine their organization from the perspective of citizens or service users accessing it from the outside. Public service adopts the outside-in perspective. It evaluates success by citizen and user satisfaction, in part, but also and primarily by measuring the degree to which the organization is achieving or delivering the public good that is its primary objective. This is measured as an outcome (rather than an output), which is typically qualitative as well as quantitative. It includes user satisfaction, but other public service values as well, such as equity, fairness, and accessibility.

Public value requires a reinterpretation of classic notions of accountability as well. Politicians continue to be accountable to the electorate, and public servants to their political bosses, but now public servants are directly accountable to the public as well. The relationship between public servants and the public they serve is much more important in the public service model than in others. The level of interaction between the public and public servants is much deeper and broader than it is in most other models of governance. Consider the following from Coats and Passmore:

> Establishing the purpose of a public service demands that organisations provide a coherent answer to the second question: to whom are we accountable? Accountability is about more than the simple fact of periodic elections from which politicians derive an electoral mandate.

> Public value tells us that public managers as well as politicians have to explain and justify what they do to the public. Successful public service delivery depends on a continuous dialogue with citizens, who should be thought of as stakeholders on a par with government, experts, industry representatives, the media, the judiciary and service users. In the language of public value, organisations must therefore seek democratic legitimacy for their actions by engaging with their "authorising environment."9*

Under the classic model, politicians justify public decisions, and civil servants remain anonymous and invisible to the public. This older model cannot be sustained if the public service is to engage in meaningful dialogue with citizens and service users, provide relevant information, and manage public expectations appropriately. This then complicates both the simple upward model of accountability (from public servants to ministers or other elected officials), and our understanding of democracy (from representative government to deliberative governance).

There is much more to the public value approach than this brief sketch can convey. What is particularly attractive about this model of public sector governance should, however, be clear enough. By focusing on what public good or public value is to be achieved by provision of a given service, we can develop a framework for subsequent decision making. "How should the service be designed and delivered so as to achieve its objective?" and "How should we measure success?" both become more manageable against a shared understanding of what the service is for, what good it is designed to achieve. Moreover, focusing on the public nature of the value opens the space in which citizens can be engaged, *qua* citizens, in the design and delivery of public services. The satisfaction of service users is important, especially with respect to goods that are accessed individually (like health care, housing, or education). But user satisfaction is not the only measure of success, nor even the most important one, from the point of view of democratic legitimacy. Rather, user satisfaction matters only if the service they are using is one that provides public value, i.e., only if the good provided is one to which they have a right, or if it is a public good in the sense discussed earlier in this book. Only if provision of the good is democratically legitimate should we then turn to the issue of how best it should be provided, whether it can be delivered most effectively by the public

*David Coats and Eleanor Passmore, "Public Value: The Next Steps in Public Service Reform," (London: The Work Foundation, 2008).

service itself or if it should be outsourced to the private sector or civil society organizations. And its democratic legitimacy can be established only through processes that involve public participation in the articulation of its purposes and foster a shared understanding of its public value.

QUESTIONS FOR FURTHER DISCUSSION

1. What features constitute "culture" or "administrative culture"?
2. List and explain the so-called collective Canadian values. How does each relate to public sector ethics?
3. What challenges does multiculturalism present for ethical practices?
4. How might multiculturalism create challenges for the delivery of services for new immigrants?
5. What is the relationship between free expression and ethical practices?
6. Explain all the different ways that section 15 of the *Canadian Charter of Rights and Freedoms* promotes equality rights.
7. Why is formal equality inadequate as a conception of equality in public service?
8. How can adopting the public values perspective support democratic legitimacy?
9. What is most promising about the public values approach? What are its greatest dangers?
10. Why does adopting public values require that we re-think the traditional relationship between public servants and a) elected officials, b) members of the public, c) service users, and d) other participants in the policy process?
11. Why might one worry that adopting the public values approach might "politicize" the public service?

Consider Cases 1, 2, 3, 5, 6, 7, 11, 15, 16, 18, 20, 22, 23, 24, 25, 27, and 28 in relation to this chapter.

NOTES

[1] P. K. Kuruvilla, "Administrative Culture in Canada: Some perspectives," *Canadian Public Administration* 16:2 (1977): 284–297, p. 286.

[2] O. P. Dwivedi and James Gow, *From Bureaucracy to Public Management: The Administrative Culture of the Government of Canada* (Peterborough, ON: Broadview Press, 1999).

[3] See Will Kymlicka, *Multicultural Citizenship* (Oxford: Clarendon Press, 1995) and *The Rights of Minority Cultures* (Oxford: Oxford University Press, 1995).

[4] See John Stuart Mill, *On Liberty* (1859).

[5] The term originated with Professor Mark Moore of the Kennedy School of Government: *Creating Public Value: Strategic management in government* (Cambridge, MA: Harvard University Press, 1995); see also the numerous resources made available by the "The Work Foundation" in the United Kingdom at www.theworkfoundation.com, and especially David Coats and Eleanor Passmore, *Public Value: The Next Steps in Public Service Reform* (London: The Work Foundation, 2008). For a more critical view, see R. Rhodes and J. Wanna, "The Limits to Public Value, or Rescuing Responsible Government from the Platonic Guardians," *The Australasian Journal of Public Administration* 66:4 (2007): 406–421.

[6] Coats and Passmore 2008, p. 7.

[7] The Work Foundation was founded in 2002, and describes itself as a not-for-profit organization that studies work and its future. Its mission is to offer its independence, expertise, and networks to organizations, policy makers, and opinion leaders in order to improve the quality of working life and the effectiveness of organizations.

[8] Coats and Passmore 2008, p. 8.

[9] Coats and Passmore 2008, p. 4. The idea of citizens being the "authorizing environment" comes from Moore 1995.

CHAPTER 7

People Values

In this chapter we examine some of the central elements of the people values to which the public service in Canada is committed. We begin with the values that must animate public servants who deal directly with members of the public, that is, with individual citizens as well as NGOs, civil society organizations, and community groups. These are the values essential within public administration for the design and delivery of public services and programs. We then turn to people values in the workplace.

7.1 RESPECT, COURTESY, AND FAIRNESS

Many civil servants serve the public directly. When they do, they must act with respect, courtesy, and fairness. Here perception is important; how members of the public perceive the service they receive from civil servants is as important as the quality of the service assessed by internal criteria.[1] The guiding value in public service is the dignity of every person, and the principles by which the dignity of persons is respected are respect, courtesy, and fairness.

One of the duties of public servants is to make government services open and genuinely accessible to all who qualify for them, without partiality, bias, or discrimination. It is imperative in a multicultural society such as Canada, which enjoys considerable diversity in its population and depends upon ongoing immigration, that public servants be sensitive to cultural differences in their clients, and the barriers that some individuals might face in accessing government services. There must be an ongoing commitment to identifying barriers to service and to finding creative solutions to them. There must be recognition that genuine equality sometimes requires unequal services or opportunities for accessing services; this is an implication of our commitment to substantive rather than formal equality.

An ethical organization does not shy away from complaints from its clients. Nor does it isolate managers from hearing complaints. It is poor institutional practice to establish public relations or complaints departments that are separate from the rest of the organization. When organizations take this approach, it quickly becomes the goal of such departments to minimize the number of complaints, and to isolate complainants from the rest of the organization. This is very bad practice. No organization is perfect, and even very good organizations can improve the quality of their service. But doing so depends critically on those in positions of authority and who design service delivery knowing where the organization is failing to achieve good results for its clients. Good institutional design empowers workers on the front lines to bring complaints forward so that they can be dealt with in an appropriate manner. Good institutional design also empowers every person in the organization to deal with complaints as they arise. If an individual hearing a complaint cannot personally remedy it, he or she ought to bear direct responsibility for finding the person who can. And there should be regular institutionally mandated opportunities for employees and managers to discuss emerging trends in the kinds of complaints that are being received.

Public servants also have a duty to promote knowledge of the work their ministry, department, or agency does. They must promote knowledge of government services among the wider public, and certainly among members of the public that make contact with their organization. It is not sufficient for ethical public servants to be entirely reactive, responding to just the requests for services that are made to them. They must also make known to their clients other services that might be of benefit to them in their particular circumstances. Suppose, for example, that a civil servant is working for Canada Pension and is contacted by a person approaching age 65 who wants to apply for her Canada Pension. It would not be adequate service if the public servant simply provided direction to the appropriate forms and nothing more. It would be proper for the public servant to inquire as to the prospective pensioner's level of income, for example, to determine whether she might also be eligible for additional income security made available by Canada Pension.

It is important that public servants meet the reasonable expectations of their clients. Sometimes, clients have unreasonable expectations, of course. In that case, the educative element of public service becomes paramount. It is not good enough to simply refuse to meet unreasonable expectations in the first instance; the public servant has a duty to explain *why* the request is unreasonable, i.e., cannot reasonably be met.

It is also important that public servants provide *reasons for decisions* affecting members of the public. Sometimes those decisions will make reference to rules and procedures, but sometimes a better explanation will also make reference to the principles and values that animate the rules and procedures. When rules and procedures are applied in isolation from the values and principles they help to realize, they may seem arbitrary or unfair. And public servants must be alive to the possibility that application of rules and procedures in an all-or-nothing inflexible way may actually give rise to unfairness or create barriers to access that were not intended. In such cases, appealing to the principles and values might assist public servants in finding creative solutions to problems.

This thought leads to another, which is vitally important. Public servants often make decisions that have profound implications for the lives of real people. But public servants are people too, and as such they are fallible. Everyone makes mistakes. Everyone makes decisions based on partial information or under conditions of uncertainty. Our fallibility is partly what defines our humanity. And it is essential that public servants who hear complaints from the public recognize their own and their colleagues' fallibility. They must be open to the possibility that a mistake has been made, that a decision is in error, and be prepared to admit the error and fix the mistake. This perhaps sounds trivial, or obvious, but it is in fact very difficult to do. We are all more or less uncomfortable with criticism and having our decisions challenged. Our egos get involved, we take affront, we get defensive, and we dig in our heels. A number of very serious mistakes made by public servants, that produced real and serious harm to members of the public, have come to light over the years. In the very worst cases, the civil servants involved seemed incapable of admitting they had made a mistake, even once it was painfully obvious that they had in fact done so. These cases should not be dismissed as aberrant, or just reflective of a few pig-headed individuals. They stem from perfectly normal and commonplace responses. Nonetheless, they must be avoided. The dangers articulated here are even more pressing in the public service than in private sector organizations, because the lack of competition for services provided in the public sector can breed complacency that further inclines against ongoing improvement in the delivery of services to the public.

When dealing with the public, civil servants must show respect for the dignity of every person. This requires treating members of the public honestly and fairly, without discrimination or partiality, and with openness and transparency.

When dealing with the public, civil servants must also display loyalty to the government and maintain their political neutrality. It would be improper for a public servant to treat members of the public differently in the delivery of government services and programs based on political affiliation, just as it would be on the basis of colour, ethnicity, sex, religion, or disability. It would also be inappropriate for a public servant to criticize the government or its policies when interacting with members of the public.

Emphasis on *service to the public* in "public" service has been increasingly stressed in the past three decades. The federal government commissioned a Task Force to examine service to the public, which issued a report in 1981. The report expresses ten enduring values of public service:

> …service delivery should be consumer-oriented, timely, sensitive to the public's needs, and equitable; it should also be accompanied by appropriate levels of information and be provided with due regard for the rights of individuals, their comfort, convenience, safety, and security; and finally, the public must be provided with recourse and response in the event of dissatisfaction.[2]

These values continue to define good public service today. We might add to them a requirement that governments make available avenues for meaningful and broad-based public input on program development, assessment, and delivery. Together with the requirements that public services be delivered in ways that are efficient and effective in realizing their objectives and meeting the needs they are intended to meet, these values ought to inform all interactions between the public service and the public. Efficiency, effectiveness, consistency, fairness, competence, responsiveness, and accessibility are all values to be realized, none of which trumps the others or has automatic priority over the others. Thus public servants must exercise judgment in determining how to achieve a proper balance between them when they conflict or compete with one another, and will have to be sensitive to the needs of those who rely upon government services in determining which values are most important to realize in any specific case. Such judgments should be guided by a commitment to delivering public service in a way that respects the individuality and dignity of clients.

7.2 PEOPLE VALUES AND ETHICAL WORKPLACES

Public servants not only interact with members of the public, of course, but with each other in their workplaces. In that capacity, they have duties to respect another set of people values: collegiality, integrity, honesty, and competence, as well as respect, courtesy, and fairness.

It is an ethical (and a legal) requirement that public service workplaces be free from harassment and discrimination. Information about the legal requirements can be obtained from the Canadian Human Rights Commission, and from provincial and territorial commissions. It is required by the *Canada Labour Code* that organizations have anti-harassment policies. There is no one policy or code that is appropriate for all workplaces; the size of an organization, the number of employees it has, and the nature of its work all influence the kind of policy that is appropriate for any given workplace. Nonetheless, all employers are responsible for preventing workplace harassment, and ensuring a healthy work environment for their employees.

7.2.1 Harassment

Harassment is any behaviour that demeans, humiliates, or embarrasses a person, and that a reasonable person should have known would be unwelcome. Some codes define workplace harassment quite broadly, such as the *Ontario Occupational Health and Safety Act*: "'workplace harassment' means engaging in a course of vexatious comment or conduct against a worker in a workplace that is known or ought reasonably to be known to be unwelcome."[3] It includes actions (e.g., touching or pushing), comments (e.g., jokes or name-calling), or displays (e.g., posters or cartoons). The *Canadian Human Rights Act* prohibits harassment on the basis of race, national or ethnic origin, colour, religion, age, sex, marital status, family status, disability, pardoned convictions, and sexual orientation. The City of Toronto goes even farther in specifying prohibited grounds of harassment, including race, ancestry, place of origin, colour, ethnic origin, citizenship, creed, sex (including pregnancy, breast feeding, and gender identity), sexual orientation, age, record of offences, marital status, family status, disability, level of literacy, political affiliation, personal harassment, and membership in a union or staff association. The City of Toronto guarantees that "every person has a right to equal treatment with respect to employment with the City without discrimination or harassment because of [these] prohibited grounds and any combination of these grounds."[4]* Every member of an organization has a duty to his or her co-workers not to engage in conduct that harasses another, or creates a poisoned work environment.

Given the above, different forms of harassment may include: sexual, racial, psychological, bullying, defamation of character, disability, electronic, stalking (both on-line and offline). It may include both Code and Personal (non-Code) harassment. Thus, for example, the City of Toronto Code distinguishes between Code and Personal Harassment this way.

> 1.8 Code Harassment: Means improper comment or conduct based on one or more of the prohibited grounds

---

*City of Toronto Human Resources Policies: *Human Rights and Anti-Harassment Policy*. Reproduced by permission.

> listed in the Ontario Human Rights Code, that a person knows or ought to know would be unwelcome, offensive, embarrassing or hurtful . . . *

Code Harassment

Examples of Code harassment based on prohibited grounds include, but are not limited to: slurs or derogatory remarks; threats; inappropriate jokes, innuendos, name-calling, teasing; insulting gestures; practical jokes that result in embarrassment; displaying pin-ups, pornography, racist, homophobic, or other offensive materials; use of electronic communications such as the Internet and e-mail to harass; actions that invade privacy; spreading rumours that damage someone's reputation; refusing to work with another; condescending or patronizing behaviour; abuse of authority that undermines performance or threatens careers; unwelcome touching, physical assault, or sexual assault.

There is no legal obligation for an individual to tell a harasser to stop. The fact that a person does not explicitly object to harassing behaviour, or appears to be going along with it, does not mean that the behaviour is not harassing or that it has been consented to.

> Personal (non-Code) Harassment: Personal (non-Code) harassment is harassment that is not related to a prohibited ground identified in the Ontario Human Rights Code. Personal harassment is improper comment and/or conduct, not related to a legitimate work purpose, directed at or offensive to another person or persons in the workplace and that the individual knows or ought reasonably to know would offend, harm or is derogatory, demeaning or causes humiliation or embarrassment.

Personal Harassment

Personal harassment often involves a course or grouping of behaviours. However, a single serious incident of such behaviour that has a lasting harmful effect on an employee may also constitute personal harassment.

Examples of personal harassment include:

- frequent angry shouting/yelling or blow-ups
- regular use of profanity and abusive or violent language
- physical, verbal, or e-mail threats, intimidation

*City of Toronto Human Resources Policies: *Human Rights and Anti-Harassment Policy*. Reproduced by permission.

- violent behaviours—slamming doors, throwing objects
- targeting individual(s) in humiliating practical jokes
- excluding, shunning, impeding work performance
- spreading gossip, rumours, negative blogging, cyber-bullying
- retaliation, bullying, sabotaging
- unsubstantiated criticism, unreasonable demands
- insults, name-calling
- public humiliation
- communication that is demeaning, insulting, humiliating, mocking.

Personal harassment does *not* include:

- legitimate performance/probation management
- appropriate exercise and delegation of managerial authority
- operational directives
- a disagreement or misunderstanding
- conflict between co-workers
- work-related change of location, co-workers, or job assignment
- appropriate discipline
- less than optimal management
- a single comment or action, unless it is serious and has a lasting harmful effect
- rudeness, unless it is extreme and repetitive.[5]

Sexual Harassment

Sexual harassment is a special kind of harassment, specifically identified by its sexual content, and where the insulting, demeaning, humiliating, or embarrassing conduct is specifically related to the sex or sexual orientation of the victim. The City of Toronto Policy is useful again:

> 4.11 Sexual Harassment: Harassment on the ground of sex. This includes a sexual advance or solicitation from anyone if they know or ought to know the advance is unwelcome, especially if the advance is from a person in a position to give or deny a benefit or to engage in a reprisal or if a threat of reprisal is made if the advance is rejected. Other examples are sexually suggestive or

obscene remarks or gestures, leering (suggestive staring) at a person's body, unwelcome physical contact, having to work in a sexualized environment (bragging about sexual prowess, or discussions about sexual activities), circulation or posting of sexist jokes or cartoons, display of pin-up calendars or other objectifying images, negative stereotypical comments based on gender, sex or sexual orientation and gender related comments about an individual's physical characteristics or mannerisms.[6]*

Harassment on the basis of sex often involves unwelcome sexual advances, requests for sexual favours, and other verbal or physical conduct of a sexual nature when (1) submission to such conduct is made either explicitly or implicitly a term or condition of an individual's employment, (2) submission to or rejection of such conduct by an individual is used as the basis for employment decisions affecting such individual, or (3) such conduct has the purpose or effect of unreasonably interfering with an individual's work performance or creating an intimidating, hostile, or offensive working environment. Conduct described under (1) or (2) is "quid pro quo" harassment, while action under (3) is "hostile-environment" harassment.

Quid pro quo sexual harassment includes the demanding of sexual favours in return for employment, advancement or promotion, favourable assignments, raises, and the like. This form of harassment typically involves power imbalances between the harasser and the victim, since the harasser must be in a position to influence the conditions of the victim's employment or make employment decisions affecting the victim; it is a form of sexual exploitation of those who are relatively vulnerable by those who are in positions of authority or power, in this case because of differential positions in a workplace. Obviously it is unethical for an employer or supervisor to demand sexual favours in exchange for giving a person a job, promotion, vacation, or the like. But many harassers do not see their conduct that way. They think a subordinate should be flattered by their sexual advances, or that they are engaged in harmless sexual banter, or that any resulting sexual relationship is consensual. From the victim's point of view, however, things may seem very different. The victims of sexual harassment often feel that they cannot say no to sexual relations with their superior, for fear of being fired or suffering other reprisals. The potential for abuse of power inevitably attends such relations. Thus considerable care must be taken in managing sexual relations in the workplace, especially between those who occupy different positions of power with the organization.

*City of Toronto Human Resources Policies: *Human Rights and Anti-Harassment Policy*. Reproduced by permission.

Some power imbalances are so extreme and so systemic that sexual relations between people in those contexts always raises reasonable doubts as to the ability of the weaker or more vulnerable party to provide genuine consent to the relationship. Interactions between parents (or other adults) and children, students and teachers, psychiatric care givers and patients, physicians and patients, prison guards and prisoners, police and detainees, clergy and penitent, and others, may be included in this group. In the contexts in which these groups interact, and given the extreme power imbalance and vulnerability within them, no sexual relations may be genuinely consensual, because the more vulnerable may feel compelled to comply with a request for sex even if the more powerful party did not engage in any activity that could be considered intimidating, threatening, or coercive. Sexual relations in such contexts may be barred through legal regulation, through a professional code of conduct imposed by professional bodies on their members, or discouraged through civil law remedies.

Sexual harassment may also create a hostile work environment for some members because of their sex. Hostile environment harassment is offensive or humiliating behaviour that is related to a person's sex, as well as behaviour of a sexual nature that creates an intimidating, unwelcome, hostile, or offensive work environment. People have the right to be free from sexual harassment that is so pervasive as to alter the conditions of employment and create an abusive working environment. Subjecting an employee to sexually stereotyped insults and demeaning propositions can affect the working environment because of their impact upon the psychological and emotional well-being of the employee, and so can constitute hostile-environment sexual harassment.

A determination of sexual harassment creating a hostile environment requires a showing of two elements. First, the behaviour must consist of unwelcome sexual advances, requests for sexual favours, or exposure to other offensive conduct because of one's sex. Whether the behaviour is unwelcome is a purely subjective matter. Because different individuals may welcome different kinds of sexual behaviour, a complainant must express, in words or actions, that the conduct is unwelcome in order for the behaviour to be actionable (despite what many Codes actually say on this matter). Second, the conduct must be sufficiently severe or pervasive to alter the conditions of the victim's employment and create an abusive working environment. Whether the conduct rises to the level of creating a hostile work environment sufficient to interfere with the victim's ability to perform her duties is determined by a "reasonable woman" standard. The specifically gendered standard of the reasonable woman reflects the fact that women perceive and respond to sexual overture, innuendo, and conduct in the workplace differently than men do. This is in large part because of the fact that women experience sex in the workplace differently than men. Sexual stereotypes differentially impact men and women; men and women are differentially secure in their workplaces and in society; and women may find sexual advances coercive given their experience of sexual violence. Thus assessing claims of sexual harassment on the basis of how the "reasonable man" would respond to the totality of the activities and contextual factors involved is simply not a reliable guide to whether those activities created an environment that is abusive and hostile to women. Similarly, paying attention to the differences between men and women is important for understanding sexual harassment as more than just offensive. To be sexually harassed is not merely to be offended; it is abusive, intimidating, degrading, and demeaning. Such behaviour defines women by their sex, and degrades them on the same basis.[7]

Racial Harassment

This is harassment on the ground of race. More specifically, it may be based on the grounds of colour, ancestry, religious belief, where a person was born, ethnic background, citizenship, cultural identity, or a person's language. Examples of racial harassment thus include: racial slurs or jokes, any form of ridicule or different treatment based on racial identity, posting/e-mailing cartoons or pictures that may degrade persons of a particular racial group, or any name-calling because of a person's race, colour, citizenship, place of origin, ancestry, ethnic background, or creed.

Bullying

Bullying is often thought of as an irrational abuse of power that can manifest itself physically, verbally, or non-verbally. The bullying behaviour is such that it humiliates, intimidates, or demeans the targeted person.

> Bullying is a form of aggression in which there is an imbalance of power between the bully and victim. The bully (or bullies) is always more powerful than the victim (or victims). Bullying can be physical, verbal and/ or psychological. It can be direct (face-to-face) or indirect (behind someone's back). Indirect bullying includes exclusion and gossip."[8]

Key elements of bullying include power imbalance; the bully's intent to harm; the victim's distress; and patterns of conduct repeated over time, through which reputations and power differentials become consolidated.

Psychological Harassment

Codes and legislation dealing with psychological harassment often refer to "inappropriate" conduct that has adverse psychological effects on its victims.[9]

In one recently amended definition, unlawful harassment now includes inappropriate conduct that

> ...adversely affects the worker's psychological or physical well-being and that the person knows or ought to know would cause a worker to be humiliated *and* constitutes a threat to the health or safety of the worker....

To constitute unlawful harassment under this expanded definition, the harassment must:

- involve repeated action or display, or

- involve a single, serious occurrence that has been established to have caused a lasting harmful effect on the worker, and

- not be any reasonable action that is taken by an employer or supervisor relating to the management and direction of the employer's workers or place of employment.[10]

Defamation of Character

This involves an attack on someone's reputation, either by slander or libel. Strictly speaking, libel involves a defamation in writing, such as in a newspaper, letter, or even via electronic means such as e-mail and other Internet or electronic-based forms of communication. Slander, by contrast, involves a verbal or spoken defamation. It may also be important to note what does *not* constitute a defamation of character. For example, general statements made about undefinable groups of people or organizations cannot be considered defamation. A specific example may include the following: "Politicians are liars." Since there is no specific identifiable victim, this is not considered a defamation of character.

Disability Harassment

Disability harassment may involve some form of intimidation or abusive behaviour toward another based on a disability. Disability harassment may also include denying another's right to participate in and benefit from services or opportunities because of his disability. This harassment may take the form of verbal or non-verbal actions, including name-calling, written statements, or any conduct that may be threatening, harmful, or humiliating. For employers, it is imperative to recognize that disability harassment also occurs if a person with disabilities is excluded or denied equal opportunity to receive program benefits and services.[11]

Electronic/Cyber Harassment

Harassment need not occur face-to-face anymore, of course, and cyber-bullying and other forms of intimidating or demeaning conduct perpetrated over the Internet or on social networking sites such as Facebook, Twitter, and MySpace are equally objectionable forms of harassment. They are also prohibited, and if committed by employers, managers, co-workers, or employees against others with whom they work, the employer or manager has a duty to address such conduct as harassment. Some forms of cyber-bullying and other on-line conduct are even criminal.

Criminal harassment can be conducted through the use of a computer system, including the Internet. Although this type of conduct is described in various ways, not all such conduct falls within Canada's definition of criminal harassment. For example, "cyber-stalking" or "on-line harassment" is often used to refer to (1) direct communication through e-mail; (2) Internet harassment, where the offender publishes offensive or threatening information about the victim on the Internet; and (3) unauthorized use, control or sabotage of the victim's computer. In some cyber-stalking situations, criminal harassment charges may be appropriate; however, depending on the activity involved, charges under sections 342.1 (unauthorized use of a computer), 342.2 (possession of device to obtain computer service), and subsection 430(1.1) (mischief in relation to data) should also be considered. Activities that can be considered cyber-stalking can include delivering threatening or harassing messages through one or more of the following:

- e-mail;

- chat rooms;

- message boards;

- newsgroups; and

- forums.

Other variations of cyber-stalking include the following:

- sending inappropriate electronic greeting cards;

- posting personal advertisements in the victim's name;

- creating Web sites that contain threatening or harassing messages, or that contain provocative or pornographic photographs, whether the images have been altered or not;

- sending viruses to the victim's computer;

- using spy-ware to track Web site visits or record key-strokes the victim makes; and

- sending harassing messages to the victim's employers, co-workers, students, teachers, customers, friends, families, or churches, or sending harassing messages forged in the victim's name to others.[12]*

Stalking

Stalking is a criminal offence, defined by Canada's *Criminal Code*, section 264, as the following:

Criminal harassment

264. (1) No person shall, without lawful authority and knowing that another person is harassed or recklessly as to whether the other person is harassed, engage in conduct referred to in subsection (2) that causes that other person reasonably, in all the circumstances, to fear for their safety or the safety of anyone known to them.

Prohibited conduct

(2) The conduct mentioned in subsection (1) consists of

(*a*) repeatedly following from place to place the other person or anyone known to them;

(*b*) repeatedly communicating with, either directly or indirectly, the other person or anyone known to them;

(*c*) besetting or watching the dwelling-house, or place where the other person, or anyone known to them, resides, works, carries on business or happens to be; or

(*d*) engaging in threatening conduct directed at the other person or any member of their family.[13]†

*Department of Justice Canada, "A Handbook for Police and Crown Prosecutors on Criminal Harassment" March 2004 at [http://www.justice.gc.ca/eng/pi/fv-vf/pub/har/ch_e-hc_a.pdf]. Accessed February 12, 2011. Copyright © Her Majesty the Queen in Right of Canada, represented by the Minister of Justice and Attorney General of Canada.

†*Criminal Code*, R.S.C. 1985, c. C-46.

It is important to note that stalking, too, can be done on-line, in what has come to be known as cyber-stalking, which can involve any of the following:

- Repeatedly sending unwanted/ inappropriate e-mails
- Pretending to be the victim and engaging in online activities such as online chats, posting personal advertisements, sending e-mails
- Circulating information on-line about the victim that may be threatening, harassing, or inappropriate (e.g., circulating altered pictures of the victim)
- Sending viruses to the victim's computer
- Tracking Web sites visited by the victim.

Employees may be afraid or silenced if an organization has no policy and procedures for identifying harassment in the workplace. And a lack of effective anti-harassment policies leaves public sector organizations open to the myriad of costs that have been associated with harassment in the workplace. Harassment costs organizations (whether public or private) money, and it is therefore in an organization's financial interest to deal with harassment. Apart from lawsuits, which can be quite costly to employers, it must also be noted that reports show that "[e]mployees who are being harassed can suffer from headaches, ulcers, tension, depression, insomnia, and other illnesses that either keep them away from work or reduce their well-being and productivity. An employee who is being harassed may resign, which penalizes that individual financially, and means that a new employee must be trained."[14] This costs both time and money.

While some employers may think that creating and maintaining policies is also costly, it is crucial to realize that "[e]ffective anti-harassment policies do not cost much to develop or to maintain. They cost much less than sick leave, poor performance, employee turnover, human rights complaints, constructive dismissal suits, workers' compensation, legal costs, and compensation for lost wages, pain and suffering."[15] Also keep in mind that sexual harassment is bad publicity for any organization. Thus, apart from being a basic moral requirement, taking the appropriate measures to avoid harassment is in the financial interest of any employer.

Unresolved workplace harassment leaves employers open to significant legal liability, should a victim of workplace harassment successfully bring an action against a harasser. Damage awards can be significant in such cases, and can be extremely harmful to an organization's reputation with the broader public. This liability is especially important for public organizations, since lawsuits against the government are inherently damaging to the perception of the government and trust in it by the public at large. Awards for damages from government agents, moreover, take vital funds away from the mission of the government, which is to serve public interests. Thus it is in the interest of public organizations to put in place clear anti-harassment policies and procedures for investigating complaints and correcting harassing conduct. Such policies must emphasize that harassment will not be tolerated, and should make explicit reference to the fact that it is against the law. In addition to setting up procedures for investigating complaints (in a way that is speedy and confidential), employers should put in place programs of ongoing education for employees and managers to prevent harassment. Such educational programs should make known the wide array of conduct that might be considered harassing, and include the use of examples. They should also include a clear statement that every employee has a right to a harassment-free workplace. Procedures for investigating allegations of harassment should make the process clear, and articulate who has responsibilities under the policy, for what, timelines, and what remedies or corrective actions are available under the policy.

Anti-harassment policies should also include protections against victimization, reprisal, or retaliation for those who make allegations of harassment in good faith. A complainant must have the following rights: to file a complaint and have it dealt with properly without fear of embarrassment or reprisal; to have a person of her choice accompany her during the process; to have no record of the complaint placed on her personnel file if made in good faith; to be informed of the progress of the complaint; to be informed of corrective measures resulting from an investigation into the complaint; and to receive fair treatment.

Both natural justice and fairness also require that the accused enjoy certain rights under anti-harassment policies and procedures, of course. Individuals accused of harassment must be informed of the complaint; given a written statement of the allegation and an opportunity to respond; have a right to have a person of their choice accompany them during the process; be informed of the progress of complaint; and to receive fair treatment.

In fulfilling their responsibilities to treat all employees with respect, supervisors, managers, and employers must investigate all complaints of harassment in a fair and timely way. In addition, they must model harassment-free conduct, setting a good example for others in the organization.

7.2.2 Discrimination

Discrimination means treating people differently, negatively, or adversely because of race, national or ethnic origin, colour, religion, age, sex (including pregnancy), sexual orientation, marital status, family status, physical or mental disability (including dependence on alcohol or drugs), or a pardoned criminal conviction.

What makes discrimination wrongful is often misunderstood. After all, we discriminate between people in countless ways, and are fully entitled to do so. We discriminate between people when choosing a spouse or sexual partner, when choosing friends or squash partners. We discriminate between people when choosing to whom to award a contract, a literary prize, and even a job.

Discrimination is only wrongful when it is based on characteristics that are arbitrary from the point of view of the decision being made, and when those characteristics reflect prejudice or stereotypes projected onto individuals simply because of their membership in a specific group. Thus it is perfectly proper to choose a spouse, sexual partner, or friend based upon quite idiosyncratic considerations: looks, common interests, common experiences, shared values, shared religion, shared tastes, and so forth. These might all be relevant to the choice in question. When choosing a squash partner, similar considerations might be brought to bear in the decision. But presumably also relevant would be squash-related abilities and interests, punctuality and shared commitment to the game, similar goals with respect to the development of squash-related skills, and so on. When choosing a recipient of a government contract, a literary award, or a job, there will be considerations that are centrally relevant: quality of product, service, and reputation among past clients; literary skills and impact, as determined by some mix of objective indicators and the judgment of learned assessors; and qualifications for the position, past employment experience, judgment of past employers, and skills that are likely to make the person a good employee, especially for the particular position in question. Of course, a responsible contractor, judge, or employer will discriminate among potential beneficiaries to identify the person most deserving of the benefit to be conveyed. Imagine the contrary: government contracts, literary awards, or jobs are distributed randomly, say by pulling a name out of a hat!

Discrimination is unethical when it is based on irrelevant or morally arbitrary characteristics, such as race, ethnic origin, religion, or sex. These characteristics are not significantly correlated with those that are relevant to the decisions in question. Moreover, the identified grounds on which persons are not permitted to discriminate have two further features in common: they are characteristics associated with groups rather than individuals, and they are characteristics around which serious negative stereotypes have been held. One feature of unjust discrimination is that it often involves the use of stereotypes based on group membership rather than individual evaluation of a person to determine whether he or she has the relevant characteristics one is looking for.

Human rights codes that prohibit discrimination on the basis of various characteristics do not typically prohibit all forms of discrimination. Persons are allowed to use religion as a basis for discriminating between potential marriage partners, for example. Rather, they prohibit discrimination in the distribution of various public goods and services. Thus they prohibit such discriminatory practices as the denial of goods, services, facilities, or accommodation on the basis of a prohibited ground; discriminatory denial of commercial premises or residential accommodation, employment, and membership in employee organizations are likewise prohibited.

In saying that employment and promotion within the public service should be based on merit, we have already expressed a commitment to non-discriminatory hiring and promotion practices. Because race, religion, sex, and the other prohibited grounds are not correlated with individual merit, they obviously cannot be the basis of hiring and promotion decisions in the public service. And, of course, gone are the days of advertisements indicating that Jews, or women, or persons with physical disabilities need not apply. Nowhere do we see promotion criteria that explicitly exclude some groups from promotion, or make membership in a specific racial, ethnic, or religious group a requirement for promotion. Such *prima facie* discriminatory policies are a thing of the past. And yet we know that members of visible racial and ethnic minorities, women, persons with disabilities, persons of aboriginal heritage, and others, are still under-represented in the public service relative to their percentage of the population. The public service has made great strides in becoming more diverse, and reflecting in its members the multicultural nature of Canada. And yet the most senior positions in the civil service are still often filled by non-disabled, heterosexual, white men (and sometimes white women).

The effects of past prejudices in our society linger yet, even while we disavow them. More insidious now than overt discrimination is *adverse effect discrimination*, which is more indirect and less visible. While people today (we hope) rarely explicitly intend to deny benefits to individuals on the basis of prohibited grounds, or to put barriers in the path of their success based on prejudice and stereotyping, many policies, institutional arrangements, and workplaces are characterized by adverse effect discrimination. Adverse effect discrimination can come about even from *prima facie* neutral policies and institutional structures and practices. To rely upon a low point of Canadian human rights jurisprudence, the Canadian Human Rights Tribunal once ruled that a corporation that denied maternity benefits to pregnant women did not discriminate on the basis of sex, since the policy denied maternity leave to men and women equally. This is an example of a facially neutral policy, applying seemingly equally to everyone, that has unequal effects. Another, more recent example, concerns the provision of sign language interpreters for deaf patients in British Columbia when seeking medical care. The province took the position that its not funding such interpreters did not constitute discrimination against deaf patients, because no patients received interpreter assistance. Of course the effect on deaf patients was very different than the effect on hearing patients, and the difference resulted in a significantly lower level of care for deaf persons.

These cases demonstrate that people can be discriminated against, even if they are treated equally with others. This usually results when persons of unequal need are treated equally with those who don't have the specific needs. Having no law requiring public enterprises to make their places of business accessible to wheel-chairs treats everyone equally, but has a very different effect on those with mobility impairments and those without. Workplaces that establish normal working hours from 9:00 a.m. to 5:00 p.m. may not be intending to discriminate against anyone, but they may have differential impacts upon those who have primary responsibility for child care, who, statistically, are still overwhelmingly women.

The impact of various institutional arrangements may generate what has come to be known as *secondary stereotyping*. If it is true at the societal level that women are still the primary caregivers of children, even if they work outside the home, then the following kind of situation can arise. When a child is ill and so cannot attend day care or school, the woman must stay home to provide care for the child. When situations of this kind are compounded (for multiple children, elder care, etc.), the woman's commitment to her employer may come to be questioned. She may receive poor performance reviews, or just not be considered for promotion or advancement because she is seen as less committed to the organization than a male counterpart who does not bear such family responsibilities. In this way secondary forms of sexism can be created. While it is acknowledged that women might be as capable as men in general, their level of commitment might be questioned, given their additional responsibilities.

Public servants are responsible for non-discrimination at a number of different levels. First, they must advise their political bosses when they identify adverse effect discrimination in government policies, regulations, or practices. Second, they must ensure that their delivery of services to the public is free of both intentional discrimination (based on prejudice or group stereotypes), and adverse impact discriminatory effect. Finally, as members of a public service workplace, they must ensure that they act in non-discriminatory ways when dealing with their fellow public servants. Although managers and employers bear special responsibility for ensuring that their workplaces are free of discrimination, all workers have a role to play in identifying and eliminating unjust discrimination.

Before leaving the topic of discrimination, it must be said that even in ethical workplaces some forms of discrimination are permitted, even if they are based on sex, age, physical or mental ability, and so forth. There may be *bona fide* requirements for a particular job, for example, that require setting conditions for employment that have the effect (and are known to have the effect) of discriminating in favour of members of one group or to the detriment of others. Certain jobs require a level of physical strength and stamina that contingently prevents most women from successfully competing for them. When such requirements are genuinely necessary for satisfactory performance of the job, even if the requirements are discriminatory in effect, they can be justifiable. This assumes, however, that women are permitted to compete for the position, so that even if most women cannot in fact meet the physical requirements, those who are able to do so and want the position may compete for it; they must not be excluded just on the basis of a stereotype about women's strength in general. Similarly, some jobs may require a level of experience that would justify age conditions, or language skills that would favour certain ethnic groups over others. Sex may even be a *bona fide* condition of employment, say for some prison guards in a female prison, or for physicians dealing with ethnic groups for whose members it is not permissible for a patient to be examined by a doctor of the opposite sex. The rationale for such exceptions must be explicit, and there must be no alternative available that is less discriminatory and still compatible with achieving the desired result. Similarly, mandatory retirement may be permissible, even though constituting discrimination based on age, and different rates of pay may be prescribed by guidelines that are based on reasonable criteria/factors, relative to the position being remunerated.

Finally, we must say something about affirmative action programs in the public service. Under the federal *Employment Equity Act*, section 15(b) of the *Canadian Charter of Rights and Freedoms*, and similar provincial legislation, differential treatment of individuals based upon group membership is permitted or even required. For this reason, critics of such equity regimes often call them "reverse discrimination," suggesting that we are permitted to discriminate in favour of those from historically disadvantaged and stereotyped groups. Employment equity or affirmative action regimes actually aim at eliminating prohibited discrimination in hiring and promotion decisions. They are based upon the presumption that members of historically disadvantaged groups continue to suffer from stereotypes and other forms of prejudice that unfairly disadvantage them in competitions for jobs and for advancement within organizations, including public service organizations. Their goal is to ensure that individuals from historically disadvantaged groups are able to effectively compete for positions within the public service. They do not require employers to hire or promote less qualified candidates over more qualified ones; rather, they require that when two candidates are of comparable quality (on relevant measures), then employers should choose the individual who is also from a disadvantaged group. This is important not only as a means of overcoming the effects of stereotyping, prejudice, and secondary sexism, but also for attaining the goal of having a public service that reflects the population it serves. The goal of employment equity is to ensure that positions are open to all persons on fair terms. And the goal of affirmative action programs is to ameliorate the conditions of disadvantage, and ensure that people are treated in substantively—not just formally—equal ways.

7.3 FOR MANAGERS—ETHICAL LEADERSHIP

Ethical conduct begins with ethical leadership, at all levels of the organization. Ethical conduct is constituted by the day-to-day ethical practices of the members of an organization. Many writers on managerial ethics suggest that the big challenge in instituting ethical values in the workplace is teaching people (especially managers) to "walk the talk," as they say. But before you can "walk the talk," you need to "talk the talk." That is, ethical managers need to learn to use ethical principles and values in their day-to-day interactions and decision making. They need to learn to explain their decisions by reference to the ethical principles and values of the organization. In this way those values become living values; they animate the activities of decision-makers, and frame the discussion of issues and outcomes. Explaining decisions in part by reference to the values and principles of the organization, as well as its more specific institutional mandate, encourages an appropriate level of transparency within organizations; it makes transparent the factors that figure into the various decisions, utilizing the central mandate of the organization and its shared values as the shared standards of justification for such decisions.

Ethical leadership involves many inter-related skills and activities. There is no single trick to ethical leadership; it consists, rather, of an orientation and a set of practical commitments. No single consideration is always more important than all the others, and so we describe some of the most important components of ethical leadership in what follows, in no particular order.

1) Encourage discussion of ethical issues.

Good leaders encourage employees to ask questions about ethical matters or issues. This requires providing regular opportunities for discussion of problems, complaints, questions, dilemmas, and the like. Having a regular agenda item at staff meetings for "emerging trends" or "extraordinary situations" opens up space for employees to raise ethical concerns that have emerged and allows group discussion of how they might be resolved.

2) Provide a mechanism for confidential disclosure of suspected wrongdoing.

Providing a safe opportunity for employees to report suspected wrongdoing can often identify problems before they become scandals. It is essential to ensure that employees understand that the point of making the internal disclosure of suspected wrongdoing safe and easy is to identify wrongdoing so that it can be corrected. The entire tenor of the disclosure regime must be preventive and corrective, rather than putative or retributive. The point must be to positively encourage ethical behaviour, not to punish bad conduct.

3) Practise non-discrimination.

Ethical managers not only avoid engaging in discriminatory practices themselves, but they convey in their everyday actions that discrimination will not be tolerated in their departments or organizations. This may be harder than it sounds, especially in organizations that are committed to equity or substantive equality, and not merely formal equality or equal treatment. Organizations that are governed by affirmative action or employment equity programs for historically disadvantaged groups must be led by individuals who can explain that such programs are not themselves discriminatory in an objectionable sense. We have already discussed non-discrimination above, but a few additional words are needed here.

Treating employees in a non-discriminatory way requires, of course, that promotion be based on merit. But it requires much more than that. It requires that personal relationships (such as close friendships) not influence decision making, in the assignment of tasks, in the distribution of holidays, in the degree to which any individual's input into decision making is favoured, or in the marginalizing of the opinions of others. It requires treating everyone as equally valuable to the organization, and an expressed, lived, recognition that every member of the group has knowledge and experience that enhances the decision making processes of the organization. It requires that stereotypes be explicitly rejected. It requires an assessment of merit that is objective and based on shared criteria, fairly applied.

Non-discrimination requires that no individual be judged on the basis of group membership. Particularized assessments, of both contributions and needs, must be relied upon, rather than stereotypes about groups. And secondary sexism must be guarded against. Secondary sexism can arise even when it is acknowledged that men and women are equally capable in general. But sexism creeps back in when work arrangements are assigned in such a way that those with primary care responsibilities for children or the aged (still typically women in our society) will find that their other responsibilities interfere with their job performance. So, for example, if it is considered essential for advancement that employees attend training sessions, or travel, and these activities are always scheduled in the evenings or on weekends, women may be systematically even if unintentionally excluded from opportunities for career advancement. The effect of workplace activities and organization may be different for different groups of workers, and such unequal effects must be considered by ethical managers. Ideally, ethical managers will routinely review the operation of their departments to identify such unintended barriers to success, and eliminate them. But secondary sexism can operate in other ways as well. If a particular female employee has care of children or elderly persons, she may be absent from work more often than a colleague without such responsibilities. If her absences are then used against her in terms of performance appraisals, or even if they simply lead to the perception that she is just not as committed to the organization as others, this is secondary sexism. Ethical managers will avoid making such false assessments, and correct others who might, but they will also try to find creative solutions to such barriers, when they produce inequity for some workers. This might require allowing caregivers to work from home in such situations, or the creation of a day care in the workplace.

4) Never allow harassment.

Ethical managers never allow harassment in the workplace. Whether it is based on racial or ethnic origins, nationality, linguistic community, religion, age, sexual orientation or sexual identity, gender, disability, or any other ground, harassment is unacceptable. Again, we have discussed harassment at length above, and so here we simply relate it to leadership. Managers must make it clear to everyone in their organizations that harassment will not be tolerated. To do this effectively they must first avoid harassment themselves, including *quid pro quo* sexual harassment. Then they must also be acutely attentive to signs of harassment by others and take steps to correct it if it is found.

Harassment produces poisoned work environments that erode productivity, collaboration, and collegiality. The victims of accepted harassment feel marginalized, unsafe, devalued, and disempowered. They dread going to work, and may develop health problems as a result of ongoing harassment. These consequences are corrosive in the extreme. And harassment affects not only the harasser and his or her victim, but others in the organization as well. Those who identify with or sympathize with the victim may express hostility toward, or at least not fully co-operate with, the perceived harasser; trust is eroded among members of the group, and proper functioning breaks down.

Good managers make it possible for harassment to be reported early, before it produces its full corrosive effects. But whether an employee will feel comfortable expressing that the harassing conduct is unwelcome, and will report it to a manager, depends upon at least two things. First, the victim must have confidence that the manager will be *willing* to deal with the problem. And, second, the victim must have confidence that the manager will be *able* to deal effectively with the problem. Both willingness and ability are necessary. And both depend upon the manager having a complex set of skills.

Managers must be sensitive to the various ways that conduct in the workplace can be unwelcome and threatening. They must understand how differentials of power can produce different perceptions of the same behaviour. What may seem like an innocent flirtation, or a genuine invitation for a sexual relationship, from the perspective of those with more institutional power or authority, may be perceived as demeaning, or an implicit threat, from the perspective of those in positions of institutional dependence or inferiority. Remarks that may seem to be good jests for some may be deeply offensive to others. Managers who tend to dismiss harassing conduct—"it's just a joke," "he doesn't mean anything by it," "it's a compliment," "don't be so sensitive," and similar responses—indicate to their staff that they do not take harassment seriously and so are not likely to be willing to deal with it appropriately. If managers refuse to see harassment for what it is, and to be sensitive to its impact on its victims, there is little reason for employees to trust that such managers will be willing to deal with it effectively.

But even if an employee believes that a manager would see the conduct as harassing, the employee may have reason to believe that the manager lacks the personal characteristics necessary to deal with it appropriately. This depends on the manager's ability to deal with conflict. Unfortunately, many people in management positions are unskilled in dispute resolution, and are uncomfortable with conflict. The first response of many managers might be to ignore the problem and hope it goes away. In many cases, they are uncomfortable with conflict, and find it difficult to discuss issues of harassment and discrimination with those alleged to have engaged in such conduct. To do so seems tantamount to accusing the alleged harasser or discriminator of being a racist, a homophobe, a sexist, or what have you. This is a very difficult thing to do, especially with respect to a person you know well and with whom you have an important working relationship. But good managers must be able to deal with conflict in a forthright and open manner. Without this, there is little reason for employees to trust them. Good leaders have both the ability and willingness to resolve disputes and disagreements.

5) Make tasks and responsibilities clear.

Good leaders assign tasks in a way that makes expectations and responsibilities clear. No matter how good the decisions of a group are, the good is not realized until the decisions are efficiently and effectively implemented. This requires that everyone responsible for executing the decision or contributing to its realization has a clear and shared understanding of who is responsible for what and when. Good managers make it clear what they expect of their employees. A common failure of new managers is leaving employees with too vague an understanding of what they are expected to do, or how their activities will contribute to a larger project. Clear expectations, with deliverables and timelines specified, are essential to the proper functioning of any complex organization. Employees cannot reasonably be expected to meet expectations that are unclear or unspecified. Nor can such expectations form a fair basis for performance appraisal by organizational superiors. As we saw earlier (5.7), clarity of tasks and responsibilities is also essential for accountability.

While it is absolutely necessary that managers assign tasks in a way that makes their expectations clear to those who are responsible for fulfilling them, it is also essential to assign tasks in a way that is realistic. Imposing responsibilities upon employees that they cannot be expected to meet, because of insufficient time, resources, information, or authority, is unfair and undermines employee morale.

Good managers also have to keep their teams focused on their tasks. And those tasks have to be sensibly related to the central mandate of the organization. This requires taking a "big picture" view of how specific projects and assignments fit into fulfilment of the overall mandate of the organization, and ensuring that the jurisdiction of one organization is properly related to those of other organizations within government. There are multiple goals being served here: the non-duplication of work, ensuring that all the tasks that must be met for the overall mandate to be fulfilled are undertaken, respect for jurisdictional boundaries and responsibilities, and overall coherence of activities.

6) Follow through.

Managers receive any number of requests, reports, complaints, recommendations, and the like. It is important that they provide timely responses to all communications received, whether from those above, parallel, or below them in the institutional structure of the organization. We have all had the experience of having worked on a report, having made a complaint, having sent a request or recommendation to another, only to be met with deafening silence. This is unacceptable. No matter what the response, negative or positive, something to be acted upon or not, good managers respond to the communications they receive.

7) Know the rules that apply to them and to others.

Managers often move from one position to another, and from one set of responsibilities to another. Different positions within the public service are governed by different rules: legislation, collective agreements, internal codes of conduct, and more. It is important for managers to make sure they familiarize themselves with the rules that govern in the various positions they occupy. Only in this way can they comply with the rules and set a proper example for others.

8) Be honest.

Honesty is a very basic ethical requirement. It requires more than merely refraining from knowingly telling falsehoods or lies, though. Lying is only one way of being dishonest. Another is withholding information altogether or telling only partial truths, that is, withholding some information in such a way that the person with whom one is communicating draws false conclusions from what you say. Exaggerating the evidence for your position is another way of being dishonest. Presenting something as certain that you know or believe is not certain, or to expressing greater confidence in some claim than your evidence for it would warrant, is less than honest.

The requirement to be honest is often summed up as the duty to tell "the truth, the whole truth, and nothing but the truth." But to see why honesty is an ethical requirement, we must recall why people are dishonest, why they might be tempted to tell untruths or partial truths, or to obscure the truth. All cases of intentional dishonesty involve deception of another person(s). But the only reason to deceive other people is to try to get them to do something they would not or might not do if they knew the whole truth. It is a form of manipulation. And it treats the person deceived, not as an autonomous decision maker, not as an equal who should be permitted to decide for himself or herself what to do, but as a tool to be manipulated into doing what the deceiver wants him or her to do. Deception shows a fundamental disrespect for the person deceived. That is what makes it unethical.

But while telling "the truth, the whole truth and nothing but the truth" may be ethically required, such truthfulness is extremely difficult. Truths can hurt those to whom they are expressed. If an employee or colleague asks whether you think she should apply for a promotion, and you believe that she is unsuited for it for some significant reason, telling the truth risks hurting her feelings at the least, and damaging your relationship at the worst. If your political superior asks for information relevant to some policy that you know to be near and dear to her heart, and the evidence suggests that such a policy would be not merely ineffective but positively damaging, telling her the truth might imperil your job. While the first situation might require tact, and the second might require courage, still the duty of honesty holds. It is tempting in such cases to consider being less than truthful as an act of kindness, as a little white lie, or as prudent. But these are rationalizations for unethical conduct. Lying is a way of avoiding conflict, but it is still deceptive. It would be better to explain in the first case the qualities that you think your employee or colleague has that would be well-suited to the position in question, while also noting that she would have to work on the areas that cause you to think she might not be fully suited for it. And in the latter case, where you are being asked by a superior about the wisdom of adopting a certain policy, you simply must tell the truth. Keep in mind that what anyone does with the information you provide is then her choice. If she chooses to ignore your information and proceed with the policy anyway, the responsibility for doing so is then hers. But if you have withheld unwelcome truths from her, and she adopts the policy, then you bear some responsibility for it as well. This is a failure of your duty to provide honest and objective advice to your superiors, but also a failure of loyalty to the Crown and to serve the public good.

9) Be consistent.

Consistency has been called the "hobgoblin of little minds," but it is a virtue in managers, when properly understood. Actually, Ralph Waldo Emerson's pithy observation is worth quoting in full: "A foolish consistency is the hobgoblin of little minds, adored by little statesmen and philosophers and divines."[16] Consistency is foolish when it replaces independent thought and responsible decision making: "that is how we have always done things" is no better justification than "I was just following orders." Emerson recognized that people in public service might be among the groups most susceptible to falling into the error of treating past practice as an authoritative guide to thought and action, regardless of whether those past practices were still appropriate to changed circumstances or in light of changing needs, values, opportunities, and understandings. Yet there is also a kind of consistency that is not foolish, and that is of considerable value within organizations. Non-foolish, virtuous, consistency is closely related to fairness and justice, insofar as it requires treating like cases alike. A manager who is consistent in his expectations, consistent in his principles and values, consistent in his treatment of others within the organizational hierarchy, consistent in his own conduct, and consistent in his directions is a person others can trust and rely upon, even if they do not agree with him on every matter. Inconsistency is disruptive, and easily leads to uncertainty, perceptions of bias or favouritism, and lack of commitment. Imagine inconsistency of an extreme kind. Imagine a manager who sometimes seems to favour conduct that meets the highest ethical standards and at others laughs off serious ethical breaches; who sometimes expects employees to work at the office during regular working hours and at other times pays no attention to workers being absent; who sometimes rewards honesty and good faith efforts and at other times harshly retaliates against those who disagree with him or who fail to meet unreasonable demands. A workplace under such a person would be a nightmare. Insecurity would undermine the effective working of the organization, as everyone tries to predict (guess, really), what he wants or values today. Obviously, then, consistency is a virtue.

But consistency should not become rigidity. The oft-forgotten second half of the requirement to treat like cases alike is to treat different cases differently. A manager who fails to modify his expectations in light of relevant differences, who imposes the same requirements on everyone, blind to the different impact of those requirements on differently situated individuals, who rigidly follows the rules though the heavens fall, is no more just or fair than one who applies different standards willy-nilly.

Consistency is required in the absence of relevant differences, and a flexible response is required when such differences are present. Accommodating relevant differences is not arbitrary. The important thing is to identify relevant differences, and why they are relevant, and make those reasons for differential actions or treatment known to all. This kind of flexibility does not undermine predictability, and need not be seen as reflecting unprincipled biases, favouritism, or caprice.

10) Monitor appropriately.

Ethical managers trust the people with whom they work, at all institutional levels. But reasonable trust is not blind trust, and managers have a responsibility to put in place appropriate mechanisms for monitoring employee activities, organizational functioning, and value for money within their operations. Such monitoring must not be so onerous that it inhibits effectiveness and efficiency; workers should not spend so much of their time meeting monitoring requirements that they cannot do their jobs effectively. The requirements of monitoring also should not convey an impression of lack of trust. Imagine an employer who called her employees every hour when she was not in the office just to make sure they were there working. Such an employer would be displaying a deep level of distrust in her employees. Such manifestations of distrust would erode productivity, create fear, and undermine morale.

A good manager monitors appropriately, neither too much nor too little. A manager bears responsibility for the conduct of employees within her organization, and so must have ways of determining how well the organization is functioning. Monitoring must illuminate problems as they arise and reveal misconduct if it develops. Unless the manager has a way of knowing what her employees are doing, she cannot fulfil her responsibilities. But, on the other hand, she must provide her employees with an environment in which they can act autonomously and exercise judgment within the bounds of their responsibilities. Trust requires not monitoring too often or too closely what those who are trusted are doing.

11) Be a mentor.

Good managers have as one of their primary responsibilities the professional and personal development of the people they oversee in the institutional hierarchy. Thus they must encourage both the creativity and motivation of their subordinates. They must also support professional development in their subordinates, and mentor them so that they may move up through the ranks of the civil service should they desire to do so. Most importantly, they must always act in such a way that the autonomy and decision making capacities of those who report to them are supported, encouraged, and continuously improved. This requires actively encouraging input from all individuals and empowering their participation. It also requires inculcating a shared sense of responsibility for the activities and accomplishments of the organization.

12) Practise ethical leadership.

Managers must encourage the organization to achieve its goals and realize its values efficiently and effectively. Their leadership should be participatory, based on open communication, empowerment, and inclusion. The activities of the organization must demonstrate respect for all its members, confidence in their abilities, and trust in their good judgment, and be organized as a co-operative venture for the public good. The spirit of the public interest must animate all their activities, thereby vesting in every member of the team a shared vision, shared commitment, shared responsibility, and shared pride in their individual and collective contribution to the public good.

An ethical workplace demonstrates in its activities and organizational structure respect for and confidence in the competence and good judgment of its members. It is not characterized by micromanaging or excessive monitoring, which undermines autonomy and disempowers and shows a lack of respect towards employees, but rather allows everyone to participate in decision making and thereby feel a shared sense of responsibility for and pride in its accomplishments. It creates the conditions under which career advancement is genuinely open to all, on terms that are fair and responsive to only morally relevant differences between individuals. It is an atmosphere in which disagreements, disputes, or conflicts are dealt with openly and promptly. It is a place where individuals can safely and in good faith report wrongdoing, without fear of reprisal. And it is place where persons can conduct their professional lives with pride, knowing that they have contributed to good government and democratic values.

13) Demonstrate integrity.

We mentioned above the "compliance approach" to ethics in the workplace, an approach that was characterized as rule-driven. This is often contrasted with what is called an "integrity approach." "An integrity approach, in contrast to a compliance approach, empowers the individual to make value judgments about right and wrong. It is values driven rather than rule driven."[17]* Ethical leadership both embodies and encourages in others such integrity. Donald Menzel describes integrity so well that he is worth quoting in full:

> Integrity: Demonstrating fairness, honesty, and ethical and legal awareness in personal and professional relationships and activities (requires knowledge of business and personal ethics; ability to understand issues of ethics and integrity in specific situations). Practices that contribute to this core content area are:
>
> - Personal integrity: Demonstrating accountability for personal actions; conducting personal relationships and activities fairly and honestly.
>
> - Professional integrity: Conducting professional relationships and activities fairly, honestly, legally, and in conformity with the International City/County Management Association Code of Ethics (requires knowledge of administrative ethics and specifically the ICMA Code of Ethics).
>
> - Organizational integrity: Fostering ethical behavior throughout the organization through personal example, management practices, and training (requires

*Donald C. Menzel, *Ethics Moments in Government: Cases and Controversies* (NY: CRC Press, 2010), p. 5.

knowledge of administrative ethics; ability to instil accountability into operations; and ability to communicate ethical standards and guidelines to others).[18]*

As this makes clear, integrity is a multifaceted virtue, which imposes duties to know as well as duties to act. It is in part for this reason that we have included such extensive discussions of discrimination and harassment policies and laws, since demonstrating integrity requires knowledge of the duties imposed by these instruments.

14) Demonstrate ethical competence.

We might summarize the various characteristics, skills, commitments, and knowledge that ethical managers possess and display as comprising ethical competence. Again, Menzel's extensive work with managers in public administration is useful in characterizing ethical competence: "[A]n ethically competent government manager is (1) committed to high standards of personal and professional behavior, (2) has knowledge of relevant ethics codes and laws, (3) has the ability to engage in ethical reasoning when confronted with challenging situations, (4) is able to identify and act on public service ethics and values, and (5) promotes ethical practices and behavior in public agencies and organizations."[19]† Understood this way, ethical competence is itself a product of more specific competencies. Those listed by Menzel (in no particular order) are the following.

Ethical Competencies:

- Be knowledgeable of ethical principles.
- Be aware and informed of relevant professional codes of ethics.
- Recognize and promote constitutional principles of equality, fairness, representativeness.
- Recognize and support the public's right to know the public's business.
- Respect the law.
- Serve the public interest.
- Engage in ethical reasoning.

*Donald C. Menzel, *Ethics Moments in Government: Cases and Controversies* (NY: CRC Press, 2010), p. 18.

†Donald C. Menzel, *Ethics Moments in Government: Cases and Controversies* (NY: CRC Press, 2010), p. 18.

- Recognize and differentiate between ethical and management issues.

- Respect and protect privileged information.

- Embrace and promote ethical behavior and practices in the workplace.

- Refuse to do something unethical.

- Maintain truthfulness and honesty.

- Guard against conflict of interest or its appearance.

- Be responsible for one's behavior.[20]*

Though put forward by Menzel as ethical competencies for managers, we think that to the extent that any public servant has authority to make decisions and bears responsibilities for the achievement or realization of public values, that public servant should try to realize these same ethical competencies in the performance of his or her work for the public. The more these competencies are shared by members of the public service, at all levels, the more likely it will be that government operations are conducted ethically.

15) Manage for public value.

Following from the public value perspective, managers must develop

- strong communication skills (to convey necessary information to the public so that the resulting dialogue is informed and public expectations are aligned with those of the organization undertaking the community engagement process);

- strong negotiation skills (because even after individuals and groups have taken on the perspective of citizens seeking public value in articulating the purpose of public service organizations and giving input to their implementation, there will often continue to be difficult priorities to set and tough choices to be made); and

- good arbitration skills (because there will still often be "losers" in the process who do not get what they want or all of what they want through participation in the policy process).

*Donald C. Menzel, *Ethics Moments in Government: Cases and Controversies* (NY: CRC Press, 2010), p. 20.

In addition, by urging that all staff in public service organizations adopt an outside-in perspective, viewing their organizations from the perspective of citizens and users, managers must empower staff to act on the feedback generated through ongoing deliberative community engagement. Here we again find ourselves in agreement with Coats and Passmore:

> A natural consequence of this line of argument is that staff must be seen as part of the authorising environment too. We might also say that Moore offers only a partial account of how high quality public management can be created and sustained because he says so little about the management of the people delivering public services. Our suggestion is that all employees should be motivated and incentivised to view their service from the "outside in," or from the perspective of the service user or citizen. The aim must be to create a reflective frame of reference where public servants have both the capacity for constructive criticism and the capability to devise creative solutions to the problems they confront.[21*]

This requires not only empowering staff, but also distributing responsibility for the delivery of public value throughout organizations. It requires an openness to local needs and local knowledge, and management systems that foster collaboration between the multitude of actors involved in the design and delivery of public services. If staff are expected to treat the public respectfully, they must in turn be treated with respect by their managers, and one way of demonstrating respect is to ensure that the contributions of staff to realizing public value are enabled and rewarded.

QUESTIONS FOR FURTHER DISCUSSION

1. Explain, in your own words, the difference between substantive and formal equality.

2. Does equality always mean identical treatment? Why or why not?

3. What three "people values" are important for public service?

4. What are some of the ways public servants can respect the dignity of persons?

*David Coats and Eleanor Passmore, "Public Value: The Next Steps in Public Service Reform," (London: The Work Foundation, 2008).

5. What does harassment mean? What forms can harassment take? Is harassment only physical and verbal in nature? In your answer, be sure to discuss all types of harassment.

6. Do you think it is appropriate for public service co-workers to become romantically involved? Why or why not?

7. What two elements are considered when determining whether sexual harassment is creating a hostile workplace?

8. Do you think that any, and all, attacks on someone's reputation are necessarily slander?

9. What are some of the costs associated with workplace harassment (for both public or private organizations)?

10. List all the features you think should be included in an anti-harassment policy.

11. What is the difference between discrimination and harassment? Do you think that discrimination is a form of harassment?

12. Is discrimination always a bad thing?

13. What is secondary stereotyping?

14. How can public servants help combat discrimination?

15. How can managers help promote non-discrimination?

16. In what ways can managers actually contribute to harassment and discrimination in the workplace? (It might be useful to think of how they can help prevent harassment before thinking of how their actions can also contribute to it.)

17. Are public servants required to always be truthful? If not, then under what conditions can a public servant elect to not be truthful?

Consider Cases 3, 4, 9, 12, 13, 14, 16, 17, 18, 19, 20, 21, 22, 28, and 30.

NOTES

[1] For a more detailed account of the importance of public perception of ethics in government, see George and David Frederickson "Public Perception of Ethics in Government" *Annals* 537 (1995): 163–172. It is generally thought that citizens typically hold a negative view of government ethics, and citizens are most likely to lump together government officials into one big category, thereby failing to take notice of the different levels within the public sector. Thus it remains of high importance that this be addressed, as it contributes greatly to the legitimacy and efficiency of governments.

[2] Report of the Task Force on Service to the Public, Feb. 2, 1981 unpublished; reported in *The Responsible Public Servant*, p. 113.

[3] *Occupational Health and Safety Act* R.S.O. 1990, Chapter 0.1 Amended 2009, c. 33, Sched. 20, s. 3.

[4] *City of Toronto Human Resources Policies: Human Rights and Anti-Harassment Policy.*

[5] Ibid.

[6] Ibid.

[7] See *Stadnyk v. Canada* (*Employment and Immigration Commission*) (2000)—Federal Court of Appeal—Date: 2000/07/21. See also Susan Dimock, "Reasonable Women in the Law," *Critical Review of International Social and Political Philosophy* 11:2 (2008): 153.

[8] Debra J. Pepler and Wendy Craig, "Making a Difference in Bullying," *LaMarsh Centre for Research on Violence and Conflict Resolution*, Report #60, April 2000.

[9] "Psychological Harassment is the term used in The [Saskatchewan] Occupational Health and Safety (Harassment Prevention) Amendment Act, 2007 to introduce statutory protection against personal harassment into the existing human-rights based definition of harassment." University of Regina Human Resources, "Types of Harassment" at http://www.uregina.ca/hr/hdpo/understanding-and-recognizing/what-is-harassment/types-of-harassment. Accessed November 2010.

[10] Ibid.

[11] Perhaps the strongest legislation dealing with harassment and discrimination based on disability is found in the *Ontarians with Disabilities Act*, 2001, S.O. 2001, c. 32.

[12] Department of Justice Canada, "A Handbook for Police and Crown Prosecutors on Criminal Harassment" March 2004 at http://www.justice.gc.ca/eng/pi/fv-vf/pub/har/ch_e-hc_a.pdf. Accessed November 2010.

[13] *Criminal Code*, R.S.C. 1985, c. C-46.

[14] Canadian Human Rights Commission, "Anti-Harassment Policies for the Workplace: An Employer's Guide" March 2006, pp. 4–5.

[15] Ibid., p. 6.

[16] Ralph Waldo Emerson, "Self Reliance" in *Essays: First Series* (1847).

[17] Donald C. Menzel, *Ethics Moments in Government: Cases and Controversies* (NY: CRC Press, 2010), p. 5.

[18] Menzel 2010, p. 18.

[19] Menzel 2010, p. 18.

[20] Menzel 2010, p. 20.

[21] David Coats and Eleanor Passmore, "Public Value: The Next Steps in Public Service Reform" (London: The Work Foundation, 2008), p. 11.

CHAPTER

Disclosure of Wrongdoing

In the foregoing we have tried to describe some of the things public service organizations can do to promote ethical conduct among their members. Yet we know that, in the real world of government work, serious ethical lapses, and even illegal conduct, can occur. When a public servant thinks that the actions of an *elected official* are seriously wrongful—an act in contravention of applicable law, a serious violation of the ethical requirements of the elected officials, a serious misuse of public funds, or an act posing serious risk to the life or health of individuals or the natural environment—the public servant faces a dilemma, a conflict of loyalties at the very least. Generally when there is a conflict between a public servant's judgment of what is in the public interest and the elected official's judgment, the civil servant's duty is to express her concerns in private and in confidence to the official, but the final authority and responsibility rest with the elected official. Yet when a public servant honestly and in good faith believes that the official is engaged in serious wrongdoing, or that a policy being pursued would place individuals at undue risk of harm, she has a duty to act. She has an ethical obligation to disclose the wrongdoing. This obligation flows both from the duty of loyalty to the Crown, and from the duty to serve the public good. To whom such wrongdoing should be reported in cases involving elected officials varies across jurisdictions.

A civil servant may also come to believe that serious wrongdoing is being perpetrated by *other civil servants*, rather than elected officials, and it is this case that will occupy us in this chapter. A duty to disclose the wrongdoing may exist in this case as well, though here the conflict will be with different values, such as collegiality, as well as loyalty to one's department or agency.

Though we will discuss one particular disclosure regime in what follows (that adopted for the Federal Public Service through the *Public Servants Disclosure Protection Act (PSDPA)* 2005), public service organizations have a choice about the approach(es) they take to reporting wrongdoing and acting on such reports. Formal mechanisms like that outlined in the *PSDPA* are only one possibility, and a pretty draconian one at that. The broad ethical approaches described at the beginning of this book suggest differing approaches that organizations might take. A Kantian deontologist might take a fairly rigid and rule-based approach to wrongdoing. Wrongdoing is wrongdoing, and participation in or complicity with wrongdoing is always itself a form of wrongdoing. Such a moral frame might lend itself to the kind of formal disclosure mechanism described below. A more consequentially minded person will weigh the costs and benefits of various possible approaches, seeking mechanisms to address wrongdoing that needs to be corrected but by methods that cause the least harm to those involved. He will look at the consequences of various possible methods to address wrongdoing and try to find those that are least harmful in their effects. Someone attracted to a virtue ethics approach might seek to discover the causes of wrongdoing in forms of personal moral corruption and to address them through remedial mechanisms. He would try to understand what caused the transgression, work with the wrongdoer to see how it compromises her character to engage in such conduct, and work to strengthen the personal virtue of the transgressor so that she can make genuine amends and move forward with greater personal integrity. This approach would be more educative and remedial than punitive or retributive. Alternatively, a person might be influenced in his approach to wrongdoing by the insights of critical social perspectives, and especially the kinds of practices that come out of some feminist and aboriginal practices. These, too, fall more on the remedial side, but they are more collectivist in their approach. Wrongdoing rarely involves just one bad apple acting out, but is rather a product of multiple failures by a number of people in an organization. They might seek mechanisms to explore the various responsibilities borne by the different players in the wrongdoing, and seek collective remedies that have support from all those involved, and explicit commitments regarding how each will support better conduct going forward. This might involve mediation, reconciliation, and healing processes. The point would be to identify how the collective made the wrongdoing possible, and it would promote a sense of shared responsibility for addressing it. Finally, those of a contractarian bent might approach wrongdoing from a variety of perspectives, depending upon its seriousness and the factors contributing to it. Some wrongdoing is such a serious violation of the rules that make mutual benefit possible that punitive responses might be needed, but other transgressions might be better dealt with by less formal processes. The point is that formal disclosure mechanisms are only one of a range of possible options, and are not necessarily always the best option. A values-based approach to ethics would insist that we create possible avenues for addressing wrongdoing that appeal to shared values and the principles needed to realize them; this approach would include significant emphasis on education and remediation.

In part, what approach it is most appropriate to take depends upon the nature of the wrongdoing and the institutional context in which it occurs. Whether formal disclosure is the best decision or not will depend, for example, on whether there is an alternative constructive approach you could take that would not involve the disclosure of wrongdoing by particular individuals. If you suspected wrongdoing, could you approach your senior officer to suggest that training was needed with respect to some activity, as an alternative to reporting it? Or could you suggest to other senior managers that a policy or procedure is needed with respect to some activity within your organization? The answer to such questions will depend in part on whether the wrongdoing is being done knowingly and intentionally, or is the result of lack of procedures or policies, clear expectations or requirements, or unresolved value conflicts. If it is the result of poor monitoring or other failures of management, then it might be the kind of wrongdoing that could be corrected with better policies, procedures, training, or monitoring.

Exploring alternatives to formal disclosure mechanisms is important because disclosure regimes have significant costs in and of themselves. First, they tend to treat wrongdoing as an individual transgression for which a specific individual is wholly responsible. This is a familiar feature of our current retributive approaches to crime and criminal punishment as well. But we know that wrongdoing is often a product of collective failures, a matter of shared responsibility, and caused by situational and institutional factors in addition to bad personal choices and vice. Such institutional and collective failures tend to be masked by formal disclosure regimes that name individual wrongdoers. Second, formal disclosure regimes can undermine morale, because they imply a sense of distrust in employees and even managers. Such regimes seem to assume that wrongdoing will occur unless there is a perpetual threat that potential wrongdoers will be turned in if they give in to temptation to do wrong. Related to this, formal disclosure mechanisms may undermine creativity and innovation, by making public servants more risk-averse. Public servants might be less willing to take risks if they believe their conduct is under continuous scrutiny from their peers and supervisors. Given the possibility of misunderstanding what others are doing and why in complex organizations, the standing possibility that others might report your conduct as wrongdoing based on such misunderstandings undermines collegiality, trust, and collaboration. These and many more potential detriments to formal mechanisms must be considered by any agency deciding what mechanism (or combination of mechanisms) might be best suited to their organization to make possible the disclosure of wrongdoing and its correction.

8.1 FORMAL DISCLOSURE MECHANISMS

Different jurisdictions have established different mechanisms and procedures for the disclosure of wrongdoing, and some have protection from reprisal for "whistle-blowers" who in good faith disclose suspected wrongdoing. An ethical organization takes steps to make sure that it has procedures for whistle-blowing or the disclosure of wrongdoing, as well as protection against reprisal or retaliation for such disclosure. But disclosure of wrongdoing cannot be an end in itself. Disclosure of wrongdoing is only instrumentally valuable, and even then, only when certain conditions are met. Whistle-blowing is valuable if, and only if:

1. it is effective in enabling the disclosure of wrongdoing (if the allegation of wrongdoing will be taken seriously, for example, and be investigated appropriately);

2. it contributes to an institutional culture of ethical conduct;

3. it enhances trust and integrity in the institution, its members, and its procedures;

4. it is fair and provides natural justice to all participants;

and, most important,

5. it is aimed at promoting "right doing" rather than the detection and punishment of wrongdoing *per se*; and

6. it has as its ultimate end the identification of wrongdoing so that it can be corrected, rather than punished.

Whistle-blower policies must be part of a larger ethics regime, an institutional orientation that expects ethical conduct from its members and encourages ethical practices. Whether a particular whistle-blower policy can achieve the goods it might make possible depends upon a large number of (sometimes inter-related) factors. First, it must make clear the kinds of wrongdoing covered by the policy. It must cover only serious wrongdoing, engaged in within a specified period of time. And it must make clear the relationship between the disclosure policy and other instruments, such as collective agreement grievance mechanisms.

One of the ways whistle-blowing policies can be useful is in establishing clear pathways for reporting wrongdoing. A good disclosure policy will provide clear guidance with respect to how wrongdoing is reported, and to whom. It will vest responsibility for dealing with allegations of wrongdoing in specific officers or managers within the organization, and will ensure that those who are responsible for receiving such complaints are trained appropriately. Allegations of wrongdoing must be dealt with as expeditiously as possible, and the person making the allegation must be informed, in writing, of the progress of the allegation, any investigation that has been conducted, and any outcome of such investigation. Such reports should include reasons for decisions at every step in the process.

Disclosures of wrongdoing must be made in good faith, and not be vexatious or frivolous. Members of an organization (whether civil servants or elected officials) must be protected against trivial or bad faith allegations. Anonymity increases the potential for abuse, for bad faith reporting of alleged wrongdoing. Disclosures should thus not be made anonymously, though the protection of the identity of those making disclosures may sometimes be very important. (For this reason, the Internet whistle-blower site Wikileaks is not an ideal construct.)

A successful whistle-blower policy will put in place good investigative procedures once wrongdoing has been reported (Stage 1). Among the elements that should be incorporated into such investigation policies is a guarantee that officials will not act on anonymous allegations (except perhaps in extraordinary situations of imminent threat of serious harm). But if anonymous reporting is to be barred, then the confidentiality of complainants and those making disclosures must be protected if there is a credible risk that the discloser will face unjust workplace reprisals for his disclosure. Ideally individuals coming forward to report wrongdoing will do so only as a last resort, and so they will have tried other routes for reform prior to disclosing. And ideally they will be sufficiently confident that serious wrongdoing is occurring and cannot be remedied by lesser steps that they will not insist on confidentiality unless reprisal is an issue. Investigations must be as informal and expeditious as possible. At the same time, investigations must be fair and conform to principles of natural justice for the accused, including the right to provide a full answer to the allegation of wrongdoing. Investigators must have the power to compel witnesses and documents. And investigators must be protected from legal liability for the proper fulfilment of their investigative responsibilities.

But putting in place mechanisms through which wrongdoing can be reported is only the first step in a disclosure policy (Stage 1). Such policies must also protect those who make good faith allegations of wrongdoing from reprisal or retribution (Stage 2). There must be protection against reprisal both for those who report suspected wrongdoing, and for those who refuse to participate in wrongdoing. There must also be protection against reprisal for those who participate in or co-operate with an investigation of alleged wrongdoing, as well as parallel processes by which allegations of reprisal can be received and investigated.

If formal mechanisms are necessary, the model we favour is that of an independent Integrity Commissioner or Ethics Officer. Such an official is specially trained in the appropriate ethics code/code of conduct/conflict of interest code under which wrongdoing is defined, as well as investigative techniques. The ethics officer must be able to recommend not only appropriate disciplinary measures if wrongdoing or reprisal is found, but also a series of practical steps to be undertaken within the organization to correct the causes of the wrongdoing, as well as having the right to monitor the progress on those steps in the future. The independence of the ethics officer must be guaranteed. There must be no undue influence from either elected officials or senior civil servants in the investigation of allegations of wrongdoing or reprisal, or with respect to the officer's recommendations concerning appropriate discipline, should such allegations be proved. One measure that assists in guaranteeing the independence of an ethics officer is ensuring that the budget of the ethics officer is not subject to political or bureaucratic control. The ethics officer should be authorized to conduct investigations into both allegations of wrongdoing and allegations of reprisal. The central mandate of such officers is to work with the parties to find a mutually acceptable resolution to problematic behaviour. The focus must be on correcting unethical conduct, in the first instance, rather than on punishment for its own sake.

Ethics officers play a further and absolutely invaluable educative role in organizations. Enforcement or ensuring compliance should be only a secondary activity for such officers. Their primary task should be promoting right-doing through various educational activities. Most importantly, members of a department or agency can seek advice from their ethics officer with respect to any matters that they might be unsure about or wish guidance in. In this way ethics officers can provide advice that prevents potential wrongdoing before it happens, rather than simply reacting to wrongdoing once it has occurred.

8.2 DISCLOSURE IN THE FEDERAL PUBLIC SERVICE: AN EXAMPLE OF ETHICAL DECISION MAKING[1]

The *Public Servants Disclosure Protection Act* (2005), and the Office of the Public Sector Integrity Commissioner (PSIC) which it created, provides a framework and operational mechanisms designed to facilitate the disclosure of wrongdoing in the public service by public servants and to protect those who disclose wrongdoing in good faith from reprisal. The *Act* similarly makes provision for disclosure of wrongdoing by members of the public. The purpose of the *Act* and the Public Sector Integrity Commission is not to detect wrongdoing for its own sake, however, but to identify wrongdoing so that it may be corrected, so that procedures and policies may be improved, and so that public trust in the integrity of our public institutions may be maintained and strengthened.

The decision to disclose wrongdoing in the public service is morally complex. Rarely will a person contemplating making such disclosure be faced with an ethically simple or clear choice between going forward and staying silent. This guide is designed to ensure that potential disclosers have considered all of the ethically important factors that should be considered in reaching their decision, and to inform potential disclosers of the range of options available to them under the *Act*. (Though the PSIC has had some difficulty in its first iteration, with the first Integrity Commissioner Christiane Ouimet resigning in disgrace after a damning Auditor's General Report, we use it just as an example against which a decision to make a formal disclosure of wrongdoing might be made. The fact that very few public servants used the PSIC process, few investigations were carried out, and no findings of wrongdoing were made, demonstrates the limited effectiveness of such tools in the absence of trust that complaints will be taken seriously and acted upon appropriately.)[2]

8.2.1 Wrongdoing

The *Public Servants Disclosure Protection Act* establishes mechanisms through which public servants may disclose serious wrongdoing in their workplace. Not all forms of wrongdoing, however, fall under the *Act* and so under the jurisdiction of the Public Sector Integrity Commission office. It limits itself (appropriately in our view) to serious wrongdoing. The kinds of wrongdoing reportable under the *Act* are:

- contravention of any Act of Parliament or legislature of a province, or of any regulations made under any such Act, with certain explicit exclusions;

- misuse of public funds or public assets;

- gross mismanagement;

- any act or omission that creates a substantial and specific danger to the life, health, or safety of persons, or to the environment;

- a serious breach of a code of conduct established by the Treasury Board applicable to the public sector or a code of conduct established within a specific organization of the public sector; and

- knowingly directing or counselling a person to commit one of these wrongs. (*PSDPA* s. 8)[*]

*Public Sector Integrity Commission Office: PSDPA s. 8.

Public servants may have a number of complaints or grievances that may not fall within the scope of wrongdoing so defined. Complaints of harassment, for example, or discontents arising from staffing practices, may be addressed under collective agreements or other mechanisms. Having a person in place, such as the Registrar of the Public Sector Integrity Commission, to point individuals toward the proper avenue for redressing complaints that fall within the jurisdiction of another office or mechanism is a valuable addition to such frameworks.

8.2.2 Good Faith Reports of Wrongdoing

Allegations of wrongdoing must be made in good faith. Good faith has the following components:

- Public rather than private interest—Disclosures of wrongdoing must serve the public interest. In making an allegation of wrongdoing, you must consider your motives in doing so (as well as possible perceptions of your motives).

- Are you trying to identify wrongdoing so as to correct it?

- Do you stand to benefit personally from the allegation? If you are alleging wrongdoing by an immediate superior, for example, whose job you might stand for should your superior be removed from the position, it may be perceived that you are motivated by personal ambition rather than the public good. Are you?

- Is your disclosure based on personal animus, jealousy, revenge, unresolved past grievances, or other conflict between yourself and the person against whom the allegation is being made? Is there any evidence that might cause a reasonable person to see it that way?

We are not suggesting that serious wrongdoing should be allowed to continue just because the person who has the evidence to bring that wrongdoing to light doesn't come with clean hands, or the purest of motives. Those to whom wrongdoing is reported must make their decision about whether to proceed based upon the strength of the evidence of wrongdoing that is disclosed, and whether the public interest will be served by an investigation into the complaint. Likewise, a member of the civil service or a member of the public may have a duty to disclose serious wrongdoing of which they are aware, regardless of their motives for disclosing. But a realistic assessment of how such disclosures will be received, and how credible a complainant is perceived to be, must include consideration of the motives of the discloser. The question to be asked is whether the public interest will be served by identification of the wrongdoing and its correction. The answer to that question will not be determined by the motives of the discloser, but in determining whether the case can be made that the public interest is served by the disclosure and subsequent investigation, the motives of the discloser may well come under scrutiny. If you are contemplating disclosure, then, you must consider how your motives will be interpreted and whether you can support the allegation of wrongdoing and the claim that disclosing it is in the public interest, even if your motives are less than pure.

8.2.3 Made on the Basis of Evidence

If you are going to make a disclosure of wrongdoing, you must have evidence that supports both the allegation that wrongdoing is occurring and that the person(s) you have identified is (are) responsible for the wrongdoing. Among the questions you might ask yourself are these:

- Do you have evidence to support your allegations? Do you have information that is material and relevant to the allegation, information that supports the specific allegation of wrongdoing and who is responsible for it?

- Would your evidence convince a reasonable person that serious wrongdoing had occurred, was occurring, or was encouraged?

- Can you provide the kind of information that is asked for on the Disclosure Form (**http://www.psic-ispc.gc.ca/doc.php?sid=29&lang=eng**)?

8.2.4 Exploring Alternative Remedies

The point of the wrongdoing disclosure regime for public servants is to enable public servants to disclose wrongdoing so that appropriate remedies can be found. It is not, in the first instance, designed as a detection and punishment exercise. Its purpose is more positive: to put in place a series of procedures by which wrongdoing can be identified and corrected. Thus good faith requires public servants to consider all the avenues available to correct wrongdoing. Have you explored other avenues to address the problem? Have you weighed the advantages and disadvantages of using the internal mechanisms provided for in the *Act* compared to reporting directly to the Commission? (These are discussed in more detail below.) If you are sure that you are acting for the public interest, to ensure the integrity of the public service and to maintain public trust in its integrity, on the basis of good evidence, and that there are no better avenues available to correct the wrongdoing, disclosure may be ethically required.

8.3 TO WHOM SHOULD YOU DISCLOSE? INTERNAL REPORTING OR DISCLOSURE TO COMMISSION

The *Act* establishes two broad mechanisms for disclosure of wrongdoing, which we might call "internal" and "Commission" for ease of reference.

8.3.1 Internal Disclosure

Every chief executive is required to establish an internal mechanism through which wrongdoing can be confidentially reported within his/her area of the public sector. A senior officer may be designated to deal with such disclosures (*PSDPA* ss. 10–12). A senior officer must be designated within every organization of the public service to receive and act on complaints of violations of the *Values and Ethics Code for the Public Service* established by the Treasury Board (*PSDPA* s. 10(2)).

Whether you should utilize the internal disclosure mechanism will depend upon a number of factors:

- Is the chief executive/senior officer implicated in the wrongdoing?
- Does the chief executive/senior officer know about the wrongdoing? Do you have any way of knowing what the senior managers know about the wrongdoing?
- Does the wrongdoing stem from a systemic or organizational defect, i.e., the lack of clear policies or procedures, or does it involve a violation of clear policies and procedures?
- Has your chief executive appointed a senior manager or put in place effective mechanisms, policies, and procedures for confidentially reporting wrongdoing?
- Is there a constructive approach you could take that would not involve the disclosure of wrongdoing by particular individuals? For example, could you approach your senior officer to suggest that training is needed with respect to some activity, as an alternative to reporting? Or could you suggest to other senior managers that a policy or set of procedures is needed with respect to some activity within your organization?
- Related to the previous: is the wrongdoing being done knowingly and intentionally, or is it the result of a lack of procedures or policies, clear expectations, or requirements? Is it the result of poor monitoring or other failures of management? Is it the kind of wrongdoing that could be corrected with better policies, procedures, training, or monitoring?

- Do you trust your chief executive/senior officer or other senior managers to deal effectively with requests for corrective action such as those suggested above (education, training, adoption of specific policies or procedures)?

- To trust your chief executive/senior officer to take appropriate corrective action to address wrongdoing requires that you think he or she is both competent to do so and willing to do so. Does your senior officer have the personality (strength of character, commitment to ethics, courage, comfort in dealing with difficult issues in an open and constructive manner) and ability needed to put in place effective mechanisms to correct wrongdoing without outside intervention? Do you think he or she will be open to the kinds of constructive proposals suggested here? Do you know?

- Do you trust your chief executive/senior officer to treat you fairly, in accordance with principles of procedural fairness and natural justice?

- Do you have genuine access to your chief executive/senior officer? In practical terms, can you access such people confidentially, without others in the organization knowing you have done so?

8.3.2 Disclosure to Commission

You may want to report the wrongdoing through the Commission (*PSDPA* s. 13) rather than disclose wrongdoing internally if any of the following apply to you:

- You do not have realistic confidential access to your chief executive/senior officer;

- You do not believe your chief executive/senior officer is willing and able to put in place corrective measures;

- You do not believe your chief executive/senior officer will respect the principles of procedural fairness and natural justice in his/her treatment of you, or that he/she is willing and able to keep your identity and the information you share with him/her confidential;

- You believe your chief executive/senior officer knows of the wrongdoing, is complicit in the wrongdoing, is participating in the wrongdoing, is benefitting from the wrongdoing, or is counselling or directing the wrongdoing;

- You have tried to get your chief executive/senior officer or other senior managers to put in place corrective measures such as training, policies, procedures, and monitoring mechanisms and they have failed to act effectively in doing so;

- You think that there is a significant danger to the life, health, or safety of persons or the environment that cannot be resolved in a timely enough manner by pursuing internal procedures for disclosure; or,

- You think that wrongdoing is so systemic (pervasive, historically ingrained, part of the very culture of the organization, unrecognized as wrongdoing because it is so widely practised or accepted as a normal part of operations) that outside assistance is needed to rectify the situation.

8.4 INTEGRITY AND PUBLIC TRUST: THE BOTTOM LINE

Imagine that a complete and accurate description of the wrongdoing of which you are aware were to appear as the front page story on every national newspaper, including your involvement and knowledge. Don't imagine the worst spin the most disreputable journalists might put on the story, but rather that a full description of the activity or practice was presented that correctly described everyone's involvement, including yours. Could you look yourself, your children, your parents, your spouse, your friends, your colleagues, your managers, your minister, and the public in the eye after such a revelation? If not, you believe there is serious wrongdoing and that you are implicated in it, even if just because of what you think you know about it. Remember: personal conscience and the moral emotions are often reliable guides to ethical insight.

8.5 WHO ARE THE STAKEHOLDERS IN YOUR DECISION TO DISCLOSE OR NOT?

No doubt when you thought about this question, given that we are talking about wrongdoing in the public service and so in your workplace, you thought about these people as those who might be impacted by your disclosure.

1) The person(s) against whom the allegation of wrongdoing is being made.

This is a very serious consideration. All disclosures of wrongdoing involve accusations against alleged wrongdoers. What impact will your disclosure likely have on those you believe are committing the wrongdoing? In extreme cases, disclosures of wrongdoing may end careers, result in public humiliation and disgrace, even lead to criminal prosecution. These are serious effects indeed, extending often beyond the individual directly involved and impacting his or her family as well. It might be cold-hearted to suggest that wrongdoers deserve what they get, even if that may be true. There are real people involved in your decision, often persons with whom you have had a significant relationship as colleagues, possibly as friends.

To what extent do you have an obligation of loyalty to the person against whom you are making an accusation of wrongdoing? Certainly you have an obligation not to raise frivolous or vexations accusations, given the wide-ranging consequences this can have for a person's career, reputation, and family. Suspicions of wrongdoing, even if they prove unwarranted, often stick to people long after an investigation has cleared them of any actual fault. That is why it is important to have critically assessed your own motives, and your evidence, before making an allegation.

If you are also friends, you may have duties stemming from that personal relationship. If so, you should ideally be able to raise your concerns with the suspected wrongdoer as a friend. Here it will make a difference whether you think the wrongdoing is purposeful and knowing, or a result of poor training, poor systems, or other failures of management. Sensitivity and tact will be needed. If possible, it would be advisable to get advice from others as to how to approach your friend most constructively and effectively. But it is important to remember that you can be loyal to a person without endorsing everything that person does. And in the case of public servants, there are always competing loyalties in play: your loyalty to the Canadian public, the Crown, and the values of the public service. When personal interests, including personal loyalties, compete with the values of the public service and the public interest, public servants have a legal duty to resolve such conflicts in favour of the public interest.

Your disclosure may result in real harm to the person whose wrongdoing is thereby exposed. Whether that harm should be imposed depends upon the degree of harm that is risked by not reporting and allowing the wrongdoing to continue. That is why only serious wrongdoing is covered under the *Act*. But if the damage done or risked by the wrongdoing is serious enough, you may have a moral duty to disclose. In part, that will depend upon the impact of your choices on others, and in choosing whether to allow the wrongdoing to continue by remaining silent or reporting it, the interests of these others must also be considered.

2) The persons in your public service organization.

Everyone in your organization may be impacted by your decision to disclose, just as they may be by your decision to remain silent and allow the wrongdoing to continue.

Your staff, colleagues, managers, chief executive, and minister may all be affected by your decision. If you report wrongdoing that is not just an isolated case of a single individual acting in clear contravention of the policies and code of conduct in your workplace, and an investigation is warranted, your entire operation and its personnel will come under scrutiny. There is always the potential for an investigation to discover wrongs of which you were unaware. And if wrongdoing is found, it may have negative impacts on all of the members of your organization. Your minister, chief executive, and senior managers may come under criticism for mismanagement or failing to put in place policies and procedures that would have prevented the wrongdoing. Morale and collegiality may be negatively affected. Co-workers may become fearful and suspicious of one another. These are no doubt among your concerns. But the impacts on your organization will depend in part upon the route you take to deal with the suspected wrongdoing.

If you can find a constructive way of having the problem addressed, the organization may be stronger for it, and morale and collegiality enhanced by good internal processes and clear articulation of policies, procedures, and expectations. If your management takes up the request for training or other improvements, and they correct the problem, no ill effects may be felt, and it may in fact be good for your organization. If wrongdoing is disclosed internally, then damage to the reputation of the organization as a whole may again be mitigated. It is important to note, however, that if wrongdoing is found, the chief executive is under an obligation to "promptly provide public access to information that (i) describes the wrongdoing, including information that could identify the person found to have committed it if it is necessary to identify the person to adequately describe the wrongdoing and (ii) describes recommendations for corrective action made by the investigator and any corrective action taken" (*PSDPA* 11(1)(c)(i) and (ii)).

If you disclose to the Commission, the impact on your organization may be much the same as internal disclosure, except that the dynamic may be altered by having an outside agency involved. This may suggest to senior managers a lack of trust and confidence in their abilities or integrity, which may increase the danger of reprisal (more on reprisal below). On the other hand, an impartial investigator is often desirable.[3]

You must weigh these risks against the risks run by silence. What are the potential impacts if the wrongdoing continues, or is discovered and disclosed by the press?

3) The public service.

The public service as a whole—its ideals, values, and institutions—is very important. The reputation of the whole public service hangs loosely together in the minds of many Canadians. Will your disclosure, and the remedies that it makes possible, increase confidence in the public service and the mechanisms that have been put in place to ensure that public servants work for the common good rather than personal interest or the interests of political parties? Will it identify a problem that might affect other areas of the public service than just your own, so that your disclosure may identify a problem and solutions that can be implemented for the benefit of the whole sector? Will your disclosure make possible better use of public funds and assets, better delivery of public services, more responsible and responsive public service, better monitoring of value for expenditures, or better working conditions for members of the public service? Will it increase trust in our public institutions in the long run?

It may not be possible to know the answer to these questions with certainty, but the more confidence you have that your disclosure may result in improvements in the public service, the stronger the case for disclosure will be.

4) The Canadian public.

As a public servant, your first duty is to the Canadian public. It is on behalf of Canadians that your efforts should be directed, and for their good that you must act. Is disclosure in the best interest of Canadians?

This is not a simple question, because the duty of public servants to the public at large is mediated through your duty to support the duly constituted government and to implement the lawful policies of your minister. As an important institution in our parliamentary democracy, the public service must assist ministers, impartially and neutrally, under law, to serve the public interest. Thus public servants are not charged with determining what is in the public interest in the first instance, but rather with ensuring that they perform their responsibilities and carry out their professional obligations in a way that is lawful and upholds the principles and values of the public service itself, as a vital public institution for the good of Canadians.

In the case of a member of the general public, by contrast, persons thinking about disclosing should be guided by considerations of the public good directly.

5) You and your family.

Disclosure may be the only morally acceptable option if you are aware of intentional misuse of public funds, for example, or of activity that poses a serious risk of harm to persons or the environment. In the clearest cases, whistle-blowers are celebrated by history as having provided a valuable public service. But history may be slow in coming, and the more immediate effects of disclosure must be considered frankly and fully.

The *Act* guarantees that chief executives and the Commissioner will protect the identity of public servants who report wrongdoing, as well as protect them from workplace reprisal in a number of ways. But you may still fear that your identity as the discloser will become known and that you will be punished for speaking out. This concern is only reasonable and needs to be considered.

8.6 ETHICAL PRINCIPLES

When making any complex ethical decision, it is important to consider explicitly the various ethical principles that are implicated in your decision, the extent to which the various options you face would uphold and embody the following ethical principles, and to what extent each option would violate or impede the realization of those principles.

The public service is committed to four families of inter-related values, each of which requires decision making that realizes specific ethical principles (from *Values and Ethics Code for the Public Service*, 2003).

Democratic Values: Helping Ministers, under law, to serve the public interest.

- Honesty and impartiality in advice
- The duty to provide full information to Ministers
- Loyalty in implementing lawful Ministerial decisions
- The duty to act in ways that support personal and collective Ministerial accountability
- Accountability to Parliament and Canadians

Professional Values: Serving with competence, excellence, efficiency, objectivity and impartiality.

- Lawfulness
- Political neutrality
- Proper, efficient and effective use of public money

- Ethical means must be taken to achieve approved ends
- Commitment to ongoing improvement of the delivery of services
- Transparency in government within the limits of confidentiality required by law

....

Ethical Values: Acting at all times in such a way as to uphold the public trust.

- Integrity, objectivity, and impartiality
- Avoid conflicts of interest
- Decide any conflict between private and public interests in favour of the public good
- Act at all times in a way that will bear the closest public scrutiny
- Act at all times to deserve the public trust, by being trustworthy

....

People Values: Demonstrating respect, fairness and courtesy in their dealings with both citizens and fellow public servants.

- Respect for human dignity and the value and autonomy of every person
- Fairness and civility
- Organizations should be led through participation, openness, communication, and respect for diversity
- Respect for the official languages of Canada
- Appointments and promotions should be based on merit
- Public service values should guide recruitment, evaluation, and promotion

....

Public servants must also consider other duties they have under law and under specific codes of conduct and ethics codes by which they are governed. Public servants have, in common with all persons, the duty to avoid serious moral wrongdoing, including complicity in wrongdoing.

8.7 ETHICAL DECISION MAKING

The decision to report suspected wrongdoing is complex, and a person making it should consider all of the ethically relevant factors it involves. The decision to disclose should itself follow the pattern for good ethical decision making.

- What are the facts? What evidence do you have? Do you have only one side of a story? Could a reasonable person interpret the facts differently than you do?

- How serious is the wrongdoing? How seriously would trust in the public service be undermined if a full and accurate description of the wrongdoing became public?

- What solutions are possible? Have you considered alternatives to disclosure or silence that might be more constructive avenues for righting the wrongdoing?

- What ethical principles are at stake in your decision? What weight should be given to each in this specific case? To what extent would a given decision violate or uphold those principles?

- What are the likely consequences of the various alternatives for all those affected? Are you relying upon just the worst-case scenarios, or are you properly weighing the risks? Are you over-emphasizing the possible negative consequences for yourself, or ignoring the consequences for others?

- Consult with others: colleagues, family, friends, and trusted advisors.

- Do you have motives that might be leading you to make a poor decision? Are you really motivated by the public good? If your motives are mixed, or might reasonably be seen to be tainted, it is even more important to be sure that you have good evidence of serious wrongdoing, and a firm grasp on the ethical factors that make disclosing the wrongdoing the right thing to do.

- If you must disclose (to fulfil your duties to the public, to act in conformity with the values of the public service, to maintain professionalism and integrity), should you disclose internally or directly to the Commissioner? Make sure you know exactly why you think one alternative is better than the other.

- Justify and defend your decision. Consider all reasonable objections to your decision that others might make, and how you would answer them. Why is your decision the best available?

QUESTIONS FOR FURTHER DISCUSSION

1. What ethical elements should be included when investigating possible wrongdoing?

2. What role do integrity commissioners, or ethics officers, serve?

3. What goals does whistle-blowing aim to achieve? Is it always to determine wrongdoing and punish those responsible?

4. What does it mean to say that allegations of wrongdoing should be reported in "good faith"? Aren't all such reports done in good faith?

5. If a public servant believes that some wrongdoing is taking place but is not certain, should she or he report it? What considerations should the public servant factor into the decision?

6. To whom should public servants report when they are confident that wrong-doing is taking place?

7. Under what conditions should a public servant report wrongdoing through the Commission?

8. How might each of the moral theories discussed in Chapter 1 inform a public servant's decision to report wrongdoing? For example, should wrongdoing only be reported when disclosure promotes overall utility?

9. How extensively should disclosure regimes be relied upon, rather than other possible responses to suspected wrongdoing? Explain your answer.

10. What are the downsides to using disclosures regimes? What are their potential benefits?

Consider how the various parties described in Cases 2, 3, 5, 7, 8, 18, 22, 23, 24, 26, 27, and 29 should respond to the situation they find themselves in. Do your answers suggest that you are inclined more toward one ethical orientation than others? Do they suggest that you incline more to informal or formal methods of dealing with wrongdoing?

NOTES

[1] The following reproduces portions of *A Guide to Ethical Decision Making: Disclosure of Wrongdoing in the Public Service*, by Susan Dimock and Greg Levine (Toronto: York Centre for Practical Ethics, 2008).

[2] For Auditor General's Report, see: http://www.oag-bvg.gc.ca/internet/English/parl_oag_201012_e_34448.html, accessed July 26, 2011.

[3] The practice of the Office of the Public Sector Integrity Commissioner in its first year of work suggests that it can play a positive role in identifying misunderstandings and poor processes that can be corrected without a finding of wrongdoing. (*Annual Report 2007–08*, www.psic-ispc.gc.ca/doc.php?sid=39&lang=eng, though subsequent developments suggest that the investigative processes at the PSIC may have been too weak to find wrongdoing even where it existed.)

Values and Ethics Code for the Public Service [Federal Public Servants] Treasury Board 2003[1]*

(PUBLIÉ AUSSI EN FRANÇAIS SOUS LE TITRE CODE DE VALEURS ET D'ÉTHIQUE DE LA FONCTION PUBLIQUE)

TABLE OF CONTENTS

*Values and Ethics Code for the Public Service, http://www.tbs-sct.gc.ca/pubs_pol/hrpubs/tb_851/vec-cve1-eng.asp, Treasury Board of Canada Secretariat, 2011. Reproduced with the permission of the Minister of Public Works and Government Services Canada, 2011. Applications Section: The Public Service Staff Relations Act was repealed and the application of the Code is to department and agencies listed in Schedules I and IV of the Financial Administration Act.

CHAPTER 1: STATEMENT OF PUBLIC SERVICE VALUES AND ETHICS

THE ROLE OF THE PUBLIC SERVICE OF CANADA

The Public Service of Canada is an important national institution, part of the essential framework of Canadian parliamentary democracy. Through the support they provide to the duly constituted government, public servants contribute in a fundamental way to good government, to democracy, and to Canadian society.

The role of the Public Service is to assist the Government of Canada to provide for peace, order, and good government. The *Constitution of Canada* and the principles of responsible government provide the foundation for Public Service roles, responsibilities, and values. The democratic mission of the Public Service is to assist Ministers, under law, to serve the public interest.

Objectives of this Code

The *Values and Ethics Code for the Public Service* sets forth the values and ethics of public service to guide and support public servants in all their professional activities. It will serve to maintain and enhance public confidence in the integrity of the Public Service. The Code will also serve to strengthen respect for, and appreciation of, the role played by the Public Service within Canadian democracy.

The Code sets out Public Service values as well as Conflict of Interest and Post-Employment Measures.

The Code should be read in the context of the duties and responsibilities set out in *A Guide for Ministers and Secretaries of State*.

Ministers are responsible for preserving public confidence in the integrity of management and operations within their departments and for maintaining the tradition of political neutrality of the Public Service and its continuing ability to provide professional, candid, and frank advice.

Public Service Values

Public servants shall be guided in their work and their professional conduct by a balanced framework of public service values: democratic, professional, ethical, and people values.

These families of values are not distinct but overlap. They are perspectives from which to observe the universe of Public Service values.

Democratic Values: Helping Ministers, under law, to serve the public interest.

- Public servants shall give honest and impartial advice and make all information relevant to a decision available to Ministers.

- Public servants shall loyally implement ministerial decisions, lawfully taken.

- Public servants shall support both individual and collective ministerial accountability and provide Parliament and Canadians with information on the results of their work.

Professional Values: Serving with competence, excellence, efficiency, objectivity, and impartiality.

- Public servants must work within the laws of Canada and maintain the tradition of the political neutrality of the Public Service.

- Public servants shall endeavour to ensure the proper, effective, and efficient use of public money.

- In the Public Service, how ends are achieved should be as important as the achievements themselves.

- Public servants should constantly renew their commitment to serve Canadians by continually improving the quality of service, by adapting to changing needs through innovation, and by improving the efficiency and effectiveness of government programs and services offered in both official languages.

- Public servants should also strive to ensure that the value of transparency in government is upheld while respecting their duties of confidentiality under the law.

Ethical Values: Acting at all times in such a way as to uphold the public trust.

- Public servants shall perform their duties and arrange their private affairs so that public confidence and trust in the integrity, objectivity, and impartiality of government are conserved and enhanced.

- Public servants shall act at all times in a manner that will bear the closest public scrutiny; an obligation that is not fully discharged by simply acting within the law.

- Public servants, in fulfilling their official duties and responsibilities, shall make decisions in the public interest.

- If a conflict should arise between the private interests and the official duties of a public servant, the conflict shall be resolved in favour of the public interest.

People Values: Demonstrating respect, fairness, and courtesy in their dealings with both citizens and fellow public servants.

- Respect for human dignity and the value of every person should always inspire the exercise of authority and responsibility.
- People values should reinforce the wider range of Public Service values. Those who are treated with fairness and civility will be motivated to display these values in their own conduct.
- Public Service organizations should be led through participation, openness, and communication and with respect for diversity and for the official languages of Canada.
- Appointment decisions in the Public Service shall be based on merit.
- Public Service values should play a key role in recruitment, evaluation, and promotion.

Application

This Code applies to all public servants working in departments, agencies, and other public institutions listed in Part I, Schedule I, of the *Public Service Staff Relations Act.*

This Code is a policy of the Government of Canada. Public service institutions not covered by this Code should respect its spirit and should adopt similar provisions for their organizations.

RESPONSIBILITIES, AUTHORITIES, AND ACCOUNTABILITIES

Overall Responsibility of All Public Servants

All public service activities should be consistent with the *Values and Ethics Code for the Public Service.* Where questions arise about its application, see Chapter 4, "Avenues of Resolution."

In addition to the stipulations outlined in this Code, public servants are also required to observe any specific conduct requirements contained in the statutes governing their particular department or organization and their profession, where applicable. They are also required to observe the relevant provisions of more general application including the following:

- *Access to Information Act;*
- *Criminal Code of Canada;*
- *Financial Administration Act;*
- *Official Languages Act and Regulations;*

- *Privacy Act;*
- *Public Service Employment Act;*
- *Public Service Staff Relations Act.*

Related Treasury Board policies:

- *Contracting Policy;*
- *Policy on the Internal Disclosure of Information Concerning Wrongdoing in the Workplace;*
- *Policy on the Prevention and Resolution of Harassment in the Workplace.*

PUBLIC SERVANTS

This Code forms part of the conditions of employment in the Public Service of Canada. At the time of signing their letter of offer, public servants acknowledge that the *Values and Ethics Code for the Public Service* is a condition of employment. All public servants are responsible for ensuring that they comply with this Code and that they exemplify, in all their actions and behaviours, the values of public service. In particular, they have the following obligations:

a) Public servants must report, within 60 days of their first appointment or any subsequent appointment, transfer or deployment, all outside activities, assets, and direct and contingent liabilities that might give rise to a conflict of interest with respect to their official duties. To this end, a Confidential Report must be filed with their Deputy Head.

b) Every time a major change occurs in the personal affairs or official duties of public servants, they must review their obligations under this Code. If a real, apparent, or potential conflict of interest exists, they must file a new Confidential Report with their Deputy Head.

c) When negotiating financial arrangements with outside parties, public servants must assure compliance with the Conflict of Interest and Post-Employment Measures in accordance with directives on this matter issued by Treasury Board. When in doubt, public servants must immediately report the situation to their supervisors in order to seek advice or direction on how to proceed.

When faced with an ethical dilemma, public servants are encouraged to use the opportunities and mechanisms established by their Deputy Head to raise, discuss, and resolve issues of concern related to this Code.

Public servants who feel they are being asked to act in a way that is inconsistent with the values and ethics set out in Chapter 1 of this Code should first attempt to raise the matter using the usual reporting relationship. Further avenues for resolution are contained in Chapter 4 of this Code.

Deputy Heads

Deputy Heads and senior managers have a particular responsibility to exemplify, in their actions and behaviours, the values of public service. They have a duty to infuse these values into all aspects of the work of their organizations. It is expected that they will take special care to ensure that they comply at all times with both the spirit and the specific requirements of this Code.

In particular, Deputy Heads have the following obligations:

a) To ensure that the letter of offer, for an initial appointment, includes the following: "You will find enclosed a copy of the *Values and Ethics Code for the Public Service*. This Code is a key policy for the management of human resources and is part of your conditions of employment." Deputy Heads must ensure that public servants are provided with a copy of the Code on any subsequent appointment. They must ensure that public servants in their organization are informed of the requirements of this Code on an annual basis.

b) To encourage and maintain an ongoing dialogue on public service values and ethics within their organizations, in a manner that is relevant to the specific issues and challenges encountered by their organizations.

c) To ensure that mechanisms and assistance are in place to help public servants raise, discuss, and resolve issues of concern related to this Code. This includes designating a senior official to assist public servants to resolve issues arising from the application of the Code.

d) To determine the appropriate method for a public servant to comply with the Code, as set out in Chapters 2 and 3, in order to avoid conflicts of interest. In doing so, the Deputy Head will try to achieve mutual agreement with the public servant.

e) To ensure that the personal information in Confidential Reports is secured in a central repository and treated in complete confidence, in accordance with the *Privacy Act*.

Deputy Heads may add compliance measures beyond those specified in this Code to reflect their department's particular responsibilities or the statutes governing its operations. They must consult with the Treasury Board of Canada Secretariat and ensure that bargaining agents are consulted at the departmental level in advance of implementing new measures. The Deputy Head will inform the Treasury Board of Canada Secretariat, in writing, of any additional measures and their effective dates.

Deputy Heads may delegate responsibilities and authorities for the implementation of the Code, but they may not delegate their accountability for ensuring that the Code is fully upheld and advanced within their organization or for the specific matters outlined in this section.

Treasury Board

Treasury Board will ensure through its Secretariat that information and educational materials related to the *Values and Ethics Code for the Public Service* are widely available. It will also maintain an advisory support service for Deputy Heads and for designated departmental officials on the interpretation and promotion of the Code.

Treasury Board, through its Secretariat, will monitor the implementation of the Code in departments and agencies. On a regular basis, Treasury Board, through its Secretariat, will review the performance of departments in the implementation of the Code through its modern management accountability framework.

The *Values and Ethics Code for the Public Service* will be subject to a review five years after it comes into effect.

Public Service Integrity Officer

The role of the Public Service Integrity Officer is to receive, record, and review disclosures of wrongdoing in the workplace, including breaches to the Code, and to make recommendations where warranted to Deputy Heads for resolution. Further, the Public Service Integrity Officer may report on any cases dealing with breaches of the Code as part of his or her annual report to the President of the Privy Council that is tabled in Parliament.

Effective Date

The effective date of the *Values and Ethics Code for the Public Service* is September 1, 2003.

CHAPTER 2: CONFLICT OF INTEREST MEASURES

OBJECTIVE

The objective of these measures is to establish rules of conduct respecting conflict of interest and to minimize the possibility of conflicts arising between private interests and public service duties of public servants. These measures serve to uphold the Public Service Values set out in Chapter 1, as well as the Post-Employment Measures in Chapter 3.

MEASURES TO PREVENT CONFLICT OF INTEREST

Avoiding and preventing situations that could give rise to a conflict of interest, or the appearance of a conflict of interest, is one of the primary means by which a public servant maintains public confidence in the impartiality and objectivity of the Public Service.

These Conflict of Interest Measures are adopted both to protect public servants from conflict of interest allegations and to help them avoid situations of risk. Conflict of interest does not relate exclusively to matters concerning financial transactions and the transfer of economic benefit. While financial activity is important, it is not the sole source of potential conflict of interest situations.

It is impossible to prescribe a remedy for every situation that could give rise to a real, apparent, or potential conflict. When in doubt, public servants should seek guidance from their manager, from the senior official designated by the Deputy Head, or from the Deputy Head, and refer to the Public Service Values stated in Chapter 1 as well as the following measures as benchmarks against which to gauge appropriate action.

Public servants have the following overall responsibilities:

a) In carrying out their official duties, public servants should arrange their private affairs in a manner that will prevent real, apparent, or potential conflicts of interest from arising.

b) If a conflict does arise between the private interests and the official duties of a public servant, the conflict should be resolved in favour of the public interest.

Public servants also have the following specific duties:

a) They should not have private interests, other than those permitted pursuant to these measures, that would be affected particularly or significantly by government actions in which they participate.

b) They should not solicit or accept transfers of economic benefit.

c) They should not step out of their official roles to assist private entities or persons in their dealings with the government where this would result in preferential treatment to the entities or persons.

d) They should not knowingly take advantage of, or benefit from, information that is obtained in the course of their official duties and that is not generally available to the public.

e) They should not directly or indirectly use, or allow the use of, government property of any kind, including property leased to the government, for anything other than officially approved activities.

Methods of Compliance

For a public servant to comply with these measures, it will usually be sufficient to submit a Confidential Report to the Deputy Head. The Confidential Report outlines the public servant's ownership of assets, receipt of gifts, hospitality, or other benefits, or participation in any outside employment or activities that could give rise to a conflict of interest.

There will be instances, however, where other measures will be necessary. These include the following:

a) avoiding or withdrawing from activities or situations that would place the public servant in real, potential, or apparent conflict of interest with his or her official duties; and

b) having an asset sold at arm's length or placed in a blind trust where continued ownership would constitute a real, apparent, or potential conflict of interest with the public servant's official duties.

In such cases, the Deputy Head will make the decision and communicate it to the public servant. In determining appropriate action, the Deputy Head will try to achieve mutual agreement with the public servant in question and will take into account such factors as:

a) the public servant's specific responsibilities;

b) the value and types of assets and interests involved; and

c) the actual costs to be incurred by divesting the assets and interests, as opposed to the potential that the assets and interests represent for a conflict of interest.

Assets

The types of assets and interests that should be included in a Confidential Report, those that need not be declared, as well as procedures for divesting assets are all set out in Appendix A.

It is to be noted that a public servant may not sell or transfer assets to family members or others for purposes of circumventing the compliance measures.

Outside Employment or Activities

Public servants may engage in employment outside the Public Service and take part in outside activities unless the employment or activities are likely to give rise to a conflict of interest or in any way undermine the neutrality of the Public Service.

Where outside employment or activities might subject public servants to demands incompatible with their official duties, or cast doubt on their ability to perform their duties in a completely objective manner, they shall submit a Confidential Report to their Deputy Head. The Deputy Head may require that the outside activities be curtailed, modified, or terminated if it is determined that real, apparent, or potential conflict of interest exists.

Gifts, Hospitality, and Other Benefits

Public servants are called upon to use their best judgment to avoid situations of real or perceived conflict. In doing so, public servants should consider the following criteria on gifts, hospitality, and other benefits, keeping in mind the full context of this Code.

Public servants shall not accept or solicit any gifts, hospitality, or other benefits that may have a real or apparent influence on their objectivity in carrying out their official duties or that may place them under obligation to the donor. This includes free or discounted admission to sporting and cultural events arising out of an actual or potential business relationship directly related to the public servant's official duties.

The acceptance of gifts, hospitality, and other benefits is permissible if they

a) are infrequent and of minimal value (low-cost promotional objects, simple meals, souvenirs with no cash value);

b) arise out of activities or events related to the official duties of the public servant concerned;

c) are within the normal standards of courtesy, hospitality, or protocol; and

d) do not compromise or appear to compromise in any way the integrity of the public servant concerned or his or her organization.

Where it is impossible to decline gifts, hospitality, and other benefits that do not meet the principles set out above, or where it is believed that there is sufficient benefit to the organization to warrant acceptance of certain types of hospitality, a public servant shall seek written direction from their Deputy Head. The Deputy Head will then notify the public servant in writing whether the gifts, hospitality, and other benefits are to be declined or retained by the department, donated to charity, disposed of, or retained by the public servant concerned.

Solicitation

At no time should public servants solicit gifts, hospitality, other benefits, or transfers of economic value from a person, group, or organization in the private sector who has dealings with the government.

In the case of fundraising for charitable organizations, public servants should ensure that they have prior authorization from their Deputy Head to solicit donations, prizes, or contributions in kind from external organizations or individuals. The Deputy Head may require that the activities be curtailed, modified, or terminated where it is determined that there is a real or apparent conflict of interest or an obligation to the donor.

Legal Framework

The above provisions are designed to ensure the *Values and Ethics Code for the Public Service* is consistent with paragraph 121(1)(c) of the *Criminal Code*, which states the following:

> ....
> … every one commits an offence who, being an official or employee of the government, demands, accepts, or offers or agrees to accept, from a person who has dealings with the government, a commission, reward, advantage or benefit of any kind directly or indirectly, by himself or through a member of his family or through any one for his benefit, unless he has the consent in writing of the head of the branch of government that employs him or of which he is an official, the proof of which lies on him.
> ....

Avoidance of Preferential Treatment

When participating in any decision making related to a staffing process, public servants shall ensure that they do not grant preferential treatment or assistance to family or friends.

When making decisions that will result in a financial award to an external party, public servants shall not grant preferential treatment or assistance to family or friends.

Public servants should not offer any assistance to entities or persons that have dealings with the government, where this assistance is not part of their official duties, without obtaining prior authorization from their designated superior and complying with the conditions for that authorization.

Providing information that is easily accessible to the public to relatives or friends or to entities in which public servants or their family members or friends have interests is not considered preferential treatment.

CHAPTER 3: POST-EMPLOYMENT MEASURES

OBJECTIVE

The objective of these measures is to establish rules of conduct respecting post-employment. These measures complement the Public Service Values set out in Chapter 1, as well as the Conflict of Interest Measures in Chapter 2.

OVERALL RESPONSIBILITY

Without unduly restricting their ability to seek other employment, former public servants should undertake to minimize the possibility of real, apparent, or potential conflicts of interest between their new employment and their most recent responsibilities within the federal public service. Before leaving employment, public servants should disclose their intention of future employment and discuss potential conflicts with their Deputy Head.

APPLICATION

The overall responsibility cited above applies to all public servants covered by the Code. The measures that follow apply specifically to those public servants staffed in executive positions (EX) or their equivalent as well as EX minus 1 and EX minus 2 positions and their equivalent (e.g., PM-06, IS-05, AS-07).

A Deputy Head may designate other positions as being subject to these measures (where the position involves official duties that raise post-employment concerns), or exclude positions from the application of the post-employment measures (when the official duties of these positions do not raise concerns for post-employment). Before doing this, the Deputy Head must consult the Treasury Board of Canada Secretariat as well as appropriate bargaining agents when applicable.

BEFORE LEAVING OFFICE

Public servants must disclose, in a Confidential Report to their Deputy Head, all firm offers of employment that could place them in a real, apparent, or potential conflict of interest situation. They must also disclose immediately the acceptance of any such offer.

LIMITATION PERIOD

Former public servants shall not, within a period of one year after leaving office

a) accept appointment to a board of directors of, or employment with, entities with which they personally, or through their subordinates, had significant official dealings during the period of one year immediately prior to the termination of their service;

b) make representations for, or on behalf of, persons to any department or organization with which they personally, or through their subordinates, had significant official dealings during the period of one year immediately prior to the termination of their service; or

c) give advice to their clients using information that is not available to the public concerning the programs or policies of the departments or organizations with which they were employed or with which they had a direct and substantial relationship.

REDUCTION OF LIMITATION PERIOD

A Deputy Head has the authority to reduce or waive the limitation period of employment for a public servant or former public servant. Such a decision should take into consideration the following:

a) the circumstances under which the termination of their service occurred;

b) the general employment prospects of the public servant or former public servant;

c) the significance to the government of information possessed by the public servant or former public servant by virtue of that individual's position in the Public Service;

d) the desirability of a rapid transfer of the public servant's or former public servant's knowledge and skills from the government to private, other governmental, or nongovernmental sectors;

e) the degree to which the new employer might gain unfair commercial or private advantage by hiring the public servant or former public servant; and

f) the authority and influence possessed while in the Public Service, and the disposition of other cases.

A decision by a Deputy Head to waive or reduce the limitation period will be recorded in writing.

EXIT ARRANGEMENTS

A Deputy Head must ensure that a public servant who is intending to leave the Public Service is aware of these post-employment measures.

RECONSIDERATION

A public servant or former public servant may apply to the Deputy Head for reconsideration of any determination respecting his or her compliance with the post-employment measures.

CHAPTER 4: AVENUES OF RESOLUTION

PUBLIC SERVICE VALUES AND ETHICS

Any public servant who wants to raise, discuss, and clarify issues related to this Code should first talk with his or her manager or contact the senior official designated by the Deputy Head under the provisions of this Code, according to the procedures and conditions established by the Deputy Head.

Any public servant who witnesses or has knowledge of wrongdoing in the workplace may refer the matter for resolution, in confidence and without fear of reprisal, to the Senior Officer designated for the purpose by the Deputy Head under the provisions of the Policy on the Internal Disclosure of Information Concerning Wrongdoing in the Workplace.

Furthermore, any public servant who believes that he or she is being asked to act in a way that is inconsistent with the values and ethics set out in Chapter 1 of this Code can report the matter in confidence and without fear of reprisal to the Senior Officer, as described above.

If the matter is not appropriately addressed at this level, or the public servant has reason to believe it could not be disclosed in confidence within the organization, it may then be referred to the Public Service Integrity Officer, in accordance with the *Policy on the Internal Disclosure of Information Concerning Wrongdoing in the Workplace.*

It is expected that most matters arising from the application of this Code can and should be resolved at the organizational level.

MEASURES ON CONFLICT OF INTEREST AND POST-EMPLOYMENT

With respect to the appropriate arrangements necessary to prevent conflict of interest or to comply with the post-employment measures described in Chapters 2 and 3 of this Code, it is expected that most situations will be addressed by discussing the matter with the public servant, identifying avenues of resolution and taking appropriate action. When a public servant and the Deputy Head disagree on the appropriate arrangements to prevent conflict of interest or to comply with the post-employment measures in this Code, the disagreement shall be resolved through the established grievance procedures.

FAILURE TO COMPLY

A public servant who does not comply with the requirements of this Code is subject to appropriate disciplinary action, up to and including termination of employment.

ENQUIRIES

Enquiries about this Code should be referred to the responsible departmental officer who, in turn, may direct questions regarding policy interpretation to the following:

Office of Values and Ethics

Policy and Planning Sector

Human Resources Management Office (HRMO)

Treasury Board of Canada Secretariat

FORM

Confidential Report

This form can be accessed through the Treasury Board of Canada Secretariat Web site at the following address: **www.tbs-sct.gc.ca/**

APPENDIX A—ASSETS, LIABILITIES, AND TRUSTS

ASSETS AND LIABILITIES SUBJECT TO A CONFIDENTIAL REPORT

Public servants must carefully evaluate on a regular basis whether their assets and liabilities need to be included in a Confidential Report. In doing so, they must take into consideration the nature of their official duties and the characteristics of their assets and liabilities. If there is any real, apparent, or potential conflict between the carrying out of their official duties and their assets and liabilities, a Confidential Report must be filed. If there is no relationship, no report is required.

The following is a list of examples of assets and liabilities that must be reported in a Confidential Report if they do, or could, constitute a conflict of interest. *This list is not exhaustive.*

a) publicly traded securities of corporations and foreign governments, and self-administered Registered Retirement Savings Plans (RRSPs), and self-administered Registered Education Savings Plans (RESPs) that are composed of these securities, where these securities are held directly and not through units in mutual funds;

b) interests in partnerships, proprietorships, joint ventures, private companies, and family businesses, in particular those that own or control shares of public companies or that do business with the government;

c) commercially operated farm businesses;

d) real property that is not for the private use of public servants or their family members;

e) commodities, futures, and foreign currencies held or traded for speculative purposes;

f) assets placed in trust or resulting from an estate of which the public servant is a beneficiary;

g) secured or unsecured loans granted to persons other than to members of the public servant's immediate family;

h) any other assets or liabilities that could give rise to a real, apparent, or potential conflict of interest due to the particular nature of the public servant's official duties; and

i) direct and contingent liabilities in respect of any of the assets described in this section.

ASSETS NOT REQUIRING A CONFIDENTIAL REPORT

Assets and interests for the private use of public servants and of their family members, as well as non-commercial assets, are *not* subject to the compliance measures.

For example, such assets include the following:

a) residences, recreational properties, and farms used or intended for use by public servants or their families;

b) household goods and personal effects;

c) works of art, antiques, and collectibles;

d) automobiles and other personal means of transportation;

e) cash and deposits;

f) Canada Saving Bonds and other similar investments in securities of fixed value issued or guaranteed by any level of government in Canada or agencies of those governments;

g) Registered Retirement Savings Plans and Registered Education Saving Plans that are not self-administered;

h) investments in open-ended mutual funds;

i) guaranteed investment certificates and similar financial instruments;

j) annuities and life insurance policies;

k) pension rights;

l) money owed by a previous employer, client, or partnership; and

m) personal loans receivable from members of public servants' immediate families and small personal loans receivable from other persons where public servants have loaned the moneys receivable.

DIVESTMENT OF ASSETS

Public servants must divest assets where their Deputy Head determines that such assets constitute a real, apparent, or potential conflict of interest in relation to their duties and responsibilities. Divestment, where required, must take place within 120 days of appointment, transfer, or deployment. Divestment of assets is usually achieved by selling them through an arm's-length transaction or by making them subject to a blind trust arrangement.

Where divestment is by means of sale, confirmation of the sale, such as a broker's sales receipt, shall be provided to the Deputy Head.

Where divestment is by means of a blind trust, the Office of the Ethics Counsellor will assist the Deputy Head and the public servant to set up a blind trust and to determine whether a specific blind trust meets the requirements of the Conflict of Interest Measures. The Ethics Counsellor will also make recommendations to the Deputy Head on the reimbursement of certain trust costs to the public servant by the home organization.

NOTE

[1] From "Values and Ethics Code for the Public Service," Treasury Board 2003 http://www.tbs-sct.gc.ca/pubs_pol/hrpubs/tb_851/vec-cve1-eng.asp.

American Society for Public Administration Code of Ethics[1]*

I. SERVE THE PUBLIC INTEREST

Serve the public, beyond serving oneself. ASPA members are committed to:

1. Exercise discretionary authority to promote the public interest.
2. Oppose all forms of discrimination and harassment, and promote affirmative action.
3. Recognize and support the public's right to know the public's business.
4. Involve citizens in policy decision making.
5. Exercise compassion, benevolence, fairness, and optimism.
6. Respond to the public in ways that are complete, clear, and easy to understand.
7. Assist citizens in their dealings with government.
8. Be prepared to make decisions that may not be popular.

II. RESPECT THE CONSTITUTION AND THE LAW

Respect, support, and study government constitutions and laws that define responsibilities of public agencies, employees, and all citizens. ASPA members are committed to:

1. Understand and apply legislation and regulations relevant to their professional role.

*ASPA's *Code of Ethics* <www.aspanet.org/scriptcontent/index_codeofethics.cfm> Courtesy of The American Society for Public Administration (ASPA).

2. Work to improve and change laws and policies that are counterproductive or obsolete.

3. Eliminate unlawful discrimination.

4. Prevent all forms of mismanagement of public funds by establishing and maintaining strong fiscal and management controls, and by supporting audits and investigative activities.

5. Respect and protect privileged information.

6. Encourage and facilitate legitimate dissent activities in government and protect the whistle-blowing rights of public employees.

7. Promote constitutional principles of equality, fairness, representativeness, responsiveness, and due process in protecting citizens' rights.

III. DEMONSTRATE PERSONAL INTEGRITY

Demonstrate the highest standards in all activities to inspire public confidence and trust in public service. ASPA members are committed to:

1. Maintain truthfulness and honesty and to not compromise them for advancement, honour, or personal gain.

2. Ensure that others receive credit for their work and contributions.

3. Zealously guard against conflict of interest or its appearance: e.g., nepotism, improper outside employment, misuse of public resources, or the acceptance of gifts.

4. Respect superiors, subordinates, colleagues, and the public.

5. Take responsibility for their own errors.

6. Conduct official acts without partisanship.

IV. PROMOTE ETHICAL ORGANIZATIONS

Strengthen organizational capabilities to apply ethics, efficiency, and effectiveness in serving the public. ASPA members are committed to:

1. Enhance organizational capacity for open communication, creativity, and dedication.

2. Subordinate institutional loyalties to the public good.

3. Establish procedures that promote ethical behaviour and hold individuals and organizations accountable for their conduct.

4. Provide organization members with an administrative means for dissent, assurance of due process, and safeguards against reprisal.

5. Promote merit principles that protect against arbitrary and capricious actions.

6. Promote organizational accountability through appropriate controls and procedures.

7. Encourage organizations to adopt, distribute, and periodically review a code of ethics as a living document.

V. STRIVE FOR PROFESSIONAL EXCELLENCE

Strengthen individual capabilities and encourage the professional development of others. ASPA members are committed to:

1. Provide support and encouragement to upgrade competence.

2. Accept as a personal duty the responsibility to keep up to date on emerging issues and potential problems.

3. Encourage others, throughout their careers, to participate in professional activities and associations.

4. Allocate time to meet with students and provide a bridge between class-room studies and the realities of public service.

NOTE

[1] ASPA Code of Ethics: http://www.aspanet.org/scriptcontent/index_codeofethics.cfm. Accessed May 20, 2011.

The International City/ County Management Association (ICMA) Code of Ethics[1]*

ICMA CODE OF ETHICS

With Guidelines

The ICMA Code of Ethics was adopted by the ICMA membership in 1924, and most recently amended by the membership in May 1998. The Guidelines for the Code were adopted by the ICMA Executive Board in 1972, and most recently revised in July 2004.

The mission of ICMA is to create excellence in local governance by developing and fostering professional local government management worldwide. To further this mission, certain principles, as enforced by the Rules of Procedure, shall govern the conduct of every member of ICMA, who shall:

1. Be dedicated to the concepts of effective and democratic local government by responsible elected officials and believe that professional general management is essential to the achievement of this objective.

2. Affirm the dignity and worth of the services rendered by government and maintain a constructive, creative, and practical attitude toward local government affairs and a deep sense of social responsibility as a trusted public servant.

---

*ICMA Code of Ethics <http://icma.org/en/icma/ethics/code_of_ethics>. Reprinted with permission of the International City/County Management Association (ICMA).

Guideline

Advice to Officials of Other Local Governments.   When members advise and respond to inquiries from elected or appointed officials of other local governments, they should inform the administrators of those communities.

3. Be dedicated to the highest ideals of honour and integrity in all public and personal relationships in order that the member may merit the respect and confidence of the elected officials, of other officials and employees, and of the public.

Guidelines

Public Confidence.   Members should conduct themselves so as to maintain public confidence in their profession, their local government, and in their performance of the public trust.

Impression of Influence.   Members should conduct their official and personal affairs in such a manner as to give the clear impression that they cannot be improperly influenced in the performance of their official duties.

Appointment Commitment.   Members who accept an appointment to a position should not fail to report for that position. This does not preclude the possibility of a member considering several offers or seeking several positions at the same time, but once a *bona fide* offer of a position has been accepted, that commitment should be honoured. Oral acceptance of an employment offer is considered binding unless the employer makes fundamental changes in terms of employment.

Credentials.   An application for employment or for ICMA's Voluntary Credentialing Program should be complete and accurate as to all pertinent details of education, experience, and personal history. Members should recognize that both omissions and inaccuracies must be avoided.

Professional Respect.   Members seeking a management position should show professional respect for persons formerly holding the position or for others who might be applying for the same position. Professional respect does not preclude honest differences of opinion; it does preclude attacking a person's motives or integrity in order to be appointed to a position.

Reporting Ethics Violations.   When becoming aware of a possible violation of the ICMA Code of Ethics, members are encouraged to report the matter to

ICMA. In reporting the matter, members may choose to go on record as the complainant or report the matter on a confidential basis.

Confidentiality. Members should not discuss or divulge information with anyone about pending or completed ethics cases, except as specifically authorized by the Rules of Procedure for Enforcement of the Code of Ethics.

Seeking Employment. Members should not seek employment for a position having an incumbent administrator who has not resigned or been officially informed that his or her services are to be terminated.

4. Recognize that the chief function of local government at all times is to serve the best interests of all of the people.

Guideline

Length of Service. A minimum of two years generally is considered necessary in order to render a professional service to the local government. A short tenure should be the exception rather than a recurring experience. However, under special circumstances, it may be in the best interests of the local government and the member to separate in a shorter time. Examples of such circumstances would include refusal of the appointing authority to honour commitments concerning conditions of employment, a vote of no confidence in the member, or severe personal problems. It is the responsibility of an applicant for a position to ascertain conditions of employment. Inadequately determining terms of employment prior to arrival does not justify premature termination.

5. Submit policy proposals to elected officials; provide them with facts and advice on matters of policy as a basis for making decisions and setting community goals; and uphold and implement local government policies adopted by elected officials.

Guideline

Conflicting Roles. Members who serve multiple roles—working as both city attorney and city manager for the same community, for example—should avoid participating in matters that create the appearance of a conflict of interest. They should disclose the potential conflict to the governing body so that other opinions may be solicited.

6. Recognize that elected representatives of the people are entitled to the credit for the establishment of local government policies; responsibility for policy execution rests with the members.

7. Refrain from all political activities which undermine public confidence in professional administrators. Refrain from participation in the election of the members of the employing legislative body.

Guidelines

Elections of the Governing Body. Members should maintain a reputation for serving equally and impartially all members of the governing body of the local government they serve, regardless of party. To this end, they should not engage in active participation in the election campaign on behalf of or in opposition to candidates for the governing body.

Elections of Elected Executives. Members should not engage in the election campaign of any candidate for mayor or elected county executive.

Running for Office. Members shall not run for elected office or become involved in political activities related to running for elected office. They shall not seek political endorsements, financial contributions, or engage in other campaign activities.

Elections. Members share with their fellow citizens the right and responsibility to vote and to voice their opinion on public issues. However, in order not to impair their effectiveness on behalf of the local governments they serve, they shall not participate in political activities to support the candidacy of individuals running for any city, county, special district, school, state, or federal offices. Specifically, they shall not endorse candidates, make financial contributions, sign or circulate petitions, or participate in fund-raising activities for individuals seeking or holding elected office.

Elections in the Council-Manager Plan. Members may assist in preparing and presenting materials that explain the council-manager form of government to the public prior to an election on the use of the plan. If assistance is required by another community, members may respond. All activities regarding ballot issues should be conducted within local regulations and in a professional manner.

Presentation of Issues. Members may assist the governing body in presenting issues involved in referenda such as bond issues, annexations, and similar matters.

8. Make it a duty continually to improve the member's professional ability and to develop the competence of associates in the use of management techniques.

Guidelines

Self-Assessment.   Each member should assess his or her professional skills and abilities on a periodic basis.

Professional Development.   Each member should commit at least 40 hours per year to professional development activities that are based on the practices identified by the members of ICMA.

9. Keep the community informed on local government affairs; encourage communication between the citizens and all local government officers; emphasize friendly and courteous service to the public; and seek to improve the quality and image of public service.

10. Resist any encroachment on professional responsibilities, believing the member should be free to carry out official policies without interference, and handle each problem without discrimination on the basis of principle and justice.

Guideline

Information Sharing.   The member should openly share information with the governing body while diligently carrying out the member's responsibilities as set forth in the charter or enabling legislation.

11. Handle all matters of personnel on the basis of merit so that fairness and impartiality govern a member's decisions, pertaining to appointments, pay adjustments, promotions, and discipline.

Guideline

Equal Opportunity.   All decisions pertaining to appointments, pay adjustments, promotions, and discipline should prohibit discrimination because of race, colour, religion, sex, national origin, sexual orientation, political affiliation, disability, age, or marital status.

It should be the members' personal and professional responsibility to actively recruit and hire a diverse staff throughout their organizations.

12. Seek no favour; believe that personal aggrandizement or profit secured by confidential information or by misuse of public time is dishonest.

Guidelines

Gifts.   Members should not directly or indirectly solicit any gift or accept or receive any gift—whether it be money, services, loan, travel, entertainment, hospitality, promise, or any other form—under the following circumstances: (1) it could be reasonably inferred or expected that the gift was intended to influence them in the performance of their official duties; or (2) the gift was intended to serve as a reward for any official action on their part.

It is important that the prohibition of unsolicited gifts be limited to circumstances related to improper influence. In *de minimus* situations, such as meal checks, some modest maximum dollar value should be determined by the member as a guideline. The guideline is not intended to isolate members from normal social practices where gifts among friends, associates, and relatives are appropriate for certain occasions.

Investments in Conflict with Official Duties. Member should not invest or hold any investment, directly or indirectly, in any financial business, commercial, or other private transaction that creates a conflict with their official duties.

In the case of real estate, the potential use of confidential information and knowledge to further a member's personal interest requires special consideration. This guideline recognizes that members' official actions and decisions can be influenced if there is a conflict with personal investments. Purchases and sales which might be interpreted as speculation for quick profit ought to be avoided (see the guideline on "Confidential Information").

Because personal investments may prejudice or may appear to influence official actions and decisions, members may, in concert with their governing body, provide for disclosure of such investments prior to accepting their position as local government administrator or prior to any official action by the governing body that may affect such investments.

Personal Relationships. Member should disclose any personal relationship to the governing body in any instance where there could be the appearance of a conflict of interest. For example, if the manager's spouse works for a developer doing business with the local government, that fact should be disclosed.

Confidential Information. Members should not disclose to others, or use to further their personal interest, confidential information acquired by them in the course of their official duties.

Private Employment. Members should not engage in, solicit, negotiate for, or promise to accept private employment, nor should they render services for private interests or conduct a private business when such employment, service, or business creates a conflict with or impairs the proper discharge of their official duties.

Teaching, lecturing, writing, or consulting are typical activities that may not involve conflict of interest, or impair the proper discharge of their official duties. Prior notification of the appointing authority is appropriate in all cases of outside employment.

Representation.   Members should not represent any outside interest before any agency, whether public or private, except with the authorization of or at the direction of the appointing authority they serve.

Endorsements.   Members should not endorse commercial products or services by agreeing to use their photograph, endorsement, or quotation in paid or other commercial advertisements, whether or not for compensation. Members may, however, agree to endorse the following, provided they do not receive any compensation: (1) books or other publications; (2) professional development or educational services provided by nonprofit membership organizations or recognized educational institutions; (3) products and/or services in which the local government has a direct economic interest.

Members' observations, opinions, and analyses of commercial products used or tested by their local governments are appropriate and useful to the profession when included as part of professional articles and reports.

NOTE

[1] ICMA Code of Ethics: http://icma.org/en/icma/ethics/code_of_ethics. Accessed May 20, 2011.

American Institute of Certified Planners Code of Ethics and Professional Conduct[1]*

AICP CODE OF ETHICS AND PROFESSIONAL CONDUCT

Adopted March 19, 2005

Effective June 1, 2005

The Executive Director of APA/AICP is the Ethics Officer as referenced in the following.

We, professional planners, who are members of the American Institute of Certified Planners, subscribe to our Institute's Code of Ethics and Professional Conduct. Our Code is divided into three sections:

Section A contains a statement of aspirational principles that constitute the ideals to which we are committed. We shall strive to act in accordance with our stated principles. However, an allegation that we failed to achieve our aspirational principles cannot be the subject of a misconduct charge or be a cause for disciplinary action.

Section B contains rules of conduct to which we are held accountable. If we violate any of these rules, we can be the object of a charge of misconduct and shall have the responsibility of responding to and cooperating with the investigation and enforcement procedures. If we are found to be blameworthy by the

AICP Code of Ethics and Professional Conduct: http://www.planning.org/ethics/ethicscode.htm. Accessed 20 May 2011. Permission courtesy of American Planning Association.

AICP Ethics Committee, we shall be subject to the imposition of sanctions that may include loss of our certification.

Section C contains the procedural provisions of the Code. It (1) describes the way that one may obtain either a formal or informal advisory ruling, and (2) details how a charge of misconduct can be filed, and how charges are investigated, prosecuted, and adjudicated.

The principles to which we subscribe in Sections A and B of the Code derive from the special responsibility of our profession to serve the public interest with compassion for the welfare of all people and, as professionals, to our obligation to act with high integrity.

As the basic values of society can come into competition with each other, so can the aspirational principles we espouse under this Code. An ethical judgment often requires a conscientious balancing, based on the facts and context of a particular situation and on the precepts of the entire Code.

As Certified Planners, all of us are also members of the American Planning Association and share in the goal of building better, more inclusive communities. We want the public to be aware of the principles by which we practice our profession in the quest of that goal. We sincerely hope that the public will respect the commitments we make to our employers and clients, our fellow professionals, and all other persons whose interests we affect.

A: PRINCIPLES TO WHICH WE ASPIRE

1. Our Overall Responsibility to the Public

Our primary obligation is to serve the public interest and we, therefore, owe our allegiance to a conscientiously attained concept of the public interest that is formulated through continuous and open debate. We shall achieve high standards of professional integrity, proficiency, and knowledge. To comply with our obligation to the public, we aspire to the following principles:

    a)   We shall always be conscious of the rights of others.

    b)   We shall have special concern for the long-range consequences of present actions.

    c)   We shall pay special attention to the interrelatedness of decisions.

    d)   We shall provide timely, adequate, clear, and accurate information on planning issues to all affected persons and to governmental decision makers.

    e)   We shall give people the opportunity to have a meaningful impact on the development of plans and programs that may affect them. Participation should be broad enough to include those who lack formal organization or influence.

f)   We shall seek social justice by working to expand choice and opportunity for all persons, recognizing a special responsibility to plan for the needs of the disadvantaged and to promote racial and economic integration. We shall urge the alteration of policies, institutions, and decisions that oppose such needs.

g)   We shall promote excellence of design and endeavour to conserve and preserve the integrity and heritage of the natural and built environment.

h)   We shall deal fairly with all participants in the planning process. Those of us who are public officials or employees shall also deal evenhandedly with all planning process participants.

2. Our Responsibility to Our Clients and Employers

We owe diligent, creative, and competent performance of the work we do in pursuit of our client or employer's interest. Such performance, however, shall always be consistent with our faithful service to the public interest.

a)   We shall exercise independent professional judgment on behalf of our clients and employers.

b)   We shall accept the decisions of our client or employer concerning the objectives and nature of the professional services we perform unless the course of action is illegal or plainly inconsistent with our primary obligation to the public interest.

c)   We shall avoid a conflict of interest or even the appearance of a conflict of interest in accepting assignments from clients or employers.

3. Our Responsibility to Our Profession and Colleagues

We shall contribute to the development of, and respect for, our profession by improving knowledge and techniques, making work relevant to solutions of community problems, and increasing public understanding of planning activities.

a)   We shall protect and enhance the integrity of our profession.

b)   We shall educate the public about planning issues and their relevance to our everyday lives.

c)   We shall describe and comment on the work and views of other professionals in a fair and professional manner.

d) We shall share the results of experience and research that contribute to the body of planning knowledge.

e) We shall examine the applicability of planning theories, methods, research and practice and standards to the facts and analysis of each particular situation and shall not accept the applicability of a customary solution without first establishing its appropriateness to the situation.

f) We shall contribute time and resources to the professional development of students, interns, beginning professionals, and other colleagues.

g) We shall increase the opportunities for members of underrepresented groups to become professional planners and help them advance in the profession.

h) We shall continue to enhance our professional education and training.

i) We shall systematically and critically analyze ethical issues in the practice of planning.

j) We shall contribute time and effort to groups lacking in adequate planning resources and to voluntary professional activities.

B: OUR RULES OF CONDUCT

We adhere to the following Rules of Conduct, and we understand that our Institute will enforce compliance with them. If we fail to adhere to these Rules, we could receive sanctions, the ultimate being the loss of our certification:

1. We shall not deliberately or with reckless indifference fail to provide adequate, timely, clear, and accurate information on planning issues.

2. We shall not accept an assignment from a client or employer when the services to be performed involve conduct that we know to be illegal or in violation of these rules.

3. We shall not accept an assignment from a client or employer to publicly advocate a position on a planning issue that is indistinguishably adverse to a position we publicly advocated for a previous client or employer within the past three years unless (1) we determine in good faith after consultation with other qualified professionals that our change of position will not cause present detriment to our previous client or employer, and (2) we make full written disclosure of the conflict to our current client or employer and receive written permission to proceed with the assignment.

4. We shall not, as salaried employees, undertake other employment in planning or a related profession, whether or not for pay, without having made full written disclosure to the employer who furnishes our salary

and having received subsequent written permission to undertake additional employment, unless our employer has a written policy which expressly dispenses with a need to obtain such consent.

5. We shall not, as public officials or employees, accept from anyone other than our public employer any compensation, commission, rebate, or other advantage that may be perceived as related to our public office or employment.

6. We shall not perform work on a project for a client or employer if, in addition to the agreed upon compensation from our client or employer, there is a possibility for direct personal or financial gain to us, our family members, or persons living in our household, unless our client or employer, after full written disclosure from us, consents in writing to the arrangement.

7. We shall not use to our personal advantage, nor that of a subsequent client or employer, information gained in a professional relationship that the client or employer has requested be held inviolate or that we should recognize as confidential because its disclosure could result in embarrassment or other detriment to the client or employer. Nor shall we disclose such confidential information except when (1) required by process of law, or (2) required to prevent a clear violation of law, or (3) required to prevent a substantial injury to the public. Disclosure pursuant to (2) and (3) shall not be made until after we have verified the facts and issues involved and, when practicable, exhausted efforts to obtain reconsideration of the matter and have sought separate opinions on the issue from other qualified professionals employed by our client or employer.

8. We shall not, as public officials or employees, engage in private communications with planning process participants if the discussions relate to a matter over which we have authority to make a binding, final determination if such private communications are prohibited by law or by agency rules, procedures, or custom.

9. We shall not engage in private discussions with decision makers in the planning process in any manner prohibited by law or by agency rules, procedures, or custom.

10. We shall neither deliberately, nor with reckless indifference, misrepresent the qualifications, views, and findings of other professionals.

11. We shall not solicit prospective clients or employment through use of false or misleading claims, harassment, or duress.

12. We shall not misstate our education, experience, training, or any other facts which are relevant to our professional qualifications.

13. We shall not sell, or offer to sell, services by stating or implying an ability to influence decisions by improper means.

14. We shall not use the power of any office to seek or obtain a special advantage that is not a matter of public knowledge or is not in the public interest.

15. We shall not accept work beyond our professional competence unless the client or employer understands and agrees that such work will be performed by another professional competent to perform the work and acceptable to the client or employer.

16. We shall not accept work for a fee, or pro bono, that we know cannot be performed with the promptness required by the prospective client, or that is required by the circumstances of the assignment.

17. We shall not use the product of others' efforts to seek professional recognition or acclaim intended for producers of original work.

18. We shall not direct or coerce other professionals to make analyses or reach findings not supported by available evidence.

19. We shall not fail to disclose the interests of our client or employer when participating in the planning process. Nor shall we participate in an effort to conceal the true interests of our client or employer.

20. We shall not unlawfully discriminate against another person.

21. We shall not withhold cooperation or information from the AICP Ethics Officer or the AICP Ethics Committee if a charge of ethical misconduct has been filed against us.

22. We shall not retaliate or threaten retaliation against a person who has filed a charge of ethical misconduct against us or another planner, or who is cooperating in the Ethics Officer's investigation of an ethics charge.

23. We shall not use the threat of filing an ethics charge in order to gain, or attempt to gain, an advantage in dealings with another planner.

24. We shall not file a frivolous charge of ethical misconduct against another planner.

25. We shall neither deliberately, nor with reckless indifference, commit any wrongful act, whether or not specified in the Rules of Conduct, that reflects adversely on our professional fitness.

C: OUR CODE PROCEDURES

1. Introduction

In brief, our Code Procedures (1) describe the way that one may obtain either a formal or informal advisory ethics ruling, and (2) detail how a charge of misconduct can be filed, and how charges are investigated, prosecuted, and adjudicated.

2. Informal Advice

All of us are encouraged to seek informal ethics advice from the Ethics Officer. Informal advice is not given in writing and is not binding on AICP, but the AICP Ethics Committee shall take it into consideration in the event a charge of misconduct is later filed against us concerning the conduct in question. If we ask the Ethics Officer for informal advice and do not receive a response within 21 calendar days of our request, we should notify the Chair of the Ethics Committee that we are awaiting a response.

3. Formal Advice

Only the Ethics Officer is authorized to give formal advice on the propriety of a planner's proposed conduct. Formal advice is binding on AICP and any of us who can demonstrate that we followed such advice shall have a defence to any charge of misconduct. The advice will be issued to us in writing signed by the Ethics Officer. The written advice shall not include names or places without the written consent of all persons to be named. Requests for formal advice must be in writing and must contain sufficient details, real or hypothetical, to permit a definitive opinion. The Ethics Officer has the discretion to issue or not issue formal advice. The Ethics Officer will not issue formal advice if he or she determines that the request deals with past conduct that should be the subject of a charge of misconduct. The Ethics Officer will respond to requests for formal advice within 21 days of receipt and will docket the requests in a log that will be distributed on a quarterly basis to the Chair of the AICP Ethics Committee. If the Ethics Officer fails to furnish us with a timely response we should notify the Chair of the AICP Ethics Committee that we are awaiting a response.

4. Published Formal Advisory Rulings

The Ethics Officer shall transmit a copy of all formal advice to the AICP Ethics Committee. The Committee, from time to time, will determine if the formal advice provides guidance to the interpretation of the Code and should be published as a formal advisory ruling. Also, the Ethics Committee has the authority to draft and publish formal advisory rulings when it determines that guidance to interpretation of the Code is needed or desirable.

5. Filing a Charge of Misconduct

Any person, whether or not an AICP member, may file a charge of misconduct against a Certified Planner. A charge of misconduct shall be made in a letter sent to the AICP Ethics Officer. The letter may be signed or it may be anonymous. The person filing the charge is urged to maintain confidentiality to the extent practicable. The person filing the charge should not send a copy of the charge to the Certified Planner identified in the letter or to any other person. The letter shall accurately identify the Certified Planner against whom the charge is being made and describe the conduct that allegedly violated the provisions of the Rules of Conduct. The person filing a charge should also cite all provisions of the Rules of Conduct that have allegedly been violated. However, a charge will not be dismissed if the Ethics Officer is able to determine from the facts stated in the letter that certain Rules of Conduct may have been violated. The letter reciting the charge should be accompanied by all relevant documentation available to the person filing the charge. While anonymously filed charges are permitted, anonymous filers will not receive notification of the disposition of the charge. Anonymous filers may furnish a postal address in the event the Ethics Officer needs to reach them for an inquiry.

6. Receipt of Charge by Ethics Officer

The Ethics Officer shall maintain a log of all letters containing charges of misconduct filed against Certified Planners upon their receipt and shall transmit a quarterly report of such correspondence to the Chair of the Ethics Committee. Within two weeks of receipt of a charge, the Ethics Officer shall prepare a cover letter and transmit the charge and all attached documentation to the named Certified Planner, who shall be now referred to as "the Respondent." The Ethics Officer's cover letter shall indicate whether the Ethics Officer expects the Respondent to file a "preliminary response" or whether the Ethics Officer is summarily dismissing the charge because it is clearly without merit. A copy of the cover letter will also be sent to the Charging Party, if identified. If the cover letter summarily dismisses the charge, it shall be sent to an identifiable Charging Party by receipted Certified Mail. The Charging Party will have the right to appeal the summary dismissal as provided in Section 11. After the Ethics Officer has received a charge, the Charging Party may withdraw it only with the permission of the Ethics Officer. After receiving a charge, the Ethics Officer shall have a duty to keep an identified Charging Party informed of its status. If an identified Charging Party has not received a status report from the Ethics Officer for 60 calendar days, the Charging Party should notify the Chair of the AICP Ethics Committee of the lapse.

7. Right of Counsel

A planner who receives a charge of misconduct under a cover letter requesting a preliminary response should understand that if he or she desires legal representation, it would be advisable to obtain such representation at the earliest point in the procedure. However, a planner who elects to proceed at first without legal representation will not be precluded from engaging such representation at any later point in the procedure.

8. Preliminary Responses to a Charge of Misconduct

If the Ethics Officer requests a preliminary response, the Respondent shall be allowed 30 calendar days from receipt of the Ethics Officer's letter to send the response to the Ethics Officer. The Ethics Officer will grant an extension of time, not to exceed 15 calendar days, if the request for the extension is made within the 30 day period. Failure to make a timely preliminary response constitutes a failure to cooperate with the Ethics Officer's investigation of the charge. A preliminary response should include documentation, the names, addresses and telephone numbers of witnesses, and all of the facts and arguments that counter the charge. Because the motivation of the person who filed the charge is irrelevant, the Respondent should not discuss it. The Ethics Officer will send a copy of the preliminary response to the Charging Party, if identified, and allow the Charging Party 15 calendar days from the date of receipt to respond.

9. Conducting an Investigation

After review of the preliminary response from the Respondent and any counter to that response furnished by an identified Charging Party, or if no timely preliminary response is received, the Ethics Officer shall decide whether an investigation is appropriate. If the Ethics Officer determines that an investigation should be conducted, he or she may designate a member of the AICP staff or AICP counsel to conduct the investigation. The Respondent must cooperate in the investigation and encourage others with relevant information, whether favourable or unfavourable, to cooperate. Neither the Ethics Officer, nor designee, will make credibility findings to resolve differing witness versions of facts in dispute.

10. Dismissal of Charge or Issuance of Complaint

If, with or without an investigation, the charge appears to be without merit, the Ethics Officer shall dismiss it in a letter, giving a full explanation of the reasons. The dismissal letter shall be sent to the Respondent and the Charging Party by receipted Certified Mail. If, however, the Ethics Officer's investigation indicates that a Complaint is warranted, the Ethics Officer shall draft a Complaint and send it to the Respondent by receipted Certified Mail, with a copy to the Charging Party. The Complaint shall consist of numbered paragraphs containing recitations of alleged facts. Following the fact paragraphs, there shall be numbered paragraphs of alleged violations, which shall cite provisions of the Rules of Conduct that the Ethics Officer believes are implicated. The allegations in the Complaint shall be based on the results of the Ethics Officer's investigation of the charge and may be additional to, or different from, those allegations initially relied upon by the Charging Party. The Ethics Officer shall maintain a log of all dismissals and shall transmit the log on a quarterly basis to the Chair of the Ethics Committee.

11. Appeal of Dismissal of Charge

Identified Charging Parties who are notified of the dismissal of their ethics charges shall have 30 calendar days from the date of the receipt of their dismissal letters to file an appeal with the Ethics Committee. The appeal shall be sent to the Ethics Officer who shall record it in a log and transmit it within 21 calendar days to the Ethics Committee. The Ethics Committee shall either affirm or reverse the dismissal. If the dismissal is reversed, the Ethics Committee shall either direct the Ethics Officer to conduct a further investigation and review the charge again, or issue a Complaint based on the materials before the Committee. The Ethics Officer shall notify the Charging Party and the Respondent of the Ethics Committee's determination.

12. Answering a Complaint

The Respondent shall have 30 calendar days from receipt of a Complaint in which to file an Answer. An extension not to exceed 15 calendar days will be granted if the request is made within the 30 day period. In furnishing an Answer, the Respondent is expected to cooperate in good faith. General denials are unacceptable. The Answer must specifically admit or deny each of the fact allegations in the Complaint. It is acceptable to deny a fact allegation on the ground that the planner is unable to verify its correctness, but that explanation should be stated as the reason for denial. The failure of a Respondent to make a timely denial of any fact alleged in the Complaint shall be deemed an admission of such fact. The Ethics Officer may amend a Complaint to delete any disputed fact, whether or not material to the issues. The Ethics Officer also may amend a Complaint to restate fact allegations by verifying and adopting the Respondent's version of what occurred. The Ethics Officer shall send the Complaint or Amended Complaint and the Respondent's Answer to the Ethics Committee with a copy to an identified Charging Party. The Ethics Officer shall also inform the Ethics Committee if there are any disputed material facts based on a comparison of the documents.

13. Conducting a Hearing

a) If the Ethics Officer notifies the Ethics Committee that material facts are in dispute or if the Ethics Committee, on its own, finds that to be the case, the Chair of the Committee shall designate a "Hearing Official" from among the membership of the Committee. At this point in the process, the Ethics Officer, either personally or through a designated AICP staff member or AICP counsel, shall continue to serve as both Investigator-Prosecutor and as the Clerk serving the Ethics Committee, the Hearing Official, and the Respondent. In carrying out clerical functions, the Ethics Officer, or designee, may discuss with the Ethics Committee and the Hearing Official the procedural arrangements for the hearing. Until the Ethics Committee decides the case, however, the Ethics Officer or designee shall not discuss the merits of the case with any member of the Committee unless the Respondent is present or is afforded an equal opportunity to address the Committee member.

b) The Ethics Officer shall transmit a "Notice of Hearing" to the Respondent, the Hearing Official, and an identified Charging Party. The hearing shall normally be conducted in the vicinity where the alleged misconduct occurred. The Notice will contain a list of all disputed material facts that need to be resolved. The hearing will be confined to resolution of those facts. There shall be no requirement that formal rules of evidence be observed.

c) The Ethics Officer will have the burden of proving, by a preponderance of the evidence, that misconduct occurred. The Ethics Officer may present witness testimony and any other evidence relevant to demonstrating the existence of each disputed material fact. The Respondent will then be given the opportunity to present witness testimony and any other evidence relevant to controvert the testimony and other evidence submitted by the Ethics Officer. The Ethics Officer may then be given an opportunity to present additional witness testimony and other evidence in rebuttal. All witnesses who testify for the Ethics Officer or the Respondent shall be subject to cross-examination by the other party. The Hearing Official shall make an electronic recording of the hearing and shall make copies of the recording available to the Ethics Officer and the Respondent.

d)   At least 30 calendar days before the hearing, the Ethics Officer and the Respondent shall exchange lists of proposed witnesses who will testify, and copies of all exhibits that will be introduced, at the hearing. There shall be no other discovery and no pre-hearing motions. All witnesses must testify in person at the hearing unless arrangements can be made by agreement between the Respondent and the Ethics Officer prior to the hearing, or by ruling of the Hearing Official during the hearing, to have an unavailable witness's testimony submitted in a video recording that permits the Hearing Official to observe the demeanour of the witness. No unavailable witness's testimony shall be admissible unless the opposing party was offered a meaningful opportunity to cross-examine the witness. The hearing shall not be open to the public. The Hearing Official shall have the discretion to hold open the hearing to accept recorded video testimony of unavailable witnesses. The Respondent will be responsible for the expense of bringing his or her witnesses to the hearing or to have their testimony video recorded. Following the closing of the hearing, the Hearing Official shall make findings only as to the disputed material facts and transmit the findings to the full Ethics Committee, the Ethics Officer, and the Respondent. The Hearing Official, prior to issuing findings, may request that the parties submit proposed findings of fact for his or her consideration.

14. Deciding the Case

The Ethics Committee (including the Hearing Official member of the Committee) shall resolve the ethics matter by reviewing the documentation that sets out the facts that were not in dispute, any fact findings that were required to be made by a Hearing Official, and any arguments submitted to it by the Respondent and the Ethics Officer. The Ethics Officer shall give 45 calendar days notice to the Respondent of the date of the Ethics Committee meeting during which the matter will be resolved. The Ethics Officer and the Respondent shall have 21 calendar days to submit memoranda stating their positions. The Ethics Officer shall transmit the memoranda to the Ethics Committee no later than 15 calendar days prior to the scheduled meeting. If the Committee determines that the Rules of Conduct have not been violated, it shall dismiss the Complaint and direct the Ethics Officer to notify the Respondent and an identified Charging Party. If the Ethics Committee determines that the Ethics Officer has demonstrated that the Rules of Conduct have been violated, it shall also determine the appropriate sanction, which shall either be a reprimand, suspension, or expulsion. The Ethics Committee shall direct the Ethics Officer to notify the Respondent and an identified Charging Party of its action and to draft a formal explanation of its decision and the discipline chosen. Upon approval of the Ethics Committee, the explanation and discipline chosen shall be published and titled "Opinion of the AICP Ethics Committee." The determination of the AICP Ethics Committee shall be final.

15. Settlement of Charges

a) Prior to issuance of a Complaint, the Ethics Officer may negotiate a settlement between the Respondent and an identified Charging Party if the Ethics Officer determines that the Charging Party has been personally aggrieved by the alleged misconduct of the Respondent and a private resolution between the two would not be viewed as compromising Code principles. If a settlement is reached under such circumstances, the Charging Party will be allowed to withdraw the charge of misconduct.

b) Also prior to issuance of a Complaint, the Ethics Officer may enter into a proposed settlement agreement without the participation of an identified Charging Party. However, in such circumstances, the proposed settlement agreement shall be contingent upon the approval of the Ethics Committee. An identified Charging Party will be given notice and an opportunity to be heard by the Ethics Committee before it votes to approve or disapprove the proposed pre-Complaint settlement.

c) After issuance of a Complaint by the Ethics Officer, a settlement can be negotiated solely between the Ethics Officer and the Respondent, subject to the approval of the Ethics Committee without input from an identified Charging Party.

16. Resignations and Lapses of Membership

If an AICP member who is the subject of a Charge of Misconduct resigns or allows membership to lapse prior to a final determination of the Charge (and any Complaint that may have issued), the ethics matter will be held in abeyance subject to being revived if the individual applies for reinstatement of membership within two years. If such former member, however, fails to apply for reinstatement within two years, the individual shall not be permitted to reapply for certification for a period of 10 years from the date of resignation or lapse of membership. If the Ethics Officer receives a Charge of Misconduct against a former member, the Ethics Officer shall make an effort to locate and advise the former member of the filing of the Charge and this Rule of Procedure.

17. Annual Report of Ethics Officer

Prior to January 31 of each calendar year the Ethics Officer shall publish an Annual Report of all ethics activity during the preceding calendar year to the AICP Ethics Committee and the AICP Commission. The AICP Commission shall make the Annual Report available to the membership.

NOTE

[1] AICP Code of Ethics and Professional Conduct: http://www.planning.org/ethics/ethicscode.htm. Accessed May 20, 2011.

APPENDIX 5

Cases for Discussion

The following cases are offered as aids to classroom discussion. Discussion of cases allows students to apply the ethical principles they have learned, and to appreciate the difficulty that sometimes exists in realizing the values of the public service. Some of the cases are drawn from the real world, some are variations on real cases, and others are entirely made up. In every case we have provided only enough factual information to set the stage for discussion. If students think that how they would respond to a given case would depend upon additional factual information not provided, they should be encouraged to think about why they believe the additional information would be useful. The cases vary in complexity, and are presented in no particular order.

CASE 1: STATISTICS CANADA

Statistics Canada is an agency under the jurisdiction of the federal government in charge of compiling data in order to "help Canadians better understand their country."[1] The statistics compiled cover an extremely wide range of topics; politicians and governmental agencies, businesses, academics, and ordinary members of the public can and do use this information for a wide variety of purposes. The best-known way that Statistics Canada compiles its data is through the national census, which occurs every five years. In June 2010, Industry Minister Tony Clement created an Order in Council[2] that altered the format of the census, changing it from a mandatory long-form questionnaire to a shorter, voluntary survey. This decision caused an uproar not only with the general public, but also within the agency itself. Opponents of Minister

Clement's decision argued that the change would reduce the quality of information available to anyone and everyone choosing to conduct studies about Canadians, since there would be less specificity in the questions being asked. They also argued that the Conservative government was putting minority groups at a disadvantage, since those groups are less likely to fill out a voluntary survey.[3] The Conservative government was also accused of falsely representing the mandatory long-form version as one that invades privacy due to its supposedly intrusive questions and creates fear due to the possible punishment available for those who do not complete the questionnaire. Munir Sheikh, Chief Statistician of Canada, quit his position after it was suggested by Minister Clement that the official position of Statistics Canada was in line with his decision.[4] Reaction from the public included a court challenge from the Federation des communautes francophones et acadienne du Canada, a group representing francophones in Canada, who unsuccessfully tried to appeal the decision of the Conservative government through Federal Court on the grounds that it violated the *Official Languages Act*.[5] The Senior Economist for the Canadian Centre for Policy Alternatives, Armine Yalnizyan, wrote an open letter to Minister Clement and Dr. Sheikh in July 2010, blasting the decision for its implications on the quality of data available for the creation of new policies.[6]

> By resigning from his position, Munir Sheikh effectively decided to remove himself from the debate rather than use his position as head of Statistics Canada to argue for the re-introduction of the long-form questionnaire. What are the ethical implications of Dr. Sheikh's decision? Which values did it serve, and which did it frustrate? A great many citizens' groups attempted to intervene and have the government's decision reversed. What role, if any, should citizens' groups play in government decision making?

CASE 2: eHEALTH SCANDAL (ONTARIO)

The eHealth Ontario organization was a provincial agency established for the purpose of creating an electronic health record system for Ontario. Specifically, their mandate was directed at three issues:

1. Diabetes Management: to control and manage diabetes more effectively and reduce associated complications and costs.

2. Medication Management: to implement on-line management of prescription medications to minimize preventable adverse drug events.

3. Wait Times: to reduce waits in Ontario emergency departments and the incidence of inpatients in acute care waiting for alternate levels of care, and to continue improving wait times for acute care services.[7]

However, in October 2009, Ontario Auditor General Jim McCarter released a report outlining various problems with eHealth.[8] News reports of his findings included the following:

- This "scathing report on the eHealth Ontario spending scandal charges that successive governments wasted $1 billion in taxpayer money."[9]*

- "His report says the board of directors at eHealth Ontario felt it had little power over CEO Sarah Kramer because she had been hired by chair Alan Hudson "with the support of the premier." That, McCarter said, gave Kramer the impression she had approval to ignore normal procurement procedures."[10]

- McCarter said in his report that "Ontario taxpayers have not received value for money for this $1 billion investment."[11]

- The report is damning in its criticism of the way governments have allowed eHealth and its predecessor, Smart Systems for Health, to let spending go out of control with few safeguards to protect tax dollars.[12]

- The report concluded that the initiative to create an Electronic Health Record (EHR) was "lacking in strategic direction and relying too heavily on external consultants." Specifically, "There was a heavy, and in some cases almost total, reliance on consultants. By 2008, the Ministry's eHealth Program Branch had fewer than 30 full-time employees but was engaging more than 300 consultants, a number of whom held senior management positions." Furthermore, McCarter noted that contracts with eHealth Ontario were often awarded without an open competitive process. He also found evidence of "questionable procurement practices." He noted that the untendered contracts that were awarded supported allegations of favouritism. For example, "One firm that bid 500% more than the next qualified bidder was invited to bid again, the only company offered such an opportunity, and, after lowering its bid significantly, won the contract." The report also demonstrated the inefficient use of taxpayer money. This primarily included the following: $800 million spent to "build a computer network for health care providers that is expensive to operate and significantly underutilized . . . on average, users are utilizing less than 1% of the network's available bandwidth."[13]†

Apart from inefficient use of money, some expenditures just seemed wasteful. "Consultants were contracted by eHealth at up to $2,750 a day. They then billed

CBC News. "EHealth scandal a $1B waste: auditor", Oct. 7, 2009. Website: http://www.cbc.ca/canada/toronto/story/2009/10/07/ehealth-auditor.html

†*Auditor General of Ontario* <www.auditor.on.ca/en/news_en/newsrelease_ehealth.pdf>. © Queen's Printer for Ontario, 2009. Reproduced with permission.

taxpayers for out-of-pocket expenses that included $1.65 for a cup of tea and $3.99 for cookies."[14] "The agency paid consultants millions of dollars for—among other things—watching TV, reading *The New York Times* and holding a conversation on the subway."[15] "Kramer billed thousands of dollars for limousine rides, including one $400 trip from Toronto to London, Ont., before she resigned from her $380,000-a-year job in June. She was given a $317,000 severance package and received a $114,000 bonus after just 10 months on the job."[16] "She also was lambasted for $51,500 spent on her office renovation."[17] Furthermore, in regards to the untendered contracts, "Documents released by the government since then showed the value of those untendered contracts was closer to $16 million, with the biggest ones going to companies the opposition parties say have ties to the Liberal government."[18] In addition, "[e]xecutives at two companies that were awarded untendered contracts from eHealth Ontario had close personal connections to the CEO and board chairman, CBC News learned."[19]*

"In his report, the auditor general also slammed unnamed officials at the Ministry of Health for thwarting his efforts to get investigators into the ministry for a routine audit in the summer of 2008. In the end, the audit didn't happen until February 2009."[20] Health Minister David Caplan resigned because of the report. Sarah Kramer was fired as CEO on June 7 in the middle of the scandal. Alan Hudson, Chairman of the Board, stepped down ten days later, on June 17, 2009.

> What ethical issues does this scandal raise? What would need to be done to improve the functioning of this agency?

CASE 3: DEPARTMENT OF VETERANS AFFAIRS DISCLOSES CONFIDENTIAL MEDICAL INFORMATION OF VOCAL CRITIC

Consider the following story from the *Globe and Mail*, which is quoted in full.[21]

> The Department of Veterans Affairs has a proud record. Founded in 1944 to care for and reintegrate into civil society the more than one million men and women who served in Canada's armed forces during the Second World War, it was an ornament of government. The Veterans Charter, the package of programs created by the Mackenzie King government, gave the department the funding it needed to care for the wounded in body and mind. There was money to send vets to university or for training, to give them farms or to set up businesses,

---

*CBC News. "Head of Ehealth Ontario is fired amid contracts scandal, gets big package", June 7, 2009. Website: www.cbc.ca/news/canada/story/2009/06/07/ehealth-kramer.html

and to put cash in their hands and a new suit on their backs. While there were inevitable complaints, the department still cares well for Canada's world war vets, and it does fine work on remembrance and military heritage.

Now all this is in jeopardy. Under its new name, Veterans Affairs Canada has besmirched its record, perhaps irrevocably. Modern-era veterans, those who served in the Persian Gulf, the former Yugoslavia or in Afghanistan, have long believed themselves short-changed by the department and successive governments, and some of the complaints have become vociferous. The Veterans Ombudsman, Colonel Pat Stogran (who commanded the Princess Patricia's Canadian Light Infantry in Afghanistan in 2002), has pushed the department hard to make improvements in benefits. So, too, has retired captain Sean Bruyea, a 14-year air force vet with service in the Persian Gulf war.

And what was the bureaucratic response? After Mr. Bruyea started criticizing the department in 2005 over a new Veterans Charter that changed the compensation package for wounded vets (with its plan to pay lump sums), he suddenly found access to the treatment he required to treat his post-traumatic stress disorder cut off. The department then demanded that he get a psychiatric assessment at a hospital of its choosing. When Mr. Bruyea later secured access to his file, he discovered that his records had been passed around Veterans Affairs' offices. "Folks, it's time to take the gloves off here," one senior official wrote.

So off came the gloves, and Mr. Bruyea lost access to the care and treatment he needed. In other words, the bureaucrats decided to try to shut up a critic who was interfering with the implementation of their plans, and they used his medical records to help them do so. We can almost hear them saying: Pay no attention, deputy minister, he's crazy and a crank.

It's important to note that Mr. Bruyea's shameful treatment began in 2005 under a Liberal government and continued under the Conservatives. Politics was surely involved, but this sorry story smacks of nothing so much as officials protecting themselves and the programs they wanted against the assaults of critics.

One instance of this bureaucratic persecution would be plenty, but Col. Stogran, the Ombudsman, shouted so loudly that the government declined to renew his appointment. Col. Stogran said he had discovered that some 400 Veterans Affairs officials had scoured his personal files for evidence that could be used to shut him up. Other vets soon came forward with similar stories.

Canada's Privacy Commissioner, Jennifer Stoddart, has confirmed Mr. Bruyea's account, and she's now looking into claims of bureaucratic abuse at Veterans Affairs as a whole. But the commissioner's powers to punish are limited. We need a formal inquiry that can summon senior officials and their ministers to explain their actions under oath and issue findings of fault. "People need to suffer the consequences of their actions, because it's the only way they would learn and other employees learn as well," said Mr. Bruyea's wife, Carolina.

She's right. Officials must learn there are limits; they must understand that veterans are citizens with rights to privacy and, because of their overseas service in times of war, even more entitlement to their nation's care and consideration. The breaches of faith are a blot on the department's record and a stain on the Canadian government. If the public's confidence is to be restored, there must be an investigation—with punishment for those who tried to smear opponents. Nothing less will suffice.[22]*

How would you analyze what went wrong here? What corrective actions should be taken?

CASE 4: PERSONNEL RATINGS

You are the general manager in the Parks, Forestry, and Recreation Department of a large municipality. You have a staff of approximately 400, engaged in a wide variety of jobs. One of your responsibilities as manager is to conduct performance reviews for the employees in your department. Annual merit-based bonuses, as well as various promotional opportunities, depend upon your annual reviews. As is to be expected, your employees range from minimally

*Jack Granatstein, "Disgrace at Veterans Affairs", *Globe and Mail* on Friday, Oct. 15, 2010 <www.theglobeandmail .com/news/opinions/opinion/the-disgrace-at-veterans-affairs-canada/article1757630> Accessed 20 May 2011.

competent to exceptional in terms of the various skills and activities upon which your reviews are to be based.

You wish to have your deputy city manager and city manager, who receive the reviews, think well of your management skills. You also know that morale in your department is boosted when performance reviews are highly positive. Finally, you also know that the managers and directors of the 13 other departments under your immediate deputy manager have for many years been inflating the reviews they give to their workers. You have resisted this pressure to inflate your reviews until now, but the result has been that fewer of your workers receive merit awards or are offered promotions. You have some worry as well that your effectiveness as manager appears weak by comparison with your colleagues, whose workers seem to be performing at a higher level due to their inflated rankings of their workers.

> You are contemplating simply inflating the rankings of all your workers by one step in the graduated ranking scheme that is used, e.g., from competent to highly competent, from very good to excellent, from excellent to outstanding. While this will misrepresent the skills you think each individual actually has displayed, this simple mechanism will at least retain the relative ranking between workers. You think this will improve morale, make your workers more competitive internally, and show you to be an effective manager to your superiors. Should you do it?

CASE 5: MISTAKES HAPPEN

You work in a mid-size municipality, in the department of social services. One of the responsibilities of your department is paying social assistance and disability benefits to city residents. A city resident has a disabled child, for whom she receives a monthly disability benefit. Four months ago your department listed the child as deceased and discontinued the benefit payment to the mother. The child has not died; this is just a mistake.

You are also a member of a local church and participate in various activities sponsored by your church as a private citizen. The mother of the disabled child belongs to the same church, and you have met both her and her child on numerous occasions, though you would not describe yourselves as friends. During a bake sale, she learned that you work for the social services department, and tells you of her plight. She has been trying unsuccessfully to have the benefit restored, but no one seems to have the authority to help her, and she has been getting what she perceives as the run-around, being sent from one part of city hall to another, without success. You offer to help the next week. You know who to talk to, and find out what forms need to be filled out. You assist the mother in the process, and her benefit is restored the next month.

> What ethical issues does this case raise?

CASE 6: PRIVATIZATION

You are a deputy city manager in a municipality that has had its garbage and recycling services performed by unionized city workers for decades. The service is considered quite good, though there have been a couple of protracted strikes by the outside workers' union that have interfered with garbage collection and created major dissatisfaction among the residents. Residents are divided as to who bore primary responsibility for the breakdown in collective bargaining that led to the strikes (some think it was a failure of management, others unreasonable demands by the union), but all agree that the strikes were a blight on the city, hurt tourism, were a major inconvenience to residents and business, and posed a potential health hazard.

In the current municipal election, the two mayoral candidates who are widely acknowledged to be the front-runners have opposing views on privatizing garbage collection in the city. One is promising to privatize garbage collection within his first year in office, claiming that this will not only eliminate the risk of future strikes, but save the city millions of dollars. The other is opposed to privatizing city services, arguing that having public sector city jobs is good for the city overall, and that the savings being touted by his opponent are exaggerated.

> You are strongly opposed to privatization. You have done some research on the subject and believe that the savings being suggested by the proponent of privatization are much exaggerated. You also believe in strong public sector jobs and want to retain city services within the municipal government structure. You are asked by the campaign director of the mayoral candidate who is opposed to privatization to join in a public information campaign against the proposal. Should you do so? You are also considering leaking the information you have collected through your research to either the union representing the outside workers whose jobs will be affected if the services are privatized (who have been actively promoting the opposing candidate on this and other issues) or to the media. Should you leak the information you have? Is there something else you should do?

CASE 7: SAFE INJECTION SITE

You work in the public health department of a large municipality that has an alarming problem with intravenous drug use. Drug use creates a number of public health concerns: addicts leave dirty needles in public areas where children and pets play; there is a significant rise in the rates of infectious diseases, including HIV and hepatitis C, among drug users in the city; there have been a number of drug overdoses in the city; and unsafe drug use practices are putting a strain on emergency medical services in local hospitals. You have been asked to head a team researching the effectiveness of safe injection sites, places where users can access clean needles and inject their drugs in a sterile and medically supervised location, and to recommend a course of action.

Your research reveals that safe injection sites save lives, both through the prevention of direct deaths through overdose and through the prevention of the spread of infectious diseases. They also mitigate the other health concerns that intravenous drug use creates. But your research also reveals that there has often been quite significant opposition from residents and businesses in neighbourhoods where such sites have been proposed or located, and that there may well be significant political opposition within your City Council to any proposal to open a safe injection site in the city, much of which is ideological, in your view.

You are convinced, however, that the benefits of a safe injection site far outweigh the costs, and that such a site should be established in your city. In order to bolster your case, however, and in order to try to deflect some of the anticipated opposition to your proposal, you inflate the benefits of such sites in your report. You over-estimate the number of lives that will be saved, the benefits that such sites provide in terms of facilitating the treatment of drug addiction and getting addicts into rehabilitation programs, and the costs to the local health care system. You also under-estimate the cost of providing the safe injection site. You reason that the benefits of the site really do vastly outweigh the costs of it, and that it really will be in the public interest. You are just trying to make the case as compelling as possible, because you know that both members of the public and politicians are ill-informed about the issues and cannot be relied upon to make good decisions on the evidence, especially given the role of ideological biases that you think colour many of the reactions of both members of the public and political leaders.

Is your action morally acceptable? Is there something better you could do?

CASE 8: HOLLOWING OUT THE GRANT

You work for the employment services department of a growing municipal government. One of the responsibilities of your department is to provide employment-related services to new immigrants. Much of your funding comes, not directly from the city, but from various grants from the federal government. The grants are to provide the immigrant-settlement services related to employment, including language training, apprenticing, and job training. As it happens, this year the number of immigrants to your city requiring this kind of assistance is lower than in previous years. This may be in part, you speculate, because the economy has been particularly strong and so employment opportunities are up in virtually all sectors, and it may be because a number of the immigrant groups you serve have now reached a critical mass such that they are providing assistance to new members of their groups in the community through non-government agencies and programs. But whatever the reasons, you are approaching the end of the budget year and have about $200,000 of unspent federal grant money. What should you do?

On the one hand, if the money is unspent at the end of the fiscal year, it will be returned to the federal government (you cannot roll surpluses over across budget years). This will, presumably, make it available for immigrants elsewhere who need it. But you know that if you do not spend your entire grant this year, you may be at a disadvantage arguing that you need the full amount next year. And within your municipal organization, a certain prestige and importance in the hierarchy of agencies seems to be tied to budget allocations. Furthermore, the city managers expect you to seek the maximum amount of federal funding possible. Your merit pay is in part tied to your success in this function. Finally, you worry that if your budget decreases, you may be forced to reduce the workforce in your department.

> What should you do? Should you hollow out the grant, i.e., spend the money on something that is not strictly necessary? What if you also know that this is standard practice in the city?

CASE 9: THE LINE BETWEEN THE PERSONAL AND THE PRIVATE

You are a mid-level manager in the financial planning department of a small municipality. You have noticed that a number of employees in your department are unhealthy, because they smoke cigarettes or are overweight. No one's job performance has yet been affected by their smoking or weight conditions; absenteeism due to illness is not yet a problem. But you are aware that health benefits for municipal employees are a major cost to the township, and that both smoking and obesity are statistically likely to cause increased health care costs and absenteeism in the future. Therefore you decide to set a no smoking policy for all employees that prohibits employees from smoking, not only at work or on municipal property grounds, but even during their off-duty hours and in their private homes. You also introduce a mandatory fitness program at lunch time in an effort to combat obesity among employees.

> Are these acceptable policies for a public employer to adopt? Why or why not, and where and how do you draw the line?

CASE 10: PERCEPTIONS, DAMNED PERCEPTIONS

You notice that contracts for services from your agency always go to outside private for-profit organizations that are now headed by former public servants. As far as you can tell, nothing wrong is being done: confidentiality and lobbying rules seem to be being respected. Yet you have this nagging suspicion that their success must have something to do with the experience of the former civil servants.

What should you do?

CASE 11: MAKING PROVINCIAL LIQUOR RETAILER MORE PROFITABLE

Many provinces in Canada own and operate liquor retail outlets (e.g., Liquor Control Board of Ontario LCBO, Alcool NB Liquor/ANBL). They are among the most profitable provincial services. Suppose that you work for the provincial government and are asked to explore ways and make recommendations to make your provincial liquor retailer even more profitable than it is, as a means of increasing revenue for the provincial government.

What ethical issues does this request raise, and what should you do?

CASE 12: ACCOMMODATING PEOPLE IN THE WORKPLACE

Suppose you are a mid-level manager at Canada Post, in one of their central sorting locations. Canada Post has a uniform that employees are expected to wear on the job, which consists of pants and shirt. You have over the past few years increased the racial, religious, and ethnic diversity of your workforce, and those new employees are now being promoted through the system. As a result, two Muslim women who had been employed in other areas of the organization have recently been transferred into your department as a result of their promotions. They indicate to you that they have cultural and religious objections to wearing pants, and want to wear floor length skirts. How should you respond to their request?

Now consider this variation: the dress code includes not just a uniform requirement, but more specific restrictions on those who directly serve the public. It includes prohibitions on visible tattoos or body piercings other than a single piercing in each ear lobe. One day a female employee of Indian origin comes to work with a henna tattoo on her hand. She explains that she is the bridesmaid in the wedding of her sister, and their cultural practice includes elaborate tattooing of the hand and wrist; the tattoo will become darker and more extensive over the next couple of weeks, at which time the wedding will take place, and the tattoo will fade over the course of about four weeks thereafter to a point where it is no longer visible. Or consider a young man who comes to work with piercings of his eye brow and lower lip. He explains that such piercings are part of his ethnic heritage and he refuses to remove them at work, stating that it would constitute an insult to his ancestors to do so.

> Would your response to these situations be any different than to the Muslim workers? Why or why not?

CASE 13: WHO TO FIRE, AND WHEN

You are the manager of a city department in a municipality that has been losing population to emigration for many years. The city's tax base is shrinking, and the number of people served by city services is declining. You have been told by the city manager that there are going to be job losses in the range of 15 to 25 percent overall, and that your department is going to lose at least three people. You have to recommend who should be let go.

You consider the following options. You might fire the longest serving employees, on the grounds that they have the highest salaries. You think: maybe that way I will lose only three employees, but not more, given the savings to be realized. That choice is hard, however, because they have been loyal employees for many years, they have valuable experience accumulated over that time, and they will likely face difficulty as older workers finding new employment at comparable wages. Yet they are also the workers that cost the most in terms of health benefits, due to their age, and they lack some skills that younger members of your team have.

On the other hand, perhaps you should let those with the least seniority go instead. True, their salaries and health care costs are lower, so you might lose even more than three junior employees, but they are likely to find employment elsewhere and there is something to be said for the fairness of using seniority as a decision consideration.

Finally, you consider not using any such general mechanism for deciding, but instead think you should engage in a robust performance review of each member of the department and recommend that the least effective workers be the ones to be dismissed, regardless of seniority or salary.

> Which would be the better decision procedure to use? Can you think of others? Are all of the factors listed relevant to making your decision?

CASE 14: RELATIONSHIPS ON THE JOB

You are a mid-level manager. Your supervisor has married a subordinate in your agency. The subordinate spouse does not report directly to your supervisor, but rather is under your supervision. You feel a certain constraint in performing your management functions with respect to the subordinate spouse. Sometimes your supervisor asks you to do things that don't feel quite right, like assigning vacation time to the subordinate out of order so that both spouses are guaranteed time off together. There is a growing perception of favouritism over time among other members of the organization, and morale is being adversely affected. You feel very uncomfortable reviewing the subordinate spouse's work performance, given the relationship with your supervisor.

What should you do?

CASE 15: WHEN THE EVIDENCE IS AGAINST YOU

You have become convinced, after years working in correctional services, that custodial punishments are less effective, and often do more harm than good overall, than non-custodial sentences for a range of offenders. You want to recommend some significant policy changes. In order to bolster your case, you contract an outside third party (say a university research team) to do research and provide data on the matter. The researchers come back in due course with a report, but it does not match your opinion or support the policy recommendations you wanted to make.

What should you do with the report?

CASE 16: WHEN CONSCIENCE COLLIDES WITH PUBLIC DUTY

Suppose you are a member of the municipal standards and licensing department. Your job includes issuing marriage licences and permits for public parades. You are asked to issue a licence of marriage to a same-sex couple, something that is legal in your jurisdiction, and a permit to the organizers of a Gay Pride parade. Your personal view, based in religious conviction, is that homosexuality is morally wrong and a sin.

What should you do?

CASE 17: DISCLOSURE IN AN INTERVIEW

You started out your career working with victims of sexual violence, moving through a number of not-for-profit community agencies and public agencies. For a while, your work involved outreach to sex workers. During that period of time, you were conducting an interview with a prostitute and got caught up in a sting operation. The police arrested you and charged you with a criminal offence of purchasing the sexual services of a prostitute. In relatively short order, your story was checked out, the prosecutor dropped the charges and you were cleared of all wrongdoing.

Now, many years later, you are being interviewed for a high-level deputy city manager's position. During your interview as one of three short-listed candidates for the position, you are asked if there is anything in your past that would cause embarrassment to the city if it hired you for the position. You flash back to your arrest, but reason that you can withhold the information about it since you were cleared of any wrongdoing and the charges were dropped. You say there is nothing the hiring committee needs to know. A few weeks later, when your appointment is announced, a keen municipal affairs reporter digs up your old arrest record and you open the morning news paper to read the headline: New Deputy Manager for City was Arrested for Buying Sex from a Prostitute!

Did you do anything wrong in the interview? What should you do now?

CASE 18: FALSIFYING DOCUMENTS

You work in the water department of your municipality. All the people in your organization are competent, well-trained, and carry out their responsibilities seriously and professionally. One of the responsibilities of your immediate supervisor is filing a monthly report concerning the testing of the municipal water supply. The report contains detailed records about testing, repairs, chlorination, and so forth. Your supervisor has been very distracted lately, however. You know that his son is gravely ill, and that he has been under tremendous personal strain. You also know that you and the others members of the department have been performing all the necessary tests and activities that are documented in the monthly reports. But this month, you come to realize, the records on the report are incomplete and your supervisor has failed to complete it, sign it, and file it as required. If the report is not completed, signed, and dated properly, provincial regulators must be called in to conduct a review and inspection. This will cause embarrassment to your supervisor, inconvenience to your co-workers, and cost the municipality money it cannot afford, because it will be charged for the provincial inspection team. You decide to falsify the report by filling in the missing information, back-dating it by one day, and forging your supervisor's signature on it so that it can be filed.

Have you done anything wrong?

CASE 19: ACCEPTING A RAISE

Suppose you have worked for some years in a large city government, occupying various roles, and moving up through the organization as your abilities expand and you garner the respect of colleagues and supervisors. A somewhat smaller neighbouring municipality is well aware of your talents, and when their long-serving city manager retires, they invite you to apply for the position. You are clearly the candidate they want, and they offer you a very attractive package, including not just a significantly higher salary than in your previous position, but a bonus structure under which you will receive a 5% bonus every year for the first five years, provided your performance reviews are highly favourable.

You take the job and are a roaring success. Your reviews every year are outstanding, and well deserved. But after two years on the job, the economy goes into a serious and unpredicted recession. The economic hard times are widespread, and do not reflect in any way on your performance. In the crisis, public sector salaries are frozen, and City Councillors even take a slight pay cut. But your bonus is a contractual obligation that the City Council is prepared to honour, and they offer you your negotiated 5% bonus.

Should you take it?

CASE 20: ADVOCACY OR INFORMATION

Suppose you are a city manager in a city that is debating what kind of public transit expansion to undertake: expand bus routes, expand streetcars, or expand the subway system. The costs of each proposal are in that order: buses are cheaper than streetcars, streetcars are cheaper than subway lines. As a result, the expansion of the service, both in terms of distance and commuters covered, is the inverse: the subway expansion will reach fewest new residents, the streetcars will reach more residents, and bus expansion will reach the most new residents. There are many other factors to be considered: impact of construction, impact on traffic congestion, and environmental impacts, to name a few. As well, there are considerable differences between the residents who will be made better off by each proposal: the subways will primarily benefit well-off inner city residents, the street cars inner city and inner-suburban residents who are extremely well off, and the buses will mostly benefit poorer residents in the outer suburbs.

Your city council is divided on which option is better, as are city residents and businesses. One councillor, a proponent of the subway option, asks you, as the manager of transportation services, to gather some information on the benefits of the subway. She makes it clear that she wants information that is favourable to the subway expansion, rather than an exhaustive report detailing the pros and cons of each of the options.

What should you do?

CASE 21: PRIVATE OR PUBLIC AGAIN

Suppose you have an employee who performs his duties to your organization with competence and whose performance is in every respect very good. Yet he has been gaining an increasing amount of public attention recently, not because of his work-related activities, but because he has become a very vocal spokesperson for an anti-abortion activist group. Abortion is not a matter that concerns your agency or even your level of government, and his actions are taken entirely on his own time. He makes it clear that he is engaged in his activist protests and other activities as a private citizen, not as a city employee. But his anti-abortion organization uses many questionable tactics, designed to shock the public, such as displaying large posters of aborted fetuses outside hospitals that provide abortion services, and chanting that abortion providers and users are damned for eternity. The publicity generated by his activities is causing increasing discomfort among some of his fellow employees, and you worry that it is also tarnishing the reputation of your department and the municipal government in general.

What, if anything, should you do?

CASE 22: GO ALONG FOR THE SAKE OF THE DEPARTMENT

You are a newly hired restaurant inspector. During your first few weeks of training, you accompany more experienced inspectors as they perform their inspections. You are shocked to discover that they seem to be ignoring a wide range of health code violations. They sometimes issue warnings to the owners but do not write up the violations, and in other cases you think they may even be taking bribes from the owners to ignore the violations and issue a passing inspection report (though you have no proof that this is occurring).

You decide to talk to your boss about what you have seen. She indicates that she is aware of the practices, and seems quite unconcerned about them. She suggests that a certain latitude is granted to inspectors so as to maintain good relations with the restaurant community, who have made it very clear over the years that strict compliance with some of the regulations would put them out of business, and that the violations are not serious enough to worry about. She hints that you might want to just go along if you want to be happy in your new position, though she does not threaten you with dismissal or discipline if you do not. After a couple more weeks, you have even graver concerns, worrying that some of the code violations may actually expose members of the public to illness. You again speak to your boss. This time she lets you know in no uncertain terms that she expects you to keep quiet and go along with the way things are done. She indicates that this is necessary to protect the reputation of the department, to avoid a public scandal, and to maintain public confidence in the inspection system. If you take your concerns any further up the chain of command, she lets you know, you will be causing significant and needless harm to your department and co-workers. And, after all, even the relatively lax inspection system we have is better than what is in place throughout most of the world, and no one gets seriously ill.

What should you do?

CASE 23: THE BOSS ASKS YOU TO LIE

You work for the local school board, in the area of property maintenance. A school is in need of significant repairs, but the Board lacks funds to do the maintenance work required. One wing of the building, in particular, is currently unusable because of structural concerns, caused by erosion around the foundation.

A hurricane has hit your town, and there has been widespread property damage. A state of disaster has been declared, and provincial inspectors are coming in to access the damage, for which compensation will be paid. Your boss instructs you to include the school in your damage report, even though the damage was not caused by the hurricane. You believe the lie would be successful.

Should you lie?

CASE 24: HELPING RESIDENTS OUT?

You work for a municipal water department as an engineer. You are tasked with assessing the pipes in the city that need to be replaced because they are lead, and lead piping exposes resident to possible lead contamination, which can be serious, especially for young children. The city will replace the portion of the pipes that is on municipal property, but residents must replace the portion of the pipes on their private property, from the roadway into the home, at their own expense. The policy states that the city portion can only be replaced if the private portion is or has been replaced too. You see the financial difficulty that the policy has on some homeowners, who simply cannot afford to replace the pipes they are responsible for. In some cases, you falsify the records so that it appears the private portion has already been replaced; that way the public portion of the pipes can be replaced. You rationalize your decision this way: replacing some of the lead piping to which residents are exposed is better than nothing, and this way the private portion can be done at a later date, once the resident can afford to do the work. It is not clear how long the program will last, so it is better to get at least the public portion of the pipe system switched to non-lead piping while you can.

How sound is this rationale?

CASE 25: LAND DEVELOPERS AND INCENTIVES

Land developers frequently seek support for rezoning of land from neighbours and city councils. This support is often secured by the developer offering to make improvements to nearby existing neighbourhoods, improvements which are overseen by a local government agency. Suppose the manager of a local property office insists that part of the incentive package must include provision of some service (e.g., a park, a road expansion) that the City Council had promised residents but cannot now afford to provide.

Is there anything wrong with such a demand?

CASE 26: INSIDER INFORMATION?

You have Sunday dinner with your family every week. It is a ritual, and includes the extended family, including your grown and married children, their partners, and their children. In the course of dinner, you not infrequently talk about events at work, as most people do. On this occasion, you mention that a road expansion has just been approved in your township. It was an interesting decision, because there was some controversy about which of a number of possible routes should be expanded. Finally, you say, a decision has been made and now you can move on to something else.

Your daughter-in-law, who was at dinner, recognizes that the land in the area of the road expansion is likely to increase in value as a result of this decision. The next day, unbeknownst to you, she begins the process of purchasing a large parcel of land in that area.

What should you do?

CASE 27: TAINTED MEAT

You are a meat inspector, and you discover that meat has been contaminated at a local meat packing plant. The manager of the plant assures you (with relevant evidence) that the problem has been corrected. There have been no reported cases of

CASES FOR DISCUSSION • 303

illness from the meat products, which have been shipped across three provinces to various retail and commercial outlets. The manager of the plant asks you to refrain from making the information public and from issuing a recall of the products, because of the impact it will have on the plant. The meat packing plant is an important local business in an economically depressed small community, employing 450 full-time employees; you worry that if you go public with your finding, the plant may have to go out of business and all of these people may lose their jobs.

What should you do?

CASE 28: SEX AT WORK

You are a manager who discovers, unhappily, that two of your most senior and valuable employees are having an affair. One is the manager of long-term care homes and senior services, and the other the manager of technical services. Neither reports to the other, and there is no conflict generated by their affair, given the organizational structure of your city government. But city policy strictly forbids intimate personal relationships between employees. You don't want to lose either of them; each is a very valuable employee and the city would be worse off without them. Because each rose through the ranks, moreover, you expect that you could not replace them in their senior positions for the same salary as they receive.

Should you report them? Confront them?

CASE 29: THE BOSS ASKS FOR A FAVOUR

Your agency has put out a call for proposals for a very important project, worth a considerable amount of money. The deadline has just passed, and you have only three proposals, none of them very strong. That is when your boss calls to ask if you would receive a final proposal, from a friend of his who is a contractor and who wants to bid on the project.

Should you accept the proposal?

CASE 30: CHARITY AT WORK

Your supervisor announced one day that your agency was going to participate in fundraising for a well-known and well-respected charitable organization. She set a target amount that she hoped the agency would reach by a certain date, and let employees know that payroll deductions could be arranged if employees wanted to make a monthly contribution to the campaign. A short time later, employees received a large package in their mailboxes, with forms through which they could make a one-time donation, as well as the forms to set up ongoing payroll deductions. It also contained a letter written personally by the head of the agency, extolling the virtues of the charity and the good work it does, restating the overall fundraising goal that had been set, providing a report on progress to date in reaching the goal, and urging all employees to give generously.

Is there anything wrong with such activities in the workplace? Under what conditions, if any, might they be acceptable?

NOTES

[1] http://www.statcan.gc.ca/about-apercu/about-apropos-eng.htm.

[2] http://www.gazette.gc.ca/rp-pr/p1/2010/2010-06-26/html/order-decret-eng.html.

[3] http://www.thestar.com/news/canada/census/article/840595--ex-statscan-chief-says-he-quit-to-protect-agency-s-credibility.

[4] http://www.theglobeandmail.com/news/politics/let-top-statistician-resolve-census-issue-former-civil-servants-urge-pm/article1703274/.

[5] http://www.montrealgazette.com/life/Francophones+drop+legal+fight/3680421/story.html.

[6] http://www.policyalternatives.ca/newsroom/updates/ccpa-senior-economist-calls-statistics-canadas-census-decision-senseless.

[7] E-health Ontario Web site: http://www.ehealthontario.on.ca/about/strategy.asp.

[8] The full report can be found at http://www.auditor.on.ca:81/isysnative/RDpcSU5FVFBVQlxVU0VSV0VCU1xPUEFcRU5ccmVwb3J0c19lblxlaGVhlthHRoX2VuLnBkZg==/ehealth_en.pdf#xml=http://www.auditor.on.ca:81/isysquery/irl5f40/3/hilite.

[9] CBC News, "EHealth scandal a $1B waste: auditor," October 7, 2009, Web site: http://www.cbc.ca/canada/toronto/story/2009/10/07/ehealth-auditor.html.

[10] Ibid.

[11] Ibid.

[12] Ibid.

[13] Information and quotes taken from: Office of the Auditor General of Ontario, "News Release: Electronic Health Record: Running Late, Too Many Consultants," October 7, 2009, Web site: http://www.auditor.on.ca/en/news_en/newsrelease_ehealth.pdf.

[14] CBC News, "EHealth scandal a $1B waste: auditor," October 7, 2009, Web site: http://www.cbc.ca/canada/toronto/story/2009/10/07/ehealth-auditor.html.

[15] CBC News, "Head of eHealth Ontario is fired amid contracts scandal, gets big package," June 2009, http://www.cbc.ca/canada/story/2009/06/07/ehealth-kramer.html.

[16] CBC News, "EHealth scandal a $1B waste: auditor," October 7, 2009, http://www.cbc.ca/canada/toronto/story/2009/10/07/ehealth-auditor.html.

[17] CBC News, "Examining eHealth Ontario," October 8, 2009, Web site http://www.cbc.ca/canada/story/2009/07/22/f-ehealth-players-0722.html.

[18] CBC News, "EHealth scandal a $1B waste: auditor," October 7, 2009.

[19] CBC News, "Head of eHealth Ontario is fired amid contracts scandal, gets big package," June 2009.

[20] CBC News, "EHealth scandal a $1B waste: auditor," October 7, 2009.

[21] Published as an opinion piece in the *Globe and Mail* on Friday, October 15, 2010, 5:00AM EDT.

[22] This extract is by historian J.L. Granatstein who is a senior research fellow at the Canadian Defence and Foreign Affairs Institute.

GLOSSARY

A

according to rule corruption When a bribe is paid in order to receive preferential treatment for something that the bribe receiver is already required to do by law. p. 116

accountable To stand in a position to give an account of oneself, or of one's decisions and actions. p. 29

act tokens An act token is a specific instance of an act type. If killing is a type of action (an act type), then Brutus stabbing Caesar to death on a particular day and in a particular location is a specific token of that type. p. 24

act utilitarianism To assess the consequences of individual actions, and choose the action that will produce the best overall outcome, is the morally right thing to do. p. 38

administrative justice Administrative justice requires that the conduct of people be evaluated according to rules or standards with the following characteristics: the rules are made known in advance; they are applied prospectively; the rules are clear and consistent with one another; and persons are judged according to the rules in ways that are fair and satisfy the principle that "like cases should be treated alike." p. 82

affirmative action programs Programs that aim at eliminating prohibited discrimination in hiring and promotion decisions. Such programs are premised upon the presumption that members of historically disadvantaged groups continue to suffer from stereotyping and other forms of prejudice that unfairly disadvantage them in competitions for jobs and for advancement within organizations, including public service organizations. The programs' goal is to make sure that individuals from historically disadvantaged groups are able to compete effectively for positions within the public service. They do not require that employers hire or promote less qualified candidates over more qualified ones; rather, they require that when two candidates are of comparable quality (on relevant measures), then employers should choose the individual who is also from a disadvantaged group. p. 63

against the rule corruption When a bribe is paid to obtain services that the bribe receiver is prohibited from providing. p. 116

amoral Without moral standing, not having to do with morality. p. 60

apparent conflict of interest When it appears that an official's private interests may have the potential to interfere with the proper performance of that official's duties. p. 125

applied ethics General ethical theories—consisting of a coherent set of values, principles, rules, evaluative standards, duties, rights, and virtues—are applied to solve moral problems and answer moral questions that arise within a given field of activity, such as medical research (known as bioethics), environmental activities (known as environmental ethics), business activities (known as business ethics), or military activities (known as military ethics). p. 23

Auditor General Independent Parliamentary Officer charged with monitoring and holding the federal government accountable for its use of public funds. p. 80

autonomy Self-rule; refers to our capacity to set ends for ourselves. For professions, the ability to self-govern their practice. p. 43

C

care ethics (or relational ethics) An approach to moral thinking that is associated with feminist thought; it focuses on meeting the needs of specific individuals in concrete relationships, rather than on abstract principles of justice or rights and duties. p. 49

categorical imperative The ultimate principle of morality in the moral philosophy of Immanuel Kant. Only actions for which the motives can be universalized and that treat every person with the respect due to them as ends in themselves can be moral. What matters in accessing the morality of one's actions is that they are motivated by a good will, rather than that they produce good consequences. p. 41

claim rights Rights that have corresponding duties. Claim rights are relational, governing the relation between the person with the right and the person who owes the corresponding duty. p. 18

compensatory justice Concerning what persons who have suffered harm deserve or are owed. p. 62

conflict of interest Any situation in which a public employee, either for himself or herself, or for some other person(s), attempts to promote a private or personal interest which results in or appears to result in either of the following:

(a) an interference with or impediment to the objective, neutral, and impartial exercise of his or her duties in the public service, or

(b) a gain or advantage by virtue of his or her position in the public service. p. 125

consequentialist moral theory A moral theory that has as its central focus the consequences of one's actions, rather than the intentions or motives behind the act. What is morally right is whatever action will produce the best consequences. p. 34

constitutive goods Goods that are valuable, ultimately, because they contribute to a good, i.e., happy, life. For instance, time spent with loved ones or engaged in meaningful work is typically treated as a constitutive good. p. 34

constitutive value Values that constitute what one thinks makes a happy life. p. 34

contractarianism (or the social contract tradition) Identifies moral rules as those a group of people would agree to be governed by because being so governed serves the interests of each of them. Its proponents ask us to imagine that we are going to form a new society from a non-moral and pre-political state of nature; what moral rules and political institutions would it be rational for us to adopt? Those that we would rationally adopt, because they would best serve our interests and allow us to live peacefully and cooperatively together, are then identified as the moral rules. p. 51

conventional morality The idea of morality in a descriptive, sociological, or anthropological sense, to refer to whatever set of moral beliefs and values a particular group of people hold. This sense of morality can be thought of as changing over time, and differing between groups. p. 23

co-operative strategy It is often the case that whether we get what we want or not is determined not just by our own choices, but the choices of all of us together. In such cases, it is often best if we collectively decide on a course of action, rather than having each individual try to decide for himself what to do. Adopting such collective strategies for choice is essential for mutually beneficial cooperation. p. 71

corruption The misuse of power for private gain. p. 115

critical morality Consists of that set of values, norms, rights, duties, virtues, and rules that is most rationally defensible, an ideal moral code that, if followed, would actually make peaceful co-operation for mutual benefit possible, would enable people to live good lives and pursue what is truly valuable, and would result in a distribution of rights and duties that can be defended as serving interests in an impartial way. p. 4

D

democracy A means of civil organization wherein citizens vote for their leader or legislative assembly. A liberal democracy follows the same procedural mechanism; however, there is an added layer of individual rights and protections, which are generally protected under a constitution. p. 76

deontology Refers to duty-based moral theories, of which there are a considerable number of variants. Deontologists deny that what makes an action right are its consequences. Rather, they think some actions are right and others are wrong just by virtue of what they are; actions are right or wrong depending on their intrinsic properties, independently of any good or harm the action might do. p. 41

diminishing marginal utility Utility is a measure of happiness, well-being, preference satisfaction or other valued state. Many goods have diminishing marginal utility, in the sense that beyond a certain specific point, further increases in that good going to a person add to their utility at a decreasing rate. Suppose a person has an annual income of $50,000. Imagine now that we give that person an additional $50,000 every ten minutes. For the first few hours, maybe even days, every additional $50,000 will add to her happiness at a steady rate. But at some point she will have so much money that the next additional $50,000 will add to her happiness less than the first $50,000 did. That is the point at which money begins to diminish in its value, or utility, for her. Money is a good that has decreasing marginal utility, as do all consumptive goods and physical pleasures. p. 37

discrimination To treat people differently, negatively, or adversely because of race, national or ethnic origin, colour, religion, age, sex (including pregnancy), sexual orientation, marital status, family status, physical or mental disability (including dependence on alcohol or drugs), or a pardoned criminal conviction. Discrimination is only wrongful when it is based on characteristics that are arbitrary from the point of view of the decision being made, and when they reflect prejudice or stereotypes projected onto individuals simply because of their membership in a particular group. p. 79

distributive justice Distributive justice concerns the distribution of goods and services, and burdens and benefits, in society. There are many potential principles attached to distributive justice, based upon assessments of what people are owed or entitled to. Among these principles are individual merit, need, contribution, ability, and equality. p. 62

dogmatist One who unjustifiably asserts his or her opinions, and is not open to evidence that is contrary to those opinions. p. 90

E

ethics code A code of conduct that sets out guidelines for ethical conduct and behaviour within an organization. p. 74

ethics of care An approach to ethics that arose out of empirical research conducted into differences between how men and women think about ethical problems, especially as found in the work of moral psychologist Carol Gilligan. She observed that while men often relied upon abstract principles (especially principles of rights and justice) in deciding how to resolve moral dilemmas, women by contrast typically approached moral issues in a more concrete way, attending to the specific context, the relationships between the parties to the dispute, and the needs of the individuals involved. Women try to resolve moral conflicts in ways that make it possible for relationships to be maintained and needs can be met. This approach may have arisen from the traditional role of women as caregivers and mediators within families. p. 49

ethics regime An institutional orientation that expects ethical conduct from its members and encourages ethical practices. p. 74

F

felicific calculus The measurement of happiness used in utilitarian moral theory. p. 34

fidelity Loyalty that is promised to a person or group or organization. p. 107

fiduciary One who acts or decides for the benefit of another, putting their interests ahead of his or her own. Fiduciary relationships depend on trust. p. 146

formal equality Treating all cases alike, regardless of relevant differences. p. 183

fortitude The strength to bear disappointments and hardship, resilience, grit, inner strength. p. 46

G

generality Dealing with the general circumstance or situation, as opposed to specific cases. p. 83

general rule A rule that is meant to apply to all, in a generalized way. For instance, "one should not lie" is a general rule that is meant to apply independent of the circumstance and individual. p. 11

golden mean An idea deriving from Aristotle, the golden mean is the point of virtue between two extremes of vice. For example, generosity is the mean (the virtuous mid-point) between the extremes of liberality and miserliness. p. 47

greatest happiness principle Always act so as to produce the greatest amount of happiness for the greatest number of people possible. p. 34

H

harassment Any behaviour that demeans, humiliates, or embarrasses a person and that a reasonable person should have known would be unwelcome. p. 79

honesty A very basic ethical requirement. It requires more than merely refraining from knowingly telling falsehoods or lies, though. Lying is merely one way to be dishonest. Another is withholding information altogether or telling only partial truths, that is, withholding some information in such a way that the person with whom you are communicating draws false conclusions from what you say. Exaggerating the evidence that supports your position is another way of being dishonest. To present something as certain that you know or believe is not certain, or to express greater confidence in some claim than your evidence for it would warrant, is less than honest. p. 16

human rights Also called natural rights, human rights are rights we have just by virtue of being human beings. The United Nations Declaration of Human Rights articulates a comprehensive set of such rights. The grounding of such rights must be some feature of human beings that is universal and, probably, unique. Thus human rights are often said to be grounded in our common rationality, our status as rational or autonomous agents, or our status as creatures having inherent dignity or worth. Such rights are often thought to be held against other human beings, so that other people have the corresponding duties not to interfere with actions we have a right to engage in. p. 19

I

immoral Contrary to morality. p. 60

imperative Absolutely necessary or required. For instance, a moral rule that necessarily binds one to follow the actions dictated by such rule is a moral imperative. p. 7

imperfect duties A duty is imperfect if it leaves the person who is under the duty choice or discretion about how to fulfil it, and it does not dictate a specific course of action on each and every occasion that the duty could be fulfilled. There are imperfect duties to *ourselves*, such as the duty to develop our natural talents, and imperfect duties to *others*, such as the duty to be charitable. p. 22

influence peddling To solicit or accept some kind of benefit in exchange for exercising one's authority or influence within government to aid the person or organization providing the benefit. p. 129

injustice Any act, circumstance, or arrangement that is deemed to be unfair or contrary to the demands of justice; an act that denies to someone what he or she is due or owed under a principle of justice. p. 81

instrumental value When an item, idea, or arrangement is valuable because of what it can do, or what it will lead to, or what it is a means to. For instance, money is instrumentally valuable because of what you can do with it, namely buy things; however, if one has money in an unrecognized or untradeable currency, for instance, then such money has lost its function and is no longer instrumentally valuable. p. 175

integrity The demonstration of fairness, honesty, and ethical and legal awareness in personal and professional relationships and activities. p. 148

Integrity Commissioner An officer of Parliament, legislative assembly, or municipal council who is charged with investigating the integrity of the actions of members of such Parliament, legislative assembly, or municipal council. p. 131

intellectual virtues Those virtues needed for right thinking and the pursuit of truth, knowledge, and understanding. They include a commitment to evidence, impartiality in assessing evidence, attention to detail, honesty in reporting, integrity in research, perseverance, intelligence, creativity, and judgment. These are virtuous intellectual traits because those who have them are more likely to achieve truth, knowledge, or understanding, and to make good judgments. p. 46

intrinsic When an item, idea, or arrangement is good or valuable in and of itself, and does not require any further ends to justify its worth. For instance, happiness is often considered to be intrinsically good, because it is good for one to be happy, just in virtue of what happiness is. p. 34

J

justice Justice is typically rendered as the disposition to give persons their due or what they are owed. Thus, to know what justice requires we must know what people are due or owed, what they are entitled to and by whom. Justice is complex, in part because there are at least four different kinds of justice: retributive, compensatory, distributive, and procedural. p. 76

L

law Law refers to positive law, the law as posited by those with authority to make law within our legal system, which is a constitutional parliamentary democracy. It includes all the various branches of law, including public law, family law, criminal law, regulatory law, and tort law. It includes both statutory and common law. Such laws may be wise or misguided, beneficial or harmful, just or unjust, but they are nonetheless the laws of the land, provided they have been enacted by the right authorities within their legislative competence and according to the procedures established for law-making. p. 29

legal rights Rights guaranteed by the legal system, and generally entrenched in the constitution of a country. p. 20

liberty or liberty-right These rights do not have corresponding duties. If I have a liberty-right to pursue an education, no one need have a duty to provide me with an education. Instead, what such rights entail is that there is no corresponding duty on me not to pursue an education. Liberties entitle one to do what one has a right to, and indicate that the right-holder has no duty not to do what she has a liberty-right to do. Liberty-rights are correlated with permissions; if I have a liberty-right to do *x*, then doing *x* is morally permissible for me (i.e., doing *x* would not violate any moral duty I have with respect to *x*-ing). I have a liberty-right to choose whether to marry, for example, because I have no duty to marry that is owed to anyone. Once I have promised to marry a particular person, however, I have given up my liberty-right and have thereby assumed a duty to marry. p. 20

M

maxim The maxim of the act is its underlying motive, formulated as a principle of action. p. 42

moral intuitionism An approach to morality that treats moral properties (such as goodness and rightness) as real properties existing in the world and whose proponents say our knowledge of moral properties is direct and non-inferential. We do not come to know that, for example, killing is morally wrong by inferring its wrongfulness from other things we know, such as that killing produces unhappiness or would not be agreed to by rational agents coming together to form a social contract. Instead, we either have a moral sense similar to our senses of sight or hearing, through which we directly perceive moral qualities (the empiricist form of the theory), or reason directly informs us of moral truths (the rationalist version of the theory). p. 58

moral judgments Specific judgments we make when we call some person or action or practice good or bad, right or wrong, just or unjust, virtuous or vicious. Sometimes these are called moral intuitions, when they are moral judgments we make immediately without reference to any general moral principle or moral theory. p. 6

moral principles Moral principles are general in a way that specific moral judgments are not. Principles identify *types* of actions as morally right or wrong, good or bad, and the like. These principles are then used as the foundations of competing ethical theories, which attempt to explain what it is that makes particular actions or practices or people right or good or just or virtuous. p. 6

moral sense or sentiments The idea that we have an innate faculty for moral judgment analogous to our other senses of touch, sight, hearing, smell, and taste. It is a version of moral intuitionism. p. 59

moral virtues Traits of character that make us sensitive and responsive to the moral characteristics of our circumstances. p. 46

morality A system of norms that sets standards of right and proper conduct. p. 1

morally free zone A circumstance or situation in which we do not need morality to achieve full mutual advantage. The free competitive market is a morally free zone in the sense that everyone making rational decisions just designed to serve their own self-interest will produce outcomes that also secure mutual benefit as an unintended side effect. p. 57

multiculturalism A political commitment to a pluralistic political and group identity. For instance, Canada is a multicultural society both in fact and in values. Factually, Canada is a country built upon immigration, populated by peoples from virtually every country, ethnicity, and race, and every religious, linguistic, and cultural group. Thus Canada is a multi-racial, multi-ethnic, multi-linguistic country. We are a country that is pluralistic along virtually every conceivable line. Multiculturalism is also a value to which we subscribe: We think it good that Canadians can retain their specific cultural identities and can belong to minority cultural groups while also being members of the broader Canadian society. p. 30

N

negative duties A duty not to interfere with someone else's right. p. 19

negative right A right to act in some manner without interference by someone else. For instance, if the right to life is a universal negative right, then this means that everyone must refrain from killing everyone else. p. 18

nepotism To give preferential treatment to one's own family members or friends in the distribution of some good or service, such as a job. p. 130

normative principles Principles that outline the standards of acceptable behaviour. *See also* moral principles. p. 34

O

Ombudsman An officer of Parliament, legislative assembly, municipal council, ministry, or Crown corporation who is charged with auditing or overseeing the service and success of programs offered to the public. They typically have the power to receive and investigate complaints directly from the public. p. 88

P

perfect duties Duties that dictate specific actions as required in each and every case that the duty is operative. Thus the duty not to engage in an act of avoidable killing is a perfect duty, requiring that we refrain from killing in every situation where killing is possible but avoidable. Such duties typically leave the person bound by the duty little room for choice or discretion as to how to fulfil the duty. There are (uncontroversially) perfect duties to *others*, such as the duty to tell the truth, and (much more controversially) perfect duties to *ourselves*, such as the duty not to commit suicide. (The specific examples are from Immanual Kant, who first drew the distinction between perfect and imperfect duties.) p. 44

pluralists The view that there are multiple moral values and many ways to live a good life. The plurality of values cannot be reduced to a single source or type: happiness, knowledge, friendship, and more are valuable for their own sakes. p. 15

political legitimacy A government is considered to have legitimacy when its claim to authority is acceptable. When political power is used for the good of the governed, i.e., the common or public good, rather than the private gain of those who govern, it will typically be considered legitimate. If a government is legitimate, its subjects will be under an obligation to obey its authoritative commands; most importantly, they will have a duty to obey the law. p. 107

political neutrality A position of impartiality between political parties, which is demanded of public servants. Political neutrality is essential for building and maintaining trust between politicians and public servants. The advice of the public service cannot be partisan; its delivery of government services cannot be contingent on public servants sharing the political values, ideological or philosophical perspective, or party affiliation, of the government enacting the policy. Thus public servants are required to refrain from any activity that would impair their political neutrality or the neutrality of the public service, and to avoid the appearance of political partiality. p. 107

political patronage The appointment of individuals to positions within the government, or the distribution of benefits from government, based on the recipient's connection to the political party of the current government. The distribution of favours to members of a specific political party. p. 110

positive duties A duty to assist some right-holder in realizing some positive right. For instance, if one holds a positive right to life against me, as opposed to a negative right, then I have a positive duty to assist such right-holder with anything they need to live. Parents, for example, have a positive duty to provide the necessities of life to their dependent children, and children have a positive right to receive such support. p. 19

positive right A right held by an individual, the realization of which requires the assistance of whoever has the corresponding duty. For instance, dependants, such as children, often hold a positive right to life against their parents, or guardians. p. 19

prisoners' dilemma The name given to a particular type of social interaction that requires cooperation among the parties, and a commitment on behalf of each to seek mutual benefit rather than narrow self-interest, in order to avoid an outcome that is worse for all and instead achieve an outcome that is better for each but that can be achieved only if they all cooperate. p. 54

Privacy Commissioner An officer of Parliament, legislative assembly, or municipal council who is charged with auditing, overseeing, or policing the means by which the government stores, secures, or uses the private information of citizens and corporations. Privacy Commissioners may also have the power to investigate the privacy practices of private sector organizations as well. p. 158

private goods Most of the goods we use and enjoy in our daily lives are private goods. They are private in the sense that they are exclusive and rivalrous. If a good is exclusive, then the person who owns it can exclude others from its use; that is, its being available to one person does not entail that it must be available to others. If a good is rivalrous, then either its use by one person is incompatible with its use by others, or its use by one person diminishes the amount of it available for use by others. p. 64

procedural justice Procedural justice requires that the terms of competition be fair, if competition is to lead to just outcomes. The administration of law must also meet the requirements of procedural justice, which requires among other things that judges who decide disputes do so impartially, that everyone has an opportunity to present his or her case, that like cases be treated alike, and more. p. 65

professional ethics Ethics pertaining to a particular profession, such as doctors, lawyers, engineers, and accountants. *See also* applied ethics. p. 23

professionals Professionals have mastery of a specialized, esoteric field of knowledge. They wield a considerable amount of authority. Their judgments must typically be accepted at least in part on trust. Professionals also have considerable autonomy in the exercise of their professional responsibilities, and are generally self-regulating. Because of the considerable authority professionals enjoy, and their self-regulation, professionals stand in the relationship of fiduciaries with respect to their clients. They must exercise their authority for the good of their clients rather than for personal gain. p. 42

prudence Appropriate care for one's own well-being, reasonable self-interest, an ability to resist current temptations that carry a risk of serious harm to oneself later. p. 46

public goods In contrast with private goods, public goods are non-excludable and non-rivalrous. For instance, consider a lighthouse. Suppose I build a lighthouse to aid my safe passage through a rocky strait of water. Once it is built, I cannot effectively exclude others from using it; they derive the benefit from it, even though they did not contribute to its construction. And their use does not rival or compete with mine. The benefit others derive from it in no way diminishes its usefulness to me or its availability to me. p. 64

public interest For the good or well-being of society, or the public in general. p. 82

public reasons Reasons that can gain acceptance by all members of the polity, regardless of more personal differences in interests, affections, religion, or philosophy. p. 89

R

reflective moral reasoning Reflective moral reasoning begins with the specific judgments we make when we simply respond to some action or event or person as morally good, right, or just, or when we immediately respond positively or negatively to a particular action or event. It then involves the construction of general moral principles that explain the specific judgments we make, identifying what those judgments have in common and makes them moral judgments. Reflective moral reasoning involves subjecting our specific judgments to evaluation according to their fit with our moral principles, and adjustment and refinement of our moral principles so that they support our most firmly held moral judgments. The result of reflective moral reasoning is a moral perspective that is internally coherent, and in which our judgments are explained and justified by our principles, and our principles support our moral convictions about specific moral cases. p. 25

respect for persons principle One formulations of Immanual Kant's fundamental moral law: the categorical imperative. It is a moral principle that requires that we always treat persons as ends in themselves, and not just as means to our own ends. It recognizes the fundamental dignity and worth of every person, and requires that we always act toward others (and ourselves) in ways that show proper respect for their inherent dignity and worth. p. 43

retributive justice Requires that we give people what they deserve, where what they deserve is based on whether they have purposefully benefitted or wrongfully harmed others. At its most general, retributive justice requires that we return good for good and evil for evil. The requirement that we return good for good grounds our duties of gratitude and reciprocity. Those who have done something good for us deserve that we not act in ways that make them regret their kindness or favour, at a minimum, and that we reciprocate with kindness toward them in turn. Its more common, negative, formulation requires that we give wrongdoers what they deserve, and what wrongdoers deserve is to be punished proportionately with the wrong they have done. Retributive justice is the form of justice that governs legitimate punishment. p. 61

rule of law The "rule of law" is contrasted with the "rule of men." In order to have the rule of law, rather than the arbitrary exercise of power, it is essential that those exercising power do so in accordance with the rules laid down. The rule of law can only be enjoyed when people are governed by general rules, made known to them in advance, and applied fairly and consistently by those who are authorized to do so. p. 121

rule utilitarian This version of the theory requires that we assess possible rules or principles, asking which rule or principle, if adopted as a guide to conduct, would produce the best consequences. Instead of asking every time that we might tell a lie or assault someone whether doing so would have the best consequences, we ask whether it would be better to have a general rule against lying or applying force against others without their consent. p. 38

S

seductive positions Positions characterized as those that provide their holders with extraordinary access to power, discretion, and money. Such positions test the moral character of those holding them. p. 117

social virtues The kinds of traits that are especially important to living a good life in society with others. They include empathy, humour, forgiveness, respect, charitableness, wit, a sense of justice, reciprocity, and the like. Social virtues are those traits that make us easy and agreeable companions to others, and that make our social interactions a source of joy, pleasure, or happiness to others, rather than the contrary. p. 46

state of nature Social contract theories ask us to engage in a thought experiment. Imagine that human beings lived without morality and without governments or other political institutions. This is the state of nature. They ask us to imagine what moral rules and political institutions we would adopt if we were in such a pre-moral and pre-political state. I might prefer rules and arrangements that favour me, and you might similarly prefer arrangements that favour you. But we have to find a set of rules that we can *all* agree on. Thus we can only choose rules that provide mutual benefit, and arrangements under which each of us would do as well as possible, consistently with everyone else doing as well as possible. The rules that we would all rationally agree to are the rules social contract theorists recommend to us to govern our social lives together. p. 51

substantive equality To treat persons with equal concern and respect, in ways that accommodate their differences when necessary to allow them to be full participants in all of the goods Canadian society makes possible. p. 183

U

utility A measure of value. Utility might be a measure of happiness, welfare, preference satisfaction, or anything else that is valued for its own sake. To say that one state of affairs is higher in or has more utility than another is just to say that the first contains more of what is valued: more happiness, more well-being, or more satisfied preferences, for example, than the other. Many consequential moral theories make the maximization of utility the standard of morally right action or the standard of morally good rules; what is right to do is whatever will maximize happiness, or the best rules are those which if followed would produce the most well-being. p. 34

V

vice Character traits or dispositions that are immoral. p. 46

virtue ethics Virtues are morally valuable settled dispositions or character traits. Virtues and vices not only incline us to act in certain ways, but colour our perceptions of our circumstances, make us notice certain morally salient characteristics of our situations, and determine to a large extent the kind of persons we are. Virtue ethics is the study of those traits of character that are virtuous and those that are vicious. It enjoins us to develop virtues and to manifest them in leading good lives. p. 46

W

walk the talk Acting in a manner consistent with the way one says others should act. p. 80

welfare system A system of programs and institutions designed to ensure that every person has their basic needs met. p. 63

INDEX